Microfinance and Financial Inclusion

Following the recent global financial crisis there is a growing interest in alternative finance – and microfinance in particular – as new instruments for providing financial services in a socially responsible way or as an alternative to traditional banking. Nonetheless, correspondingly there is also a lack of clarity about how to regulate alternative financial methods particularly in light of the financial crisis' lessons on regulatory failure and shadow banking's risks.

This book considers microfinance from a legal and regulatory perspective. Microfinance is the provision of a wide range of financial services, particularly credit but also remittances and savings, to low-income or financially excluded people. It combines a business structure with social inspiration, often resorts to technological innovations to lower costs (FinTech: e.g. crowdfunding and mobile banking) and merges with traditional local experiences (e.g. financial cooperatives and Islamic finance), this further complicating the regulatory picture. The book describes some of the unique dimensions of microfinance and the difficulties that this can cause for regulators, through a comparative analysis of selected European Union (EU) countries' regimes. The focus is on the EU legal framework, with some references to certain developing world experiences where relevant. The book assesses the impact and validity of current financial regulation principles and rules, in light of the most recent developments and trends in financial regulation in the wake of the financial crisis and compares microfinance with traditional banking. The book puts forward policy recommendations for regulators and policy makers to help address the challenges and opportunities offered by microfinance.

Eugenia Macchiavello is a Lecturer/Adjunct Professor in Banking Law at the University of Genoa and Senior Research Fellow at the Genoa Centre for Law and Finance.

Routledge Research in Finance and Banking Law

Available:

Fiduciary Law and Responsible Investing
In Nature's Trust
Benjamin J. Richardson

Redefining the Market-State Relationship
Responses to the Financial Crisis and the Future of Regulation
Ioannis Glinavos

Financial Stability and Prudential Regulation
A Comparative Approach to the UK, US, Canada, Australia and Germany
Alison Lui

Law and Finance after the Financial Crisis
The Untold Stories of the UK Financial Market
Abdul Karim Aldohni

Microfinance and Financial Inclusion
The Challenge of Regulating Alternative Forms of Finance
Eugenia Macchiavello

Forthcoming:

Competition Law and Financial Services
David Harrison

Institutional Structure of Financial Regulation
Theories and International Experiences
Robin Hui Huang and Dirk Schoenmaker

Banking and Society
Mapping Financial Regulation and Social Justice for the 21st Century
Gary Wilson and Sarah Wilson

Microfinance and Financial Inclusion

The Challenge of Regulating Alternative Forms of Finance

Eugenia Macchiavello

Routledge
Taylor & Francis Group
LONDON AND NEW YORK

First published 2018 by Routledge

2 Park Square, Milton Park, Abingdon, Oxfordshire OX14 4RN
52 Vanderbilt Avenue, New York, NY 10017

Routledge is an imprint of the Taylor & Francis Group, an informa business

First issued in paperback 2020

British Library Cataloguing in Publication Data
A catalogue record for this book is available from the British Library

Library of Congress Cataloging in Publication Data
Names: Macchiavello, Eugenia, 1982- author.
Title: Microfinance and financial inclusion : the challenge of regulating alternative forms of finance / Eugenia Macchiavello.
Description: Abingdon, Oxon ; New York, NY : Routledge, 2017. | Series: Routledge research in finance and banking law | Includes bibliographical references and index.
Identifiers: LCCN 2017002094 | ISBN 9781138652798 (hbk) | ISBN 9781315623962 (ebk)
Subjects: LCSH: Microfinance--Law and legislation--European Union countries.
Classification: LCC KJE2192.M53 M33 2017 | DDC 346.2407/3--dc23
LC record available at https://lccn.loc.gov/2017002094

ISBN: 978-1-138-65279-8 (hbk)
ISBN: 978-0-367-59486-2 (pbk)

Typeset in Galliard
by Taylor & Francis Books

To my kids and husband, filling my heart with joy and love and making every instant of my life special

Contents

List of illustrations

Figures

Tables

Acknowledgements

I need to start by thanking my family (children, husband and parents but also my numerous and wonderful relatives-in-law) for their constant and tireless support during all these years, as well as many friends (in particular, Vanessa Casado-Pérez).

I am extremely thankful also to my academic mentors (here listed in chronological order), Professors Giovanna Visintini, Guido Ferrarini, Geoffrey P. Miller and Antonella Sciarrone Alibrandi, for their support and for providing me with different but all precious examples and lessons about research and teaching.

My gratitude also goes to other excellent academics I had the pleasure to meet for their teaching, for inspiring me and for believing in me. Just mentioning only a few of them in alphabetic order: Marco Arato, Danny Busch, Fabrizio Cafaggi, Veerle Colaert, Kevin E. Davis, Raffaella De Matteis, Ana Demel, Giovanni Domenichini, Paolo Giudici, Robert Howse, Andrea Pericu, Andrea Perrone, Katharina Pistor, Gaetano Presti, Vittorio Santoro, Michele Siri, Joseph H. Weiler.

I am also grateful to all people and organizations (including LuxFlag, BNP-Paribas, PerMicro and EMN) I have been in contact with while conducting research for and writing this book (often mentioned in the same as references) for their kindness, willingness to share with me their experiences and opinions and for their passionate work. Special thanks, for clarifying some aspects of their respective legal systems, to Maria Doiciu, Kaloyan Ganev, Izabela Norek and Professors Kaloyan Ganev and Ugo Reifner.

I want to express my gratitude also to my editor and their team for the trust and support showed.

Although rather unusual, I want also to thank the obstacles I have encountered on my route for making me stronger and grow as a person, professional and academic.

Introduction and executive summary

Microfinance and its 'regulatory dimensions'

In the wake of the financial turmoil, two contemporary phenomena, among many others, have taken place: first, the mission of financial regulators now encompasses not only stability and market efficiency but also consumer protection and financial inclusion. Second, new instruments, alternative to traditional and mainstream banking, have started to flourish as a response to the scepticism and aversion towards the traditional financial sector (e.g. social and collaborative finance, FinTechs). My book will focus on microfinance, that is, the provision of a wide range of financial services, particularly credit (but also remittances and savings, for instance) to low-income or financially/socially excluded people.

Microfinance is an interesting form of finance with social inspiration, challenging our traditional legal categories and existing regulations. In fact, microfinance is a complex creature: it combines a business structure with social inspiration (so called 'double-bottomline'). Its adaptive and evolving nature also adds to its complexity. Even though it first had roots in both European forms of socially responsible financial activities (e.g. financial cooperatives and '*Monti di Pietà*') and ancient collective solutions to poverty in developing countries (e.g. *tontines*, rotating savings and credit associations (ROSCAs), *susus* or chit funds), it gained public attention with the Grameen Bank experience in Bangladesh. After that, it rapidly spread around the world, including economically advanced countries. Microfinance adapted to local conditions (social links and structures as a substitute for legal enforcement and institutions) and legal traditions (e.g. mutual movement, Islamic banking), while taking advantage of available cost-saving and far-reaching innovations (e.g. crowdfunding, mobile banking). In the process, microfinance has lost many of its original features and evolved in ways that make it even more complex and, thus, more difficult to regulate.

My book aims precisely at addressing the enigma of regulating such a chameleonic creature. I will start by describing the origins and main features of microfinance in the context of a renewed interest in financial inclusion. The first part of the book defines various concepts related to microfinance instrumental to the legal analysis of the issues pertaining to microfinance regulation that will be discussed later on. It will range from the causes of financial exclusion and the new role for financial inclusion within the financial sector legal framework to the analysis of the main features of microcredit and microfinance, with special reference to EU experiences.

In the second part of the book, in order to adequately tackle the problem of regulating microfinance, I will identify and discuss the most important 'dimensions' of the same. Such 'dimensions' represent the aspects and conditions that can make microfinance a desirable player in the financial system, but also an odd one requiring new regulatory measures to be taken. At the end of the analysis of each dimension, I will offer regulatory recommendations to adequately address the challenges and opportunities of microfinance, using the identified dimensions as inspirations for setting the principles this book will put forward as policy recommendations for regulators and policy makers trying to tame the chameleon.

Highlighting some of its dimensions will help illustrate this point. First, the term 'microfinance' currently refers to a varied set of activities having in common that they target a low-income population, but they can be offered by operators with very different legal forms (e.g. cooperatives, banks, foundations) and be subject to multiple laws (e.g. charity, banking, capital markets). Consequently, in order to regulate microfinance, we should first define what microfinance really is. The next steps would be to identify who can better regulate it (government or self-regulation), at what level (local, national, regional, international) and how (e.g. through prudential regulation, non-prudential regulation, charity law), also taking into account regulatory costs and implications of each alternative regulatory solution. The adaptive character of microfinance to local traditions (e.g. financial cooperatives and Islamic banking) has often made it more effective and responsive to local needs but sometimes also subject to additional regulatory obstacles.

The second essential dimension of microfinance institutions (MFIs) is its social objective (e.g. serving the unbanked or low-income). Microfinance is not single minded, like traditional banks. It does not seek only profit maximization, but also to serve 'the poor'. This may justify a differentiated regulatory treatment that enables microfinance, and does not subject it to all the constraints imposed on traditional commercial banks. At the same time, though, social objectives must be pursued effectively and how to measure its effectiveness is a daunting task, but one that needs to be considered by regulators. Furthermore, regulation must be careful in limiting MFIs' permitted activities because this could endanger the effects of financial inclusion.

The third dimension, linked to the previous one, is economic effectiveness: microfinance is also a business venture, and, thus, more desirable than other comparable philanthropic initiatives, and therefore it must be economically sustainable, having adequate funds. There is a long-standing debate about the economic sustainability of MFIs but regulators should allow various forms of funding for MFIs (e.g. donations, bank loans, crowdfunding, or microfinance investment vehicles – MIVs), and, at the same time, create safeguards to protect consumers, investors and systemic stability. A possible guiding principle would be, as current trends in EU financial regulation show, to facilitate simple and basic activities while more strictly regulating complex ventures. Management and corporate governance are also aspects that can contribute, if well regulated, to its financial profitability.

The fourth dimension is its innovative and adaptive nature: microfinance has absorbed other alternative and innovative financial inclusion instruments, such as crowdfunding and mobile banking. Again, regulators should not discourage microfinance's innovations by imposing too strict legal constraints while protecting clients and investors.

Finally, the fifth dimension is its 'alternative' character. Microfinance was born as an alternative to traditional intermediaries and banks. Hence, understanding the differences with respect to the traditional financial sector is one of the keys to optimally regulate it. Regulation should not transform microfinance into traditional banking. The adaptation of financial rules must be tailored, taking into account many aspects, including the types and complexity of activities conducted and services offered, the clients served, structures and instruments used. Not only is microfinance different from traditional banking, but it is so diverse in itself that regulation should also avoid a one-size-fits-all solution. Policing microfinance's social and economic effectiveness while not crowding out the financial inclusion effect and maintaining its adaptive and innovative nature is a fine line to walk, but this book will offer some guidance for it.

The book will also offer a portfolio of policy recommendations based on the analysis of each dimension, through the study of the legal systems and specific regulatory choices applicable to microfinance of selected EU countries both from Eastern Europe and from Western Europe.

In fact, despite the relevance of microfinance and financial inclusion policies in developing countries, in my book I will focus on the European Union framework, with some references to some developing world experiences where relevant. A global perspective is not feasible because countries are too diverse and developing countries may suffer from institutional problems that might affect microfinance. The EU is in itself homogenous and heterogeneous, making it an ideal case study. First, in the aftermath of the financial crisis, the EU has passed several groundbreaking reforms leading to a centralization of banking supervision and resolution powers (e.g. the Banking Union in the euro-area) and moving to a maximum harmonization model, consequently presenting at the moment a quite homogenous bulk of norms in the financial area. Second, the EU encompasses countries with very different traditions, institutions and financial sector development, justifying instead partial national discretions. This book will analyse whether there is also room and need for a partial harmonization in the microfinance area and instead for national reforms, taking into account recent trends (e.g. shadow banking fear, consumerization and simplification of retail finance). Since microfinance has often been presented as a new and alternative form of banking, the discussion will therefore cover typical banking areas (banking services, payment services and, in part, investment services and financial markets), with the exclusion, however, of a relevant area nowadays, micro-insurance, which would require a separate and accurate analysis.

I cannot conceal that I have been fascinated by microfinance and inspired by social finance but I also recognize hidden dangers. Consequently, I have tried to objectively analyse the main legal issues, while hoping to find an adequate balance among all interests involved. I am also optimistic about a future of more inclusive and equal financial systems.

Part 1

Description of microfinance: a creature of chameleonic nature

1 New frontiers and objectives of financial regulation

1 Financial exclusion: definition, causes and size of the phenomenon

The subprime crisis highlighted the problems linked to a system that considered financially excluded people only as a source of speculative profit. Generally, only not-for-profit alternative financial operators were addressing these issues, ignored by mainstream financial institutions and related literature.

Financial exclusion is commonly referred to as the condition of no or limited access of low-income working-age adults to mainstream financial services that are appropriate to their needs.[1] The Commission refers to financial exclusion as 'the process whereby people encounter difficulties accessing and/or using financial services and products in the mainstream market that are appropriate to their needs and enable them to lead a normal social life in the society in which they belong'.[2] In fact, the inclusion/exclusion is generally evaluated by four criteria: access (in terms of costs and proximity), quality (availability of a variety of products targeted to clients' needs and treatment), usage over time and impact/welfare (changes in clients' lives linked to the use of financial services).[3] The causes of lack of access are various.[4] A first group of causes can be referred to self-exclusion: low-income

1 *See* L. Anderloni and E. Carluccio, 'Access to Bank Accounts and Payment Services', in L. Anderloni et al. (eds), *New Frontiers in Banking Services. Emerging Needs and Tailored Products for Untapped Markets*, (Springer 2007), 7ff.; S. Carbó et al., *Financial Exclusion*, (Palgrave Macmillan 2005), ch 2; Commission, 'Financial Services Provision and Prevention of Financial Exclusion', Report, (2008), 9, <ec.europa.eu/social/BlobServlet?docId=760&langId=en>.

2 Commission, 'Financial Services', 9.

3 *See* A. Hannig and S. Jansen, 'Financial Inclusion and Financial Stability: Current Policy Issues', (2010) *ADB Institute Working Paper* 259, 3ff., <www.adbi.org/files/2010.12.21.wp259.financial.inclusion.stability.policy.issues.pdf>. *See* also Commission, 'Financial Services'.

4 *See* UN DESA-UNCDF, *Building Inclusive Financial Sectors for Development*, (UN 2006), <www.uncdf.org/sites/default/files/Documents/bluebook_1.pdf>; A. Demirgüç-Kunt et al., *Finance for All? Policies and Pitfalls in Expanding Access*, (WB 2008), 12, 28ff., <http://siteresources.worldbank.org/INTFINFORALL/Resources/4099583-1194373512632/FFA_book.pdf>; T. Beck et al., 'Banking Services for Everyone? Barriers to Bank Access and Use around the World', (2008) 22(3) *World*

people tend to avoid banks because of the idea of being inadequate for bank accounts (generally banks having quite strict requirements in terms of minimum deposit balance and credit history, high fees, etc.) or because of resentment caused by previous bad experiences with banks (also in their home countries in the case of migrants).

A second group relates to banks' decisions based on economic-business motivations and might consist, for example, in too low minimum account balances or too high fees or too demanding client profile (e.g. in terms of income, credit scoring, employment, collateral or documentation required). Moreover, products offered might not be appropriate for low-income people's financial needs and typical standardized procedures be unable to understand their risk profile, repayment and business chances and need (*see* Chapters 4, §5; 6, §2.b).

A third group of causes of financial exclusion are embedded in some societies in general: many clients might be discriminated against based on gender, religion, language, social position or age or might not be able to access and understand bank products and services because of education or geographical limitations.

In many economically advanced countries (EACs), bank branches are often located close to poor clients (in poor boroughs) but products and marketing techniques appear inadequate to serve them.[5] For instance, the majority (57.5%) of unbanked U.S. households in 2013 reported as reasons for financial exclusion not having enough money to open an account or not meeting the minimum required balance (the main reason for 35.6%), high or unexpected fees (30.8% of unbanked, the main reason for 13.4%) and distrust/dislike of banks (34.2%, the main reason for 14.9%).[6] Consequently, low-income people tend to use alternative financial services (such as pawn shops, payday lenders, cheque cashers, money

Bank Economic Review, 397 <http://siteresources.worldbank.org/DEC/Resources/WBER_Banking_services_for_everyone.pdf>; A. Demirguc-Kunt and L. Klapper, 'Measuring Financial Inclusion: The Global Findex Database', (2012) World Bank Policy Research Working Paper 6025, 18ff., <http://www-wds.worldbank.org/servlet/WDSContentServer/WDSP/IB/2012/04/19/000158349_20120419083611/Rendered/PDF/WPS6025.pdf>; F. Allen et al., 'The Foundations of Financial Inclusion: Understanding Ownership and Use of Formal Accounts', (2012), World Bank Policy Research Working Paper 6290, 11ff., <http://documents.worldbank.org/curated/en/348241468329061640/pdf/wps6290.pdf>. As regards Europe, *see* Commission, 'Financial Services', 40ff.; Commission, 'Study on the Costs and Benefits of Policy Actions in the Field of Ensuring Access to a Basic Bank Account – Final Report', (2010), 10ff., <http://ec.europa.eu/internal_market/finservices-retail/docs/inclusion/abba_cses_en.pdf>; Anderloni and Carluccio, 'Access', 10, 12–14, 86ff.; L. Nieri, 'Access to Credit: The Difficulties of Households', in Anderloni, *New Frontiers*, 110ff.; P. Molyneux, 'What Are the Specific Economic Gains from Improved Financial Inclusion? A Tentative Methodology for Estimating These Gains', in Anderloni, *New Frontiers*, 192ff.

5 However, data suggest that the lack of availability of bank facilities in Europe may affect the access to bank accounts: Commission, 'Study', 14–15.

6 *See* FDIC, '2013 FDIC National Survey of Unbanked and Underbanked Households', (2014), 6 <www.fdic.gov/householdsurvey/2013report.pdf>.

transfers, credit cards and prepaid debit cards) that are often more expensive than normal banking ones (*see* also Chapter 4, §5.b).[7]

The majority of unbanked or underserved people belong to particular societal groups, such as low-income people, unemployed or people with non-regular and unstable jobs, low financial literacy, young people, ethnic minorities, living in suburbs or agricultural areas.[8] In Europe, in particular, financially excluded people are mostly unemployed, minorities or migrants, people with disabilities, the elderly (over 65), young people and women.[9]

With special reference to credit services, studies highlight credit markets' imperfections, which make the optimal equilibrium between demand and offer unreachable, with the result of a contraction in credit availability.[10] Banks, in fact, in their decisions about loans to their clients are influenced not only by the interest rate they can charge but also by the level of risk, which because of asymmetric information is itself affected by the interest rate charged. In fact, banks cannot have complete information about loan applicants (especially when they are unemployed, immigrants or without valuable possessions as security) and consequently charge higher interest rates in order to hedge such risk. This might, on the one hand, attract high-risk borrowers (adverse selection problem: the ones willing to pay a high interest rate also expect higher profits and therefore are able to accept greater risk) and, on the other, has a negative effect on borrowers' incentives (moral hazard problem: the higher the interest rate, the greater the incentives on borrowers to engage in risky but more profitable activities). Consequently, the demand corresponding to the optimal level of interest rates is higher than the offer

7 *See* Financial Services User Group's (FSUG), '2012 FSUG Priorities Report – Ensuring Fair, Affordable and Safe Financial Products for Vulnerable Users', (2012) <http://ec.europa.eu/finance/finservices-retail/docs/fsug/papers/2012-priorities-report_en.pdf>; Anderloni and Carluccio, 'Access', 15; Nieri, 'Access', 108, 118; Molyneux, 'What Are', 194. On the U.S. market, *see* M. Fellowes and M. Mabanta, 'Banking on Wealth: America's New Retail Banking Infrastructure and Its Wealth-Building Potential', (2008) <www.brookings.edu/~/media/research/files/reports/2008/1/banking%20fellowes/01_banking_fellowes.pdf>; M. Barr et al., 'And Banking for All?', Federal Reserve Board Finance and Economics Discussion Series (2009) <www.federalreserve.gov/pubs/feds/2009/200934/200934pap.pdf>; Anderloni and Carluccio, 'Access', 71ff.; J. Morduch et al., 'An Invisible Finance Sector: How Households Use Financial Tools of Their Own Making', (2014), 8 <www.usfinancialdiaries.org/issue3-informal/>.

8 *See* Carbó, *Financial Exclusion*; J. Devlin, 'A Detailed Study of Financial Exclusion in the UK', (2005) 28 *J Consum Policy* 75; Nieri, 'Access', 110, 117. For the U.S. market, FDIC, '2013 FDIC'.

9 *See* Commission, 'Financial Services Provision', and Eurobarometer Report 2007, <www.bristol.ac.uk/media-library/sites/geography/migrated/documents/pfrc0808.pdf>; Commission, 'Study', 13–14.

10 J. Stiglitz and A. Weiss, 'Credit Rationing in Markets with Imperfect Information', (1981), 71(3) *Am Econ Rev* 393; G. Akerlof, 'The Market for "Lemons": Quality Uncertainty and the Market Mechanism', (1970) 84(3) *Q J Econ* 488, 498ff.; M. Klausner, 'Market Failure and Community Investment: A Market-Oriented Alternative to the Community Reinvestment Act', (1995) 143 *U Pa L Rev* 1561.

and the bank will deny loans even to creditworthy borrowers (typically of lower income).[11]

The market can also be affected by high transaction costs (that might be due to institutions' and market infrastructures' deficiencies): providers are thus unable to reach economies of scale and scope and they charge high fees and costs, therefore excluding poor households as clients.

Finally, the first movers face the dilemma of bearing all initial costs while newcomers can easily adopt their model once proved to be successful. Especially in a field not involving large sums of money and therefore less remunerative than others, this fact might reduce the number of providers interested in entering the market unless they receive some kind of external support even in the form of coordination among participants (*see* Chapter 7).[12]

The lack of access to formal financial services does not necessarily imply the lack of any financial instrument or the need of it. On the one hand, especially in EACs, people often do not ask, for example, for credit because they think not to need it (having internal resources or lacking a viable projects; in lower-income countries sometimes because of the limited level of financial sector development)[13] but the percentage of people having problems in accessing or using credit products is still high.[14] On the other hand, recent studies report the intense use by the poor of informal means to obtain credit or save.[15] Family members and local money lenders, Rotating Savings and Credit Associations (ROSCAs),[16] self-help groups,

11 *See* Nieri, 'Access',110.

12 *See* A. de la Torre et al., 'Innovative Experiences in Access to Finance: Market Friendly Roles for the Visible Hand?', (2007) The World Bank Policy Research Working Paper 4326, 8–9, <http://documents.banquemondiale.org/curated/fr/861901468269684103/pdf/wps4326.pdf>.

13 *See* de la Torre, 'Innovative', 3, 6ff.; Nieri, 'Access', 113 (in the survey covering France, Italy and Spain, half of the sample never approached a credit institution, in 64% of cases because they thought not to need it). The majority (56%) of unbanked European surveyed in 2011 by the Commission declared not needing a bank account (45% in EU-15 and 67% in new EU-12) while only 5% have seen their application rejected: Commission, 'Retail Financial Services Report', (2012) Special Eurobarometer 373, 25, <http://ec.europa.eu/internal_market/finservices-retail/docs/policy/eb_special_373-report_en.pdf>.

14 Nieri ('Access', 116) reports that 34% of the sample faced problems in accessing/using mainstream credit (including households having received credit but with difficulties in repaying, assuming among the causes inappropriate advice or inadequate products).

15 *See* D. Collins et al., *Portfolios of the Poor. How the World's Poor Live on $2 a Day* (PUP 2010); S. Rutherford et al., 'Clients', in J. Ledgerwood, *The New Microfinance Handbook* (WB 2013), ch. 2, 49ff. Based on Demirguc-Kunt and Klapper 'Measuring', 33ff, '[a]mong adults who report having saved or set aside money in the past year, only about 35 percent did so using a formal account in Europe and Central Asia, Latin America and the Caribbean, and Sub-Saharan Africa'; in addition, the 29% of worldwide savers preferred to save through asset accumulation or '"under the mattress"' (ibidem, 35).

16 ROSCAs are a group of people who periodically (e.g. weekly/monthly) contribute sums of money to a common pot that is disbursed to a different member each period (week/month). They have different names depending on the country (SHGs in India,

savings clubs and the 'mattress' represent for the poor valid alternatives to formal banking services, being flexible, negotiable and the creator of important social links.[17] Nonetheless, most of these informal methods have the downside of being subject to the risk of fraud and collapse as well as of not allowing enough flexibility or charging too high interest rates or even employing aggressive collection practices (*see* money-lenders/sharks).[18]

Although data are difficult to evaluate, in the region of 2.5 billion people worldwide appear not to have access to formal financial services, most located in Africa, Asia, Latin America and the Middle-East:[19] 56% of the world population does not benefit from any savings or credit product.[20]

Even in the EU, in 2011, 16% of EU citizens were unbanked (without a bank account) while 10% were financially excluded (without a bank account or credit or savings product) but with relevant differences among Member States. In fact, the unbanked population in EU-15 was 10%, while it was 40% in EU-12 (i.e. new Member States since 2004) and the financially excluded was 6% in EU-15 and

tontines in Cameron, *susu* in West Africa, *arisan* in Indonesia, *pandero* in Peru, *tanda* in Mexico and *polla* in Chile). *See* B. Armendáriz and J. Morduch, *The Economics of Microfinance* (2nd edn, MIT Press 2010), 67ff.; Demirguc-Kunt and Klapper, 'Measuring', 34.

17 *See* I. Guérin et al., 'Understanding the Diversity and Complexity of Demand for Microfinance Services: Lessons from Informal Finance', in M. Labie and B. Armendariz (eds), *The Handbook of Microfinance* (World Scientific Publishing 2011), 101ff.

18 *See* Demirguc-Kunt and Klapper, 'Measuring', 34; Rutherford, 'Clients', 62; R. Rajan, 'Separate and Unequal', (2006) 43(1) *Finan Dev* 58, 64–66.

19 A. Chaia et al., 'Half the World is Unbanked', (2009) Financial Access Initiative Framing Note, <www.mckinseyonsociety.com/downloads/reports/Economic-Development/Half_the_world_is_unbanked.pdf>; CGAP, 'Financial Access 2010. The State of Financial Inclusion through the Crisis', (2010) 5, <www.cgap.org/gm/document-1.9.47743/FA_2010_Financial_Access_2010_Rev.pdf>; Demirguc-Kunt and Klapper, 'Measuring', 2ff.

20 *See* O. Pinar Ardic et al., 'Access to Financial Services and the Financial Inclusion Agenda around the World. A Cross-Country Analysis with a New Data Set', (2011) World Bank Policy Research Working Paper 5537, 3, <http://ssrn.com/abstract=1747440>; J. Kendall et al., 'Measuring Financial Access around the World', World Bank Policy Research Working Paper 5537, 24, <www.cgap.org/gm/document-1.9.43130/Measuring_Financial_Access_Around_World.pdf>) calculated 160 million or 19% of all adults in EACs 'as unbanked and at 2.7 billion adults or 72%' in DCs. Financial inclusion is calculated using the data on the number of deposits and loans in each country; these data come from population surveys as well as banks' information to their national supervision authorities: nonetheless, this kind of estimate does not solve the problem of possible informal means, of accounts of the same person at different financial institutions or, on the contrary, of accounts used by more than one member of a family group or of existing but not used accounts. *See* CGAP, 'Access to Financial Services 2009. Measuring Access to Financial Services around the World', (2009), <www.cgap.org/sites/default/files/CGAP-Financial-Access-2009.pdf>. Recent studies adopt a different approach calculating banked and unbanked people through a global individual-based database that accounts for informal means, individual or collective accounts and other characteristics: *see* Chaia, 'Half'; Demirguc-Kunt and Klapper, 'Measuring'.

25% in EU-12, with the highest figures in Bulgaria, Romania, Hungary and Poland, followed, unexpectedly by Italy (*see* Figures 1.1 and 1.2).[21] In the same year, of the 56 million EU consumers not having a bank account, 6 million had their application rejected.[22]

Consequently, financial exclusion represents an important issue both in developing and ECA countries. However, while the credit crunch consequential to the financial crisis has made access to credit an urgent issue, traditional or new savings instruments (e.g. basic bank accounts) in Europe provided by postal services, public institutions and cooperative banks make the deposit side of the problem less pressing in the EU context (*see* Chapters 3, §5.a; 4, §6.b).

In Europe the attention is also focused on the access to funding by small and medium enterprises (SMEs). SMEs in fact represent 99% of the European non-financial enterprises (99.8% of EU-28 non-financial enterprises in 2014) and a good part of the aggregated production and jobs creation (78% of total employment

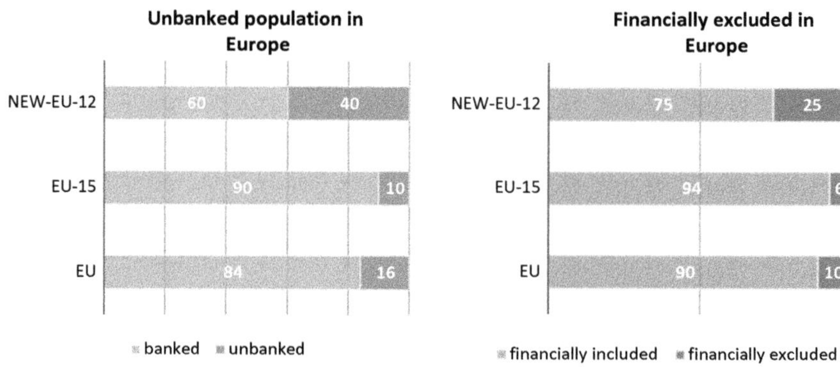

Figure 1.1 Unbanked and financially excluded population in Europe in 2011 (%)

21 Commission, 'Retail Financial', 10–14. EU citizens are most likely to have a bank account (84%), insurance (51%), credit card (40%), life insurance (31%), mortgage (19%), personal loans (13%), shares and bond (11%) and investment funds (7%): ibidem, 9.

22 Commission, 'Impact Assessment Accompanying the Proposal for a Directive on the Comparability of Fees Related to Payment Accounts, Payment Account Switching and Access to Payment Accounts with Basic Features', SWD(2013)164 final, 53. The Commission calculated that in 2009 there were '30.1 million consumers without access to a bank account' (7% of EU consumers), of which '11.6 million are likely to be at high risk of financial exclusion and 6.6 million more may be at risk, whereas the remaining 11.9 million are likely to be in a society where the use of bank accounts is not yet almost universal', but at present financial products are increasingly widespread and needed. *See* Commission, 'Study', 18. About U.S. financial exclusion, *see* FDIC, '2013 FDIC National Survey', 4 (7.7% of US households unbanked, corresponding to about 16.7 million adults and 8.7 million children and 20% underbanked – having an account but served by alternative providers – corresponding to 50.9 million adults and 16.6 million children).

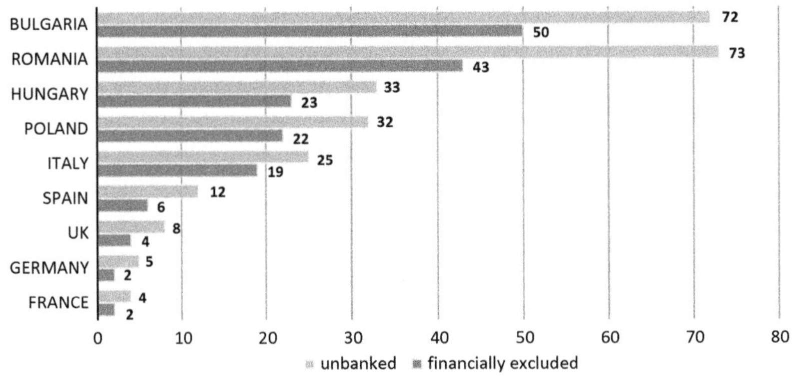

Figure 1.2 Unbanked and financially excluded in selected EU countries in 2011 (%)

and 71.4% of employment generation in 2014).[23] Among SMEs, micro-enterprises (with less than ten employees and turnover below €2 million) correspond to 92% of European businesses but only to a small part of the sector income.[24]

A recent survey depicts the restricted access to financing as one of the most urgent problems for SMEs.[25] SMEs mostly rely on bank financing since banks can partially overcome the asymmetric information related to the lack of verifiable public information about SMEs (and relative adverse selection and moral hazard problems) through the direct access to client-SMEs' savings account information (*see* Chapter 6, §2.b–c).[26] According to the same survey, about one third of SMEs applied for bank funding but obtained only a part of the amount requested or were rejected or refused the loan because of the high costs. In fact, bank loans were most likely assigned to the largest enterprises as well as larger and more

23 *See* Commission, *Annual Report on European SMEs 2014/2015. SMEs Start Hiring again*, (Brussels 2015), 3 and 7–8. *See* also Commission, 'An Action Plan to Improve Access to Finance for SMEs', (Communication) COM(2011)870, 1 (linking to SMEs more than half of the total value added in the non-financial business economy and 80% of all new jobs in Europe in the previous five years). Another study report that SMEs account for about 67% of the employment in the non-financial business economy, of which 20% is by small enterprises and 17% by medium-sized enterprises: EIM Business & Policy Research, 'Do SMEs Create More and Better Jobs?', (2011), <http://ec.europa.eu/enterprise/policies/sme/facts-figures-analysis/performance-review/files/supporting-documents/2012/do-smes-create-more-and-better-jobs_en.pdf>.

24 EIM, 'Do SMEs'.

25 'Access to finance' ranked second (after 'finding customers') among the most pressing problems for SMEs in the opinion of 15% of European SMEs managers. The percentages were higher in some countries such as Cyprus (40%), Greece (32%), Spain and Croatia (23%), Slovenia (22%), Italy and Ireland (20%): Commission, '2013 SMEs' Action to Finance Survey. Analytical Report', (2013), 6, 15ff., <http://ec.europa.eu/enterprise/policies/finance/files/2013-safe-analytical-report_en.pdf>.

26 Commission, 'European Financial Stability and Integration Report 2012', SWD (2013)156 final, 125.

mature SMEs, registering smaller and younger SMEs a rejection rate of, respectively, 18% and 27% (versus the 3% of larger firms). While lending to large firms has already recovered its 2003–2004 pre-crisis level, lending to SMEs has not.[27] Anyway, SMEs obtaining credit experienced a rise in interest rates,[28] shorter maturities of loans and increased requests of collateral.[29] Finally, the introduction of additional capital requirements through the Capital Requirements Directive IV/ Capital Requirements Regulation (CRDIV/CRR) package has likely had a negative impact on SME lending.[30]

The importance of SMEs for the EU economy and its job market, combined with their difficulties in accessing financing, explains the focus of microfinance in Europe and of EU institutions in the promotion of SMEs financing (*see* Chapter 2, §2 about microfinance in Europe; Chapter 4, §2 about MFIs' missions).

2 Financial inclusion: a new financial regulator's objective

Until recently, the presence of financial regulators' objectives besides stability and efficiency has been considered distortive. While the development of financial markets had been linked to economic development, growth and general wealth, equity and financial inclusion were secondary targets of which financial regulators (among the most powerful in intervening in economic activity) were not necessarily perpetuators. The belief that financial development and growth would end up benefiting the whole population supported such order.[31] However, recently, inefficiencies within the financial system, related costs and social exclusion have been emphasized.[32]

The literature about the nexus between financial development and growth,[33] on the one side, and poverty alleviation and equality, on the other, is not unanimous.

27 *See* EBA, 'Report on SMEs and SMEs Supporting Factor', EBA/Op/2016/04, 45ff.

28 *See* Commission, '2013 SMEs', 7–10 and 34ff.; OECD, 'Financing SMEs and Entrepreneurs 2013: An OECD Scoreboard – Final Report', (2013), 27, <www.oecd.org/officialdocuments/publicdisplaydocumentpdf/?cote=CFE/SME(2012)12/FINAL&docLanguage=En> (only 12 countries registered a significant increase in interest rate spreads between SMEs and large firms); EBA, 'Report', 56ff.

29 OECD, 'Financing', 27–28.

30 EBA, 'Assessment of SME Proposals for CRD IV/CRR', (Sept. 2012), <www.eba.europa.eu/documents/10180/16148/EBA-SME-Report.pdf>.

31 *See* M. Sriram et al., 'Too Big to Fail versus Too Small to be Counted', (BIS conference 'Financial Sector Regulation for Growth, Equity and Stability', Mumbai, 15–16 Nov. 2011), 95–96, <www.bis.org/publ/bppdf/bispap62j.pdf>. For a summary on the literature about finance, growth and equality, *see* A. Demirgüç-Kunt, 'Finance and Economic Development. The role of government', in A. Berger et al., *The Oxford Handbook of Banking*, (OUP 2012), 729ff.

32 Anderloni and Carluccio, 'Access', 6–7.

33 Instead, the recent literature agrees on the fundamental role of financial sector development in facilitating growth: *see* R. Levine, 'Finance and Growth: Theory and Evidence', (2004), NBER Working Paper 10766, <www.nber.org/papers/w10766>; A. Demirgüç-Kunt and R. Levine, 'Finance, Financial Sector Policies, and Long-Run Growth', (2008) World Bank Policy Research Working Paper 4469, <http://ssrn.com/abstract=1081783>; R. Rajan and L. Zingales, 'Financial Development and Growth', (1998) 88

A part of the literature believes that financial development benefits only the rich and powerful.[34] On the contrary, some studies suggest that financial development generally leads also to the reduction in income inequalities and to the growth of the lowest income share.[35] Finally, some others have found that the distributional effect of financial development depends on the general level of economic development where only at high levels of economic development does financial development broaden poor access.[36] Alternatively, it might be significant only in the long run and thanks to the indirect effects of growth (e.g. more people in the labour market and higher wages)[37] or, considering the initial high level of inequalities, reached only through specific enabling regulations.[38] Most reconnect inequalities to financial underdevelopment and capital imperfections are often recognized as responsible for the negative relationship between growth and inequalities:[39] a real reduction in poverty through growth and financial sector development has more chances to happen if the process is inclusive, with policies able to reduce inequalities. In fact, recent studies seem to reconnect expanded access to poverty reduction and long-term economic growth.[40]

Am Econ Rev 559; J. Zhuang et al., 'Financial Sector Development, Economic Growth, and Poverty Reduction: A Literature Review, (2009) ADB Economics Working Paper 173, 3, 15ff., <www.adb.org/publications/financial-sector-development-economic-growth-and-poverty-reduction-literature-review>. Nonetheless, it is not clear what kind of reforms each legal system needs, considering the experimented failures in transition economies: *see* K. Pistor et al., 'Law and Finance in Transition Economies', (2000) 8 *Econ Transit* 325; K. Davis and M. Trebilcock, 'The Relationship Between Law and Development: Optimists versus Sceptics', (2009) 57(1) *Am J Com Law* 895; Zhuang, 'Financial', 6ff.

34 N. Lamoreaux, *Insider Lending: Banks, Personal Connections, and Economic Development in Industrial New England* (CUP 1994); S. Haber (ed.), *How Latin America Fell Behind?* (SUP 2005), 146–178.

35 *See* T. Beck et al., 'Finance, Inequality and the Poor' (2007) 12 *J Econ Growth* 27; P. Aghion and P. Bolton, 'A Theory of Trickle-Down Growth and Development', (1997) 64 *Rev Econ Stud* 151. For additional references, *see* also J. Barth et al., *Rethinking Banking Regulation. Till Angels Govern* (CUP 2006), 2.

36 J. Greenwood and B. Jovanovic, 'Financial Development, Growth, and the Distribution of Income', (1990) 98 *J Pol Econ* 1076.

37 X. Giné and R. Townsend, 'Evaluation of Financial Liberalization: A General Equilibrium Model with Constrained Occupation Choice' (2004) 74 *J Dev Econ* 269.

38 *See* M. Ravaillon, 'Pro-Poor Growth: A Primer', (2004) World Bank Policy Research Working Paper 3242, <www-wds.worldbank.org/servlet/WDSContentServer/WDSP/IB/2004/06/09/000009486_20040609104122/Rendered/PDF/wps3242growth.pdf>; Allen, 'The Foundations'; Demirguc-Kunt and Klapper, 'Measuring', 19; Chaia, 'Half', 8ff.

39 T. Beck et al., 'Financial and Legal Constraints to Firm Growth: Does Size Matter?', (2005) 60 *J Finance* 137; G. Clarke, 'More Evidence on Income Distribution and Growth', (1995) 47 *J Dev Econ* 403; T. Person and G. Tabellini, 'Is Inequality Harmful for Growth?', (1994) 84 *Am Econ Rev* 600.

40 Beck, 'Finance'; Zhuang, 'Financial', 22.

Improvements in institutions and regulation are considered the instruments for expanding access[41] while maintaining stability.[42] International and national documents, especially if issued after the financial crisis, list financial inclusion among financial regulators' tasks. The G20 group commits itself to financial inclusion and access.[43] The Basel Committee on Banking Supervision (BCBS) has adapted its Core Principles for effective banking supervision to deposits-taking microfinance institutions[44] and has also revised the same Core Principles with the aim of taking into account financial inclusion. The responsibility for attaining such new objectives can now be attributed to the financial supervisor, provided that it does not conflict with the primary objective of safety and soundness.[45] The BCBS ascribes to financial inclusion a fundamental role in assisting financial regulator's tasks: it can make central banks' interest rates policy more effective and contribute to their price stability objective. Furthermore, financial inclusion can also result in stability improvements thanks to a broader depositor base (with a resilience effect) and a more diversified lending-base.[46] Other advantages would consist of improved transparency, financial integrity, lower macroeconomic volatility and social and political instability.[47]

Financial exclusion already represented a major concern for many developing countries (DCs) even before the crisis, but EACs have recently started tackling

41 About the fundamental role of the law in financial markets, K. Pistor, 'Law in Finance', (2013) 41(2) *J Comp Econ* 311. In general about the role of law in countries' development, D. Trubeck and M. Galanter, 'Scholars in Self-Estrangement: Some Reflections on the Crisis in Law and Development Studies in the United States', (1974) 4 *Wisc Law Rev* 1062; D. Rodrik et al., 'Institutions Rule. The Primacy of Institutions Over Geography and Integration in Economic Development', (2004) 9 *J Econ Growth* 131.

42 *See* Zhuang, 'Financial', 31.

43 G20, 'Leaders' Statement. The Pittsburgh Summit', (24–25 September 2009), <www.g20.org/Documents/pittsburgh_summit_leaders_statement_250909.pdf>; G20, 'Seoul Summit Document', (11–12 November 2010), in particular 10, 12–14, Annexe II, 8ff., <www.g20.utoronto.ca/2010/g20seoul-doc.pdf>.

44 BCBS, 'Microfinance Activities and the Core Principles for Effective Banking Supervision', (2010), <www.bis.org/publ/bcbs175.pdf>.

45 Principle 1, essential criterion 2: 'The primary objective of banking supervision is to promote the safety and soundness of banks and the banking system. If the banking supervisor is assigned broader responsibilities, these are subordinate to the primary objective and do not conflict with it': BCBS, *Core Principles for Effective Banking Supervision*, (BIS 2012), 22 but *see* 4–5, 21. *See* also BCBS, *Range of Practice in the Regulation and Supervision of Institutions Relevant to Financial Inclusion*, (BIS 2015) and BCBS, *Guidance on the Application of the Core Principles for Effective Banking Supervision to the Regulation and Supervision of Institutions Relevant to Financial Inclusion – Consultative Document*, (BIS 2015), 5.

46 A. Mehrotra and J. Yetman, 'Financial Inclusion – Issues for Central Banks', 2015 (March) *BIS Quarterly Review* 83ff. *See* also Hannig and Jansen, 'Financial'; R. Han and M. Melecky, 'Financial Inclusion for Financial Stability: Access to Bank Deposits and the Growth of Deposits in the Global Financial Crisis', (2013) World Bank Policy Research Working Paper 6577, <https://openknowledge.worldbank.org/handle/10986/16010>.

47 BCBS, *Guidance*, 5.

financial inclusion issues.[48] For example, the UK lists economic growth and financial inclusion and equity as objectives for prudential and consumer protection authorities within the financial regulation reform and has a Parliamentary group dedicated to microfinance.[49] In 2010, 90% of economies appeared to have at least some aspects of financial inclusion under the purview of the main financial regulator.[50]

In fact, recent studies seem oriented towards recognizing financial inclusion as contributing in the long run not only to growth but also to stability, thanks also to diversification (although many relevant data and aspects still lack this).[51] Furthermore, financial services for low-income people would not entail systemic risk because of the small size of the sector or its institutions (*see* Chapter 6, §§1–2, 4, 6.a, 7). Nonetheless, financial inclusion might also entail some stability risks where policies are not well calibrated: as experimented with the subprime crisis, excessive credit growth with inadequate lending standards or rapid expansion of unregulated parts of the financial sector can lead to instability.[52]

Financial inclusion would also contribute to the general welfare through the reduction of an informal financial services market and therefore also of the risks of money-laundering and financing terrorism.[53]

48 *See* CGAP, 'Financial Access 2010', 16ff.; CGAP and IFC, 'Financial Access 2011. An Overview of the Supply-Side Data Landscape', 1, <www.cgap.org/sites/defa, ult/files/CGAP-Forum-Financial-Access-2011-An-Overview-of-the-Supply-Side-Data-Landscape-Jun-2012.pdf>.

49 *See* HM Treasury, 'A New Approach to Financial Regulation: Summary of Consultation Responses', (2010), 6, §2.14, <www.gov.uk/government/uploads/system/uploads/attachment_data/file/190261/summaryofcondocresponses241110.pdf>; All-Parliamentary Group on Microfinance (APPG on Microfinance), 'Helping or Hurting: What role for Microfinance in the Fight against Poverty?', 2011; Id., 'Call for Written Evidence on the Regulation of Microfinance' (2012), <www.appg-microfinance.org/documents.php>.

50 CGAP, 'Financial Access 2010', 2. A 2013 BCBS survey (BCBS, 'Range', 11) conveys partially different results (likely because of a narrower concept of financial inclusion): 37% of respondents have a national financial inclusion strategy and/or a microfinance strategy (63% among low-income countries and 17% for high-income ones); 27% of all respondents have no strategy but are in the process of developing one, 6% have neither a strategy nor a plan to develop one but have signed the Maya Declaration while the remaining 31% neither have, nor have plans to develop, a strategy and have not signed the Maya Declaration. The large majority of the respondents having a financial inclusion strategy rely on the central bank, banking supervisory authority or the Ministry of Finance to implement it.

51 *See* Demirgüç-Kunt, 'Finance and Economic', 729ff.; Proceedings from BIS Conference 'Financial Sector Regulation', 22, 45ff., 95 and 113; Hannig and Jansen, 'Financial Inclusion', 23–24; CGAP and G20, 'Global Standard-Setting Bodies and Financial Inclusion for the Poor. Toward Proportionate Standards and Guidance', (2012), 9 and 12, <www.gpfi.org/sites/default/files/documents/CGAP.pdf>. About doubts regarding the direction of causality between financial inclusion and economic development, D. Ferrand, 'Building Inclusive Financial Markets', in Ledgerwood, *The New*, 461–462.

52 Mehrotra and Yetman, 'Financial inclusion', 84, 91–93.

53 CGAP and G20, 'Global Standard-Setting', 5 and 29. *See* also FATF, 'FATF Guidance. Anti-Money Laundering and Terrorist Financing Measures and Financial Inclusion', (2013), <www.fatf-gafi.org/media/fatf/documents/reports/AML_CFT_Measures_and_Financial_Inclusion_2013.pdf>.

The shift of focus of transnational standards-setting bodies and national regulators can represent a challenge, involving a new perspective and a new equilibrium among missions, with important lessons to draw from DCs' experience in financial inclusion.[54]

However, in high-income countries, the attention of regulators as regards financial inclusion tends to focus more on consumer protection and financial literacy while in low-income and middle-income countries they also take care of the promotion of financial access.[55] Anyway, consumer protection, developed in EACs, has now found new motives and power both in the former and in DCs (although it can have the effect of restricting access through the imposition of burdensome obligations on financial institutions and so costs). Consequently, financial regulator's objectives appear now closer in the 'two worlds'.

Such relevant change in financial regulation objectives is also a reaction to speculative operations involving low-income people's financial needs (*see* subprime scandal, Chapters 4, §5 and 7, §1) and it is sometimes justified on ethical/equity grounds (e.g. the need to reintroduce ethics in the financial world and satisfy the poor's need: *see* Chapter 4) and, some others, on efficiency and stability grounds (e.g. diversification reducing risks and limitation of crises backlash: *see* above and Chapters 4, 8). New corrective measures might also be needed to react to market failures linked to consumer cognitive biases (*see* Chapter 8).

In conclusion, financial regulators now face the challenge of promoting financial inclusion without endangering stability: this task might require a varied range of policies, entailing traditional financial institutions' involvement as well as the promotion of innovative forms of finance, not focusing only on credit but on a wider array of financial services (Chapters 4, 6–7).

3 Financial inclusion and microfinance

Microfinance, as the provision of financial services to unbanked people, seems to respond to all these new needs. In fact, it contributes to financial inclusion (along with other objectives: *see* Chapter 4), advances financial education through coaching services and relationship-banking, carefully checks the client's level of indebtedness and repayment capability and present flexibility, negotiability and empowerment (aspects appreciated in informal financial instruments: *see* Chapter 2 about microfinance characteristics). In addition, it seems able to serve otherwise neglected individuals, overcoming markets failures through specific tools such as group lending, progressive lending, short maturity, frequent instalments, social networks and relationship banking (*see* Chapters 2, §1; 6).[56] Finally, it aims at increasing financial access through a hybrid model of market-based approach and public support (consistent with so-called 'pro-market activism'[57]).

54 CGAP and G20, 'Global Standard-Setting', 11, 12.

55 *See* CGAP, 'Financial Access 2010', 16.

56 *See* Demirgüç-Kunt, *Finance for All?*, 114–123. On the topic of market failures and techniques to solve them, *see* also Barth, *Rethinking*, 22ff.

57 *See* de la Torre, 'Innovative', 4, 24–26.

Microfinance has received the endorsement of powerful international organizations (World Bank, UN, G-20) and been seen as a good response not only to financial exclusion but also to poverty and people's lack of freedom (*see* Chapter 4, §1).

Nonetheless, evidence about the real 'financial inclusion effect' of microfinance is not conclusive yet. In fact, the success of microfinance is often measured by the number of clients served by the industry but, first of all, it is not always clear whether those clients would not have been served by mainstream financial institutions (although their low income and lack of previous experiences with banks may suggest their otherwise exclusion). Second, some assert that a better index of microfinance success in promoting financial inclusion would correspond to the number of clients moving from microfinance to the mainstream financial sector ('graduated' clients),[58] while donations and non-governmental organizations' (NGOs') mentality within microfinance (somewhere entailing lax screening and instability) instead discourage low-income people from saving with banks, also frustrating the development of local financial sectors.

Furthermore, studies seem to recognize a robust link only between micro-savings and certain positive effects such as increased savings, productive investment, consumption and women's empowerment while credit access appears only weakly correlated to such effects (*see* Chapter 4, §1). Moreover, while credit might not suit everybody and when excessive can lead to instability, savings and payment instruments are always needed (*see* Chapter 4, §5).[59]

On the other hand, recent scandals in the microfinance sector related to abusive collection practices and other consumers' rights violations (Chapter 8) highlight that microfinance itself is not able to solve all the financial sector's problems.

Consequently, an attentive evaluation of all interests, principles and objectives involved by regulators is needed to reach an effective regulation of microfinance and services to low-income people.

Before entering the area of discussing the issues concerning microfinance regulation, it is worth describing this new sector in order to understand its features, risks and advantages and the regulatory challenge in balancing different objectives and interests (such as innovation, financial inclusion, consumer protection and financial stability).

58 *See* C. Ahlin and N. Jiang, 'Can Micro-credit Bring Development?', (2008) 86 *J Dev Econ* 1.

59 Mehrotra and Yetman, 'Financial Inclusion', 92; Demirgüç-Kunt, *Finance for All?*, x, 14, 17.

2 Microcredit and microfinance: general characteristics

1 From microcredit to microfinance

Microfinance's origins and main activity still consists of microcredit, the provision of small loans to micro-entrepreneurs otherwise 'unbanked', relying on the cash-flow generated through their clients' economic activity.

These activities have been carried on through different types of bodies, from not-for-profit entities to commercial banks and regulated financial institutions, with varied objectives, techniques and geographic interests. Microfinance institutions (MFIs) are entities adopting varied legal forms (e.g. banks, companies, cooperatives, NGOs, non-bank financial institutions (NBFIs)) that specialize in the provision of microfinance services, specifically microcredit.[1]

Microfinance has roots in informal and rotating mechanisms of saving and financing (e.g. 'tontines' and 'ROSCAs': *see* Chapter 1, §1) as well as in the financial cooperatives movement in Europe (Chapter 3, §5.a). However, it has recently gained recognition throughout the world as an effective and profitable business with some special features adopted by Grameen Bank in Bangladesh to cope with the risks involved in the activity.[2] In fact, MFIs, having the poor as typical clients, need to deal, among other factors, with the absence of traditional collateral (i.e. something objectively valuable that can be seized or someone wealthy who can repay in case of the borrower's default), of a reliable stream of funds (informal and temporary jobs) and lack of statistical data about the borrower's ability to repay (*see* also Chapters 6, §2; 8, §1.b).

One of the better known features is group lending: in order to address asymmetric information problems and monitoring costs, loans are made to each member of a self-formed group but they are all denied further loans if they cannot cover for a defaulted member. Consequently, group members have incentives in selecting trustworthy and successful peers and in monitoring them.[3] This system

1 *See* §2.a and Chapter 5, §2 about different legal forms.

2 About Grameen Bank: M. Yunus, *Banker to the Poor: Microlending and the Battle against World Poverty* (Public Affairs 1998); A. Dowla and D. Barua, *The Poor Always Pay Back – The Grameen II Story* (Kumarian Press 2006).

3 *See* B. Armendáriz and J. Morduch, *The Economics of Microfinance*, (2nd edn, MIT Press 2005), 12ff. and 85ff.; X. Giné et al., 'Microfinance Games', (2006) *Yale*

heavily relies on social networks, cultural tradition and social norms[4] and, thus, adapts to local characteristics. Anyway, it might contribute to the exclusion of the poorest subjects or people discriminated by the group and fail in effectively screening entrepreneurial projects.[5]

An additional technique is progressive lending: in the absence of traditional forms of collateral, incentives to repay are mostly linked to the expectation of receiving a larger loan once the previous one is repaid.[6] This instrument is less effective when competition is intense since borrowers can easily find an alternative source of financing.[7]

Furthermore, MFIs have often identified women as their target-client not only because in many countries they are traditionally excluded from mainstream finance but also because they tend to be more reliable, dedicated to saving for the family instead of futile goods, more subject to social pressure to repay, less mobile and, thus, more easily monitored.[8]

A fourth characteristic is a borrowers' selection process based on a detailed analysis of the candidate's personality and business project, also through field visits and interviews with family and neighbours, performed by loan officers with deep knowledge of the market and social environment (*see* Chapter 6, §2.b).

Moreover, short maturities and frequent instalments facilitate client monitoring and support and reduce MFIs' exposure (*see* Chapter 6, §2.a).[9]

Many microfinance experiences are also characterized by high interest rates: MFIs face considerable operational expenses due to the high cost of capital, labour-intensive selection and monitoring processes, offering services in remote areas and, above all, for managing many loans and accounts of limited amount (Chapter 8, §4).

Finally, coaching services often accompany microloans, in order to increase the chances of repayment and social impact (Chapter 4, §6.e).[10]

University Economic Growth Center Discussion Paper No. 936, 4, <http://ssrn.com/abstract=912301>; D. Karlan, 'Social Connections and Group Banking', (2007) 117 Econ J F52.

4 *See* A. Cassar et al., 'The Effect of Social Capital on Group Loan Repayment: Evidence from Field Experiments', (2007) 117 *Econ J* 85.

5 R. Dyal-Chand, 'Reflection in a Distant Mirror: Why the West has Misperceived the Grameen Bank's Vision of Microcredit', (2005) 41 *Stan J Int'l* 217, 254ff.

6 *See* Armendáriz and Morduch, *The Economics*, 119, 125ff.; D. Egli, 'Progressive Lending as an Enforcement Mechanism in Microfinance Programs', (2004) 8 *Rev Dev Econ* 505.

7 *See* J. Morduch, 'The Promise of Microfinance', (1999) 37 *J Econ Lit* 1569.

8 *See* Yunus, *Banker*; Armendáriz and Morduch, *The Economics*, 13ff., 138ff. About the negative effects on women (e.g. excessive pressure, violence by the husband), *see* Dyal-Chand, 'Reflection', 261ff.

9 *See* Yunus, *Banker*; P. Mosley and D. Hulme, 'Micro Enterprise Finance: Is There a Conflict between Growth and Poverty Alleviation?', (1998) 26(5) *World Dev* 783.

10 About coaching services and their link with financial inclusion, *see* D. Karlan and M. Valdivia, 'Teaching Entrepreneurship: Impact of Business Training on Microfinance Clients and Institutions', (2006) Yale University Economic Growth Center Discussion Paper 941, <www.econ.yale.edu/growth_pdf/cdp941.pdf>; M. Sievers and P.

Nonetheless, such features have not necessarily been maintained in the spreading around the world and development of microfinance: we can now witness many individual, consumer and larger loans and mortgages instead of just small business loans,[11] entailing new risks and fewer alternative safeguards. Anyway, microcredit still results in characteristics such as small amounts and short maturities, low-income clients, lack of traditional collateral, personalized and relationship-based credit evaluation as well as, often, coaching services (*see* Chapter 3, §1).

The sector development and attempt to respond to clients' needs have led to the offering of additional services such as deposits, remittances, payments and insurance, transforming microfinance into a sort of 'micro-banking' for the poor and raising several regulatory issues (*see* Chapters 3–4, 6).

2 Microfinance in Europe: peculiar features of microfinance in a very varied region with a complex and harmonized legal framework

Although conceived to face some challenges typical of developing countries (e.g. lack of credit bureaux and of good institutions to enforce collateral repossession), microfinance has also appealed to economically advanced countries, especially after the financial crisis. It has represented a way to re-discover financial services in an ethical perspective as well as for reaching out to people excluded from the financial sector by the downsides of standardization of contracts, credit evaluation and regulatory costs rise in the banking sector (Chapter 6, §2.b).

The demand for microfinance in Europe is constantly growing, although estimates about current figures are very difficult to attempt. The Commission estimated in 2007 a demand of 700,000 microloans worth €6.2 billion (based on the number of working adults and the share of population at risk of poverty),[12] while European MFIs estimated a few years later (post-crisis) a demand corresponding to 2.9 billion microloans (based on the number of unemployed, people excluded from both the market and welfare services and other disadvantaged groups).[13] An updated estimation (2012) by Evers & Jung, based on the same methodology used by the Commission in 2007 (and therefore rather conservative, accounting only for

Vandenberg, 'Synergies through Linkages: Who Benefits from Linking Micro-finance and Business Development Services?', (2007), 14, <www.ilo.org/wcmsp5/groups/public/@ed_emp/@emp_ent/@ifp_seed/documents/publication/wcms_143167.pdf>.

11 *See* A. Jain and C. Norton, 'Microfinance: Where Do We Stand Today?', (2009) 18 MicroBanking Bulletin 9, <www.themix.org/sites/default/files/MBB%2018%20Spring%202009.pdf>.

12 Commission, 'An European Initiative for the Development of Micro-credit in Support of Growth and Employment' (Communication) COM(2007)708.

13 C. Guene, 'Microcredit Networks and Existing National Legislations with a View to the Implementation of the Microfinance instrument', (2010) European Parliament Report, <www.europarl.europa.eu/RegData/etudes/note/join/2010/451479/IPOL-EMPL_NT(2010)451479_EN.pdf>; M. Unterberg et al., *Study on the Imperfections in the Area of Microfinance and Options How to Address Them through an EU Financial Instrument – Final Progress Report*, (EU 2014), 8–10.

working adults at risk of poverty) but on a country-by-country basis, refers to 1.2 million business micro-loans, worth €6.2 billion or €5.1 billion (depending on the methodology).[14] However, a more realistic estimation would also include unemployed people wishing to become entrepreneurs and established micro-entrepreneurs and the self-employed seeking, respectively, micro-loans and to become micro-entrepreneurs. Consequently, the expected demand ranges from €5.1 billion to €41 billion (or from 667,000 to 5.1 million borrowers).[15]

The reported number of microloans disbursed in 2013 in the EU was 388,000, for a total value of €1.53 million (with a 45% increase in total value of loans and a 69% increase in the number of loans since 2011 and 400% since 2009),[16] with a significant share of unmet demand (an estimated market gap of at least €2.7 billion).[17]

Transplanted into Europe, microfinance had to adapt to a different context, sometimes losing in the process part of its originality and mission (*see* §a) but nonetheless Europe also represents a stimulating area of study because of such distinct features of European microfinance (and consequent regulatory implications) and diversity in legal traditions (Chapters 3; 6) as well as of the currently highly regulated and harmonized nature of the European financial sector (*see* Introduction, Chapter 3, §4).

a The European microfinance market: examples of Western countries (France, Germany, Italy, Spain, UK) versus *Eastern countries (Croatia, Bulgaria, Hungary, Poland, Romania) and common features*

Microcredit came to Eastern European countries ('new', since most entered the European Union after 2004) in the early 1990s, assisting their transition to a liberal economy and dominated by international NGOs and foreign aid. For instance, Romanian, Bulgarian, Hungarian and Polish microcredit grew in the 1990s as a reaction to both post-communism liberalisation and the banks' inability to serve part of the population and was mainly provided by internationally supported NGOs on an individual and progressive basis.[18] Similarly, Croatian microcredit

14 Unterberg, *Study*, 10–14.

15 Commission, 'Evaluation of the JASMINE Technical Assistance Pilot Phase – Final Report', (2013), 16–20, <http://ec.europa.eu/regional_policy/sources/thefunds/doc/instruments/jasmine/jasmine_evaluation_final_report.pdf> (*see* also 22 for an estimated demand for each EU country).

16 *See* M. Bendig et al., 'Overview of the Microcredit Sector in the European Union – 2012/2013', (2014), 7, 9, 22, <www.european-microfinance.org/docs/emn_publications/emn_overview/Overview2012-2013_Nov2014.pdf> (the survey covers 150 MFIs out of 447 from 24 countries with an overall response rate of 34% corresponding to 207,335 microloans and €1.26 billion).

17 Unterberg, *Study*, 11–15.

18 Romanian state-owned banks tended to lend to state enterprises and government institutions and to disregard low-densely populated areas: *see* M. Doiciu and D. Bialus, 'Microcredit in Romania', in B. Jayo Carboni et al. (eds), *Handbook of Microcredit in Europe. Social Inclusion through Microenterprise Development*, (Edgar Elgar 2010), 306ff.; C. Pop and P. Buys, 'Microfinance in Romania', (2015) 5 *Contemporary Legal*

supported post-war reconstruction through the financing and technical support of international organizations (first, the United States Agency for International Development (USAID) and since 2013, the EU).[19]

Nonetheless, the sector has developed very fast, turning more recently to for-profit oriented models, also following international funders' preferences and reaching a high level of maturity in terms of self-sufficiency, specialization, models, product diversification and funding sources (Chapters 4–5). Consequently, the Eastern European microfinance sector is more structured and similar to developing countries' ones, characterized by the presence also of NBFIs, financial cooperatives and even specialized microfinance banks, all fiercely competing with mainstream banks.[20] For example, Romanian microfinance has gone through an intense commercialization process under international and regulatory pressure[21] and it is now dominated by (for profit) NBFIs,[22] credit unions (collectively 95% of MFIs)[23] and SME-banks all specializing in microcredit, but also commercial banks are interested in partnerships with specialized operators thanks to government projects subsidizing

& Economic Issues 307, 310–11. Among the first donors in Bulgaria: USAID, EU PHARE Programme, Germany and Switzerland: *see* EMN and EIF, 'EIF Market Studies on Micro Lending in the European Union – Cross Country Study on Central and Eastern Europe', (2009), 131, <www.emnconference.org/archives/data/file/EIF%20Study%20Microlending_Eastern%20Central%20Europe_March%2009.zip>; K. Munev, 'The Microcredit Sector in Bulgaria', in Jayo Carboni, *Handbook*, 103. Between 1992 and 2008, the Hungarian microfinance sector was dominated by the PHARE Program (Poland-Hungary Assistance for the Reconstruction of the Economy, 21 million ECU) and National Microcredit Programme of the Hungarian Foundation for Enterprise Promotion (HFEP, initially 1,5 million ECU) funded by the EU and the Hungarian government and administered through a Local Enterprise Agencies (LEAs) national network: Bendig, 'Overview', 29; T. Szekfu, 'Hungary', (2013) EMN Legislative Mapping Report 12/2013; Id., 'The Hungarian Microfinance Legislation', in J. Durán Navarro, *TheIimportance of a Microfinance Legislation for the Development of the Sector in Spain*, (Cromoimagen 2013), 51ff.; S. Lagoa, 'Financial Institutions and Supply of Financial Services in the European Microcredit Market: A Survey of Selected Countries' Experiences', (2014) FESSUD Working Paper 73, 41, <www.fessud.eu/wp-content/uploads/2013/04/Financial-institutions-supply-of-financial-services_European-microcredit-market_WP-73.pdf>. For Poland, A. Szostek, 'The State of Microfinance in Poland', in Jayo Carboni, *Handbook*, 329ff.

19 *See* J. Borzic, 'Croatia', (2013) EMN Legislative Mapping Report 12/2013, 3, <www.european-microfinance.org/docs/emn_publications/other_emn_publications/mapping_croatia_2013.pdf>.

20 *See* Bendig, 'Overview', 20, 29–30; MFC, EMN and CDFA, 'From Exclusion to Inclusion through Micro Finance', (2007), Report 3, <www.emnconference.org/archives/data/file/programmes/from-exclusion-to-inclusion-through-microfinance-benchmarks-and-performance-measurement.pdf>; EIF, 'Microfinance in Europe. A Market Overview', (2009), 13–14, <www.eif.org/news_centre/publications/EIF_WP_2009_001_Microfinance.pdf>

21 Pop and Buys, 'Microfinance', 312.

22 Pop and Buys, 'Microfinance', 314ff.

23 Bendig, 'Overview 2014', 29.

microloans (e.g. Romanian Micro-Credit Facility).[24] It also shows intense product diversification, new risk management and debt collection procedures.[25] Bulgarian NGOs, too, have soon transformed into NBFIs or credit cooperatives,[26] with specialized (e.g. ProCredit) and mainstream banks also downscaling and competing for market segments,[27] all now fighting against the financial crisis recession.[28] Similarly, Hungarian microfinance since 2008 has attracted the attention of many for-profit investors thanks to the EU JEREMIE Program launch (*see infra* §b), which led to the creation of many MFIs (for profit and not-for-profit, with not-for-profit remaining the main actors and providing BDSs).[29] In Poland, liberalization has given the opportunity to a wide range of providers (including loan funds, private companies, associations and foundations) to offer micro-loans (Chapter 4, §6.c),[30] also with the creation of specialized microfinance banks.[31] In Croatia, the original NGOs and Savings and Loan Cooperatives (e.g. NOA, DEMOS and MikroPlus) have faced since 2000 the fierce competition of foreign-owned commercial banks (now partially withdrawing since the financial crisis)[32] and were forced by the Government in 2008 to transform into regulated credit unions or to close-down operations (Chapter 4, §6.c).[33]

Instead, microfinance reached Western countries mostly in the 2000s[34] and presents distinctive characteristics. It is in fact still a young sector with a lower but

24 Bendig, 'Overview 2014', 79, 30 (over 80% of Romanian MFIs are specialized in microcredit); Doiciu and Bialus, 'Microcredit', 309, 315–19; M. Doiciu, 'Best Practice in Microfinance in Romania', in A. Szabò, 'Microfinance for SMEs in the BSEC Region', conference proceedings (12–15 November 2014, Bucharest), 108.

25 Bendig, 'Overview', 77–79; EMN and EIF, 'Market Studies – Central and Eastern Europe', 75–76.

26 In 2007, the non-bank MFIs (covered by a recent survey) disbursed almost 10% of the microloan market in the country, with 15,294 active borrowers: EMN and EIF, 'Market Studies – Central and Eastern Europe', 28, 124.

27 *See* EMN and EIF, 'Market Studies – Central and Eastern Europe', 28, 123, 132, 138; Munev, 'The Microcredit', 105.

28 It had a 119% OSS ratio in 2013 but many recent operations appear unsustainable: Bendig, 'Overview', 49, 60.

29 Bendig, 'Overview', 29; T. Szekfu, 'Hungary', (2013) EMN Legislative Mapping Report 12/2013; Id., 'The Hungarian Microfinance Legislation', in Durán Navarro, *Importance*, 51ff.; Lagoa, 'Financial', 41.

30 Bendig, 'Overview', 74; Szostek, 'The State', 329ff.

31 The largest loan fund registered as limited liability company, Fundusz MIKRO, in 2010 transformed into a bank specializing in microfinance, expanding its offering of services and merging in 2013 with another bank (Bank Przedsiębiorczości SA): <www.fmbankpbp.pl/en/about/history/>.

32 *See* M. Bateman and D. Sinković, 'Impact of Microfinance in Croatia', in M. Bateman (ed.), *Confronting Microfinance: Undermining Sustainable Development*, (Kumarian Press 2011), 103–4. Croatia now ranks as the most difficult country in the region as regards financial access: Borzic, 'Croatia', 3.

33 Such government reaction was linked to negative experiences of money-laundering and loan sharks with cooperatives: Borzic, 'Croatia'. *See* also, for a critical analysis of microfinance in Croatia, Bateman and Sinković, 'Impact', 99ff.

34 German MFIs are among the youngest (50% of German MFIs started operations after 2010), accounting for 60% of all surveyed MFIs starting between 2010 and 2013: Bendig, 'Overview', 31.

growing demand, especially in some countries. For example, the French microcredit sector is large in terms of number and amount of loans disbursed as well as active borrowers, always ranking among the first three countries within the EU for these figures.[35] The size of the Italian microcredit market[36] is partially undefined because of different calculation methods (some including consumer credit and *prêts d'honneur*) and sample adopted[37] but it is anyway of limited size, although growing at a fast pace.[38] The Spanish microcredit sector, despite the post-crisis profound contraction (*see* below), remains the biggest one in the EU in terms of total value and number of loans disbursed (in 2013, respectively, €319 million and 56,570) as well as outstanding portfolio (€539.4 million), thanks to a few big players (e.g. MicroBank, of *La Caixa* group).[39] The potential demand for business microloans in the UK was estimated at about €1.3 billion (and potential 103,000 borrowers) in 2012[40] but it cannot be easily identified since there is no specific market segmentation. In fact, Community Development Finance Institutions (CDFIs) (non-bank providers created under many different legal forms but mostly not-for-profit and relying on public funding)[41] are considered the main microcredit providers because of their mission to finance SMEs and underserved

35 Bendig, 'Overview', 20–23 (in 2013 almost 47,000 loans for €276 million disbursed, 76,000 active borrowers and more than €432 million outstanding portfolio); *see* also M. Camdessus, 'Rapport annuel 2012 de l'Observatoire de la microfinance', <www.banque-france.fr/fileadmin/user_upload/banque_de_france/publications/Rapport-annuel_2012_Observatoire-microfinance.pdf>; Fond de Cohesion Sociale, 'Rapport d'activité 2014', <https://www.france-microcredit.org/sites/www.france-microcredit.org/IMG/pdf/ra_2014_-_fcs.pdf>.

36 On Italian microcredit, *see* Ente Nazionale per il Microcredito (ENM), 'Le multiformi caratteristiche del Microcredito. Rapporto finale di monitoraggio', (2013), <www.fgda.org/dati/ContentManager/files/Documenti_microfinanza/Le-multiformi-caratteristiche-del-microcredito—Rapporto-finale.pdf>; C. Borgomeo et al., 'IX Rapporto sul microcredito in Italia-2013', (2014), <www.fondazionedallefabbriche.coop/wp-content/uploads/2015/05/9%5E-Rapporto-sul-microcredito-in-Italia.pdf>; EMN and EIF, 'Microfinance Market Studies in the Framework of JEREMIE-Cross Country Study on Western Europe', (2009), 18, 21ff., <www.emnconference.org/archives/data/file/EIF%20Study%20Microlending_Western%20Europe_March%202009.zip>; S. Di Castri, 'The Microcredit Sector in Italy: Small Initiatives in a Dynamic Scenario', in Jayo Carboni, *Handbook*, 72ff.

37 *Compare* Evers, 'Status', Borgomeo, 'Rapporto 2007' and A. Limone and P. Vitali, *Banche e microfinanza. Esperienze e strumenti innovativi*, (Bancaria 2006), as well as Borgomeo, 'IX Rapporto' (in 2013, 165 initiatives responding to the survey, 15,344 loans for €174.9 million; in 2012, 3,579 microloans for €148.4 million) and ENM, 'Le multiformi', 11 (106 initiatives, 7,167 microloans for €63 million).

38 The number of beneficiaries and volume of loans in the 2010–2013 period have doubled. *See* Borgomeo, 'IX Rapporto', 52–53; Bendig, 'Overview', 68 (in 2013, 23 participating MFIs, 14,144 loans for €64.6 million).

39 Bendig, 'Overview', 20–23.

40 *See* CDFA, 'Inside Community Finance 2012', (2013), 8, <http://responsiblefinance.org.uk/policy-research/publications/> (CDFI in the UK have a wider coverage since they often provide loans above 25,000).

41 M. Bendig et al., 'Overview of the Microfinance Sector in Europe 2010/2011', (2012), 33, <www.european-microfinance.org/docs/emn_publications/emn_over

individuals but they generally do not distinguish (or report) based on the loan amount (with loans even above €25,000) or loan categorization (microcredit instead of other types).[42]

Western microfinance has also been traditionally characterized by not-for-profit orientation and non-specialized NGOs (conducting other non-financial/charitable activities besides microcredit).[43] For example, the French microfinance sector has been dominated by few big not-for-profit MFIs (e.g. ADIE – the first one in the country – France Initiative and France Active),[44] while the Italian market has been fragmented with a prevalence of many small not-for-profit organizations.[45] Nonetheless, in Italy, cooperatives, mutual organizations (MAG) and ethical banks also operate, while specialized for-profit organizations in the form of financial institutions (and therefore allowed to receive capital investments from banks) are only two ('PerMicro s.p.a.' and 'Microcredito di Solidarietà s.p.a.') and the recent 2010 reform seems not able to encourage new entrants.[46]

Anyway, considering the whole EU microfinance sector, the majority of MFIs are currently represented by NBFIs (29.3%), with not-for-profit institutions (NGOs and foundations), formerly the main group, still covering 22.9% of the total number of MFIs.[47] Credit unions and cooperatives form the third main institutional group (10%), while bank-MFIs represent only 5% (*see* ProCredit in

view/1.overview2010-2011-final.pdf> (100% of surveyed UK institutions were not-for-profit).

42 In 2006/2007 only 28% of CDFIs' loans could fall in the microcredit category (the average loan size among all CDFIs was €45,000): *see* EMN and EIF, 'Microfinance Market Studies – Western Europe', 18, 25–26, 55ff., 68.

43 *See* Bendig, 'Overview 2010/2011', 31–32; K. Molenaar, 'Microfinance, its Concepts and Development, Lessons to Draw from Europe', (2009), 12, <www.microfinancegateway.org/sites/default/files/mfg-en-paper-microfinance-its-concepts-and-development-lessons-to-draw-for-europe-jan-2009_0.pdf> (not-for-profit sector represented the majority of EU-15 MFIs); L. Viganò et al., 'Microfinance in Europe', (2004) Working Paper, 8ff., <www.microfinancegateway.org/sites/default/files/mfg-en-paper-microfinance-in-europe-2004.pdf> (NGOs, associations and foundations 43%; NBFIs and financial cooperatives: 50%); J. Evers et al., 'Status of Microfinance in Western Europe', (2007) 20, <www.microfinancegateway.org/sites/default/files/mfg-en-paper-status-of-microfinance-in-western-europe-an-academic-review-2007.pdf> (9 out 10 European MFIs were not-for-profit and 4 out of 10 were NGOs managing half of the entire volume of microloans).

44 The last two focus, respectively, on '*prêt d'honneur*' (to nearly bankable clients) and guarantee schemes: *see* S. Lämmermann, 'Microcredit in France: Financial Support for Social Inclusion', in Jayo Carboni, *Handbook*, 44–46.

45 *See* EMN and EIF, 'Market Studies – Western Europe', 188; Molenaar, 'Microfinance', 13.

46 C. Brusini, 'Microcredito. "La nuova legge costringe gli operatori a lavorare in perdita". Così l'albo degli intermediari resta vuoto', *Fatto Quotidiano* (6 March 2016), <www.ilfattoquotidiano.it/2016/03/06/microcredito-la-nuova-legge-costringe-gli-operatori-a-lavorare-in-perdita-cosi-lalbo-degli-intermediari-resta-vuoto/2496136/>.

47 Bendig, 'Overview', 29 (microfinance associations in 2013 corresponded to only 8% of European MFIs).

Bulgaria and Romania) but in addition to savings banks (2.7%).[48] Nonetheless, there are significant differences among countries, irrespective of the geographical region: for example, Bosnia and Herzegovina, Hungary, Italy and Poland present the highest shares of NGOs or foundations while the prevailing institutional form in Romania (95% of respondent MFIs) is the NBFI.[49]

In Western Europe, in many cases due to regulatory restrictions creating a banking monopoly on lending (Chapters 3, §4.c; 4, §6.c; 6, §3.b), MFIs often offer their services in partnership with banks. For example, in France partnerships between MFIs and commercial banks are incentivized by Social Cohesion Funds securing up to 50% of microloans and the NACRE programme for the developing of interest-free loans,[50] although banks are increasingly engaged in offering microcredit for consumption.[51] The traditional Italian microfinance model is trilateral ('linkage model'), involving mainstream banks (especially cooperative mutual banks – BCC) disbursing loans,[52] NGOs/foundations putting in contact beneficiaries and banks, monitoring the former and providing the same with supporting services and public entities (and/or foundations) supplying guarantees or subsidizing interest rates.[53] Similarly, in Germany, regional development banks disburse loans directly or through partner-banks, also cooperating with MFIs. For example, under the public scheme 'Mikrokreditfonds Deutschland' created in 2011, MFIs act as a 'front office', directly selecting and monitoring borrowers (and partially securing the loan) while the bank only formally disburses loans with public funds.[54]

In fact, European microfinance is also characterized by public support in many forms.[55] In Germany, regional development banks, in addition to directly disbursing loans or through banks, support guarantee funds for cooperation models between business support centres and banks under a complex risk-sharing and responsibilities scheme (e.g. with centres/MFIs supporting a 20% risk and monitoring repayments in exchange for a gratification payment depending on the repaid loans).[56] In Italy, EU structural funds and public resources allow the creation of guarantee funds in favour of banks and, more recently, also MFIs,

48 Bendig, 'Overview', 29.
49 Ibidem.
50 Bending, 'Overview', 62.
51 Bendig, 'Overview 2010/2011', 63–65.
52 *See* Limone and Vitali, *Banche*; ENM, 'Le multiformi', 57–58.
53 Borgomeo, 'IX Rapporto'; Commission, 'The Regulation of Microcredit in Europe', (Expert Group report) (2007), 12–13, <http://ec.europa.eu/DocsRoom/documents/3669/attachments/1/translations/en/renditions/pdf>; EMN and EIF, 'Microfinance Market Studies – Western Europe. 18, 21ff.; ENM, 'Le multiformi', 55ff.; Bendig, 'Overview', 68.
54 Bendig, 'Overview', 64; EMN and EIF, 'Microfinance Market Studies – Western Europe', 129–30; J. Evers and S. Lahn, 'Status of Microlending in Germany: An Empirical Survey of Programmes in 2006', in Jayo Carboni, *Handbook*, 164ff.
55 *See* EMN and EIF, 'Microfinance Market Studies – Western Europe', 17ff.
56 Ibidem.

providing micro-loans but sometimes even local authorities directly disburse loans.[57] The French social cohesion fund covers up to 50% of MFIs' loans.

The Spanish microcredit sector has been traditionally dominated by savings banks (*Caixas/Cajas*, devoted to providing financial services to low-income segments of society, thus combating usury), which have provided microcredit through in-house programmes or in partnerships with public entities (often without taking risks and relying on public funds or guarantees). NGOs and other private or public entities (Social Microcredit Support Organizations – SMSOs), previously also operating in the sector especially as partners of savings banks and providing fundamental supporting services,[58] have more recently filled the gap left by savings banks which, since the financial crisis have mostly ceased operations (cancelled or transformed in foundations after *ley* 26/2013).[59]

The different stage of maturity of European microfinance sectors is also evident in product offering. In Eastern and Central Europe, MFIs tend to offer not only microcredit but also a varied range of financial services, including different forms of lending, remittances, insurance and savings.[60] For example, Croatian products are personalized, flexible and creative as regards methodologies, guarantees funds and target clients[61] and in Bulgaria product offering is varied, including leasing and revolving loans.[62] Instead, Western MFIs typically offer only microcredit (Chapter 4, §6).[63] Furthermore, looking exclusively at microcredit, while in Eastern and Central Europe the main type is for business purposes (as in the EU as a whole), in Western Europe there is a preference for 'personal/social microcredit'

57 *See* Borgomeo, 'IX Rapporto', 33, 60 (50% of the 22 programmes started in 2013 were promoted by public entities, corresponding to 83.8% of loans and 82.5% of the total amount disbursed but considering all projects still active in 2013, the highest number and amount of loans have been disbursed by not-for-profit MFIs); ENM, 'Le multiformi', 29ff., 52–53.

58 *See* Bendig, 'Overview', 82ff.; Bendig, 'Overview 2010/2011', 32–33 (in 2011, 50% of Spanish MFIs were NGOs or foundations and 80% not-for-profit); EMN and EIF, 'Microfinance Market Studies', 294ff., 307ff.; S. Rico Garrido et al., 'Microcredit in Spain: The Role of Savings Banks', in Jayo Carboni, *Handbook,* 277ff.; S. Lagoa, 'Financial Institutions and Supply of Financial Services in the European Microcredit Market: A Survey of Selected Countries' Experiences', (2014) FESSUD Working Paper 73, 17ff., <www.fessud.eu/wp-content/uploads/2013/04/Financial-institutions-supply-of-financial-services_European-microcredit-market_WP-73.pdf>.

59 Bendig, 'Overview 2010/2011', 79–81 and 'Overview', 12, 80–82; M. Lacalle-Calderón and S. Rico, *Microfinanzas en España: impacto y recomendaciones a futuro* (Cromoimagen, 2012); E. González-Hernández, 'Microcréditos y nuevas formas de financiación en España', (2015), <https://repositorio.comillas.edu/xmlui/bitstream/handle/11531/6393/TFM000193.pdf?sequence=1&isAllowed=y>.

60 *See* MFC et al., 'From Exclusion', 4; M. Unterberg, 'Microfinance as a European Policy Issue – Policy Images and Venues', (2008), EMN Annual Conference, <http://tk.eversjung.de/www/downloads/Microfinance_as_a_European_policy_issue.pdf>; Molenaar, 'Microfinance', 10ff., 14; Commission, 'Evaluation', 9–12.

61 Bendig, 'Overview 2010/2011', 61–62.

62 Bendig, 'Overview', 59; EMN and EIF, 'Market Studies – Central and Eastern Europe', 16, 27, 148; Munev, 'The Microcredit', 119.

63 Bendig, 'Overview', 29 (46% of surveyed MFIs focus only on microcredit).

and 'emergency microcredit' (*see* Chapters 3, §1; 4, §§ 2 and 6.c).[64] For example, the current prevailing form of Italian microloans is social/emergency micro-loans (but entrepreneurial micro-loans present a lower number of loans but higher amounts)[65] as in the UK (in contrast to previous surveys).[66] Instead, in Poland and Hungary business microcredit dominates.[67] However, deviations from this scheme are frequent and the sector is evolving: in France, microcredit for business purposes is the predominant form as regards both volume and number of loans (in 2013, 82% of loans) with personal microcredit and microcredit for consumption growing fast.[68] In Spain, business and personal loans present similar figures in terms of amount disbursed (respectively, €175 million and €144 million) but the latter shows the highest number of loans (40,700 *versus* 15,900).[69] The majority of Romanian microloans are for business activity (54%) but personal loans represent the remaining 46% and the main one in case of credit unions.[70] Croatian micro-loans are split between business microcredit and personal/consumption ones.[71] In Bulgaria, the prevailing form used to be business micro-loans but it has recently shifted to personal/consumption purposes (62.5%).[72]

Differences between Western and Eastern MFIs also exist in terms of loan size and volume, with the latter presenting a lower loan size (because of lower gross national income (GNI) per capita) but a higher number of loans per institution.[73] In 2007, though considering the lack of unanimous results, the average microloan size was €11,000 in Western Europe and €7,700 in Eastern and Central Europe (compared to $100 in developing countries).[74] However, this also depends on the type of loan (personal *versus* entrepreneurial)[75] and disbursing institution[76] and in some cases

64 Ibidem, 29, 32 (in 2013, 67% of surveyed MFIs provided personal loans; 79% of the total value of microloans and 56% of the number of total loans were for business purposes, while 21% of total value and 44% of the total number were for personal consumption).
65 Ibidem, 68; ENM, 'Le multiformi', 11.
66 Bendig, 'Overview', 20–23; N. Goggin, 'The Microcredit Sector in the United Kingdom: The Role of CDFIs', in Jayo Carboni (eds), 17ff.
67 Bendig, 'Overview', 20, 22.
68 Ibidem, 25.
69 Ibidem, 83.
70 Ibidem, 79.
71 Bendig, 'Overview 2010/2011', 64.
72 Bendig, 'Overview', 60.
73 Western MFIs reported 59% of the total volume of microloans while Eastern MFIs 64% but only 41% of the total value of microloans reported: Bendig, 'Overview', 30–31.
74 *See* Unterberg, 'Microfinance', 8; Molenaar, 'Microfinance', 6, 15; EIF, 'Microfinance in Europe', 6; Viganò, 'Microfinance', 11; Commission, 'The Regulation', 16; Evers, 'Status', 11ff.
75 E.g., Italian average micro-loan size ranges from €3,000 (personal) to €23,000 (entrepreneurial): *see* ENM, 'Le multiformi', 51.
76 For example, in Germany business loans provided by MFIs in partnership with banks have a maximum size of €20,000 (in 2013 on average €5,700), while promotional banks disburse loans of maximum amount ranging from €15,000 to €25,000 (in 2013 on average €18,000): Bendig, 'Overview', 65.

differences are less striking than described. For instance, in 2013 the average loan size in France was around €2,300 for personal loans and €11,800 for business loans[77] while in Bulgaria, respectively, €2,800 and €10,200.[78] Furthermore, Hungarian law permits micro-loans above the EU-accepted maximum microcredit level (up to €33,000 for not-for-profit and €165,000 for-profit), determining an average loan size of €15,900.[79] Anyway, the average loan amount for the whole EU in 2013 was €9,234 (in 2011, €7,129).[80]

Moreover, in the West loan maturities are longer, with, for example, an average duration of four years in France and Italy compared to two years in Croatia and Bulgaria.[81]

Also MFIs' objectives tend to diverge: in the Centre-East, the prevailing mission is, as in developing countries, enterprise development, while in the West it is social and financial inclusion of the unbankable, immigrants, unemployed people and temporary workers (*see* Chapter 4, §2).[82] However, there are differences among different types of providers: for instance, in Germany, despite some overlapping, development banks tend to target bankable entrepreneurs, MFIs non-bankable entrepreneurs and business support centres people outside the job market. Anyway, more generally, EU micro-borrowers are not the ones completely cut off from the economy (as instead in developing countries) but the ones at the margins of the mainstream economy (e.g. not qualifying as mainstream but neither for poverty relief).[83]

77 The respective figures for other countries are: €1,400 and €15,300 in Spain; €3,100 and €4,800 (but €9,623 in 2009) in the UK: Bendig, 'Overview', 25, 32–33, 48–49; Goggin, 'The Microcredit', 26; EMN-EIF, 'Microfinance', 83.

78 Bendig, 'Overview', 25, 33. In Poland the average loan size is €12,000 but €5,000 for most MFIs: Ibidem, 32.

79 Ibidem, 32, 49, 67–69; EMN, 'The Collection', 4–5; I. Kovács, 'The Microlending Sector in Hungary: Microlending to SMEs', in Jayo Carboni, *Handbook*, 190ff.

80 Bendig, 'Overview', 24.

81 Ibidem, 33. In Germany the duration is up to ten years (with 6 to 24 months grace period). However, in the UK the average duration is 36–39 months, while in Poland four years. *See* Ibidem, 32–33, 48–49, 75; Goggin, 'The Microcredit', 26; EMN-EIF, 'Microfinance', 83.

82 For example, in France, microloans are mostly directed to unemployed (83%) and financially excluded (65%) and in the UK to ethnic minorities (65%), women (58%), financially excluded (55%) and unemployed (48%). Instead, in Hungary MFIs focus primarily on enterprise promotion and economic development (not targeting socially/financially excluded) and in Romania and Bulgaria in 2012/2013, only, respectively 13% and 18% of loans went to unbankable clients. *See* Bendig, 'Overview', 20, 22, 40–41, 65, 79. However, in Croatia unbankable clients in 2010–2011 were the most served (79%), followed by women (53%), rural people (50%), ethnic minorities (40%) and clients below the poverty line (25%): Bendig, 'Overview 2010/2011', 64.

83 *See* R. Copisarow, 'An Example of Micro-finance in the North: Fundusz Mikro (Poland)', in C. Guene and E. Mayo (eds), *Banking and Social Cohesion. Alternative Responses to a Global Market*, (Carpenter 2001), 54; J. Carr and Z. Yi Tong (eds), *Replicating Microfinance in the United States*, (Woodrow Wilson Center Press 2002), 204, 213–214.

Moreover, in Western countries, microcredit is perceived almost as a charitable activity, therefore interest rates tend to be low while Eastern and Central countries tend to replicate developing countries' experience with interest rates higher than mainstream ones (but *see* Chapter 8, §4).

Finally, funding sources reflect distinct maturity stages: while Western MFIs tend to rely primarily on grants and concessional funding, Eastern ones also resort to commercial banks loans and securitizations (Chapter 5, §§ 3–4). Furthermore, Western MFIs are rarely self-sufficient: based on a 2006 survey, the 40% of MFIs relied on subsidies to cover three-quarters of operational costs (linked to personalized services and targeted to the needs of single clients) and only 10% of MFIs (mostly banks) are funding their capital for loans through the revenues from their activity (*see* Chapter 5, §1).

Nonetheless, EU MFIs also present common characteristics. For instance, microfinance has partially merged with the experiences of financial cooperatives, credit unions and charitable financial institutions (Chapter 3, §5.a).

Furthermore, European micro-loans are almost entirely individual[84] and not progressive. In fact, MFIs have found it difficult to replicate group lending in European cities because of the lack of the same sense of community and social bonds typical of developing countries' villages, this preventing adequate self-selection of borrowers and peer-pressure on repayment (*see* Chapter 5, §1.b).[85] MFIs, consequently, have started recurring to new instruments such as checking landlord references, bill payments, referrals from local not-for-profit associations and accompanying services to improve repayment (e.g. in France)[86] (*see* Chapter 6, §2.b). Similarly, progressive lending has appeared ineffective since borrowers are able to obtain money from charities or government programmes.[87]

Finally, also thanks to EU support (below §b), both Western and Eastern MFIs often benefit from guarantee funds, providing collateral, protection against defaults (often up to 75–80% of loan amounts: *see* Hungary, Romania, Italy, Germany, UK) or subsidized interest rates.[88] In some countries MFIs benefit primarily from public guarantees provided by development banks and EU funds (e.g. Bulgaria, Poland) or national and local governments (e.g. France, Germany, UK, Romania, Poland), while, in others, guarantees might be set up under private schemes (*see* Spain, France, Hungary).[89]

84 In 2010/2011, 92% of loans were individual: *see* Bendig, 'Overview 2010/2011', 36.

85 *See* Carr and Yi Tong, *Replicating*, 26–27; 223ff., 340ff.; N. Bhatt and S. Tang, 'Making Microcredit Work in the United States: Social, Financial, and Administrative Dimensions', (2001) 15(3) *Econ Dev Q* 229; Dyal-Chand, 'Reflection'.

86 *See* Carr and Yi Tong, *Replicating*, 26–27, 55; Bhatt and Tang, 'Making', 236.

87 *See* Carr and Yi Tong, *Replicating*, 208.

88 TrustLaw, 'Creating Jobs in Europe Legal and Regulatory Frameworks of Microenterprises and Microcredit in Europe', (2011), 17, <www.trust.org/contentAsset/raw-data/ac56cbae-2724-4226-bbfe-1903c01bb68b/file>.

89 TrustLaw, 'Creating', 25, 56, 58, 62, 75, 115, 124, 141.

Table 2.1 Features of microcredit in Europe

<table>
<tr><th colspan="2">Features of microcredit in Europe</th></tr>
<tr><th>Eastern Europe/DCs</th><th>Western Europe</th></tr>
<tr><td>• Mature, specialized and competitive sector
• Mainly for-profit orientation, self-sufficient and varied sources of funding
• High interest rates
• Microcredit and additional financial services (including deposits)
• Average two-years maturity
• Small-size loan
• Main mission: enterprise development

(in DCs but not in Eastern Europe: shorter maturity, very small loan size, group lending, progressive lending, women and completely cut-off from the economy as targets)</td><td>• Young sector with extensive public support
• Mainly not-for-profit orientation, not self-sufficient and relying on subsidies and concessional loans
• Low interest rates
• Mostly microcredit (but MFIs often conducting also charitable activities)
• Average four-years maturity
• Medium-size loan
• Main mission: social and financial inclusion</td></tr>
<tr><th colspan="2">In common (Eastern and Western Europe)</th></tr>
<tr><td colspan="2">• Relationship-based and personalized borrower screening
• No group lending or progressive lending but use of alternative instruments: e.g. landlord references, bill payments, references and referrals from local not-for-profit associations, coaching services
• No real collateral
• Guarantee funds
• Frequent instalments
• Coaching services
• Evolving sector: many different actors (including increasing number of NBFIs)</td></tr>
</table>

b EU programmes to support microfinance

The EU has looked at microfinance as an instrument to promote several of its objectives reinforced after the Lisbon Treaty, including SMEs promotion, employment and social inclusion (Chapter 3, §4.a). Consequently, MFIs and micro-enterprises can resort to many programmes to develop their activities through various forms of funding and technical support.

Some of these programmes can be ascribed to the category of initiatives in support of SMEs. For example, the 2007–2013 Competitiveness and Innovation Framework Programme (CIP) has made available a €1 billion budget to provide SMEs encountering difficulties in funding with guarantees for loans, micro-loans, securitizations and equity financing managed by the European Investment Fund (EIF),[90] and, similarly, the 2007–2013 Joint European Resources for Micro and

90 *See* <www.european-microfinance.org/docs/microfinance_in_europe/microfinance_eu/CIP_QuasiEquity_Lender.pdf>.

Medium Enterprises (JEREMIE).[91] In parallel, the EU has also taken action in favour, specifically, of micro-enterprises, simplifying applicable European laws (*see* the Small Business Act).[92]

Other programmes have been instead specifically targeting microfinance and MFIs. The Joint Action to Support Micro-finance Institutions in Europe (JASMINE; 2007–2013 extended to 2020) is designed to co-finance (along with financial institutions) start-up non-bank MFIs close to self-sufficiency through loans and equity investments, as well as to provide consulting services and technical assistance and promote a European debate about microcredit regulatory framework and best practices.[93] Furthermore, the European Progress Microfinance Facility (managed by EIF) has made available since 2010 different types of loans (senior, subordinated and risk-sharing), equity financing and risk-sharing instruments to intermediaries (for profit or not-for profit), enhancing the financial access of micro-enterprises and self-employed (including groups excluded from the traditional banking system, such as women, youngsters, minorities or people with a disability). The programme ended in April 2016, channelling its fund to the European Programme for Employment and Social Innovation (EaSI).[94] This is a fund managed by the Commission to promote 'smart, sustainable and inclusive growth' under the 2014–2020 European Strategic Framework, specifically to advance 'employment, social policy and labour mobility across the EU'. It represents an umbrella to coordinate other EU programmes aiming at promoting employment, social protection, social inclusion and working conditions, such as the Programme for Employment and Social Solidarity (PROGRESS), European Employment Services (EURES) and the above mentioned Progress Microfinance. It provides European financial intermediaries with guarantees to extend loans to vulnerable groups, micro-enterprises and social enterprises as well as technical assistance (e.g. for institutional assess-

91 Among various programmes since 1998: 'Growth and Employment Initiative' (1998–2000), 'Multi-annual Programme for the Promotion of enterprises and entrepreneurship' (2001–2005), securitizations of micro-loans by the EIF in Western Balkans and South-eastern Europe.

92 *See* Commission, 'Minimizing Regulatory Burden for SMEs. Adapting EU Regulation to the Needs of Micro-enterprises', (Report) (2011), <http://ec.europa.eu/governance/better_regulation/documents/minimizing_burden_sme_EN.pdf>. Other relevant programmes include: COSME 2014–2020 (loan guarantees and risk capital for SME funds), InnovFin Programme (Horizon 2020-loans and guarantees for innovative businesses and R&D), 'SME instrument' (funding and coaching to innovative SMEs), 'Creative Europe' (loans to SMEs in the cultural and creative sectors): *see* G. Ford, 'Microcredits in Europe', (*Finance Watch*, 30 October 2015), <www.finance-watch.org/hot-topics/blog/1172-microcredits-in-the-eu>.

93 *See* European Parliament and Council Decision No. 283/2010/EU [2010]OJ L87/1.

94 <www.eif.org/what_we_do/microfinance/progress/funded_instruments/index.htm>.

ments and microfinance institutional ratings and staff training) and for capacity building.[95]

The Commission has also promoted the adoption of the European Code of Good Conduct for non-bank MFIs as well as recommended Member States to simplify the microcredit and micro-enterprises regulation (*see* Chapters 3–6, 8).

95 *See* <www.european-microfinance.org/docs/microfinance_in_europe/microfinance_eu/DGEMPL_EaSI_EN.pdf> and <www.eif.org/what_we_do/microfinance/easi/index.htm>.

Part 2

Analysis of microfinance 'dimensions' from a regulatory point of view

3 Dimension I: Microfinance as a multi-faceted creature: the legal enigma and different levels of regulation

1 Difficulties in defining microfinance and regulatory implications

In the first chapters, we have generally referred to microfinance as the provision of a varied range of financial services to low-income people. Nonetheless, this appears too wide and vague a definition for regulatory purposes. In fact, if we want to create special rules or an *ad hoc* regime for microfinance, we first need to clearly identify microfinance. The Basel Committee on Banking Supervision (BCBS) reports that in 2010 59% of respondent countries (19 out of 27) had some sort of definition of microfinance/microcredit (mostly microcredit).[1] In a more recent BCBS survey (2013), 67% of respondent countries (35 out of 52) declared having a definition of microcredit/microfinance, while six countries (out of 52) affirmed to have plans to introduce it in the near future. However, looking exclusively at high-income countries, only 8 countries out of 18 (44%) presented similar definitions and none planned to introduce them.[2]

The choices made about the definition of microfinance will obviously have relevant practical consequences: the definition of microfinance identifies the characteristics that make, from a regulatory point of view, microfinance special and deserving of special rules. It also defines the limits for regulatory arbitrage, setting the conditions that may determine some outsiders to opt for the microfinance regime to take advantage of its favourable provisions. It also shapes the future market since microfinance operators will structure their business accordingly to maximize the regime benefits. Considering the lack of a universal notion of microfinance/microcredit, regulators should therefore elaborate their own definition.

The first fundamental choice pertains to the kind of main services offered: several countries, especially in Europe, have chosen to restrict microfinance to its microcredit dimension (i.e. micro-loans provision). As we will discuss later (*see* Chapters 4, §6; 6), this simplifies the legal implications of offering microcredit or the adjustments required to existing regulations since the simple provision of loans

1 *See* BCBS, *Microfinance Activities and the Core Principles for Effective Banking Supervision*, (BIS 2010), 34.

2 *See* BCBS, *Range of Practice in the Regulation and Supervision of Institutions Relevant to Financial Inclusion*, (BIS 2015), 37.

is generally less regulated than the banking activity (deposits plus credit) or even than payment services.

However, defining microcredit is not an easy task. Some countries have adopted wide definitions: as an example, the 2006 Bangladeshi Microfinance Regulatory Authority Act[3] defines microcredit (microfinance) as 'loans facilities offered by micro-credit organization certified under this Act for poverty alleviation, employment generation and facilitate a small entrepreneur' (Art. 2.22), authorizing MFIs to offer deposits to members and insurance products as well as loan and business development services to clients (Art. 24.2). Peru (with its *Resolución* No. 11356/2008[4]) identifies microcredit by loans' purpose (production, commercialization of products and offering of services: Art. 4.5) and with the aim of limiting the level of indebtedness (loans directed to people or entities whose level of indebtedness, excluding home mortgage, is below 20,000 *Nuevos Soles* – about €5,500).[5]

Other countries have relied on quantitative criteria to define microcredit/microfinance with reference to clients' socio-economical characteristics (though not always easy to measure), such as income, assets, sales, revenues, number of employees or to the level of loans or deposits balance (setting a threshold based on the average poverty level and income in the country).[6] For example, Colombian microcredit consists of credit operations directed to micro-enterprises (defined through a certain level of assets and number of employees) with limited total indebtedness (not above 120 minimum monthly wages, corresponding in 2010 to USD61.8 million), of limited amount (below 25 minimum monthly wages, USD12,750,000).[7]

Other countries insert references also to the short term and/or frequent instalments or underwriting methodology.[8] For instance, Zambia identifies microfinance with

3 <http://mra.gov.bd/images/mra_files/mra_act_2006_english.pdf>.

4 <http://intranet1.sbs.gob.pe/IDXALL/FINANCIERO/DOC/RESOLUCION/PDF/11356-2008.R.PDF>.

5 Based on the previous regulation, *Resolución* No. 808/2003 (Art. 1.2), instead, the limit was USD30,000. About the new regime *see* V. Frisancho-Robles, 'Signaling Creditworthiness in Peruvian Microfinance Markets: The Role of Information Sharing', (2012) IDB Working Paper 347, 6, <https://publications.iadb.org/bitstream/handle/11319/4084/Signaling%20Creditworthiness%20in%20Peruvian%20Microfinance%20Markets%3a%20The%20Role%20of%20Information%20Sharing.pdf;jsessionid=9FB826708E615054BB33CBA7BFBFDEA3?sequence=1>.

6 *See* P. Meagher, 'Microfinance Regulation in Developing Countries: A Comparative Review of Current Practice', (2002), 8, <www.arabic.microfinancegateway.org/sites/default/files/mfg-en-paper-microfinance-regulation-in-developing-countries-a-comparative-review-of-current-practice-2002.pdf>; J. Trigo-Loubière et al., 'Supervising & Regulating Microfinance in the Context of Financial Liberalization. Lessons from Bolivia, Colombia and Mexico', (2004), 36ff.; K. Druschel, 'The Ultimate Balancing Act: Investor Confidence and Regulatory Considerations for Microfinance', (2005) *USAID microNote* 10, 22ff., <http://pdf.usaid.gov/pdf_docs/Pnadf314.pdf>.

7 Art. 39 *Ley* 590/2000 modified by *Ley* 905/2004. *See* Banco de la Repùblica, 'Situación actual del microcrédito en Colombia: caracterìsticas y experiencias', (2010), <www.banrep.gov.co/docum/Lectura_finanzas/pdf/Tema1_sept.pdf>.

8 BCBS, *Microfinance*, 15.

the provision of services primarily to small or micro-enterprises or low-income customers, including the provision of credit usually with frequent repayments and remittances.[9] A recent Indian reform, in addition to business purpose, borrower's annual income and total indebtedness indexes, identifies as relevant also loan tenure (12 months for amounts below Rs15,000, otherwise 24), repayment frequency (monthly, fortnightly or weekly) and absence of collateral.[10]

In the EU context, there is not a legally binding definition of microcredit. Nonetheless, a widespread concept of microcredit refers to the provision of loans below €25,000 to encourage entrepreneurship through self-employment and micro-enterprises (i.e. firms employing less than 10 people or with a turnover below €2 million). Such definition has been inferred from documents briefly mentioning microcredit/microfinance[11] while explicitly defining microenterprises (Art. 2(3) of the Commission Recommendation No. 2003/361)[12] and does not account for relevant differences in gross domestic products (GDPs) per capita among EU countries.[13] EU microcredit is therefore limited to its business sphere and identified only through three indexes: maximum loan amount, firm size and loan purpose, without reference, for instance, to social objectives, collaterals, instalments frequency and/or accompanying services. However, other documents identify as main determinants of microfinance:

> [targeting] micro-entrepreneurs, the self-employed and socially excluded people lacking access to traditional sources of capital; [having as object] the

9 Banking and Financial Services Microfinance Regulations 2; *see* also C. Chiumya, 'The Regulation of Microcredit in Zambia', (International Conference 'Microfinance Regulations: Who Benefits?', 15–17 March 2010, Dhaka-Bangladesh), 6–7, <www.microfinancegateway.org/sites/default/files/mfg-en-paper-the-regulation-of-microfinance-in-zambia-jan-2010.pdf>.

10 The amount of loans for income generation should not be below 50% of total loans (including loans for personal expenses and emergencies): *see* RBI, 'FAQs on Non-Banking-Financial-Company-Micro-Finance-Institutions (NBFC-MFIs)', <www.rbi.org.in/scripts/FAQView.aspx?Id=102>.

11 *See* Commission, 'Implementing the Community Lisbon Programme: Financing SME Growth-Adding European Value', (Communication) COM(2006)349 final, 7: 'Member States are also invited to ensure that national legislation facilitates the provision of microfinance (loans of less than €25,000). Such loans offer an important means to encourage entrepreneurship through self-employment and micro-enterprises, in particular among women and minorities. This instrument favours not only competitiveness and entrepreneurship, but also social inclusion.' *See* also Commission, 'Commission Staff Working Document' SEC(2009)907, 4: 'Micro-credit in the EU means loans under €25,000. It is tailored for micro-enterprises, employing less than 10 people (91% of all European enterprises), and unemployed or inactive people who want to go into self-employment but do not have access to traditional banking services.'

12 Commission 'Recommendation 2003/361/EC of 6 May 2003 Concerning the Definition of Micro, Small and Medium-sized Enterprises', [2003]OJL124/36.

13 *See* European Parliament Resolution of 24 March 2009 with recommendations to the Commission on a European initiative for the development of micro-credits in support of growth and employment, [2010]OJC117E/85.

> creation or expansion of income-generating and job-creating activities or micro-enterprises, whose principal need is usually the financing of initial investment or of the working capital; the small amount of the individual loans required which in turn relates to the limited debt servicing capacity of the target clientele; [...] a more labour-intensive delivery system for making loans, involving greater knowledge of borrower capacity and a close relationship with the borrower, especially during the start-up phase of the micro-enterprise, through mentoring and general business support.[14]

Moreover, current surveys about microcredit in Europe also include in the definition of microcredit personal microloans, i.e. loan under €25,000 for covering clients' personal consumption necessities such as rent, personal emergencies and education (in 2013 reaching 21% of the total value of all microloans disbursed).[15] Nonetheless, the European Code of Good Conduct for Microcredit Provision (European MFIs Code),[16] promoted by the Commission, has limited its scope to productive microcredit.

Turning now the attention to single Member States (MSs), Romanian law No. 240/2005 used to define microcredit as the provision of loans up to €25,000, with a reimbursement period of maximum 60 months, to entrepreneurs and micro and small enterprises for developing an activity, business or project, or encouraging projects for community and economic development, initiatives of local communities and social programmes with a view to improve the living standard of local communities (Art. 2.b).[17] However, the creation of a general category of non-bank financial institutions (NBFIs), allowed to provide varied financial services without restrictions, has made this definition useless and microcredit is now offered by NBFIs in combination with other financial services without any requirements as regards loan amount, collateral or social mission (*see* Chapter 4, §6.c).

France has lacked for years an official definition of microcredit despite several laws referring to the same and a 2005 law (No. 32/2005 of 26 July) introducing microcredit providers an opportunity to benefit from a social cohesion fund. The *Conseil National de l'Information Statistique* (CNIS) (a public statistical institution) has therefore worked out a definition of microcredit for statistical purposes, distinguishing between professional and social microcredit. Professional microcredit consists in an onerous (charging interest rate) loan below €25,000, disbursed by a credit institution or a specialized association, accompanied by coaching services ('*accompagnement*'), to a young firm (less than five-years life), with less than ten employees and a turnover below €2 million (*see* EU definition of micro-enterprise). 'Personal

14 Commission, 'A European Initiative for the Development of Micro-credit in Support of Growth and Employment', (Communication) COM(2007)708 final, Annex 1, 12.
15 *See* M. Bendig et al., 'Overview of Microcredit Sector in the European Union-2012/2013', 20, (2014), <www.european-microfinance.org/docs/emn_publications/emn_overview/Overview2012-2013_Nov2014.pdf>.
16 Available at <http://ec.europa.eu/regional_policy/sources/thefunds/doc/code_bonne_conduite_en.pdf> (2013, version 2.0).
17 Available at <www.microfinancegateway.org/sites/default/files/mfg-en-paper-romania-law-regarding-micro-financing-commercial-companies-2007.pdf>.

microcredit', instead, targets individuals with difficulties in accessing credit, for the reintegration in the job market or society, in an amount below €3,000, with or without interest rates and with a maturity below 36 months.[18] Art. 23 of Law No. 737/2010 (on consumer credit) and subsequent implementing acts basically confirm the definition of personal microcredit, adding as requirements a fixed interest rate, a service of '*accompagnement social*' and a public guarantee.[19] In particular, Art. R518–61, as modified by Decree No. 2009–682 (and subsequent reforms, e.g. Law 22/2016 elevating loan amount thresholds), now requires loans provided by authorized associations/foundations to charge interest rates, be covered by a guarantee fund and be directed either to enterprises no more than five years old (or seven, in case of subsequent loans) and with no more than three employees, with a size not above €12,000 or, as regards personal microcredit, to people with financing difficulties but repayment capacity and '*accompagnement social*' for re-employment or social-inclusion projects, with loan amount not exceeding €5,000.[20]

The Italian regulator has introduced in 2010[21] a twofold definition of microcredit: 'commercial microcredit' refers to loans not above €25,000, not assisted by collateral in the forms of mortgage or pledge, disbursed in favour of individuals or partnerships or associations or cooperatives (or a special form of limited liability company: *S.R.L. semplificata*), for the creation or development of a business initiative or the reintegration in the job market (self-employment, including educational costs), along with the provision of supporting and monitoring services and duration below seven years (Artt. 111.1 of the Italian Banking Act-*TUB*; 4.4 of the Ministerial Decree 176/2014). Entrepreneurs with a VAT registration for more than three or five years, companies with more than ten employees and individual entrepreneurs with more than five employees (therefore partially restricting European definition) are excluded from the beneficiaries group (Art. 1.2 Decree 176/2014). The social microcredit is identified, instead, with loans of a maximum of €10,000, disbursed in favour of individuals in conditions of particular economic or social vulnerability, not assisted by collateral in the forms of a mortgage or pledge, aiming at the social and financial inclusion of the borrower, at conditions more favourable than market ones, combined with ancillary services of financial, educational and technical support and with a below five-years maturity (Artt. 111.3 *TUB*, 5 Decree).

Portugal has recently adopted a specific regulation about microcredit financial corporations (*societades financieras de microcrédito*–MCIs) authorized to provide financing up to €25,000 to small business or professional projects capable of

18 *See* M. Camdessus, 'Rapport Annuel de l'Observatoire de la Microfinance 2009', (2010), 3ff., <www.banque-france.fr/fileadmin/user_upload/banque_de_france/publications/microfinance-2009.pdf>.

19 *See* M. Camdessus, 'Rapport Annuel de l'Observatoire de la Microfinance 2012', (2013), 8, <https://www.banque-france.fr/fileadmin/user_upload/banque_de_france/publications/Rapport-annuel-2012-Observatoire-microfinance.pdf>; P. Valentin et al., 'Le microcrédit', (2011) Rapport d'un groupe de travail du CNIS 125, 12ff., <http://www.unaf.fr/IMG/pdf/RAP_2011_125_microcredit.pdf>.

20 Valentin, 'Le microcrédit', 16.

21 Legislative Decree No. 141/2010 implementing Consumer Credit Directive 2008/48.

maintaining sustainable jobs (self-employment) and facing difficulties in obtaining credit from mainstream operators.[22]

Spain does not have an official microcredit definition (nor UK or Germany) but a 2013 legislative proposal (not approved) advanced by the national microcredit association (*Fondo de MicroFinanzas* – now *Associación Española de Microfinanzas*) refers to microcredit as loans below €25,000, without real security, provided in combination with accompanying services, with fixed interest rate, for the purposes of re-employment, entrepreneurship, social and financial inclusion and/or combating poverty.[23]

Definitions need not to be too detailed to allow innovation but must clarify what characterizes microfinance/microcredit for legal purposes and, consequently, justify the application of special norms. In fact, such justification might lie in the social mission/impact or, on the contrary, also in the use of a specific model (e.g. small loans, for business purposes, short maturity, BDS) able, in regulators' opinion, to limit risks. This implies a preliminary decision by regulators about whether to focus on microfinance and therefore identify specific technical features in the regulatory definition (e.g. small sums involved, certain targeted clients, basic services, no traditional collateral but also frequent instalments, short maturity and accompanying services) or, instead, to build a regime around a generic idea of social finance (mission, types of services and targeted clients) and thus centre the definition on the social mission also embedded in adequate structures. While the second approach will ensure better competition among alternative operators (MFIs but also financial cooperatives, peer-to-peer platforms, etc.), the first one allows a more tailored approach and better adaptation of financial regulation to the specificities of such activity. As a result, regulators should favour a restrictive or at least mixed approach: under the latter, they could in fact design a specific regulation for microfinance but simultaneously introduce common facilitations and provisions for all social financial services as well as, in case, specific regimes for other alternative social financial operators.

2 Regulation and microfinance: some aspects to consider. Cost issues and different types of regulation

Having addressed the fundamental problem of defining microfinance, we need to tackle additional relevant issues.

First, leaving microfinance unregulated can impose significant costs on a country's financial sector and population. In fact, it can negatively affect MFIs' clients (as

22 Decree-Law No. 12/2010 of 19 February 2010; Orders (*Portarias*) No. 1315/2010 of 28 December 2010 and 59/2011 of 31 January 2011. *See* also TrustLaw, 'Creating Jobs in Europe: Legal and Regulatory Frameworks of Microenterprises and Microcredit in Europe' (2011), 119, <www.adie.org/sites/default/files/links/AdieTrustlaw_2011.pdf>.

23 EMN, 'Legislative Mapping Report – Spain', (2015), 2, <www.european-microfinance.org/docs/emn_publications/other_emn_publications/Legislative%20Mapping%20Report%20Spain.pdf>.

Table 3.1 Microfinance/microcredit identification internationally (trends)

<table>
<tr><th colspan="2">Microfinance/Microcredit identification internationally (trends)</th></tr>
<tr><td>Microfinance = financial services (e.g. deposits, payment, insurance) to unbanked, financially excluded, low-income (threshold based on country's poverty levels)</td><td>Microcredit = (small) loans for poverty alleviation, employment creation and small enterprises development directed to low-income people (frequent instalments, short term, no collateral) (not over-indebted)</td></tr>
<tr><td colspan="2">Microcredit definition based on EU documents (business microcredit only)</td></tr>
<tr><td colspan="2">Loan up to €25,000, for self-employment or SME development directed to micro-enterprises (firms with less than ten employees and €2 million turnover) (official)
Also labour-intensive loan disbursement, close relationship with the borrower, mentoring and general business support services (unofficial)</td></tr>
<tr><td colspan="2">Trends in defining microcredit in Europe (business and social microcredit)</td></tr>
<tr><td colspan="2">– Small loans (up to €25,000) accompanied by coaching services, directed to micro-entrepreneurs or un-employed for economic activity/self-employment, with short maturity (frequent instalments, without real security, sustainable)
– Small loans (up to €10,000 or €5,000) to socially excluded and people in difficult economic conditions/emergency situations, accompanied by coaching services, with short maturity (frequent instalments, without real security) (covered by guarantee fund) (more favourable conditions)</td></tr>
<tr><td colspan="2">(in brackets features present only in some countries)</td></tr>
</table>

depositors of a failing institution or borrowers victim of abusive practices) and aggravate their social and financial exclusion, also with detrimental effects on the welfare system. It can also attract distrust on the financial system as a whole as well as damage investors.

Nonetheless, regulation also entails costs, directly affecting operators, public authorities and customers. The former will have to face the burden of being informed, trained and advised about applicable rules and of complying with the same ('compliance costs', implying, e.g., transmission of reports and data, new information systems, organizational requirements).[24] Moreover, compliance costs exhibit economies of scale, with higher costs for smaller and start-up institutions, therefore disproportionately affecting MFIs (*see* Chapter 6, §6.a).[25] Such costs

24 About different types of costs included in the regulatory burden, *see* S. Hoskins and M. Labonte, 'An Analysis of the Regulatory Burden on Small Banks', (2015) Congressional Research Service Report, 2, <www.fas.org/sgp/crs/misc/R43999.pdf>.

25 *See* G. Elliehausen and R. Kurtz, 'Scale Economies in Compliance Costs for Federal Consumer Credit Regulations', (1988) 1(2) *J Financ Serv Res* 147; Hoskins and Labonte, 'An Analysis', 28, 31ff.; B. Armendáriz and J. Morduch, *The Economics of Microfinance*, (2nd edn, MIT Press 2010), 259; R. Christen et al., 'Microfinance Consensus Guidelines. A Guide to Regulation and Supervision of Microfinance', (2012), 21, <www.cgap.org/sites/default/files/Consensus-Guideline-A-Guide-to-Regulation-and-Supervision-of-Microfinance-Oct-2012_0.pdf>; R. Cull et al., 'Does Regulatory Supervision Curtail Microfinance Profitability and Outreach?', (2011) 39(6) *World Dev* 949.

might negatively affect MFIs' clients, being partially transferred to the same through higher prices or lower quality of services or restricted access to microfinance for certain clients ('opportunity costs').

Public authorities, on the other hand, will generally need to monitor the newly regulated operators and enforce the new rules, facing costs partially borne by tax-payers. Consequently, while regulation is necessary, it is also important to avoid excessive burdens, which might restrain economic activities, competition and innovation as well as involve regulatory capture, extraction of private benefits by regulators or their inability to understand and monitor operators (as underlined by the 'self-interest' approach to regulation).[26] Excessive regulation may be especially detrimental to MFIs considering their expensive and labour-intensive business model as well as limited financial and human resources.[27]

Second, not only such costs but also available instruments in terms of enforcement, supervision and other relevant aspects highly depend on the type of regulation to which MFIs are subject. In particular, banks are traditionally targeted by prudential regulation, which focuses on risks and on maintaining stability (of both single institutions and the financial system)[28] and resort to rather strict, prescriptive and rigid rules (e.g. specific capital and reserve requirements, organizational rules, structural separation) and instruments (e.g. early intervention, inspections, reporting requirements, authority's power to remove directors) (Chapter 6).[29]

Such type of regulation and supervision entails high costs, which might also affect microfinance services' availability and outreach. The literature has explored the impact of prudential regulation on MFIs' efficiency and outreach with conflicting results: some studies attest a lower level of outreach of regulated MFIs (finding a correlation between prudential regulation and reductions in the number

26 *See* J. Barth et al., *Rethinking Banking Regulation. Till Angels Govern*, (CUP 2006), 34ff.; L. Dragomir, *European Prudential Banking Regulation and Supervision. The Legal Dimension*, (Routledge 2010), 53; C. Goodhart et al., *Financial Regulation. Why, How and Where Now?*, (Routledge 1998), 2–3.

27 *See* Cull et al. 'Does', 2ff.; D. Porteous et al., 'Prudential Regulation in Microfinance', (2010) FAI Policy Framing Note 3, <www.microfinancegateway.org/sites/default/files/mfg-en-paper-prudential-regulation-in-microfinance-jan-2010.pdf>.

28 *See* F. Allen and R. Herring, 'Banking Regulation versus Securities Market Regulation', (2001) Wharton Financial Institutions Center Working Paper 29, 3, <http://finance.wharton.upenn.edu/~allenf/download/Vita/0129.pdf>; Dragomir, *European*, 53ff.; W. White, 'The Prudential Regulation of Financial Institutions: Why Regulatory Responses to the Crisis Might Not Prove Sufficient', (2013), <www.policyschool.ucalgary.ca/sites/default/files/research/prudential-regulation-white.pdf>.

29 *See* N. Moloney, 'The Legacy Effects of the Financial crisis on Regulatory Design in the EU', in E. Ferran et al. (eds.), *The Regulatory Aftermath of the Global Financial Crisis*, (CUP 2012), 117, 120–124; H. Hu, 'Disclosure Universes and Modes of Information: Banks, Innovation, and Divergent Regulatory Quests', (2014) 31(3) *Yale J on Reg* 565, 574; Dragomir, *European*, 56.

of female or impoverished clients)[30] but no effects on sustainability.[31] Instead, other studies do not find any significant impact of regulation on MFIs.[32] Nonetheless, a recent study, adopting a more complete methodological approach, links microfinance regulation with lower outreach in for-profit institutions and lower profitability in more socially oriented ones.[33]

Moreover, supervising microfinance activities might prove particularly expensive because of the existence of numerous small institutions[34] with different business models, structures and products, requiring a more labour-intensive supervisory work. For instance, a study conducted in Peru showed that MFIs' supervision in this country was thirty times more costly than traditional financial supervision (2% of assets instead of 0.06%).[35]

Non-prudential regulation has instead varied goals such as consumer protection, prevention of fraud, money-laundering and terrorism (AML-CT laws)[36] and can traditionally rely on less intrusive instruments such as disclosure, *ex-post* enforcement and competition.[37] Consequently, it generally entails lower costs. Other types of regulation, such as charity law, are even less costly but have different priorities and less incisive instruments, which might result in a lack of adequate response to the risks posed by microfinance (*see* below §3).

Consequently, the impact of regulation on the sector varies significantly based on the type of regulation and supervision. Furthermore, there are many different models and practices of supervision in the financial sector, which influence the choices about microfinance regulation. Such models have also been affected by the

30 *See* Cull et al., 'Does' (finding that regulation is correlated with larger average loan size and a reduced proportion of loans to women, which is consistent with the hypothesis that 'profit-oriented MFIs that have to comply with prudential supervision respond by curtailing their outreach to segments of the population that are more costly to serve').

31 Ibidem (the entities subject to supervision appear mature, asset rich, profit seeking and self-sustainable).

32 *See* V. Hartarska and D. Nadolnyak, 'Do Regulated Microfinance Institutions Achieve Better Sustainability and Outreach? Cross-Country Evidence', (2007) 9 *Appl Econ* 1207, 1220 (finding that 'regulatory involvement does not affect sustainability or outreach but that better capitalized MFIs have better sustainability'); R. Mersland and R. Øysten Strøm, 'Performance and Corporate Governance in Microfinance Institutions', (2009) 33(4) *J Bank Finan* 662 (finding regulation to be insignificant in predicting MFI performance).

33 Cull et al., 'Does'.

34 BCBS, *Microfinance*, 28.

35 *See* R. Christen and R. Rosenberg, 'The Rush to Regulate: Legal Frameworks for Microfinance', (2000) CGAP Occasional Paper 4, 7 (Box 4), <www.cgap.org/sites/default/files/CGAP-Occasional-Paper-The-Rush-to-Regulate-Legal-Frameworks-for-Microfinance-Apr-2000.pdf>.

36 D. Llewellyn, 'The Economic Rationale for Financial Regulation', FSA Occasional Paper, 10ff., <www.fep.up.pt/disciplinas/pgaf924/PGAF/Texto_2_David_Llewellyn.pdf>.

37 *See* Moloney, 'The Legacy', 120–21; D. Langevoort, 'Global Securities Regulation After the Financial Crisis', (2010) 13(3) *J Int Econ Law* 799; Hu, 'Disclosure', 574, 602, 610, 660.

financial crisis, often leading to the creation of separate authorities ('twin picks' model), respectively, for prudential supervision and consumer protection (*see* in the UK, the Netherlands and Belgium).[38]

However, countries tend to apply banking regulation and supervision to MFIs when accepting deposits, often creating a specialized microfinance unit[39] but many countries subject also credit-only MFIs to the same regime.[40] Based on a 2009 world survey, in 58 countries over 130 participating (35%), the MFIs represent a separate category and are regulated and supervised by the banking authority. In some other countries, MFIs are regulated by another authority (8%) or by both (9%), while in 48% of countries they are not regulated.[41]

Some countries have introduced a favourable 'special window' for microfinance, also in consideration of its different nature from mainstream banking because of its social and development aid spheres. Special regimes can favour the creation of dedicated operators serving low-income clients but can, at the same time, create a justification for mainstream ones to ignore that same part of the population. However, we might also observe the opposite effect, with a non-dedicated microfinance regime nullifying the incentives for providing services to low-income clients. For instance, the 2009 cancellation in Romania of the special regime for MFIs through the creation of a general NBFI category might have reduced the number of specialized microfinance providers as well as of served clients among unbankable people and those living in remote areas[42] (*see* Chapters 4, §6.c; 6, §6.a).

Furthermore, with the aim of reducing supervisory costs some countries have resorted to forms of hybrid or self-supervision (below §3).[43] For instance, the

38 *See* about post-crisis institutional reforms, R. Hui-Huang and D. Schoenmaker (eds), *Institutional Structure of Financial Regulation*, (Routledge 2015); E. Ferrán, 'Institutional Design. The Choices for National Systems', in N. Moloney et al. (eds), *The Oxford Handbook of Financial Regulation*, (OUP 2015), 97ff.; E. Wymeersch, 'The Structure of Financial Supervision in Europe: About Single Financial Supervisors, Twin Peaks and Multiple Financial Supervisors', (2007) 8(2) *EBOR* 237; Group of Thirty, 'The Structure of Financial Supervision: Approaches and Challenges in a Global Marketplace', (2008), 12–14, 23ff., <www.group30.org/images/PDF/The%20Structure%20of%20Financial%20Supervision.pdf>.

39 BCBS, *Microfinance*, 42 (90% of respondents subject ODTIs to bank supervision and half of them have specialized teams).

40 BCBS, *Range*, 20 (69% of respondents).

41 CGAP, 'Financial Access 2009 – Measuring Access to Financial Services around the World', (2009), 8–9, <www.cgap.org/sites/default/files/CGAP-Financial-Access-2009.pdf>.

42 C. Pop and P. Buys, 'Microfinance in Romania', (2015) 5 *Contemporary Legal & Economic Issues* 307; EMN, 'A Collection of Case Studies on the Legal and Regulatory Framework for Microfinance Provision', (2012) electronic Bulletin 12(1), 18, <www.microfinancegateway.org/sites/default/files/mfg-en-case-study-a-collection-of-case-studies-on-the-legal-and-regulatory-framework-for-microfinance-provision-dec-2012.pdf>.

43 Meagher, 'Microfinance', 9.

recent Italian microcredit reform has mandated the creation of a private authority (funded by MFIs) to monitor and sanction (backed by financial supervisor's powers) microfinance operators once their number reaches a certain relevant level (Art. 113 *TUB*).

3 Levels of regulation and supervision[44]

The decision about microfinance definition is only the first of many choices that countries need to take when facing the problem of regulating microfinance. Microfinance has in fact puzzled regulators worldwide because of its multi-faceted nature (*see* Introduction). As evidenced above, microfinance services can be offered by a varied range of different operators (from not-for-profit organizations and foundations to cooperatives, commercial banks, NBFIs) and with a double-bottom line. Microfinance has also been seen as a tool for poverty eradication and economic development, involving international organizations (IOs) devoted to such missions. MFIs resort for funding to donations and international aid as well as to capital markets, securitizations and innovative tools such as crowd-funding and microfinance investment vehicles (Chapter 5, §§3–5). Such a hybrid and highly varied nature of microfinance can trigger the application of multiple types of regulation, with distant aspirations and governing principles, challenging our traditional legal categories. Consequently, a number of different regulations (and authorities) might interact and compete with each other without a clear scheme.

As a result, before discussing the best regulatory approach to microfinance in Europe, it is also important to clarify different possible types of regulation and supervision affecting microfinance and deal with the division of competences among regulators at such different levels. My analysis will address three facets of the problem: the horizontal one, pertaining to the attribution of rule-making and supervisory powers among different sectors of the law and related authorities (e.g. development assistance, financial authority, charity authority); the vertical one, regarding the geographical level of organization (i.e. local, regional, or international level); finally, the nature of the authority and regulation (private, public or hybrid). This appears to be crucial considering the multitude of various potential regulators, both public and private, and the benefits from clear principles of competence and coordination among authorities.[45]

44 This chapter partially relies on the research work and results presented in E. Macchiavello, 'Microfinance Regulation and Supervision: A Multi-faced Prism of Structures, Levels and Issues', (2012) 9(1) *NYU J L & Bus* 125; Id., 'Private Regulation and Enforcement in Microfinance: A Multi-Layered and Polycentric Puzzle', in F. Cafaggi and G. Miller (with al.), *The Governance and Regulation of International Finance*, (Edward Elgar Publishing 2013) (to which I refer for a detailed discussion and proposal for an optimal division of competences among different levels as well as further references).

45 *See* BCBS, 'Basel Core Principles for Effective Banking Supervision' (revised 2012), Principles 1 and 3.

a Horizontal perspective

Microfinance cuts across many different sectors, each often regulated by a specialized authority and governed by different principles and rules. Because of the financial nature of MFIs' activity, financial regulation comes usually into play and might restrict MFIs' activities. For example, depending on the country, financial regulation may prohibit NGOs from providing credit directly (thus also microcredit, *see* Chapter 4, §6.c) or instead expand their funding sources and permitted activities (*see* Chapters 5, §3; 6). From a different perspective, microfinance activities can be affected by foreign investment treaties when provided by foreign entities and may conflict with protective domestic financial regulation or be regulated by the World Trade Organization (WTO) as a business activity. With its hybrid nature, it is also attracted by the development aid sphere, having been regarded as an additional tool for alleviating poverty (*see* Chapter 4, §1).

The prevalence given to one aspect over another has consequences from the point of view of authorities entitled to take action, authorized types of measures, kind of regulation and so on.

Anyway, the financial sphere currently appears as the prevailing one. In fact, the financial crisis has further focused the attention of regulators on financial regulation and the need for reform, also for NBFIs, in particular to protect from systemic risk. In Europe, this has entailed fundamental reforms in the supervision area as well as deeper harmonization and broader reach of financial regulation (§4), potentially restricting microfinance opportunities. At the same time, financial regulation is one of the strongest instruments used by local and domestic governments in developing countries (DCs) to react to problems and give a political message (*see* in India and Nicaragua microfinance clients crises: *see* Chapters 6, §2. a; 8, §4).[46] Furthermore, considering the recognized link between finance, financial regulation and growth (Chapter 1, §2), DCs have often used financial regulation reforms (either deregulating or reinforcing financial rules) to show their commitment to investors and IFIs.[47]

b Vertical perspective

The vertical dimension concerns different allocations of power and functions across authorities at the international, regional, national and local levels. The global character of the financial crisis has suggested the need to allocate certain powers at international level, especially for monitoring systemic risk, leaving to

46 For a synthesis *see* Microfinance Focus, '6 Microfinance Crises that the Sector does not Want to Remember', (22 Apr. 2010), <www.microfinancefocus.com/6-microfinance-crises-sector-does-not-want-remember>.

47 About DCs adopting Basel principles under the influence of IOs,*see* D. Tarullo, *Banking on Basel: The Future of International Financial Regulation*, (Institute for International Economics 2008), 206; Barth, *Rethinking*, 71; C. Bradley, 'Private International Law-Making for the Financial Markets', (2005) 29 *Fordham Int'l L J* 127, 137.

discussion whether to centralize these powers or allow competition among regulators. Post-crisis reforms support the integration process at international and regional levels and the adoption of common standards and coordination mechanisms among countries to prevent crises (*see* §4 about the EU).[48]

Similarly, microfinance might require an international approach because it is a geographically widespread phenomenon and involves participants from different countries and internationally-set standards (e.g. Basel Accord, AML-CT). However, it also presents many country-specific aspects, very different levels of development, resilience to the global economy (instead connection with local events: *see* Chapter 6, §3.b) and almost non-existent trans-border activities, this justifying lobbying for adaptation of international standards to the sector's local characteristics.

However, considering the growth rate and commercialization trend of the sector (*see* Chapters 4, §4; 5, §1.a), problems related to cross-border activities and systemic risk at least for a particular country or a region should not be ignored. In particular, some big MFIs in DCs are starting to export their model to neighbouring countries and foreign banks or other international entities have been creating subsidiaries or branches in DCs with a low level of access to financial services.[49] This entails classical home-host country problems[50] in supervision as well as the risk of supervisory holes.[51] Protective measures adopted by domestic regulators in DCs limiting foreign investments rights might trigger some treaties'

48 *See* generally, e.g., the work of the BCBS, IOSCO, IAIS and OECD. *See* the Larosière Group, 'The High Level Group on Financial Supervision in the EU-Report 6', (2009), 59–60 <http://ec.europa.eu/internal_market/finances/docs/de_larosiere_report_en.pdf>; FSB, 'Improving Financial Regulation. Report of the Financial Stability Board to G20 Leaders', (2009), 10 <www.financialstabilityboard.org/publications/r_090925b.pdf>.

49 *See* T. Black and A. Martinez, 'Compartamos Draws Gartmore as UBS Projects 20% Rally', *Bloomberg* (20 April 2010), <www.bloomberg.com/news/2010-04-20/compartamos-draws-gartmore-on-mexico-s-rebound-as-ubs-projects-22-rally.html> (about Banco Compartamos' projects of expansion cross-borders); A. Gelpern, 'Wal-Mart Bank in Mexico: Money to the Masses and the Home-Host Hole', (2007) 39 *Conn L Rev* 1513 (addressing the rare case of an unregulated entity in the home country, the U.S., operating through a subsidiary in the host country, Mexico, and consequently under the supervision of the latter only, instead of a consolidated supervision of the home country).

50 This would also include phenomena like the deficiency in supervision in some DCs and the consequent domination of EAC home countries' supervisors, as well as possible protective responses by DCs such as the imposition of a subsidiary organization instead of branches, territorial liquidity requirements or limitations in the transfer of capital: Warwick Commission, 'The Warwick Commission on International Financial Reform: In Praise of Un-level Playing Fields', (2009), 26, <www2.warwick.ac.uk/research/warwickcommission/financialreform/report/uw_warcomm_intfinreform_09.pdf; K. Pistor, 'Into the Void: Governing Finance in Central & Eastern Europe', Columbia Law and Economics Working Paper 356, <http://ssrn.com/abstract=1476889> (exploring home-host country frictions in supervision between DCs and EACs).

51 *See* Gelpern, 'Wal-Mart'.

provisions (e.g. 'non discrimination' and 'national treatment' clauses in Bilateral Investment Treaties – BITs or GATS).[52]

Anyway, a rationale for international regulation in microfinance might also come from a development aid perspective, which is closely tied with financial regulation, with a high number of IOs (e.g. UN, World Bank, IMF, G20, BCBS and WTO) involved in regulating microfinance (*see* above §a).

c Nature of the authority: the role of self-regulation. The special case of the European Code of Good Conduct for Microcredit Provision

Rules are not exclusively set by public authorities but can present a self-regulatory, private or hybrid nature. Private regulation refers to various forms of private entities' involvement in the creation of norms, including contractual or organizational norms, consultation during the co-regulation decision process, delegation by the public regulator or *ex post* adoption of private rules by the public regulator.[53] Self-regulation has been playing an important role in the financial sector in North America, Latin America and Asia while only a minor one in Europe and in the Middle East.[54]

In the microfinance field, we can consider guidelines, standards and codes of conduct, standardized terms of private contract or network affiliation agreements, originated by varied types of private regulators such as associations or networks of MFIs, industry participants, practitioners, professionals, other stakeholders, IOs and development banks, as well as rating agencies and labelling agencies. Private bodies might alternatively be in charge of the supervision and monitoring compliance of government-issued rules.

There are various rationales for the existence and development of private regulation, such as, in presence of information asymmetries and public regulator's inefficiency, choosing as authority a body with possibly better understanding and access to information, improving rules' legitimacy and compliance.[55] In the context of microfinance, private regulators can supplement or substitute public authorities addressing the disproportion between supervisory costs and dimensional relevance

52 As regards GATS, however, protective prudential measures might be acceptable since GATS recognizes a 'prudential carve-out', allowing restrictive measures targeting foreign entities when introduced 'for prudential reasons, including the protection of depositors, policy holders or person to whom a fiduciary duty is owned by a financial service supplier, or to ensure the integrity or stability of the financial system'. *See* Barth, *Rethinking*, 170–71; Cranston, *Principles of Banking Law*, (2nd edn, OUP, 2002), 428.

53 *See* F. Cafaggi, 'Rethinking Private Regulation in the European Regulatory Space', EUI Law Working Paper 2006/13, <http://ssrn.com/abstract=910870>; J. Black, 'Constructing and Contesting Legitimacy and Accountability in Polycentric Regulatory Regimes', (2008) 2 *Regulation & Governance* 137, 139.

54 J. Carson, 'Self-Regulation in Securities Markets', (2011) World Bank Policy Research Working Paper 5542, 2, <http://siteresources.worldbank.org/FINANCIALSECTOR/Resources/WPS5542_Self_Regulation_in_Securities_Markets.pdf>.

55 *See* F. Cafaggi, 'Private Regulation in European Private Law', in A. Hartkamp et al. (eds), *Towards a European Civil Code* (4th edn, Wolters Kluwer 2010), 91; Ferran, 'Institutional', 110–11; Carson, 'Self-Regulation', 15–16.

of the sector (above §2), reduce political influence, improve trust and attract investments. Furthermore, as in other new and innovative sectors, private regulation can more easily respond to evolving needs, spur innovation and provide adequate special knowledge. Other reasons include historic or traditional structures, the political or economic power of some actors (e.g. NGOs or IOs) or, finally, the ease in reaching an understanding informally among private actors rather than through the bureaucratic public machine.[56] Such rules are generally applied voluntarily by the members of the issuing association or even by non-members because of competition forces or other reasons. Private regulation can be observed at all vertical levels of government (national, local or transnational level).[57]

For example, we can find self-adopted codes of conduct or certain levels of capital ratios self-imposed by local MFIs or their associations to meet investors' expectations.[58] There is also a growing role of supra-governmental organization at international level to monitor and label MFIs and MIVs,[59] such as specialized rating agencies and the Microfinance Information eXchange (the MIX, *see* next note). Particularly interesting is the growing role of the Consultative Group to Assist the Poor (CGAP) in the production of guidelines, collection and disclosure of data on MFIs and MIVs and the provision of technical assistance, whose hybrid nature, however, does not ensure the needed levels of accountability and legitimacy to become an official authority for microfinance.[60]

Moreover, many international, regional or bilateral developmental organizations, such as the UN, UNDP, IADB, IMF and USAID, as well as non-profit organizations (e.g. Ford, Rockefeller, Citi and Gates Foundations) and microfinance networks (e.g. SEEP, Acción, EMN, Pro Mujer) have contributed to addressing many challenging issues in the sector, suggesting or reporting best practices, guidelines and setting standards.[61]

56 Cafaggi, 'Private'; Id., 'New Foundations of Transnational Private Regulation', (2011) 38(1) *J Law Soc* 20.

57 *See* Cafaggi and Miller (eds.), *The Governance*; J. Benjamin et al., 'Law and Regulation for Global Financial Markets: Markets as Rule-Makers-Enforcement, Dispute Resolution and Risk', (2008) 2 *LFMR* 321.

58 For an overview and discussion of such forms of private regulation in microfinance, Macchiavello, 'Private'.

59 On supra-governmental organizations and self-regulation, *see* E. Meidinger, 'Competitive Supragovernmental Regulation: How Could It Be Democratic?', (2008) 8 *Chi J of Int'l L* 513.

60 CGAP is an independent organization specialized in microfinance, housed at World Bank and gathering together the main funders of the sector, both IOs (IFIs and development aid) and private funders. CGAP created the MIX in 2002 in partnership with for profit as well as not-for-profit entities (such as Open Society Institute, Citibank and Deutsche Bank): *see* <http://www.cgap.org/p/site/c/template.rc/1.11.124130/1.9.41938/> and CGAP, 'Annual Report 2002', 27, <www.cgap.org/gm/document-1.9.41930/CGAP_Annual_Report_2002NoSig.pdf>. For an evaluation of CGAP role, *see* Macchiavello, 'Private' and 'Microfinance'.

61 On various forms of self-regulation and regulation by donors or commercial funders, *see* M. Fiebig, 'Prudential Regulation and Supervision for Agricultural Finance', (2001), 75–87, <www.redcamif.org/uploads/tx_rtgfiles/afr5_e.pdf>.

Nonetheless, private regulation also has its downsides, raising issues regarding risks of self-interest,[62] anti-competitive effects, accountability and legitimacy deficiencies (in terms of procedures and organization)[63] as well as toothless enforcement.[64] For instance, the reliability of private rules might be questioned when issued by a self-regulatory organization for its members but affecting other subjects, without contemplating the participation of other stakeholders (e.g. clients) and without an adequate monitoring system or correct alignment of interests. In fact, issues related to the incentives of private regulators/supervisors in the financial sector have also been raised.[65] Enforcement might be problematic too: for instance, when the exclusion of the member violating the standards does not drive such member out of the market, no other sanctions are left.[66] Even forms of public–private regulation can lead to regulatory capture, preferential treatments or unbalanced regulation instead of increased legitimacy and democracy.[67]

However, adequate participatory procedures and structures can be implemented and studies show that close-knit groups tend to cooperate in a socially beneficial way, highlighting instead the limits of public regulation such as capture, incompetence and bureaucratic failures.[68] Moreover, when behaviours are observable and rule compliance is price and investment sensitive, the private authority has an interest in enforcing the rules and members in complying with the same.[69]

A relevant initiative in the European microfinance sector has been the above mentioned European MFIs Code, promoted by the Commission[70] but drafted by

62 *See* D. Snyder, 'Private Lawmaking', (2003) 64 *Ohio St LJ* 371, 434.

63 *See* J. Black and D. Rouch, 'The Development of the Global Markets as Rule-makers: Engagement and Legitimacy', (2008) 2 *Law and Fin Markets Rev* 218, 223.

64 *See* D. Awrey, 'The Dynamics of OTC Derivatives Regulation: Bridging The Public-Private Divide', (2010) 11 *EBOR* 155, 184; Ferran, 'Institutional', 111.

65 H. Jackson, 'Centralization, Competition, and Privatization in Financial Regulation', (2001) 2 *Theoretical Inq L* 649, 671 n. 58; L. Dragomir, 'Private Parties' Involvement in Prudential Banking Regulation – Some Thoughts on the Underlying Accountability Mechanisms', (2007), <www.iilj.org/GAL/documents/DragomirPrivateBankReg.pdf>; Tarullo, *Banking*, 152ff.

66 *See* D. Rozas and S. Sinha, 'Avoiding a Microfinance Bubble in India: Is Self-Regulation the Answer?', *Microfinance Focus* (10 January 2010), <www.microfinancefocus.com/news/2010/01/10/avoiding-a-microfinance-bubble-in-india-is-self-regulation-the-answer/>; J. Macey, 'Public and Private Ordering and the Production of Legitimate and Illegitimate Legal Rules', (1997) Faculty Scholarship Paper 144, 1133, <http://digitalcommons.law.yale.edu/fss_papers/1449> (quoting Professor Cooter about the advantages of public enforcement).

67 *See* Bradley, 'Private'; Black and Rouch, 'The Development'.

68 Macey, 'Public', 1131–32.

69 *See* also IOSCO, 'Objectives and Principles of Securities Regulation', (2003), 11–12, <www.iosco.org/library/pubdocs/pdf/IOSCOPD154.pdf>; Carson, 'Self-Regulation', 7.

70 *See* Commission, 'A European Initiative', 9, 29; Commission, *Methodology to Monitor the Implementation of the 'European Code of Good Conduct for Microcredit Provision' by Microcredit Providers. Microcredit Provider Guidelines*, (EU 2013).

experts collecting best practices from the sector and its stakeholders, representing a form of private regulation. Absent is a common regulatory framework for microfinance in Europe (*see* below §4), it aims at creating shared standards to spread customer-friendly practices and facilitate financing and sustainability, especially for (un-regulated) non-bank MFIs. In fact, it has been designed for non-bank MFIs, with banks and other regulated operators as possible endorsers but not subject to the same. The Code is divided into five sections: customer and investor relations, governance, risks management, reporting and management information system. It contains 186 clauses with different weights attached, depending on their importance (20 are 'priority clauses'), and 10 only apply to large MFIs (i.e. with more than 7,000 borrowers and 70 employees). MFIs can voluntarily adhere to the Code but compliance with the same (assessed by an external evaluator paid by the Commission and formally recognized by a steering committee composed of experts and Commission's representatives) will be evaluated in the context of MFIs application to European funding programmes, creating in principle strong incentives.[71] Furthermore, part of the data provided by MFIs will be published online and be publicly accessible on the EaSI-MicPro portal (*see* Chapter 2, §2.b), after being verified by an external evaluator (at best against available ratings or documentation or, otherwise, checked for consistency with other data, raw data or with comparable providers or verified by the board).[72] Nonetheless, at present, only seventeen MFIs have signed up to the Code (and only 66% of MFIs surveyed in 2013 showed the intention to implement the Code) while no data have been published on the web platform yet,[73] suggesting a low level of enforcement at least for the moment or rather slow implementing process (*see* Chapter 4, §§2–3). Furthermore, the Code applies only to non-bank providers and only to business microcredit (MFIs can choose to apply its clauses to other products). More generally, in consideration of the diversity among European microfinance experiences (in terms, e.g., of national frameworks, missions and size), the Code allows for proportionate and case-by-case evaluations (not all clauses apply to all MFIs), increasing flexibility but reducing comparability and therefore incentives for compliance. However, the existence of a minimum compliance threshold (all priority clauses and 80% of the weighted total of other applicable clauses) and the fact the respect of the same will be assessed by an external evaluator, partially restores comparability (rising costs, covered anyway with EU funds).

71 *See* Commission, 'A European', 10, 30; conditions of the EaSI program (*see* Chapter 2, §2.b): <www.eif.org/what_we_do/microfinance/easi/easi-call-for-expression-of-interest/easi-guarantee-annex-ii_microfinance-direct-guarantee.pdf>.

72 *See* K. Dayson and P. Vik, 'Toward an Architecture of Microcredit Regulation: The Case of the European Code of Good Conduct', (2014) 28(2) *Cost Management* 18; Commission, *Methodology*.

73 As of August 2016: *see* <https://webgate.ec.europa.eu/easi-micpro/Jasmine.jsp#CoGCPlace> (for a list of organizations adopting the Code); Bendig, 'Overview 2012/13', 54.

d Sectioning the prism: basic criteria for the attribution of rule-making power

All the above considered, I believe it is possible to draw some principles about the allocation of rule-making power among different levels, based on the type and purpose of regulation, interests involved, incentives, costs, benefits, timing, effectiveness, powers and measures available, effects on different stakeholders, legitimacy, as well as centralization, competition and privatization issues.[74]

Starting with the consumer protection area, this kind of regulation aims at protecting consumers from abuses and exploitation due mainly to market failures. Many actors might be interested in regulating this field: domestic government to defend a traditional general interest, private actors to promote social investments and avoid government intervention or development agencies to show to stakeholders a positive and socially responsible impact. Especially when no regulation is adopted by local governments or anyway to ensure a minimum common level of consumer protection worldwide in the sector for reputational reasons, forms of self-regulation or international guidelines are more than welcome, and frequent in practice (as a response to the financial crisis and microfinance scandals: Chapter 8).

These standards are also likely to be efficient since self-regulation can work when all participants agree about the shared benefits from compliance and credible enforcement is implemented. In fact, microfinance providers and their associations recognize the importance of the sector's reputation for their functioning and investors and donors can make financing contingent upon social performance reporting and results (*see* Chapter 4).[75] One example of a successful form of microfinance private regulation in the consumer protection area is the Client Protection Principles (CPPs) initiative, promoted by CGAP and other organizations (*see* Chapter 8, §3.b). Its enforcement ranges from mere endorsement (frequent) to certifications (still quite rare), to incorporation in financing contracts or in networks' affiliation agreements or into investors' due diligence process (the most effective), to MIVs social performance indicators (*see* Chapter 5, §5). In fact, at first, contrary to expectations and hope, CPPs have found wide endorsement only recently through the efforts of the 'Smart Campaign' (led by the network Acción),[76] and many channel enforcement largely based on investors' action (due diligence and financing contracts).[77] In fact, CPPs can become financial

74 *See*, more extensively, Macchiavello, 'Microfinance Regulation' and 'Private Regulation'. About centralization, competition or privatization as methods of regulating corporate governance, securities regulation and financial institutions *see* generally Jackson, 'Centralization', 650.

75 However, this works, in particular, under the threat of government intervention in case of failure: *see* E. Ostrom, *Governing the Commons: The Evolution of Institutions for Collective Action*, (CUP 1990); with particular reference to new sectors, A. Newman and D. Bach, 'Self-Regulatory Trajectories in the Shadow of Public Power: Resolving Digital Dilemmas in Europe and the U.S.', (2004) 17(3) *Governance* 387.

76 *See* <http://www.smartcampaign.org/about/campaign-endorsers> (as of May 2016, 4,639 endorsers, of which 1,671 MFIs and 186 investors and donors).

77 *See* S. Forster et al., 'Implementing the Client Protection Principles. A Technical Guide for Investors', (2011), <www.cgap.org/sites/default/files/CGAP-Technica

obligations and be enforced through suspension of financing or even, in some cases, litigation in courts or through ADRs,[78] forcing, for example, the adoption of certain consumer redress mechanisms or internal controls about staff behaviour (although such clauses are not so widespread yet and their concrete enforceability relies heavily on their wording).[79] Recently, the Smart Campaign has added a new instrument, the Smart Campaign Certification conducted by specialized rating agencies and attesting the respect of CPPs by MFIs through 30 standards (corresponding to over 90 indicators).[80] However, the results are public only for MFIs passing the test.[81]

CPPs and other forms of consumer protection principles have also been applied through international or regional networks of MFIs (or of investors and guarantors), which require their members, through the membership agreement and leveraging MFIs' financial or technical dependence, to adopt codes of conduct, certain structures and systems consistent with the network's consumer pledge. Such rules might be more specific than CPPs (especially as regards responsible and fair pricing) and include transparency and reporting requirements.[82] The industry (SEEP network) has even developed indicators to assess the ability of networks to play such roles, measuring their coverage and MFI-members' performance.[83] Rating agencies and social investors have developed their own social performance indicators sending messages to the MFIs regarding how to behave in order to obtain financing (*see* Chapters 4, §3; 8).[84]

l-Guide-Implementing-the-Client-Protection-Principles-A-Technical-Guide-for-Investors-Jan-2011.pdf>; E. Lahaye and K. McKee, 'Investors Implementing the Client Protection Principles in Microfinance', (2010) <https://openknowledge.worldbank.org/bitstream/handle/10986/9465/567260BRI0CGAP1rotection1Principles.pdf?sequence=1&isAllowed=y>.

78 About the enforcement of private regulation through financial obligations, *see* Benjamin, 'Law', 321–22; Bradley, 'Private', 176.

79 *See* in this respect Macchiavello, 'Private'.

80 <https://centerforfinancialinclusionblog.files.wordpress.com/2013/08/certification-standards_english-1-22-mb.pdf>. As of April 2016, the certified MFIs were 55 and listed here: <www.smartcampaign.org/certification/certified-organizations>.

81 *See* FAQs: <www.smartcampaign.org/certification/certification-frequently-asked-questions-faq#What_happens_if_an_organization_passes_or_fails_certification>.

82 Among the networks adopting consumer pledges (not necessarily the CPPs) and disclosure requirements binding their members: SEEP, MicroFinance Network (MFN), European Microfinance Network (EMN), Acción and Women's World Banking (WWB). Some of them, like Opportunity International, Pro-Mujer or Acción have equity stakes or governance roles in their member organizations: *see* J. Isern and T. Cook, 'What is a Network? The Diversity of Networks in Microfinance Today', (2004), CGAP Focus Note 26, 3, 7, <www.cgap.org/sites/default/files/CGAP-Focus-Note-What-Is-a-Network-The-Diversity-of-Networks-in-Microfinance-Today-Jul-2004.pdf>.

83 P. McAllister and D. Dezso, 'Building Vibrant and Inclusive Financial Sectors: Success Indicators for Microfinance Associations', (2010), <www.seepnetwork.org/filebin/SuccessIndicatorsforMFAs_web_en.pdf>.

84 Some guarantor networks (like MicroCredit Enterprises, *see* www.mcenterprises.org/for-mfis) provide coverage protection only if some conditions (e.g. women and rural focus, low interest rates) are met by MFIs.

The European MFIs Code, containing also social-performance indicators and CPPs, can contribute to this goal under the condition of improving its enforcement mechanisms (*see* above §c; Chapter 4).

For both these bottom line and economic factors, the microfinance market might be trusted more than the mainstream financial sector for implementing proper private norms and controls. However, this assumption should be verified for all particular local circumstances and be contingent upon the existence of some general conditions such as the prestige of the rule-making and monitoring authority, adequacy of its internal functioning, effective enforcement mechanisms and large adherence by participants.[85]

Furthermore, such forms of private regulation allow flexibility, therefore also adaptation to local needs and differentiation among investors' preferences and objectives.[86] Moreover, the existing competition among regulators appears beneficial.[87] The combined efforts of NGOs, specialized rating agencies, CGAP, MFI networks, investors, and international agencies should be preferred to regulation only through international public law instruments. The interaction of different regulatory authorities can lead to both differentiated requirements depending on local conditions and some minimum uniformity and comparability among MFIs benefiting investors.

Moving now to financial and prudential regulation, the attribution of power and functions to one regulator instead of another can significantly affect the outcomes and effects of regulation and supervision because of the different priorities and perspectives among regulators. For instance, the small size of MFIs or their not-for-profit nature can be seen by some DCs regulators or IOs as a reason to expand their permitted activities while, at the same time, excluding them from prudential regulation/supervision, in order to improve financial inclusion without endangering stability or excessively raising costs.[88] The same aspects, instead, can be used by some economically advanced countries (EACs) or international prudential regulators as a reason to restrict the range of permissible activities based on a presumption of inadequate organization (*see* Chapters 4, §§3, 6; 5, §2.a; 6, §6.f).[89]

Also, the costs of regulation on MFIs should be carefully considered since being regulated can entail improved trust and therefore an increased number of clients and consequent outreach but also severe supervisory costs on domestic regulators

85 *See* D. Porteous, 'Consumer Protection in Credit Markets', (2009) FAI Policy Focus Note 2, 13–15, <www.microfinancegateway.org/sites/default/files/mfg-en-paper-consumer-protection-in-credit-markets-jul-2009.pdf>; F. Cafaggi, 'Gouvernance et responsabilité des régulateurs privés', (2005) EUI Working Paper Law 2005/6, <http://cadmus.eui.eu/bitstream/handle/1814/3326/law05-06.pdf?sequence=1>.

86 *See*, among others, Cafaggi, 'New Foundations', 25, 36.

87 On the beneficial effects of competition among private as well as public regulators, *see* L. Catá-Backer, 'Economic Globalization and the Rise of Efficient Systems of Global Private Law Making: Wal-Mart as Global Legislator', (2007) 39 *Conn L Rev* 1739, 1776–77.

88 *See* Christen, 'Microfinance', 45, 47; Christen and Rosenberg, 'The Rush', 11.

89 BCBS, *Microfinance*, 2–3, 14–15.

(*see* §2; Chapter 5, §2.a). While international developing organizations might be interested in promoting innovative financing of MFIs, many EACs might be concerned with protection of their national investors resorting to microfinance investment funds or peer-to-peer platforms (*see* Chapters 5, §§3–4; 7, §3).

Furthermore, microfinance does not involve systemic risk at an international level but it does locally where additional rationales for government intervention might primarily apply, such as a 'too sensible to fail' approach (*see* Chapter 6, §2.a).[90] Domestic authorities have better information and experience on local conditions and can better supervise activities or take decisions aimed at expanding financial access through significant exemptions of MFIs from prudential regulation.

Moreover, prudential rules have impact on the correct functioning, competition and balance within local financial markets. Liberalization imposed internationally on these aspects in a DC's context might not be optimal towards maintaining control over the financial system and stable development. Going forward, local governments should still be able to impose restrictions on foreign ownership, transfers in foreign currency and usury since these decisions greatly affect public objectives and have effects on competition among financial providers, capital controls, imbalances inside the country and dependence on foreign funds.[91] Nonetheless, this might discourage investments and therefore convince international actors to lobby for special windows.

Thus, as a general matter, domestic governments should retain the power to set micro-prudential standards (including capital requirements and reserves) but transnational or regional liquidity and resolution facilities can appear useful to improve crisis management (*see* Chapters 6, §§4, 6.f; 5, §4). On the opposite side, AML-CT rules should be elaborated internationally in order to better control the phenomenon but adaptation to local markets and business models is also required for a proportionate approach.

Nonetheless, first, current wide microfinance geographic expansion and global economic interconnection as well as increased use of technologies (*see* Chapters 6–7) can entail more diffuse systemic risk and the classical problems of regulatory arbitrage, competition and home/host country coordination.[92] Consequently, forms of cooperation relying on some existing regional structure for regulation, supervision and sharing of information might be desirable. The continuous comparative research work conducted by IOs and private research centres can be useful but should not be regarded as the final word.

Second, the scarcity of available public resources might negatively affect local governments' ability to effectively regulate and supervise microfinance and be a determinant in some regulatory choices such as regulation only of deposit-taking

90 S. Shankar and M. Asher, 'Regulating Microfinance: A Suggested Framework', (2010) 45 *Economic & Political Weekly* 15, <http://ssrn.com/abstract=1607704>.

91 *See* Warwick Commission, 41–50; Pistor, 'Into the Void'; Meagher, 'Microfinance', 15; Barth, *Rethinking*, 170–73; Cranston, *Principles*, 427–28.

92 E. Kane, 'Financial Regulation and Market Forces', (1991) 127 *Swiss J Econ & Stat* 325, 334–36.

institutions (compulsory savings included or not), specialized supervisory unit or instead delegated supervision (*see* §2; Chapters 4, 6). However, the use of self-regulatory bodies in the prudential sector has been highly debated: for instance, the adoption through the Basel II Accord of capital adequacy rules based on internal assessment models (IRB) by more sophisticated banks has been criticized (*see* also Chapter 6, §6c),[93] resulting, *de facto*, in a delegation of supervision to the regulated institutions because of the complexity of the monitoring process.[94] Allowing an almost complete delegation of regulation and supervision to the microfinance industry can lead either to efficient solutions or disastrous consequences,[95] but a partial delegation would be based on a cost–benefit analysis and presumably have a less serious impact on the system than deficient supervision. Determinations about supervisory architecture are undoubtedly domestic because they depend on available resources, effectiveness of other existing forms of self-regulation, recognized priorities and existing structures and institutions,[96] also considering the failure of previously prevailing liberal models of development.[97]

Moreover, the uncertainty about the link between microfinance and economic development (Chapter 4, §1) might make IOs' liberalization measures not even justified under the development aid scheme. Thus, even in a capacity building and development perspective, international authorities should limit their role to cooperation with domestic authorities to build strong infrastructures useful for the development of the financial and microfinance sector without imposing strict and specific parameters usually conceived for Western systems.

Finally, another relevant area is disclosure of financial standards. Disclosure has traditionally vested a fundamental role in the financial area (especially in the securities field), under the assumption of market ability to reflect in prices all available information (efficient market hypothesis – EMH)[98] and with the aim of ensuring market efficiency and, consequently, investor protection.[99] Regulators have mandated disclosure to overcome asymmetric information and agency problems

93 *See* Tarullo, *Banking*, 152ff.; Dragomir, *European*, 265.

94 Ibidem.

95 For openness to self-supervision, *see* BCBS, 'Microfinance', 288ff. *Contra*, Christen, 'Microfinance', 44ff.; Christen and Rosenberg, 'The Rush', 2, 20.

96 With reference to the conventional financial system, *see* Barth, *Rethinking*, 316 ('Given our findings regarding the connections between the operation of the political system and both the selection and influence of banking policies, our work sheds a sceptical light on attempts by international agencies to develop uniform best practice checklists for countries.').

97 *See* H. Rogers, *The Global Financial Crisis and Development Thinking*, (2010), World Bank Policy Research Working Paper 5353, <http://elibrary.worldbank.org/content/workingpaper/10.1596/1813-9450-5353>.

98 *See* J. Coffee Jr., 'Market Failures and the Case for a Mandatory Disclosure System', (1984) 70 *Va Law Rev* 717; R. Gilson and R. Kraakman, 'The Mechanisms of Market Efficiency', (1984) 70 *Va Law Rev* 549.

99 *See* IOSCO, 'Objectives', Principle 4.2.1; Joint Forum, 'Review of the Differentiated Nature and Scope of Financial Regulation Key Issues and Recommendations', (2010), 88ff., <www.bis.org/publ/joint24.pdf>; S. Solaiman, 'Revisiting Securities Regulation in the Aftermath of the Global Financial Crisis: Disclosure-Panacea or Pandora's

(self-protection) of self-disclosure. Disclosure has appeared a cheap, not-invasive and widely acceptable instrument, also able to reduce conflict of interests and frauds and improve corporate governance.[100] In the banking sector, however, it has showed peculiar features, aiming at improving bank risk management and stability through transparency about main bank risks (*see* Basel third Pillar).[101] Anyway, the financial crisis and other scandals have revealed disclosure as an ineffective instrument, also because of complex banks' opaqueness.[102]

In the microfinance field, absent disclosure requirements in domestic law, self-reporting mechanisms have developed to reassure investors and stakeholders, also through the elaboration of common standards. MIX Market and MicroBanking Bulletin – MBB – (information platforms created by CGAP) and Microcredit Summit Campaign have been collecting relevant financial information from worldwide MFIs (presumably only the best-in-class). However, the availability to the public is scarce: the MIX, although to improve data review and quality, has recently restricted the availability of detailed information to paying clients; data collected by MBB (and Microcredit Summit Campaign) are not public with reference to single MFIs (providing only benchmarks or only summary information). Anyway, many independent or joint efforts have been made by networks and associations (e.g. SEEP, CGAP, USAID, EMN and MFC) to promote uniform performance ratios and reporting standards (also in line with international ones like IASB and IFRS) for MFIs worldwide or in certain regions, otherwise left to a fragmented scenario at the expenses of financing opportunities. In fact, the interest of investors and IOs in the accuracy of such data and in monitoring at least partially ensure reliability. Nonetheless, some common definitions are still lacking[103] and international campaigns have appeared rather ineffective for transparency on pricing despite some steps forward (*see* Chapter 8, §4). The European MFIs Code mandates the disclosure of several financial ratios (outstanding portfolio, active

Box?', (2013) 14(4) *JWIT* 646; M. Andenas and I. Chiu, *The Foundations and Future of Financial Regulation*, (Routledge 2013), 22–23.

100 *See* Hu, 'Disclosure'; O. Ben-Shahar and C. Schneider, 'The Failure of Mandated Disclosure', (2011) 159 *U Penn L Rev* 647, 681–84; E. Avgouleas, 'The Global Financial Crisis and the Disclosure Paradigm in European Financial Regulation: The Case for Reform', (2009) 6(4) *ECFLR* 440; N. Moloney, *EU Securities and Financial Markets Regulation*(3rd edn, OUP 2014), 54.

101 *See* Hu, 'Disclosure', 568ff., 602ff.

102 *See* eg Avgouleas, 'The Global'.

103 E.g. of default and delinquent loans: *see* R. Rosenberg, 'Measuring Microcredit Delinquency: Ratios Can Be Harmful to Your Health', (1999) CGAP Occasional Paper 3, <www.cgap.org/gm/document-1.9.2698/OP3.pdf>; SEEP, 'Financial Reporting Standards Initiative. Survey Results Brief,' (2008), <www.seepnetwork.org/filebin/pdf/resources/MFRS_Survey_Brief_English.pdf>;. MFC et al., 'From Exclusion to Inclusion Through Microfinance. Report 3: Benchmarks and Performance Measurement', (2007), <www.emnconference.org/archives/data/file/From%20exclusion%20to%20inclusion%20through%20microfinance%20%20Benchmarks%20and%20performance%20measurement.pdf>. *See* current EBA efforts in harmonizing definitions of default related to capital adequacy: <www.eba.europa.eu/-/eba-harmonises-the-definition-of-default-across-the-eu>.

borrowers, financial and operating revenue, expenses, PAR-30, write-off, allowances, assets, operational sustainability ratio: clauses 4.1.1–4.1.15) and external audit (2.39 priority clause). Once operative the enforcement mechanisms should ensure comparability, effectiveness while allowing flexibility in case of distinct requirements in domestic law to avoid double-imposition (*see* Chapter 5, §1.a).

4 Differences in perspectives between EACs and DCs. In particular, the EU context

We have primarily referred so far to issues involving microfinance regulation and supervision in DCs. Different conclusions may be reached regarding microfinance regulation and supervision in EACs. In these countries, financial regulation is substantial and often burdensome but, especially after the financial crisis, microfinance has been regarded as a possible solution to social and financial exclusion. For instance, in the European Union, despite some relevant difference due to national discretions in implementing European directives, quite a substantial system of rules regarding banking and financial systems exist, especially after the financial crisis which has led to the adoption of more detailed instruments and centralization reforms in the sector (§b).

Nonetheless, in the EU, while, on the one hand, the financial sector has gone through an intense integration process, on the other, MSs present very diverse microfinance experiences as well as different stages of financial sectors' development, especially between Western countries and Eastern ones (the latter with weaker institutions but more mature microfinance sectors, then sharing some aspects with DCs' experiences, while the former *vice versa*) (Chapter 2, §2).

Consequently, first, prudential measures targeting microfinance should also be adopted at EU level (as it will be proposed in the next paragraphs) to overcome some obstacles in EU laws. Second, in consideration of the significant differences among MSs in the financial inclusion and microfinance sector, such rules should allow flexibility locally. Third, some considerations illustrated above might apply also to Eastern/Central European countries in relation with the EU and international investors.

a The EU Treaty and different legal bases available for European microfinance initiatives

EU programmes in the microfinance and micro-enterprises fields have been grounded so far in the new areas of solidarity and social inclusion, which had the effect of expanding, through the 2001 Nice Treaty, first, and then the 2007 Lisbon Treaty, EU scope and interest beyond competition and economic integration.[104] Nonetheless, such new social objectives and concurrent powers seemingly should still be read in the light of the main economic objectives (i.e. market

104 *See*, e.g., Art. 3(3) TEU, Artt. 9, 149, 151ff., 166, 175 TFEU; Artt. 29, 34, 36, 38 of the 'Charter of Fundamental Rights of the European Union'.

integration and competition, higher in the 'priority hierarchy') and anyway respect the internal market *acquis* (including competition rules), the EU having traditionally built its legitimacy on its technical expertise and as perpetrator of economic efficiency.[105]

Furthermore, relevant differences exist between the social area and the single market area. In fact, EU actions within social policies are lightly intrusive (typically involving only cooperation and even explicitly excluding harmonization),[106] leaving more room for MSs' discretion and acknowledging the great differences among MSs' welfare systems, political traditions and conceptions of the State. Moreover, in the same area, MSs appear over-sensitive and inclined to see violations of their sovereignty. For example, the German Constitutional Court in the *Solange II* and *Lisbon* judgments,[107] despite recognizing EU primacy, has reaffirmed its role in protecting the core values of the German Constitution and German people's sovereignty (based on the argument of EU 'democratic deficit'), limiting EU intervention in some areas, including social policy/security and education.

Instead, the integration in the financial sector has far more ancient and solid origins, counting on now highly intrusive instruments and with little space left to MSs' discretion (Artt. 50, 53, 114 TFEU; below §b). EU intervention in the financial sector was in fact conceived as a part of the economic integration and growth process (not having the Treaties' specific provisions about the financial sector).[108] The early objective was the attainment of a level-playing field in this area through convergence of regulations concerning credit institutions and supervisory homogenization (*see* First Banking Directive 77/780/CE). The White Paper of 1985 moved a step forward trying to overcome the significant differences in the sector's traditions and approaches and divergent interests among MSs, laying the grounds for a series of fundamental legal texts (e.g. subsequent banking and own funds Directives, MiFID and many others). It introduced the principles of

105 *See* G. Majone, 'The European Community between Social Policy and Social Regulation', (1993) 31(9) *JCMS* 153, 156 ('[...] measures by the Commission in the social field must be compatible with the "economic constitution" of the Community, that is, with the principles of a liberal economic order'); M. Daly, 'EU Social Policy after Lisbon', (2006) 44(3) *JCMS* 461, 463–64, 475; F. Scharpf, 'The European Social Model: Coping with the Challenges of Diversity', (2002) 40(4) *JCMS* 645, 647, 655.

106 *See* Art. 149 TFEU on the promotion of MSs' actions in the employment sector without regulatory harmonization; Art. 153 on the complementary action of the UE for the integration of people excluded from job market – through cooperation action or *de minimis* directives – and against social exclusion – only through cooperation. On the weakness of the instruments of EU action in social policy, *see* Daly, 'EU Social', 468.

107 *Re Wuensche Handelsgesellschaft*, BVerfG decision of 22 October 1986 [1987] 3 CMLR 225, 265; *Zitierung*, BVerfG, Case No. BvE 2/08 of 30 June 2009, Absatz-Nr. (1–421), 123 BVERFGE 267 2 (in particular, §§226, 351, 393), <www.bundes verfassungsgericht.de/entscheidungen/es20090630_2bve000208en.html>. *See* A. Fischer-Lescano et al. (eds), *The German Constitutional Court's Lisbon Ruling: Legal and Political Science Perspectives*, ZERP-Diskussionspapier 1/2010, 21ff., 41ff., 83ff.

108 *See* Dragomir, *European*, 66ff.

mutual recognition, home-country control, minimum harmonization of fundamental banking regulation and supervisory standards and regulatory competition, all confirmed by the 1999 Financial Services Action Plan, the 2005 White Paper and subsequent innumerable Directives (also thanks to the faster Lamfalussy system of regulatory process), eliminating EU regulatory lacunae.[109]

In particular, European banks must fulfil various requirements (e.g. authorization process, safe and sound administrative, risk-management and accounting procedures, adequate internal controls, capital adequacy, liquidity and solvency ratios, limitations on large exposures) to ensure stability and competition but are facilitated in cross-border activities (*see* Chapter 6). In fact, the 'European passport' allows them to operate through branches or free provision of services in any MS under the exclusive supervision of the home country's banking authority, except for the competences expressively attributed to the host country's authority (e.g. liquidity requirements and conduct of business: *see* Artt. 41.1 and 41.2, 29–37 CRD) and the rules set by the same to protect fundamental general interests (Art. 26.1 CRD).

However, the financial crisis has revealed the presence of more serious deficiencies in the EU system, which had allowed the survival of significant differences in MSs' banking regulations and were not able to ensure a real and prompt cooperation among supervisors and effective immediate responses to the crisis, leading to a new and revolutionary wave of reforms.

b Post-crisis reflections, the 'Banking Union' and other path-breaking reforms

The post-crisis wave of EU financial regulation, although not questioning the pre-existing framework, moves towards more detailed prudential standards (also to improve risk-management and risk-internalization) and a more EU pervasive role in the financial field, while, at the same time, focusing on stability and effective supervision rather than just competition.[110]

In the process, EU involvement has grown to such a level to, first, transform banking from an area of minimum harmonization to a (shared) EU competence based on a maximum harmonization regime (with a post-crisis increased use of Regulations or detailed Directives),[111] with common principles, rules, guidelines and technical standards for the creation of 'single rulebooks' in the areas of

109 *See* Dragomir, *European*, 33ff., 90, 105ff., 152; N. Moloney, 'New Frontiers in EC Capital Markets Law: From Market Construction to Market Regulation', (2003) 40 (4) *CML Rev* 809, 813ff.

110 Post-crisis reforms chose to compose the 'financial trilemma' favouring stability and integration over national determination. About the 'financial trilemma', *see* M. Obstfeld and A. Taylor, 'The Great Depression as a Watershed: International Capital Mobility over the Long Run', (1997) NBER Working Paper 5960, <www.nber.org/papers/w5960>; D. Schoenmaker, 'Financial Trilemma', (2011) 111(1) *Economics Letters* 57.

111 *See* Dragomir, *European*, 151ff.; Moloney, 'New Frontiers', 817–20; Ferran, *The Regulatory*, 63ff.

banking supervision, crisis prevention and management and deposit insurance (*see* Directive CRDIV 2013/36/EU and Regulation CRR 575/2013; Directive BRRD 2014/59/EU; Directive DGS 2014/49/EU).[112] For instance, CRR (Regulation) sets detailed and directly prescriptive prudential rules about capital, liquidity, large exposures, executives pay, transparency and leverage. CRDIV (Directive) leaves instead MSs with more discretion about the authorization process, exercise of freedom of establishment and free movement of services, prudential supervision, capital buffers, corporate governance and sanctions. However, the CRDIV/CRR package frequently assigns to the Commission (often based on a European Banking Authority – EBA draft: *see* below) the task of clarifying or technically specifying concepts and standards through level 2 measures (Implementing or Delegated Acts: ITS or RTS, Artt. 290–291 TFEU), while, at level 3, EBA adopts guidelines and recommendations, further restricting MSs' discretion also with reference to less significant banks.[113]

Second, the supervisory cooperation model has evolved for Euro-area countries towards a more centralized one, through the creation of a 'Banking Union',[114] based on three pillars, the last of which (Single Deposit Insurance) has not yet been realized.[115] The aim of the reform has been to sever the link between banks and sovereigns and respond to some shortcomings (e.g. home-country bias, slow and intricate procedures).[116] The first pillar, the Single Supervisory Mechanism – SSM (*see* Regulations 1024/2013 and 1022/2013) – consists of a complex system of banking supervision with competencies shared between the European Central Bank (ECB, through the creation of a Single Supervisory Board – SSB) and National Competent Authorities (NCAs). The former has been invested with the responsibility of the functioning of the system and with specific and direct supervisory powers over the largest and most significant European banks (generally, with assets above €30 billion or constituting at least 20% of their home country's GDP or so considered by their NCAs or with EFSF or ESM financial support) of the Euro-area (or from countries opting-in), also setting standards and instructions on how to perform the supervisory function. NCAs retain in principle direct supervisory powers over less significant banks (but which can be advocated by ECB since small banks can also pose systemic risk:[117] Art. 6(5) Reg. 1024/2013)

112 On the 'single rulebooks', *see* G. Ferrarini and F. Recine, 'The Single Rulebook and the SSM. Should the ECB Have More Say in Prudential Rule-making?', in D. Busch and G. Ferrarini (eds), *European Banking Union*, (OUP 2015), 118ff.
113 *See* Moloney, *EU Securities*, 212–15.
114 About the Banking Union, *see* among others, Busch and Ferrarini, *European*; N. Moloney, 'European Banking Union: Assessing its Risks and Resilience', (2014) 51 (6) *CML Rev* 1609.
115 *See* Commission, 'Towards the Completion of the Banking Union', (Communication) COM(2015)587 final; Id., 'Proposal for a Regulation of the European Parliament and of the Council Amending Regulation (EU) 806/2014 in Order to Establish a European Deposit Insurance Scheme', COM(2015)586 final.
116 Ferrarini and Recine, 'The Single', 126; Moloney, 'European'.
117 *See* Commission, 'Legislative Package for Banking Supervision in the Eurozone' – 'FAQs', MEMO/13/780.

and perform significant tasks in cooperation with the SSB (e.g. day-to-day verifications and joint-inspection teams, freedom of establishment communications). Furthermore, they maintain their competencies in areas traditionally excluded from EU-credit institutions' sphere (e.g. lending-only, payment and e-money institutions, AML-CT, business conduct: Artt. 1, 4–6). The SSM represents an enormous jump forward in the integration process compared to the previous system of European Supervisory Authorities (EBA, EIOPA, ESMA for, respectively, banking, insurance and securities sectors) created by Regulations No. 1092 and 1096/2010 but lacking significant direct binding powers over market actors being mainly consultative agencies.[118] The second pillar, the Single Resolution Mechanism (Regulation No. 806/2014 and Council Document 8457/0214), has created a similar system for bank-crises prevention and management, with a Single Resolution Board – SRB (an agency) – vested with the role of resolution authority for significant banks, investment firms and cross-border groups in the Euro-area (this time along with the ECB, Commission and the Council according to the *Meroni* doctrine) and managing a Resolution Fund.

The integration process in the financial regulation area should progress also through the Capital Markets Union – CMU – initiative,[119] a broader and less-defined programme with the aim of strengthening (ensuring stability and investor confidence) and promoting non-bank-funding (e.g. securitization, crowdfunding, venture capital) especially for SMEs, also through harmonization. This appears to inspire and gather a varied range of reforms and initiatives (e.g. simple securitizations, covered bonds, simpler prospectuses, ELTIFs, EuVECA/EuSEF, green investments, SMEs credit information: *see* also Chapters 5, 7).

The decision of British people of 23 June 2016 to leave the EU has opened a heated debate about the future of UK–EU relations, especially in the financial sector. Nonetheless, it is still not possible to predict the effects of Brexit on the described integration process or on British microfinance (in terms of applicable law, passport and reliance on EU funds).

c Grounds for an EU regulatory action

European Institutions have promoted various programmes to provide financial and technical assistance to MFIs under the Lisbon and social cohesion strategy (*see* Chapter 2, §2.b) but never adopted a legislative binding text in this area. Nonetheless, the Economic and Social Committee of the European Parliament and the

118 *See* E. Ferran and V. Babis, *The European Single Supervisory Mechanism* (2013), University of Cambridge Faculty of Law Research Paper 10/2013, <http://ssrn.com/abstract=2224538>; Moloney, 'European'.

119 Commission, 'Green Paper. Building a Capital Markets Union', (Communication), COM(2015)63 final; Id., 'Action Plan on Building a Capital Markets Union', COM (2015)468 final. *See* also N. Véron, 'Defining Europe's Capital Markets Union', (2014) Bruegel Policy Contribution 2014/12, <http://bruegel.org/wp-content/uploads/imported/publications/pc_2014_12_cmu.pdf>.

Parliament itself[120] have proposed that the Commission adopt a harmonized regime for bank and non-bank MFIs (for the latter e.g.: easy authorization process, simplified accounting standards and supervision; generally, a guarantee fund for microloans, a European database about beneficiaries, collection of microloan data), recommend higher national interest rate caps for MFIs, tax advantages, reporting about microcredit, collection of best practices and guidelines, along with reforms to EU legislation in the areas of competition, state-aid and AML-CT. Instead, the Commission has so far only recommended to MSs the creation of a favourable regulatory and institutional framework for microcredit (e.g. easier authorization processes, guarantee facilities, securitization systems, more flexible usury laws for MFIs, tax breaks, access to credit bureaux and the creation of a European database about defaults, loan losses and ratings). It has also recognized the need to apply prudential regulation and supervision only in the case of deposit mobilization and recommended to take into account costs and risks in regulating microcredit (Chapter 6, §3.b).[121] Finally, it has promoted the European MFIs Code (above §3.c; Chapters 4, §2; 8, §§3–4).

Anyway, existing or prospective EU financial regulation can have a significant impact on the development of microfinance. On the one hand, MFIs willing to also offer deposits have to be authorized as banks and respect European requirements (§a–b and Chapters 4, 6), even in the case of only domestically active banks and not entailing systemic risk. In fact, their home countries would not be legitimated to create a new type of entity (Art. 9 CRR) or introduce lighter requirements (save in exceptional and specific cases: e.g. Artt. 12(4) CRDIV about initial capital, 129(2) about capital conservation buffer, 130(2) about the countercyclical capital buffer).[122] European laws can also be relevant in the case of the offering of additional services, such as consumer credit, residential mortgages, payment services or electronic money (Chapters 4, §6; 9).

On the other hand, MSs, while now allowed to impose stricter rules only in the case of specific bank risk profile and on stability grounds,[123] can extend banking regulation to operators not considered credit institutions under EU law (although more recently not to call the same 'credit institutions'). This has implied in some

120 European Parliament Resolution 24/3/2009.

121 Commission, 'A European Initiative'.

122 Art. 9(2) CRD IV allows national or EU laws to specifically exempt undertakings from the general prohibition of taking deposits or repayable funds without a credit institution status provided that these are subject to regulations and controls protecting depositors and investors but this exemption has been interpreted restrictively and only with reference to some already existing and traditionally operating undertakings. *See* Chapter 6.

123 The Capital Adequacy Directive included a general provision allowing MSs to impose stricter requirements (*see* recital 8) while the CRD IV/CRR package envisions national stricter rules only with reference to specific items (e.g. of own funds, risk buffers, capital conservation buffer, public disclosure or large exposure: recital 15, Artt. 133(1) CRD IV and 458 CRR) and after a EU approval process. *See* also Commission, 'Capital Requirements – CRD IV/CRR – FAQs', MEMO/13/690, 5, 8 and 10; Dragomir, *European*, 76–78, 113–14, 154.

countries bank requirements on credit-only institutions (*see* Greece, Germany), often indirectly impeding microcredit development (§§2; Chapters 4, 6).

Consequently, an EU legislative act might be required to facilitate bank-MFIs or just promote at a European level non-bank MFIs, eliminating disparities and competitive distortions.[124] In fact, a European microfinance reform would facilitate the circulation of expertise, innovations and best-practices among MSs in the social financial services area, responding not only to the objective of economic and financial cohesion, but also of the fundamental Treaty freedoms, removing barriers to providers' activity and to customers' access to the internal market and therefore to comparable basic financial services across MSs. On similar grounds, the EU has introduced the right to a basic payment account (Recommendation 2011/442 and Directive 2014/92/EU: *see* Chapter 4, §6.b).[125]

Furthermore, the EU regulatory role has recently moved from opening up markets and removing obstacles,[126] to regulating such markets. Consequently, EU regulatory intervention (based on Artt. 50, 114 or 5 TFEU: *see* again Directive on basic payment account) would be justified by the need to address market failures in the credit market, also partially determined by EU financial and competition regulations.

d National reforms: microfinance and EU competition law

In the absence of an EU legislative act, MSs have been interested in creating national regimes for microfinance. However, regulatory advantages and forms of financial support to microfinance might conflict, not only with EU financial regulation, but also with European competition law, which has also the effect of limiting MSs' ability to reach social and economic development goals through State aid or public enterprises or financial regulation measures (with some exceptions: *see infra*).[127]

124 EU intervention need to be justified not only by mere disparities but also by competitive distortions: case C-376/98 *Germany v. Parliament and Council* (*Tobacco Advertising*) [2000] ECR I-8419.

125 EU action would bring to all EU consumers the advantages of the Single Market by facilitating financial inclusion: *see* Commission, 'Impact Assessment Accompanying the Document "Commission Recommendation of 18 July 2011 on Access to a Basic Payment Account"', Staff Working Paper SEC(2011)906, 13 and Commission, 'Impact Assessment Accompanying the Proposal for a Directive on the Comparability of Fees Related to Payment Accounts, Payment Account Switching and Access to Payment Accounts with Basic Features', SWD(2013)164 final, 53.

126 *See* Dragomir, *European*, 155.

127 *See* Scharpf, 'The European', 648. For example, the ECJ has affirmed (case C-342/96 *Spain v Commission* [1999] ECR I-2459, paras 22–23) that, although MSs have exclusive powers in the social field, 'they are required in any event to comply with Community rules on competition' and 'the social character of State aid is not sufficient to exclude it outright from being categorised as aid for the purposes of Article 92 of the Treaty'.

State aid under Art. 107 TFEU is identified by the ECJ as an intervention by the State or anyway through State resources, with the ability to affect the trade between MSs in an advantageous way (with an economic advantage not obtainable under normal market conditions, disregarding any consideration of social or philanthropic nature – 'private investor test'[128]), for the recipient (selective economic advantage) and with the effect of distorting competition in the Internal market.[129]

Consequently, measures, exempting microfinance providers from general provisions or simplifying existing requirements, although assigning a (even financial) competitive advantage, should generally not be considered State aid as long as they do not entail a direct financial burden on the State (in the form of expenditure or reduced income: 'resource transfer' criterion)[130] or can be justified by the 'nature or general scheme of the statutory system' ('selectivity' criterion).[131]

Instead, subsidies, but also mitigations of charges normally included in an undertaking's budget (including costs from regulatory obligations)[132] and provision of services and goods at preferential terms, including tax reliefs and loans at preferential terms or state guarantees (if not available otherwise on the market)[133] or even tax incentives for investors,[134] can be regarded as State aid. Furthermore, measures targeting particular sectors (e.g. banking) or a part of the undertakings in the sector (e.g. MFIs instead of all financial institutions) are generally considered selective economic advantages (being a derogation from a general scheme),[135] unless justified by the nature or general scheme of the statutory system (social

128 *See* case C-482/99 *French Republic v Commission*, [2002] ECR I-04397, para 69; case C-39/94 *SFEI and Others* [1996] ECR I-3547, para 60; *Spain v Commission*, para 41.

129 *See* case C-280/00 *Altmark Trans GmbH and Regierungspräsidium Magdeburg v Nahverkehrsgesellschaft Altmark GmbH*, [2003] ECR I-07747, paras 75ff.

130 Case 82/77 *Openbaar Ministerie v Van Tiggele* [1978] ECR 25, paras 8 and 25e; Joined Cases C-72/91 and C-73/91 *Sloman Neptun Schiffahrts* [1993] ECR I-887, paras 20–21; Commission, 'Notice on the Notion of State Aid as Referred to in Article 107(1) of the Treaty on the Functioning of the European Union', (2016/C 262/01), paras 47, 56 (a derogation from employment law, although reducing social security contributions or payable taxes, does not account to state aid); R. Plender, 'Definition of Aid', in A. Biondi et al., *The Law of State Aid in the European Union*, (OUP 2004), 18–19.

131 *See* Opinion of Advocate General Maduro in case C-237/04 *Enirisorse SpA v Sotacarbo SpA*, [2006] ECR I-2843, paras 48–52.

132 Commission, 'Notice', para 69; case T-538/11 *Belgium v Commission* [2015] OJ C-155/24, paras 74–78.

133 *See Guarantee Scheme for Banks in Ireland* (case 48/2008) Commission decision C (2008)6059 final, [2008] OJ C6059, para 48; K. Bacon, *European Community Law of State Aid*, (OUP 2009), 26ff.

134 *SFEI and Others*, paras 58–59; *Spain v Commission*, para 42; case C-241/94 *France v Commission – 'Kimberly Clark'*, [1996] ECR I-4551, para 34; case C-75/97 *Belgium v Commission* [1999] ECR I-3671, para 23.

135 *See* Opinion of Advocate General in joined cases C-72/91 and C-73/91 *Sloman-Neptun*, paras 50, 58; Plender, *Definition*, 20; C. Ahiborn and C. Berg, 'Can State Aid Control Learn from Antitrust? The Need for a Greater Role for Competition

welfare or tax)[136] (in our case, MSs' general policy in favour of SMEs and low-income people). In fact, beyond such cases, the measure's social purpose does not exclude the qualification as aid (being relevant the effects, not the aim), nor does the undertaking's not-for-profit nature when it provides goods or services (engaging in an economic activity) on the market and, consequently, in competition with other providers.[137]

To verify the distortive effects on competitors and consumers, the Commission primarily employs the 'cross-price elasticity of demand criterion', to detect products and services concerned, considering the relevant market the one with replaceable products.[138] In the European microfinance case, we might consider that the segment of population (low-income and unbanked people) typically served by MFIs is not the same as mainstream financial providers' and therefore their products are not replaceable except for traditional providers specialized in serving low-income communities (e.g. credit unions, financial cooperatives, savings banks: §5).

Anyway, to be relevant under EU law, measures need to have the ability to affect the internal trade. The financial sector is generally characterized by an intense level of trade among MSs[139] and liberalized, and therefore advantages are

Analysis under the State Aid Rules', in Biondi et al, *The Law*, 51–52; Bacon, *European*, 81–82.

136 *See* case 173/73 *Italy* v *Commission*, [1974] ECR 709, para 13; *'Kimberly Clark'*, paras 20–21; *Belgium v Commission*, case C-75/97, paras 25 and 34; *Spain* v *Commission* para 23. *See* also C-222/04 *Ministero dell'Economia e delle Finanze v Cassa di Risparmio di Firenze SpA and others*, paras 137–138, referring to an exemption in favour of Italian Banking Foundations: 'It derogates from the ordinary tax regime without being justified by the nature or scheme of the tax system of which it forms part. The derogation is not based on the measure's logic or the technique of taxation, but results from the national legislature's objective of financially favouring organisations regarded as socially deserving. Such an advantage is therefore selective'; Commission, 'Notice on the Application of the State Aid Rules to Measures Relating to Direct Business Taxation', (1998) C384/3, para 16; Bacon, *European*, 25, 90–93; Plender, *Definition*, 7, 27; Ahiborn and Berg, 'Can', 60–61.

137 *See* C-222/04 *Cassa di Risparmio di Firenze*, paras 103–108, 120–23. *See* also Commission, 'Services of General Interest, Including Social Services of General Interest: A New European Commitment', (Communication) COM(2007)725 final, 5; Bacon, *European*, 35–36; W. Sauter, 'Services of General Economic Interest and Universal Service in EU Law', TILEC Discussion Paper 2008–017, 20–21, <http://ssrn.com/abstract=1136105>. *See* also *United Kingdom-Credit Union* Commission Decision 244/2003 about Irish Credit Union provision of access to basic financial services, [2005] OJ C223, paras 41, 64.

138 *See* Commission, 'Common Principles for an Economic Assessment of the Compatibility of State Aid Under Article 87.3', (2009), 16–17, <http://ec.europa.eu/competition/state_aid/reform/economic_assessment_en.pdf>; R. Nitsche and P. Heidhues, *Study on Methods to Analyse the Impact of State Aid on Competition*, (Commission 2006), 120ff.; Ahiborn and Berg, 'Can', 49.

139 *See* Commission, 'Guide to the Application of the European Union Rules on State Aid, Public Procurement and the Internal Market to Services of General Economic Interest, and in Particular to Social Services of General Interest', Staff Working Document, SWD(2013)53 final/2, 20; *Italy v Commission*, para 19.

presumed aid but microfinance is still generally offered only locally (and not yet EU-harmonized).[140] However, the Commission tends to exempt only small and with low turn-over undertakings, not able to attract foreign operators, customers or investors (e.g. small local swimming pools for residents),[141] but in principle has also applied it to the banking field.[142]

In any case, measures in favour of microfinance might escape EU law when falling within one of the SME and employment sectors' 'block exemptions'[143] or *de minimis*.[144]

Furthermore, microfinance providers might be regarded as charged with public service obligations and thus their advantages not considered aid as long as the services are clearly defined as public service obligation, the parameters for determining the compensation are objective, transparent and established in advance, there is no over-compensation, the selection is based on public procurement procedures or other methods ensuring efficiency ('compensation' approach under the *Ferring* case).[145] Traditional forms of aid in favour of certain financial undertakings providing basic financial services (e.g. public financial institutions or credit cooperatives also targeting social housing and SMEs) have been admitted in case of a clear identification of the service, specific appointment, choice based on public procurement procedures or anyway impeding over-compensation and no other less disruptive measures.[146]

140 *See* Joined cases C-15/98 and 105/99 *Italian Republic and Sardegna Lines v Commission* [2000] ECR I-8855, paras 68–770.

141 *See* Bacon, *European*, 97–100; Commission, 'Notice', paras 190–98.

142 *See* Commission, 'Services of General Economic Interest in the Banking Sector', Report (1998), <http://ec.europa.eu/competition/state_aid/studies_reports/archive/report_bank_en.html>: 'Thus, in principle, locally operating savings banks or similar credit institutions of purely local impact benefiting from such measures would not be caught at all by Article 92(1)' [now 107]. *See* also Commission, 'Guide', 35 (question 35).

143 *See* Commission Regulation (EC) 800/2008 on the application of Articles 87 and 88 of the Treaty declaring certain categories of aid compatible with the common market-General Block Exemption Regulation (GBER), [2008] OJ L214/3 2008.

144 Commission Regulation (EC) 1998/2006 on the application of Articles 87 and 88 of the EC Treaty to *de minimis* aid [2006] OJ L379/5 (the threshold is set at €200,000 over three fiscal years per undertaking). In case of SGEIs, the threshold is set at €500,000 over three fiscal years per undertaking: *see* Art. 2 of Commission Regulation (EU) 360/2012 on the application of Articles 107 and 108 of the Treaty on the Functioning of the European Union to *de minimis* aid granted to undertakings providing services of general economic interest, [2012] OJ L 114/8.

145 Case C-53/00 *Ferring* case, [2001] ECR I-9067. *See* also Bacon, *European*, 57ff.; Ahiborn and Berg, *Can*, 61; C. Rizza, 'The Financial Assistance Granted by Member States to Undertakings Entrusted with the Operation of a Service of General Economic Interest', in Biondi et al., *The Law*, 67ff.

146 *See* Commission, 'Services' (Report); Commission, 'European Union Framework for State Aid in the Form of Public Service Compensation', (Communication) [2011] OJ C8/15, paras 39ff. (introducing MSs' duty to set compensation incentives promoting efficiency, although not at the expense of quality).

Otherwise, they might be considered aid but exempted as providers of a service of general economic interest (SGEI)[147] under Artt. 14 and 106(2) TFEU (and 36 of the Charter of Fundamental Rights of the European Union), provided that the proportionality principle is respected ('State aid' approach under *Altmark* case),[148] i.e. there is a formal entrustment, the measure is needed to ensure the service (necessity test), there are no other less restrictive means available (proportionality test; including the not-over-compensation test) and the effect on trade is not contrary to the Community interest.[149] SGEI is a rather uncertain concept, not officially defined in EU regulation not to excessively constrain MSs' discretion and the continuously evolving nature of such services.[150] The Commission has anyway identified SGEIs as 'economic activities, which the MSs subject to specific public service obligations by virtue of a general interest criterion' because they 'consider that market forces do not provide such services, or not at conditions considered as satisfactory'.[151] Their typical characteristics have been identified with equality of access, universal accessibility, continuity, affordability, high quality and consumer protection,[152] but not limited to universal services (being admissible also services to only a part of the population or confined to a certain territory).[153]

147 *See* recently, Monti's suggestion to include among the service of general economic interest basic financial services: M. Monti, 'A New Strategy for the Single Market at the Service of Europe's Economy and Society', (2010), 74ff., <http://ec.europa.eu/bepa/pdf/monti_report_final_10_05_2010_en.pdf>.

148 *See* also case T-106/95 *FFSA and others v Commission*, [1997] ECR II-229, paras 99–101, 167–78, 185–93. *See* Ahiborn and Berg, *Can*, 62–63; Rizza, 'The Financial', 68ff.

149 *See* Commission, 'The Application of the European Union State Aid Rules to Compensation Granted for the Provision of Services of General Economic Interest', (Communication) [2012] OJ C8, 4, paras 43, 62; *see* also Commission Decision 842/2005 of 28 November 2005 on the application of Article 86(2) of the EC Treaty to State aid in the form of public service compensation granted to certain undertakings entrusted with the operation of services of general economic interest, [2005] OJ L 312; Bacon, *European*, 59–63, 134ff.; Sauter, 'Services', 23, 32–35. Specifically for sectors other than transport with compensation not exceeding €15 million and the sector of 'access to and reintegration into the labour market' and 'social inclusion of vulnerable groups', with duration below ten years, *see* Commission Decision 2012/21/EU of 20 December 2011 on the application of Article 106(2) of the Treaty on the Functioning of the European Union to State aid in the form of public service compensation granted to certain undertakings entrusted with the operation of services of general economic interest, [2012] OJ L7/3.

150 *See* Commission, 'Green Paper on Services of General Interest', COM(2003)270 final, para 16–17; Commission, 'A Quality Framework for Services of General Interest in Europe', (Communication) COM(2011)900 final, 4–5; case T-289/03 *BUPA v Commission*, [2008] ECR II-81, paras 165–67; Sauter, 'Services', 10–11.

151 *See* Commission, 'The Application of EU State Aid Rules on Services of General Economic Interest since 2005 and the Outcome of the Public Consultation', (2011) Staff Working Paper SEC(2011)397, 5; Commission, 'Services of General Interest in Europe of 2000', (Communication) [2001] OJ C 17/4, para 14 and annex II; Commission, 'Green Paper', para 22; Commission, 'Guide to the Application', 21–22, 26.

152 *See* Commission, 'Green Paper', para 49.

153 *BUPA v Commission*, para 186; Bacon, *European*, 134.

The EU itself has started viewing the offering of basic financial services as SGEI.[154] Nonetheless, since the financial service sector is highly harmonized and competitive, restrictions to competition must be analysed carefully with a case-by-case approach.[155] For instance, in a 2005 Decision[156] the Commission upheld the national qualification as SGEI of the provision of basic financial services to financially excluded people and other vulnerable groups by the Scottish Credit Unions, exempting the aid under Art. 106(2) TFEU. In fact, although recognizing its nature of aid (lacking the fourth condition of *Altmark*-tender procedure), it verified the respect of SGEI conditions (formal and transparent entrustment, need for the aid, proportionality, alignment of the objective of financial inclusion with EU objectives and policies).

Anyway, MSs retain the discretion to entrust with SGEIs only some types of providers or entrust all providers but treat them differently accordingly to their respective differences.[157] Consequently, while measures in favour of all microfinance providers (including commercial banks) would more easily pass the test, also measures only favouring MFIs or only partially banks (through differentiated measures) might be acceptable.[158] Directive 2014/92 (also) on basic payment accounts (*see* Chapter 4, §6.b) underlines that designating only a smaller group of providers needs to be carefully justified since it runs the risk of stigmatizing certain consumers (Recital 38).

Other Treaty provisions allow the Commission to authorize specific MSs' aid measures (not for operating expenses), after verifying the presence of common interest objectives, instrument appropriateness (correct incentives and proportionality), limited distortions (considering selection procedures, conditions, type of market and size) and necessity. For instance, Art. 107(3)b refers to the execution

154 *See* European Parliament, 'Resolution on the Commission Communication "Services of General Interest in Europe", COM(2000)580, para 68; Commission, 'A Quality', 10; Commission, 'Guide', 25; Commission Recommendation 2011/442/EU of 18 July 2011 on access to a basic payment account, [2011] OJ L 190/87.

155 *See* Commission, 'Services' (Report); Commission, 'The Application' (2011), 22–23; Commission, 'Guide', 23–24; P. Rossi-Maccanico and V. Sansonetti, 'Survey of State Aid in the Lending Sector: A Comprehensive Review of Main State Aid Cases', (2007) 18(6) EBL Rev 1353, 1354; Sauter, 'Services', 26ff.

156 Commission Decision 244/2003, para 69.

157 *See* Commission, 'Guide', 35 (question 32), 62 (question 112) and 95 (question 209). *See* also Commission Recommendation on access, recital 9 and para 2.

158 *See* Commission, 'Services' (Report): 'In the Commission's view, if each credit institution is free to offer the services on behalf of the Member State on the same conditions and with the same compensation this should in principle not cause problems under the competition rules of the Treaty, in so far as the question of aid to the service provider is concerned. On the other hand, if the performance of a task is entrusted to only one or a limited number of credit institutions it has to be ensured that this is done in a way which is compatible with the rules of the Treaty. However, any state aid nature can per se be eliminated if all institutions have the opportunity to compete on an equal basis for the service to be rendered. By establishing precise specifications a Member State can ensure that the service is rendered at the desired quality and price level. Free competition between interested service providers is thus ensured.'

of an important project of common European interest,[159] which might be represented by microfinance, considering the number of EU initiatives in the field.[160] Art. 107(3)c about facilitating the development of certain economic activities or of certain economic areas might be relevant too (when measures target all microfinance providers).[161] Other categories of exemptions can be introduced by the Council *ex* Art. 107(3)e based on a Commission proposal.

In conclusion, on a case-by-case basis and depending on each MS's system, we might be able to affirm the compatibility of microfinance measures, when measures:

- do not entail a financial burden for the State and are justified in the framework of MS's policies/system;
- are not to be considered aid under *Altmark* and *BUPA* cases because, other conditions satisfied, they simply remunerate public service obligations of serving financially excluded (not a real economic advantage), without overcompensation, through transparent, predetermined and clear selection and remuneration criteria;
- (ideally accessible by other – EU-providers and thus irrespective of the home country[162]) do not affect the internal market (at least until the proposed EU harmonization) being strictly local-targeted microfinance activities;
- do not qualify as aid because their size do not reach the *de minimis* thresholds;
- are aid but microfinance is considered SGEI and therefore microfinance providers exempted as long as Art. 106(2) TFEU conditions are met (i.e. need, formal entrustment, proportionality including SGEI compensation and distortion effect in relation to the Community interest);
- (less likely) are specifically authorized by the Commission under Art. 107(3)b TFEU as parts of an EU common project or as 'certain economic activities' (if not against the common interest) or fall within the categories listed in Council's decisions under Art. 107(3)*e* TFEU.

159 *See North Rhine-Westphalia DTT* Commission Decision C-34/2006, para 141; Commission, 'Vademecum. Community Law on State Aid', (2008), 11–14, <http://ec.europa.eu/competition/state_aid/studies_reports/vademecum_on_rules_09_2008_en.pdf>.

160 Instead, the exemption based on measures' nature of remedy to a 'serious disturbance in the economy of a Member State' (in our case, post-crisis financial exclusion) could hardly apply, considering the Commission's restrictive interpretation in the framework of national recovery plans for certain relevant banks (only exceptional circumstances jeopardizing the functioning of the entire financial system): *see* Commission, 'The Application of State Aid Rules to Measures Taken in Relation to Financial Institutions in the Context of the Current Global Financial Crisis', (Communication) [2008] OJ C-270/8, paras 4, 7–10, 14–16, 26, 39 (now replaced by Commission, 'State Aid Rules to Support Measures in Favour of Banks in the Context of the Financial Crisis', (Communication) [2013] OJ C 216/1); Bacon, *European*, 122–23.

161 Bacon, *European*, 124–25, 421; Commission Decision 244/2003, para 58.

162 *See Tax Measures for Banks and Banking Foundations Implemented by Italy* (case C (2001) 3955) Commission Decision 2002/581/EC, [2002] OJ L 184/27.

5 Microfinance adaptability to local traditions and structures: some European examples

a Financial cooperatives, savings banks and other double-bottom-line financial institutions

One of the major strengths of microfinance worldwide has been the ability to adapt to local conditions taking advantage not only of strong social and cultural links where no adequate legal institutions were available, but also of existing legal forms (self-help groups, financial cooperatives or banks), favourable public policies and private initiatives. Microfinance has found in many European countries pre-existing social-oriented financial service providers or programmes dedicated to low-income people, which could represent hard competitors and justifications for rejecting a microfinance model as redundant (Chapter 2, §2.a). Nonetheless, in most cases microfinance has instead taken the shape of such possible competitors, benefiting from their experience and (sometimes) favourable legal regimes.

For instance, many European MFIs have been operating as financial cooperatives. This term generally refers to member-owned and member-controlled financial institutions, characterized by the 'one member, one vote' principle, restricted distribution of profits, limited participation transferability (with only the right to redeem at nominal value), providing loans and often accepting deposits and serving mainly members (but partially also non-members) within a restricted geographic area but forming regional networks (with very diverse governance structures). These include credit unions (pooling shares and deposits to provide loans, restricted to members: UK, Ireland, Romania, Poland), building societies (member savings are used to grant loans for property acquisition which also represent the collateral: Austria, Germany, Romania, Hungary, Croatia), cooperative banks (authorized credit institutions generally partially open also to non-members: Austria, Germany, Italy, France, Spain, Netherlands), *caisses/cajas/*savings banks (often with public-owned or charitable origins: Austria, Belgium, France, Germany, Italy, Spain), and savings and credit cooperatives.[163] In the UK, we also have Community Development Finance Institutions CDFIs) (more recently, 'Responsible Finance') which similarly include social banks, mutual guarantee or credit companies, loan funds, credit unions and are regulated by FCA only when

163 BCBS, Range, 6; E. Liikanen et al., 'High-level Expert Group on Reforming the Structure of the EU Banking Sector', (2012), 56–58; W. Fonteyne, 'Cooperative Banks in Europe – Policy Issues', (2007) IMF Working Paper 159, 6ff., <www.imf.org/external/pubs/ft/wp/2007/wp07159.pdf>; H. Groeneveld, 'Governance of European Cooperative Banks: Overview, Issues and Recommendations', (2015) TIAS School for Business and Society Working Paper, 8ff., <www.globalcube.net/clients/eacb/content/medias/publications/annual_reports/20160411_HG_EACB_FINAL_Snapshot.pdf>; F. Lang, 'The Role of Cooperative Banks and Smaller Institutions for the Financing of SMEs and Small Midcaps in Europe', (2016) EIF Working Paper 36, 10ff., <www.eif.org/news_centre/publications/eif_wp_36.pdf>.

conducting a regulated activity such as mortgage lending.[164] In Italy, MAGs (*Mutue di Autogestione*), mutual financial cooperatives, have been providing microcredit as unregulated providers until recently, when they have been included in the regime for social microcredit providers but allowed to lend larger and longer loans to their members (up to €75,000 and ten years) while being subject to special provisions as regards, for example, dividend distribution, transparency of capital structure and lending activity, mandatory membership of staff and participants to the capital, socio-environmental evaluation of credit applications and interest rate (Artt. 112.7 *TUB* and 16 Ministry of Finance Decree 176/2014).

Such a diverse group implies several differences not only among various types (e.g. savings banks often used to be public banks while cooperatives are member-based entities) but also within the same type across different countries (e.g. cooperatives with different group structure and level of openness to external financing). Their origins mostly lay in urban and rural cooperatives established in Germany by Schulze-Delitzsch and Raiffeisen at the end of the nineteenth century, then spread also, among others, in Austria, Italy, Switzerland, Belgium, the Netherlands and even Canada and the U.S.[165] They still play an important role in the European banking system, accounting for approximately 26% of deposits (mostly in Western Europe).[166]

Financial cooperatives regulation sometimes entail waivers or favourable terms (e.g. lower minimum capital, tax incentives, public guarantees, no interest caps). For instance, credit unions in Ireland, UK and Portugal are expressly exempted from CRDIV despite offering deposits and loans, in reason of their historical public benefit role, limited permissible activities and operations restricted to members (Art. 2(5) points 8, 19, 23).[167] However, in many countries they have been assimilated into the commercial banks regime (*see* in Germany, Austria,

164 *See* <www.fca.org.uk/firms/apply-authorisation/banks-lending-alternatives>; <www.bankofengland.co.uk/pra/Documents/authorisations/newfirmauths/alternativestobeingabank.pdf>; S. Lagoa, 'Financial Institutions and Supply of Financial Services in the European Microcredit Market: A Survey of Selected Countries' Experiences', (2014), FESSUD Working Paper 73, 26, <http://fessud.eu/wp-content/uploads/2013/04/Financial-institutions-supply-of-financial-services_European-microcredit-market_WP-73.pdf.>.

165 About financial cooperatives, Fonteyne, 'Cooperative'; R. Ayadi et al., *Investigating Diversity in the Banking Sector in Europe – The Performance and Role of Savings Banks*, (CEPS 2009); D. Bülbül et al., 'Savings Banks and Cooperative Banks in Europe', (2013) SAFE White Paper 5, <http://safe-frankfurt.de/uploads/media/Schmidt_Buelbuel_Schuewer_Savings_Banks_and_Cooperative_Banks_in_Europe.pdf>. About microfinance and financial cooperatives, *see* A. Hollis and A. Sweetman, 'Microcredit: What Can we Learn from the Past?', (1998) 26(10) *World Dev* 1875; T. Guinnane, 'The Early German Credit Cooperatives and Microfinance Organizations Today: Similarities and Differences', in Labie and Armedáriz, *The Handbook*, 80ff.

166 Lang, 'The Role', 12; Commission, 'Impact Assessment (2013)', 13.

167 EBA, 'Report to the European Commission on Matters Relating to the Perimeter of Credit Institutions', (2014), 38ff., <www.eba.europa.eu/documents/10180/534414/2014+11+27+-+EBA+Report+-+Credit+institutions.pdf>.

Spain, partially Portugal).[168] Their attractiveness for microfinance was then more represented by cooperatives' double-bottom line, local roots, relationship-banking and traditional banking services focus, comparative advantages to commercial banks and common features with many MFIs (*see* Chapters 5, §2.a; 6, §2.b–c). Nonetheless, during 1990s, the cooperative banking model faced significant pressure towards transformation into commercial banking. In addition to the liberalization trend in the EU (e.g. against public guarantees for German cooperative banks), the idea prevailed that cooperative banks were affected by weak governance: absent profit-maximization and free share transferability, there is a risk of weak monitoring and consequently of managers' or a particular member class's appropriation and no market discipline. Moreover, in a crisis situation, capital calls from members are difficult and external funding inexistent (*see* Chapters 5, §2.a; 6, §6.f).[169] Because of this and of technological change, cooperative banks in some countries (e.g. Italy and Spain contrary to Germany and Austria) lost part of their features in favour of the commercial bank model and sometimes consequently suffered from competition, riskier business lines and the effects of the financial crisis. In some countries, the financial cooperative model even disappeared (i.e. savings bank in Belgium and Italy; cooperatives in the UK) or shared many characteristics with commercial banks (*see Banche Popolari* in Italy, especially after the 2014 reform).[170]

However, financial cooperatives have tended to perform better through the financial crisis than their commercial counterparties,[171] showing better capitalization, less volatile earnings, lower leverage, more prudent management (focused on traditional banking services with strong client base) because of limited external funding and lower asymmetric information in lending as well as thanks to certain governance correctives (e.g. deposit withdrawal threat, issuance of hybrid instruments, liquidity from regional network).[172] This, along with the commercial bank model failure, has determined a partial renaissance of the cooperative/dual-bottom line model, underlying the importance of European banking diversity.[173] Nonetheless, post-crisis reforms have been designed with shareholder-based banks in mind, disregarding financial cooperatives specificities.[174] Consequently, Basel

168 Ayadi, *Investigating* (2010), 35, 51, 86.

169 Fonteyne, 'Cooperative'.

170 Bülbül, 'Savings'.

171 Ayadi, *Investigating* (2009) and (2010); H. Groeneveld, 'The Value of European Cooperative Banks for the Future Financial System', (2011), <www.helsinki.fi/ruralia/materiaalit/ICA2011/Groeneveld.pdf >.

172 Groeneveld, 'The Value'; Ayadi, *Investigating* (2010); Lang, 'The Role', 12ff. About bank performance before and after the crisis, R. Ayadi et al., *Banking Business Models Monitor 2015 Europe*, (IRCCF HEC Montréal, 2016), 35ff.

173 Ayadi, *Investigating*; G. Ferri and G. Pesce, 'Regulation and the Viability of Cooperative Banks', (2011 ICA Global Research Conference, Mikkeli – Finland), <www.sommetinter.coop/sites/default/files/article-scientifique/files/22-ferri.pdf>. *See* also Recitals 42, 46, 72 CRR.

174 Instead, the U.S. have exempted from Basel III rules credit unions and community banks: *see* Ferri and Pesce, 'Regulation'; Ayadi, *Banking*, 5–7.

III capital and liquidity requirements as well as CRDIV governance rules might attribute to such entities a riskier profile and result in an excessive burden for the same, which have restricted access to capital markets, mostly relying as buffers on member deposits and retained earnings, exhibit fixed compliance costs and peculiar governance structures. This might lead to fierce competition in deposit base with commercial banks and restricted lending (*see* also Chapter 6, §§2 and 6 about small banks and the proportionality principle).[175]

However, while MFIs have often resorted to the cooperative form, the two cannot be completely assimilated (e.g. typical cooperatives offer longer and larger loans, serve richer clients and heavily rely on deposits). In fact, the EIF has recently implemented a new programme (EREM CBSI instrument) supporting European cooperative banks offering loans between €25,000 and €500,000 to SMEs and midcaps (up to 500 employees) to fill the demand gap in relation to other EU programmes, such as EaSI, which only target microfinance and smaller credit providers, therefore recognizing a different client-base among traditional cooperatives and MFIs.[176] As mentioned, diversity in banking models represents a fundamental value for Europe, also in a stability perspective, therefore suggesting the need to promote the existence of multiple types of providers covering different demands.[177]

Anyway, many regulatory issues are similar between cooperatives and MFIs (also because of the small size and double-bottom-line character) so that we will often refer to financial cooperatives within this book (see Chapters 5, 6).

b Islamic banking and other experiences (CRA and priority sector lending)

In other countries, microfinance has found different policies promoting financial inclusion to confront with.

In the U.S., for instance, the 1977 Community Reinvestment Act (CRA)[178] creates an incentives-based system for spurring bank investments (including lending and services) in community services or low-income areas relying on reputation and market incentives. Such investments, in fact, are publicly disclosed and positively evaluated by bank authorities in the context of their decisions about licensing the opening of new branches or mergers and acquisitions, also influenced by powerful consumer associations' campaigns. Consequently, banks have a reputational and economic interest in investing in communities to avoid negative publicity and supervisory refusal in their expansion programmes, despite post-crisis

175 Ferri and Pesce, 'Regulation'; Groeneveld, 'The Value', 8; Groeneveld, 'Governance', 16; Ayadi, *Banking*, 92–95 (signalling a misalignment of regulatory risk indicators to underlying risks of European banks).

176 Lang, 'The Role', 31–35.

177 *See* Groeneveld, 'The value', 10; Ayadi, *Investigating* (2010).

178 *The Community Reinvestment Act* (CRA), 12 U.S.C. §§ 2901–906. *See* also R.S. Carnell et al., *The Law of Banking and Financial Institutions*, (Aspen 2009), 357ff.; M. Barr, 'Credit Where It Counts: The Community Reinvestment Act and Its Critics', (2005) 80 *NYU L Rev* 513.

critics to the CRA.[179] Recently, also microcredit has been qualified as community investment and therefore can benefit from the CRA regime.[180] Anyway, a system like this can work only in presence of strong consumer associations.

A different (and more prescriptive) approach exists in India. In fact, regulation requires banks to allocate a high percentage (40%) of their credit (also indirect) or equivalent off-balance sheet exposures to so called 'priority sectors' (e.g. agriculture, micro and small enterprises, education, housing, recently also microcredit and, since 2015, medium firms, renewable energy and social infrastructures).[181] However, as recent scandals have showed, such a system is effective only when banks exercise an adequate monitoring on the financed MFIs to avoid abuses and runs the risk of creating a separate and segregated financial sector for the poor (*see* above). The Reserve Bank of India (RBI), indeed, revised its priority sector lending (PSL) guidelines in 2012 and 2015 also to ensure that NBFI-MFIs receiving PSL respect certain conditions set for microfinance provision.[182]

Not so differently, some EU countries and, recently, the EU, have imposed on financial operators the provision of certain basic financial services (*see* Chapter 4, §6.b).

Another challenge for microfinance is to offer *Sharia'a* compliant services to their Muslim clients, as required by certain DCs' regulations or to meet certain clients' needs in Europe. In fact, the *Sharia'a* condemns *riba*, which has been interpreted as any form of interest rate on a loaned sum (any addition to the principal), since this would protect the lender from the risk of project failure while

179 CRA would have contributed to subprime mess incentivizing, in combination with irresponsible housing policies and credit to low-income people even when not creditworthy: C. Jones-Harvard, 'To Lend or Not to Lend: What the CRA Ought to Say about Sub-prime and Predatory lending', (2005) 7 *Fla Coastal L Rev* 1. *Contra* (linking only a very limited part of subprimes to CRA), Federal Reserve Bank, 'Staff Analysis of the Relationship between the CRA and the Subprime Crisis', (2008) <www.federalreserve.gov/newsevents/speech/20081203_analysis.pdf>; R. Kroszner, 'The Community Reinvestment Act and the Recent Mortgage Crisis', (2008), <www.frbsf.org/publications/community/cra/cra_recent_mortgage_crisis.pdf>; R. Brescia, 'The Community Reinvestment Act: Guilty, but Not as Charged', (2014) 88(1) *St. John's Law Review* 1; Federal agencies 2010 proposal of CRA review: <www.fdic.gov/regulations/laws/federal/2010/10proposeAD60.pdf>.

180 M. Richardson, 'Increasing Microlending Potential In the United States through A Strategic Approach to Regulatory Reform', (2009) 34 *J Corp L* 923; O. Walker, 'The Future of Microlending in the United States: A Shift from Charity to Profits?', (2011) 6 *Ohio St Entrepen Bus LJ* 383.

181 *See* M. Gandhi, 'Enhancing Effectiveness of Directed Priority Sector Lending for Inclusive Growth Agenda for India', (2014) 3(4) *IJTGBP* 1298; U. Thorat, 'Financial Regulation and Financial Inclusion – Working Together or at Cross-purposes', (10th annual international seminar on Policy challenges for the financial sector, 4 June 2010), <http://rbidocs.rbi.org.in/rdocs/Speeches/PDFs/GDUTWE070610.pdf>.

182 For RBI's Master circulars on PSL, <www.rbi.org.in/scripts/BS_ViewMasCirculardetails.aspx?id=9815> and on NBFC-MFIs <https://rbi.org.in/scripts/NotificationUser.aspx?Id=6857&Mode=0> and <https://rbi.org.in/Scripts/NotificationUser.aspx?Id=9651&Mode=0>.

ensuring a return, eliminating mutual assistance, equitable distribution of resources and productive investments.[183] Consequently, any conventional loan (but also deposit) contract would violate such prescription. Islamic banking has therefore created alternative contracts, generally involving forms of profit and loss sharing and partnerships between banks and clients. For instance, a *Mudaraba* is a contract in which the bank invests (equity) in a project sharing profits with the entrepreneur based on a predetermined ratio and bearing most financial losses (while the entrepreneur agrees to manage the capital and then return it with the agreed part of profits, bearing only the losses from his/her time and labour). *Musharaka* instead involves either capital investment also from the entrepreneur or management powers by the bank and losses are shared in proportion to capital contributions. Deposit and savings accounts are similar to non-Islamic ones but cannot envision a remuneration (nor a guarantee): banks, consequently, tend to reward clients at the end of the year with donations or preferential credit conditions. Moreover, participation-deposits can be used, with the depositor investing in certain projects bearing losses but sharing profits.[184] These contracts entail for banks asymmetric information, moral hazard and adverse selection more than in non-Islamic banking but reputational risk might adjust the balance. Furthermore, deviating from conventional bank contracts, Islamic finance might conflict with EU banking law: for instance, the absence of collateral and the burden of the entire financial risk would make the activity extremely expensive under Basel rules; the absence of deposit guarantee would make unlawful banking activity within the EU (in case of redeemable funds and therefore deposits).[185] Consequently, MFIs offering Islamic products in the EU might face such additional regulatory issues.

6 Principles and guidelines for regulators

The first obstacle encountered in regulating microfinance is its definition. Regulators should decide whether to create a general social responsible finance sector for all providers with social objectives or restrict a special treatment only to microfinance. In the former case, rules should be however adapted to the different models allowed (e.g. financial cooperatives, Islamic finance, microfinance). In the latter case, financial regulators should avoid too rigid definitions in order to allow innovation and adaptation to market's demands but identify the features that justify a special regime, such as the social goal, certain targeted clients (e.g. based on income, job, family), the maximum amount, the instruments used to reduce typical risks (e.g. social collateral, progressive lending, relationship banking, peculiar lending process). Since the EU presents only a too generic indication (up-to €25,000

183 B. Kustin, 'Islamic (Micro)Finance: Culture, Context, Promise, Challenges', (2015), 6ff., <https://docs.gatesfoundation.org/Documents/Islamic%20(Micro)%20Finance%20Culture,%20Context,%20Promise,%20Challenges.pdf>; B. Kettel, *Introduction to Islamic Banking and Finance*, (Wiley 2011), 31ff.

184 M. Khan and M. Porzio (eds.), *Islamic Banking and Finance in the European Union. A Challenge*, (Edward Elgar 2010), 27ff., 54ff.

185 Khan and Porzio, *Islamic*, 71ff.

loan for business purpose), MSs adopting a definition of microcredit tend to focus on a maximum loan size, the presence of accompanying services, SMEs/start-up as beneficiaries, short maturity and purpose of self-employment or business activity. With reference to social microcredit, MSs generally set lower size thresholds, require more favourable conditions, public or private guarantees but absence of real security and, as beneficiaries, low-income or people in particularly vulnerable conditions. However, requiring interest rates below certain levels or certain contractual terms might be counter-productive (*see* above Table 3.1).

Before discussing specific issues concerning the regulation of microfinance, I have laid down some general but fundamental considerations on regulation, considering the factors influencing microfinance regulation, such as costs and different levels of regulation, their different effectiveness, legitimacy, risks, principles and objectives involved. As a general matter, I have identified financial regulation as the main framework for regulating microfinance (with some room for the development aid perspective). Then, I have recognized prudential regulation as more domestic and government-led, although proposing for transnational regulators, in some cases, a more technical and development-based support for the creation of infrastructures and, in other cases, a more market-based approach for building know-how. Instead, the consumer protection and transparency fields appear more able to benefit from competition among different regulators with an important role played by transnational forces and private regulation.

Anyway, the level of legal harmonization within the EU financial sector, especially after the crisis, provides strong argument for a common approach to microfinance also in the prudential field. I have in fact proposed an EU regulatory initiative in the framework of internal market policies (Artt. 50, 114 TFEU) targeting microfinance and/or social financial services justified by the need to eliminate the risk of violating EU law by national special regimes, distortive effects in the internal market and facilitate the circulation of expertise and innovations for social financial services.

In the absence of such EU reform, I have attempted to identify the conditions under which national regimes favouring microfinance might avoid violations of EU state aid law (e.g. regulatory measures without burden for MS, financial advantages but public service or SGEI qualification – certain conditions standing – or size below *de minimis*), especially when entailing advantages for all microfinance providers or different ones based on reasonable grounds (differences in terms of costs, results, specialization, organization, efficiency), without discriminating based on the country of origins.

Finally, microfinance's multiform nature has also allowed the same to develop benefiting from existing legal regimes or private initiatives in MSs. Nonetheless, in certain cases this adds further legal dilemmas (*see* discussions about cooperative efficiency and governance and Islamic banking regulatory obstacles). Anyway, post-crisis reflections have highlighted the importance of diversity in the European banking system, making us also appreciate the need of different types of providers serving different types of clients' needs.

4 Dimension II: The social objective within the business structure and social effectiveness

1 Microfinance social objectives: financial inclusion, poverty reduction and empowerment

Another fundamental dimension of microfinance is represented by its social objective. MFIs might have as an objective profit maximization but to mark a difference from mainstream operators must present an additional mission. The scope of such additional mission can significantly vary but has to incorporate the satisfaction of external needs, primarily of disadvantaged people. In my opinion, this additional mission contributes to justify regulatory facilitations although adjustments to financial regulations might be required also on technical grounds, because of microfinance specificities (e.g. specific risks: *see* Chapter 6).

What are such additional missions? Microfinance is nowadays described, especially in economically advanced countries, as a useful instrument of financial and social inclusion, able to respond to current market gaps and failures (*see* Chapter 1).

Nonetheless, microfinance has been assigned various and ambitious missions. In fact, microfinance has been identified also as an instrument to eradicate poverty and spur countries' economic development (Chapters 1, 3). In particular, the UN and the World Bank (WB) at first regarded microfinance as a miraculous tool to spur development, reserving to the same a special role within the 'Millennium Development Goals'.[1] However, the same organizations have recently acknowledged microfinance's limits from a macroeconomic point of view. The WB in fact asserted in 2009 that 'the tiny loans usually provided under microcredit schemes do not seem to lift large numbers of people out of poverty'[2] (though recognizing

1 UN, 'The Monterrey Consensus', (2003), 8, point 18, <www.un.org/esa/ffd/monterrey/MonterreyConsensus.pdf>; Id., 'Microfinance and Millennium Development Goals', (2005), <www.yearofmicrocredit.org/docs/MF_MDGs.pdf>; UN General Assembly, 'Resolution No. A/RES/53/197–International Year of Microcredit 2005', (1999).

2 D. Narayan et al., *Moving Out of Poverty–Volume 2. Success from the Bottom Up*, (Palgrave-WB 2009), 33. *See* also A. Demirgüç-Kunt et al., *Finance for all? Policies and Pitfalls in Expanding Access*, (WB 2008), 13.

microfinance as a useful instrument of financial inclusion, only indirectly leading to economic development and a more equal society).[3]

Not only traditional literature is unconvinced about SMEs' potential to spur the economy[4] but also specific research on microfinance impact on growth has been inconclusive. While in some countries microfinance reforms have led to development and growth (e.g. Bangladesh), in others the microfinance effect appears negligible (e.g. Thailand).[5] Nonetheless, more recent studies return to assign a more significant role to microfinance in poverty reduction.[6]

Also looking from a microeconomic perspective, focusing on the impact of microfinance on clients' lives, results are mixed. Some studies (based on a non-experimental approach) attest an objective improvement in micro-entrepreneurs' welfare (e.g. in terms of monthly income, consumption level, assets acquisition, children spending).[7] On the contrary, other studies employing randomized field experiments (currently considered a more rigorous methodology because of selection bias and causality)[8] have reached different conclusions. For instance,

3 Demirgüç-Kunt, *Finance*, X, 2ff., 73ff., 106; Independent Evaluation Group, 'The World Bank's Country Policy and Institutional Assessment', (2009), XXII, 18, 110, <http://siteresources.worldbank.org/EXTCPIA/Resources/cpia_full.pdf>.

4 *See* R. Cooter and H. Schaefer, *Solomon's Knot: How Law Can End the Poverty of Nations*, (2011), ch. 8 (manuscript), <http://works.bepress.com/cgi/viewcontent.cgi?article=1163&context=robert_cooter>; M. Barr, 'Microfinance and Financial Development', (2004) 26 *Mich. J. Int'l L.* 271; R. Dyal-Chand, 'Reflection in a Distant Mirror: Why the West has Misperceived the Grameen Bank's Vision of Microcredit', (2005) 41 *Stan. J. Int'l* 217, 254. About microfinance's inability to fill the gap of 'missing middle' (i.e. creating a sustainable SMEs sector) in South Eastern Europe, *see* M. Bateman (ed.), *Confronting Microfinance. Undermining Sustainable Development*, (Kumarian Press 2011).

5 *See* Demirgüç-Kunt, *Finance for All?*, 102–104; J. Ledgerwood (ed.), *The New Microfinance Handbook*, (WB 2013), 113ff.

6 *See* K. Imai et al., 'Micro-finance and Poverty: A Macro Perspective', (2012) 40(8) *World Dev* 1675; K. Miled and J. Rejeba, 'Microfinance and Poverty Reduction: A Review and Synthesis of Empirical Evidence', (2015) 195 *Procedia-Social and Behavioral Sciences* 705.

7 On the topic *see* B. Armendáriz and J. Morduch, *The Economics of Microfinance*, (2nd edn, MIT Press 2010), ch. 9; K. Odell, 'Measuring the Impact of Microfinance. Taking Another Look', (2010), <www.grameenfoundation.org/resource/measuring-impact-microfinance>.

8 Without randomized experiments, it is difficult to exclude that a client would not have been richer even without microfinance (e.g. because of a selection bias: micro-entrepreneurs selected by MFIs are richer and smarter than others). *See* Armendáriz and Morduch, *The Economics*, 269 (about the critics to randomized studies: 306); D. Roodman and J. Morduch, 'The Impact of Microcredit on the Poor in Bangladesh: Revisiting the Evidence', (2009) Center for Global Development Working Paper 174, <www.cgdev.org/files/1422302_file_Roodman_Morduch_Bangladesh.pdf>; D. Karlan and J. Zinman, 'Expanding Credit Access: Using Randomized Supply Decisions to Estimate the Impacts', (2010) 23(1) *Rev Financ Stud* 433. About critics to such RCTs on methodological and ethical grounds, G. Gloukoviezoff, 'Evaluating the Impact of European Microfinance. The Foundations', (2016) EIF Working Paper

McKernan,[9] studying the MFI Basix in India, observed an income increase only in half of micro-entrepreneurs, while 25% of micro-entrepreneurs did not change their condition before the loan and another 25%, instead, was subject to an income decrease.[10] However, more effective appear micro-savings programmes: in a field experiment in Kenya, the availability of a savings account determined an increment in investments in entrepreneurial activity by female clients and a decrease in 'temptation goods'.[11] Anyway, subsequent studies also report some positive impact of micro-lending, such as increase in income, food consumption, job retention, decision-making.[12] In general, microcredit seems to have a positive but not transformative impact for most borrowers.[13] It is worth acknowledging that the results of all these studies appear highly context-specific, depending on clients' profile, services offered and institutional framework.[14]

Another mission assigned to microfinance consists of the improvement of the poor's 'freedoms' (in Amartya Sen's sense),[15] ie in terms, for instance, of women's empowerment, self-confidence, networking, contraception, education and attention to health issues. Such aspects are even more difficult to measure and many studies are not able to reach statistically significant results.[16]

More generally, researchers recognize difficulties in isolating microfinance's effects and account for all possible consequences (e.g. more business revenues by female entrepreneurs might lead to a decrease in the time spent at home with children or in fertility and in children's schooling levels because of the need to help with the family business or at home) and in finding a methodology free of flaws, leading to generalized results.[17]

In conclusion, additional research is still needed to clarify microfinance's role in reducing poverty and improving low-income people's conditions. Anyway, there is a common understanding: microfinance can – at least partially – advance financial and social inclusion and provide instruments to better face financial difficulties, although with results depending on several factors.

2016/033, 23ff., <http://comptrasec.u-bordeaux.fr/sites/default/files/pdf_book/livret-6-impact-global.pdf>.

9 S. McKernan, 'The Impact of Micro-Credit Programs on Self-Employment Profits: Do Non-Credit Program Aspects Matter?', (2002) 84 *Rev Econ Stat* 1, 93.

10 *See* also A. Demirgüç-Kunt et al., *Finance*; Karlan and Zinman, 'Expanding'.

11 P. Dupas and J. Robinson, 'Savings Constraints and Microenterprise Development: Evidence from a Field Experiment in Kenya', (2013) 5(1) *Am Econ J Appl Econ* 163. *See* also Karlan and Zinman, 'Expanding'.

12 Karlan and Zinman, 'Expanding'; Odell, 'Measuring', 17ff.

13 *See* A. Banerjee et al., 'Six Randomized Evaluations of Microcredit: Introduction and Further Steps', (2015) 7(1) *Am Econ J Appl Econ* 1.

14 *See* Odell, 'Measuring', 12; Gloukoviezoff, 'Evaluating', 17ff.

15 A. Sen, *Development as Freedom*, (1st edn, OUP 1999).

16 *See* Odell, 'Measuring'. More recently, finding a positive effect of microfinance: S. Garikipati, 'Microcredit and Women's Empowerment: Through the Lens of Time-Use Data from Rural India', (2012) 43 *Dev Change* 719.

17 Armendáriz and Morduch, *The Economics*, 270–71; Gloukoviezoff, 'Evaluating', 18ff.

2 The effectiveness of European microfinance

As anticipated above, a fundamental character of microfinance is its social mission but this can vary significantly. Looking at European MFIs' declared missions, the main focus is on enterprises' promotion and job creation (among the most pressing issues in Europe: Chapter 1, §1). The most widespread mission based on a recent survey, in fact, is microenterprises' promotion (69% of respondents), followed by job creation (58%), social inclusion and poverty reduction (56%),[18] financial inclusion (50%) and SME promotion (45%), while women or minority empowerment is a shared goal only for a small minority of institutions (respectively, 29% and 20%).[19] The majority of European MFIs target registered companies with less than five employees (76.7%), followed by start-up enterprises (75%), self-employed (67.3%) and registered enterprises with between five and seven employees (51.5%).[20]

However, what really matters in order to justify a special treatment is not only the presence of a social mission but also MFIs' ability and possibility of reaching such goals. If publicly stating a social mission sufficed, mainstream operators would find profitable entering the microfinance market but then pursuing only a profit-making objective with a comparative advantage and at the expense of low-income people. The social mission should not remain an abstract declaration without consequences in case of non-adherence to the same (such as, in most cases, codes of ethics or other CSR measures) but has to represent a condition, to be verified in practice, for the application of a certain favourable regime (*see* Chapter 3). Consequently, MFIs must demonstrate, first, to have clearly identified realistic social missions and, second, to be able to fulfil them and have a measurable social impact.

Comparing the list of mostly chosen social missions with data from Chapter 1, §1 about financial exclusion, it is evident that European MFIs are mostly targeting clients needing their services (SMEs/micro-enterprises, unemployed and, although to a lesser extent, women, migrants, ethnic minorities and disabled persons). However, for example, while the client categories mostly reached by Spanish MFIs are unemployed (30%) and ethnic minorities (23%), the most marginalized might

18 There are many instruments to measure poverty, each entailing different indicators and measurements. The Grameen Bank 'Progress out of Poverty Indicators' (PPI) require direct field visits and interviews with clients to determine the poverty level based on certain questions such as regarding the number of livestock, number of family members and number of beds corresponding to the number of family members (USAID Poverty tool is similar). Other methodologies rely on more official and publicly available data such as housing index, per capita household expenditure, household income, participatory wealth ranking, means test and food security index; some data (e.g. income) are not easily available in developing countries.

19 M. Bendig et al., 'Overview of the Microcredit Sector in the European Union – 2012/2013', (2014), 37, <www.european-microfinance.org/docs/emn_publications/emn_overview/Overview2012-2013_Nov2014.pdf> (many French and British MFIs target women).

20 Bendig. 'Overview', 39–41.

remain excluded because of the importance assigned in the credit-application process to entrepreneurial skills and financial viability.[21] Most MFIs state to monitor social indicators to measure progress towards their mission,[22] but limitations in financial, technical and human resources hinder social performance efforts.

Unfortunately, data available about MFIs' outreach and impact in Europe are still limited.[23] A partial survey estimates 150,000 jobs created/preserved through micro-loans in 2012–2013.[24] Studies conducted at national level seem to show the creation of jobs and self-esteem/autonomy through microfinance,[25] although the impact on income appears limited and on the quality of life mixed (most are in better conditions but some in worse).[26] Also personal microloans appear overall to be beneficial for French micro-borrowers but rarely transformative (positively impacting only 1 to 4 dimensions of well-being out of 8) and in few but existing cases (4.4%) can have a negative impact.[27] In Italy the multiplier effect of microcredit disbursed in 2010 was estimated at 2.43 (each microloan generated 2.43 jobs included the entrepreneur's).[28]

21 Ibidem 40. At least in the past, a great part of microloans ended up in the hands of the 'less poor' regions/people: EMN-EIF, 'Microfinance Market Studies', 348; S. Rico Garrido et al., 'Microcredit in Spain: The Role of Savings Banks', in Jayo-Carboni, *Handbook*, 297.

22 M. Bénard, 'European Microfinance and Social Performance: Where Do We Stand?', (2014), 11, <www.european-microfinance.org/docs/emn_publications/other_emn_publications/IL%20SPM%20-%20EU%20MF%20and%20SPM%20where%20do%20we%20stand%20-%2020141112.pdf> (having a sample of only 35 European MFIs located in 12 countries, mostly in Eastern Europe).

23 *See* Bendig, 'Overview', 40–41.

24 The estimate is based on the assumption of on average two jobs created/preserved per enterprise supported and the data reporting 66,749 supported microenterprises and start-ups in 2012 and 75,707 supported microenterprises and start-ups in 2013: *see* Bendig, 'Overview', 38.

25 *See* Gloukoviezoff, 'Evaluating', 13ff.; MicroBank, 'Report on the Impact of Microcredits. Institute for Social Innovation', (2013), <http://itemsweb.esade.es/wi/research/iis/publicacions/Microbank_Informe_impacto_microcreditos_2013_en.PDF> (each business funded by MicroBank in Spain generated an average 1.18 jobs, in addition to the job of MFIs' clients in 64% of the cases, amounting to an average of 1.81 jobs per business); B. Balkenhol and C. Guézennec, 'Le microcrédit professionnel et l'accompagnement à la création d'entreprise en France: quel devenir des créateurs sur le marché du travail trois ans après?', (2014) France Stratégie Note d'analyse 13, <www.strategie.gouv.fr/sites/strategie.gouv.fr/files/atoms/files/na-fs-microcredit-juin201411.pdf> (each French microloan led in average to the creation of 2.6 jobs); Gloukoviezoff, 'Evaluating', 13.

26 Ibidem.

27 G. Gloukoviezoff and N. Rebière, 'Etude d'impacts des microcrédits personnels garanti–Livret 6 L'impact global sur les emprunteurs', (2013), 17–18, <http://comptrasec.u-bordeaux.fr/sites/default/files/pdf_book/livret-6-impact-global.pdf>.

28 Ente Nazionale per il Microcredito, 'Le multiformi caratteristiche del Microcredito. Rapporto finale di monitoraggio', (2013), 92–94, <www.fgda.org/dati/ContentManager/files/Documenti_microfinanza/Le-multiformi-caratteristiche-del-microcredito—Rapporto-finale.pdf>.

Although it would not be economically (and sometimes methodologically) feasible to measure the impact of MFIs on their clients' life, we can still track MFIs' main social indicators to understand whether they are heading in the right direction (in terms of internal organization and outputs).[29]

Looking at European surveys, relevant percentages of MFIs' clients are unemployed persons or on welfare benefits (21.1%) and excluded from the financial sector (41%).[30] Many MFIs clients are also women (41%) while data about migrant and minorities' clients are scarce[31] and about youth and disabled persons categories almost non-existent (despite the high share of financial exclusion among these categories: Chapter 1, §1).[32]

In fact, although a discussion about the importance of measuring social impact and outreach is currently spreading worldwide, not all MFIs track their outreach and clients' characteristics. Nonetheless, socially responsible investors, public entities and international organizations have started making their support contingent upon social performance reporting. Also the 2011 'European Code of Good Conduct for Microcredit Provision' (Chapter 3, §3.c), requiring MFIs to report on certain identified social indicators, aims at increasing the tracking, monitoring and transparency of social performance (below §3).

Anyway, there is both a low level of reporting on social indicators, especially on outcomes in connection with MFIs' social mission, and few impact investors tracking social outcomes (even among social investors' funders of the impact investment measurement movement).[33] Reasonable explanations for such a low level of social reporting can be found not only in a still limited culture about social impact/performance importance, but also in the problematic measurement of social indicators.

29 *See* also Bénard, 'European', 4.
30 The highest volume of loans to unemployed people was disbursed in France, with €230 million (corresponding to 83% of clients) while Spain reached €95 million, corresponding to 30%: Bendig, 'Overview', 41.
31 Ibidem 39. The countries most lending to women are France (€108 million, 39%) and Bosnia and Herzegovina (€98 million, 51%). The migrants' and ethnic minorities' outreach was the highest in Spain (€72 million, 23%) and Germany (€33 million, 22%): ibidem 41.
32 Only few MFIs track the loans to these categories. France, again, ranks first as regards the loan volume to young people with €56 million (39%) and to disabled (€179 million, 65%), followed, for the latter category, by Bosnia and Herzegovina (€124 million, 64%) and Spain (€80 million, 25%): ibidem 41.
33 M. Pistelli et al., 'Beyond Good Intentions: Measuring Impact Investment and Social Performance in Microfinance', (2014), <www.themix.org/sites/default/files/Beyond%20Good%20Intentions%20Publication.pdf>. A parallel survey among 125 impact investors (representing a fifth of total assets in microfinance) reports instead that 95% of surveyed impact investors claim to measure social/environmental impact of their investments: Y. Saltuk et al., 'Spotlight on the Market: The Impact Investor Survey', J. P. Morgan–GIIN (2014), <www.jpmorganchase.com/corporate/socialfinance/document/140502-Spotlight_on_the_market-FINAL.pdf>.

3 The difficult measurement of social impact and performance

The urgent need for methods to assess the 'good' done beyond financial returns is not limited to microfinance but extends to a wide range of sectors (such as socially responsible investments, social enterprise and even humanitarian projects) characterized by the double-bottom line (also just in the form of efficient use of donations).[34]

'Social impact' refers to concrete social results (outputs) in terms of, for example, jobs creation, number of people moved above the poverty line and saving of public resources. On the other hand, 'social performance' is a more comprehensive concept, looking at the entire impact-creation process, from missions and objectives to systems in place to ensure goals attainment. It denotes a more behaviours/intentions-based evaluation (instead of only a focus on results), looking, for example, also at the nature of the activity, objectives, the adoption of codes of conduct, predisposition of procedures ensuring staff ethical behaviour, transparency, responsiveness, coaching or educational services for borrowers, adequate products responsive to clients' needs and overall quality of services.[35]

Also under donors' and social investors' pressure, some MFIs have started designing their own social impact/performance indexes, grounded on their own missions and priorities without ignoring collection and monitoring costs.[36] Nonetheless, this tailor-made approach makes the comparison among MFIs complex but might respond to the variety of investors' and donors' priorities.[37] However, an increased standardization and comparability in the sector would benefit MFIs and all stakeholders as well as, especially from the particular angle of our analysis, the supervisor.

Recently, the industry has put efforts into harmonizing social performance measurement in order to facilitate comparison among MFIs and get a general sense of the state of the sector, although European MFIs still show little interest.[38] The

34 E.g., the 'Sustainability Reporting Guidelines' by Global Reporting Initiative 3 (GRI, www.globalreposrting.org) aims at providing evaluation criteria of different projects, such as charity programs or social enterprises or MFIs. *See* also proceedings of the Conferences 'Privatization of Development Assistance', (NYU School of Law, 4–5 December 2009), <http://iilj.org/research/FinancingDevelopmentConference.asp> and 'Innovation in Governance of Development Finance: Causes, Consequences and the Role of Law', (NYU School of Law, 8–9 April 2013), <www.iilj.org/newsandevents/InnovationinGovernanceofDevelopmentFinance.asp>.

35 *See* SPTF, 'FAQs', No. 6, <http://sptf.info/how-do-i-start/faqs>.

36 *See* recommendations in Imp-Act and MFC, 'Social Performance Management in Microfinance. Guidelines', (2005), <www.microfinancegateway.org/sites/default/files/mfg-en-paper-social-performance-management-in-microfinance-guidelines-2005.pdf>.

37 Interview in March 2011 with J. Trant, President of the International Association of Microfinance Investors (IAMFI). *See* also E. Macchiavello, 'Private Regulation and Enforcement in Microfinance: A Multi-Layered and Polycentric Puzzle', in F. Cafaggi and G. Miller (eds), *The Governance and Regulation of International Finance*, (Edward Elgar 2013).

38 *See* Bénard, 'European', 5, 8.

Social Performance Task Force (SPTF),[39] a group formed by CGAP and several not-for-profit organizations,[40] examined different social performance tools for MFIs in order to elaborate common social performance indicators. SPTF adopted in 2012 the Universal Standards for Social Performance Management – USSPM (updated in 2014 and 2016),[41] a manual of standards organized in six dimensions completed by 161 social indicators elaborated by CERISE in collaboration with other partners (SPI4 audit tool)[42] and also adopted by the MIX,[43] to allow MFIs to self-evaluate their social performance, including their structure coherence with the proposed objectives and mission.[44] Such dimensions are: identification and monitoring of social goals, executives' and staff's commitment to social goals, in line with CPPs,[45] clients' needs as reference for product and services' design and distribution strategies and channels; treating clients responsibly, treating employees responsibly, balancing financial and social performance (*see* Table 4.1 for examples of indicators for each dimension).

Tools available to assess MFIs' social performance are still numerous but nowadays rather harmonized as regards relevant aspects and processes.[46] Moreover, there are also tools used by specialized rating agencies, evaluating social performance. For instance, Microfinance Institutional Rating by Microfinanza Rating is a comprehensive evaluation about the long-term viability of an MFI, covering information from the MFI, clients' survey and impact assessment but focusing only on client protection and social responsibility towards the staff as possible sources of reputational risk.[47] 'Social Rating', performed by M-CRIL, Microfinanza Rating, MicroRate and Planet Rating, is an expert evaluation of a MFI's social performance, based only on information collected by the MFI and focusing on missions, design and systems to translate the first into practice.[48] In particular, it examines the country context, social performance management, social responsibility (towards clients, staff, community and environment), depth of

39 The SPTF is a working group formed in 2005 by, among others, CGAP, Smart Campaign, the Imp-Act Consortium, MFTransparency, MicroSave, CERISE, the Progress out of Poverty Index, MIX, and the International Labor Organization: <http://sptf.info/>.

40 About CGAP, *see* above Chapter 3, §3.c.

41 For the 2016 USSPM, *see* <http://sptf.info/images/USSPM-English-Manual-2016-v2.0_final.pdf>.

42 *See* <www.cerise-spi4.org/#/conduct-an-audit-1/> and <http://sptf.info/spmstandards/indicators; http://sptf.info/images/spi4%20press%20release%20english%20march%202015.pdf>.

43 About the MIX *see* Chapter 3, §3.c.

44 *See* <www.themix.org/social-performance/Indicators>.

45 About CPPs,*see* Chapters 3, §3.d; 8, §3.b.

46 Other audit tools include 'EDA Rural Social Performance Audit (SPA)' and 'MicroSave SPM': *see* <http://sptf.info/sp-tools/audit-tools>.

47 *See* A. Marti, 'Rating Guide', (2012) Rating Initiative, <http://sptf.info/images/Rating%20Guide_English_20150825.pdf>.

48 *See* H. Clark and F. Sinha, 'Social Rating Guide', (2013) Rating Initiative, <http://sptf.info/images/social%20rating%20guide_english_nov%202014.pdf> and <http://sptf.info/sp-tools/rating-tools>.

Table 4.1 Examples of USSPM/SPI4 indicators within each dimension

1) *Identification and monitoring of social goals*	4) *Treating clients responsibly*
– clear and detailed missions including specific characteristics of target clients and expected outcomes – internal processes and services/products strategies to ensure mission achievement and outcomes/outputs – collection of data referred to social goals, employees training in collecting such data – when poverty reduction is a goal, use of technical and recognized tools to measure and monitor clients' poverty – disclosure and reporting of such data	– Adequate credit evaluation including disposable income, cash-flow and client indebtedness analysis for repayment capacity assessment and other measures to address over-indebtedness – full and timely transparency on terms, conditions and prices – steps to ensure client understanding – appropriate collection practices – measures to avoid frauds and non-discriminatory practices – procedures to ensure client fair treatment and privacy – effective complaints procedures also used to improve services/products
2) *Executives and staff's commitment to social goals*	5) *Treating employees responsibly*
– board orientation, education and periodic information about social performance – board strategy and specific processes to ensure social goals – board corrective actions and minutes attesting monitoring and reliance on social performance data – existence of social performance committee – evaluation of CEO/directors based on social performance – senior management/board's accountability for operationalization of social goals – staff incentives towards social goals	– clear, easily available and non-discriminatory human resources policy – transparent and competitive market rates – measures to monitor health, safety risks for employees and employees' satisfaction and turn-over including grievance mechanisms
3) *Clients' needs as reference for product and services' design and distribution strategies and channels*	6) *Balancing financial and social performance*
– specific characteristics of products/services to improve financial access and reduce client risks – preliminary market research, clients' feedback on products and services – monitoring of client satisfaction and retention rate	– growth rate set to balance economic and social return and considering demand, penetration, MFI capability, clients' satisfaction – financial return policies and monitoring in line with social objectives and stakeholders' interest – including a written document on expectation of profit and exit strategies to ensure social goals – transparent financial structure complying with IFRS; responsible and sustainable pricing – acceptable performance ratios in line with peers – senior management compensation in line with social goals and transparent and proportionate with field staff's remuneration

outreach, quality of services and outcomes.[49] Finally, some assessment tools are used by investment funds and are not widely available in details,[50] although the SPTF has been working to align USSPM and some social investor indicators (e.g. Global Impact Investing Network-GIIN-IRIS catalogue, Global Impact Investing Rating System-GIIRS-B Impact Assessment tool).

It is evident that such indicators try to standardize social performance evaluation among MFIs in order to improve comparability and transparency but, at the same time, allow customization to accommodate different missions, focus and needs. Consequently, some indicators might be subjective or ambiguous unless clearly explained. For example, the existence of a credit insurance and the adoption of a code of conduct have been typically considered positively by most questionnaires but, on the one hand, the mandatory insurance coverage might have somewhere incentivized loan officers even to depict suicide as the easiest way to ensure repayment (Chapter 8, §3.a).[51] On the other hand, the simple adoption of a code of conduct is meaningless without systems in place to ensure compliance and social reporting to CERISE (only 1 MFI in Western Europe) or to MIX tend to be confidential (or available to premium clients) or only used to elaborate publicly available sector benchmarking (*see* Chapter 3, §3).[52]

The recent MFIs European Code includes common social reporting standards, such as social mission, average loan size (and median as a percentage of GNI), percentage of – depending on target market and mission – female or rural or below poverty line clients or clients graduating to mainstream finance or from ethnic minorities or start-up or welfare recipient clients (clauses from 4.2.1 to 4.2.10). Furthermore, an entire section ('Customer and Investor Relations') is dedicated to client protection, requiring complete and clear information about services (including costs in the form of APR), systems to ensure clients' understanding of the terms, recognition of clients' right to withdraw within 14 days at no cost, to have adequate time to review the contract terms, to early repayment compensating the operator for the reasonable costs, to see their credit history in microfinance reported to national credit bureaux, clients' repayment capacity assessment and guidance on acceptable levels of debt, clients' satisfaction and mechanisms to efficiently deal with customer complaints, non-discriminatory treatment, fair collection practices and mechanisms to ensure staff ethical behaviour and privacy protection (1.1–1.25). Consequently, the Code seems to focus, as regards disclosure, only on a limited number of social indicators (compare with Table 4.1 about SPI4) to facilitate measurement and only in connection with the

49 Clark and Sinha, 'Social Rating Guide', 1.

50 Examples of social performance tools used by investment funds are Incofin ECHOS 2009 and Grassroots Capital 2008.

51 *See* J. Nagaraju, 'MFI Agents "Forcing" Debtors to Commit Suicide: Study', *Times of India*, (Delhi, 20 October 2010), <http://articles.timesofindia.indiatimes.com/2010-10-20/india/28247030_1_mfi-agents-loan-amount-elimination-of-rural-poverty>.

52 *See* SPI4 September 2016 benchmarking <www.cerise-spi4.org/#/benchmarking/> (as of September 2016).

stated mission. This limits a general and comparable assessment of MFIs' social performance but it responds to the need for flexibility and proportionality within the diverse European microfinance sector and can at least contribute to spread the culture of measuring microfinance outreach and aligning social missions to clients served. In fact, for example, previous surveys reported that Western European MFIs, although declaring, as main missions, financial and social inclusion as well as self-employment, appeared instead to serve mostly SMEs.[53]

The Code's effectiveness still needs to be verified: participation to EU programmes will in principle depend on the Code compliance and MFIs data published online but at present only few MFIs are listed as signatories and the disclosure portal seems not operative yet (*see* Chapter 3). Furthermore, the Code applies to non-bank MFIs, with therefore banks providing microfinance not required to respect the Code and report on social performance, this reducing comparability and social performance culture in the sector. The limitation in the Code's scope can be justified only as regards financial indicators (banks being already subject to extensive financial disclosure) but not for social indicators, which do not find comparable requirements in mainstream financial regulation (*see* Chapter 3, 3.c).

4 The recent debate about commercialization and mission drift. Banking culture, corporate governance and the enforcement problem

Microfinance missions, as discussed, are quite wide and varied, being associated with different levels of social responsibility and 'dedication to the cause'. This also reflects the so called 'microfinance schism', identifying within the microfinance movement two different inspirations.[54] The first one, which can be traced back to the Microcredit Summit Campaign, praises microfinance for its added social value to the financial sector, its social outcomes, impact and performance, focusing on the importance of accompanying services as well as clients' welfare and well-being. The other one, closer to CGAP logic, values microfinance simply for serving low-income people/reducing poverty and for demonstrating that it is possible to serve the excluded profitably, consequently promoting consumer protection and coaching services in the measure they contribute to ensure stability and repayment

53 *See* K. Molenaar, 'Microfinance, Its Concepts and Development, Lessons to Draw from Europe', (2009), 11, <www.microfinancegateway.org/sites/default/files/mfg-en-paper-microfinance-its-concepts-and-development-lessons-to-draw-for-europe-jan-2009_0.pdf>; S. Lämmermann, 'Microfinance in Europe and its Outreach to Target Groups', (2011), EMN Working Paper, 5–6, <www.european-microfinance.org/data/file/Librairy/emn-target-overview-study.pdf>; M. Bendig et al., 'Overview of the Microfinance Sector in Europe 2010/2011', (2012), 8, <www.european-microfinance.org/docs/emn_publications/emn_overview/1.overview2010-2011-final.pdf>.

54 J. Bedson and A. Renzaho, 'Good Practices in Microfinance and World Vision-funded Programs: The Challenges of a Poverty Focus in an Evolving Industry', (2006), 11ff., <www.academia.edu/20614872/Good_Practice_In_Microfinance_and_World_Vision-funded_Programs_The_challenges_of_a_poverty_focus_in_an_evolving_industry>; J. Morduch, 'The Microfinance Schism', (2000) 28(4) *World Dev* 617.

capacity. According to this second way of thinking, MFIs need to reach financial sustainability and enlarge their client base, even resorting to institutional transformations, IPOs, higher interest rates, profit-oriented funders and with at least a partial sacrifice of the poorest segment of clients or of supporting services. This partial shift and evolution in microfinance mind-set has entailed, as side effects, episodes of exorbitant interest rates, abusive practices and high profits at the expenses of the poorest, all labelled as cases of mission drift and microfinance commercialization's risks (*see* Chapters 5, §1.a about Compartamos IPO and 8).

These negative events have shaken the whole sector and stressed the importance of client protection and social performance. In this context, improving social performance culture and disclosure on the social aspects of microfinance activity is fundamental to accommodate most of the interests involved. In fact, disclosure and forms of labelling might help donors and investors choose, among available MFIs, the ones reflecting their preferences in the choice between the two opposite components of the double-bottom line equilibrium. It would avoid distrust towards the whole microfinance sector in case of incidents in the only profit-oriented segment and force MFIs managers to be clearer about their entity's goals and instruments, not having the chance to put smoke in stakeholders' eyes with a promise of both high returns and social impact.

In Western Europe, the risks of mission drift and commercialization are still low because of various obstacles to sustainability and therefore to profits. This statement does not apply to Eastern Europe, where the more mature sector's stage, the higher demand for microfinance and consequent competition favour such phenomena. In both cases, however, the development of social performance culture and relative best practices would help improving monitoring and specialization, as well as contribute to expanding MFIs access to funding while containing social mission drift.

More attention to financial operators' principles of conduct and social capital has now been paid also in the mainstream sector in the wake of the financial crisis. The 2015 Basel Corporate Governance Principles[55] partially reflects the work of the G-30 Group on Culture culminated in the document 'Banking Conduct and Culture'.[56] The Group defines 'Banking Culture' as 'the mechanism that delivers the values and behaviours that shape conduct and contribute to creating trust in banks and a positive reputation for banks among key stakeholders, both internal and external'.[57] The same document recognizes banks as '"socially accountable" to the public and community at large', affirming that '[t]his call for social accountability may readjust the balance seen in the last two decades slightly away from shareholder returns, and require banks to include broader public factors in their economic and financial calculus'. Consequently, the Basel Committee assigns to the board the responsibility of developing a sound culture of the bank and to the

55 BCBS, *Guidelines. Corporate Governance Principles for Banks*, (BIS 2015).

56 G-30, 'Banking Conduct and Culture. A Call for Sustained and Comprehensive Reform', (2015), <http://group30.org/images/PDF/BankingConductandCulture.pdf>.

57 G-30, 'Banking Conduct', 17.

management of writing a code of conduct/code of ethics reflecting it (Principle 1).[58] Such a trend in the mainstream sector, in reaction to the post-crisis loss of trust in the banking sector, seems to realign the traditional financial sector with the microfinance one. Nonetheless, the two are not completely comparable. Trust in MFIs social performance is in proportion way more important than social responsibility of banks: while the very existence and justification of MFIs is grounded in their social mission, everyone (especially shareholders) expects and wants their bank to, first, make profits and be competitive on the market. A scandal in the area of consumer protection or human resources affecting the banking sector can avert some bank investors and clients but in the microfinance sector it can completely weed out the business from the country (*see* the Andhra Pradesh case, Chapters 6, §2.a; 8). MFIs are double-bottom line institutions and managers have to translate both dimensions in concrete measures, such as organization structures and procedures.

In the mainstream sector, it will be difficult to observe some practical consequences of the implementation of such a 'cultural manifesto' or conduct/ethical codes: they will likely remain solemn but empty declarations for CSR purposes. Although some banks might dare to insert limited clauses in the articles of incorporation (instead of simply making in the same a general reference to the existence of a separate code of conduct/ethics), the general wording will make it impossible to recognize any enforceable right or duty to social performance. Moreover, the G-30 document meaningfully states that 'culture cannot be regulated', denying a supervisor's role in enforcing such declarations.[59]

On the contrary, microfinance needs concrete instruments to make social inspiration part of the structure and governance. As discussed later on (Chapter 5, §2), MFIs might need internal bodies with specific duties to ensure social performance (*see* USSPMs/CERISE indicators). Furthermore, social objectives can be incorporated in clauses of investment contracts with investors, enforceable by the latter in case of failure to comply (Chapter 3, §3.d). Similarly, violations of certain specific duties in connection with social goals (e.g. to put in place adequate systems of social performance monitoring, to avoid certain abusive practices, to target certain clients) inserted in the articles of incorporation should be actionable by shareholders, staff and monitoring bodies leading to, for example, the removal/substitution of managers or decisions invalidation. Finally, we might envision supervisory mechanisms contributing to the public enforcement of social objectives and clauses. For example, U.S. banks are required by the CRA (*see* above Chapter 3, §5.b) to publicly disclose their activities in favour of their communities. This does not create *per se* specific rights or duties but banks might find their project expansion application rejected by the Authority after significant complaints from community associations. Similarly, MFIs' social performance should be taken into account by public authorities in evaluating funding applications, in selecting project partners and in some supervisory decisions.

58 BCBS, *Guidelines*, 5, 8.
59 G-30, 'Banking Conduct', 23.

5 The poor's needs and MFIs' services: the importance of targeting

a Targeting under recent EU law after the subprime scandal and clients' needs in microfinance

Choosing a target market and designing products and services to meet the targets' needs is a fundamental strategy for any enterprise. However, after the financial crisis and the subprime scandal, targeting and instruments for consumer protection have also been regarded as contributing to ensure financial stability (Chapter 8, §1).[60] Especially in the U.S., the combination of housing public policies, agents' remuneration techniques based on volumes and complexity of contracts contributed to the delivery to the consumer of products not adequate to his/her conditions/profile nor sustainable, taking advantage of clients' cognitive limits (Chapter 8, §2).[61]

Consequently, both in the banking and in the investment services sectors, in the wake of the financial crisis, the EU has introduced consumer protective rules and recognized the importance of providing products and services adequate to clients' needs.[62] For example, the recent Mortgage Credit Directive aims at enhancing consumer chances to receive the right product and make an informed choice also considering all market alternatives through specific providers obligations (Chapter 8, §2). The EBA has recently issued Guidelines on product governance for retail banking products, requiring both manufacturers and distributors when, respectively, designing or distributing the products also to take into account consumers' interests, objectives and characteristics, to avoid conflict of interests, to identify specific target markets and to ensure that the final customer belongs to such target group and is able to make an informed decision, to test the product, to monitor the abidance of product governance arrangements and periodically review the same.[63] On the investment services side, the MiFID II/MiFIR package,[64] among multiple protective norms, stresses the importance of designing, manufacturing, offering and delivering products adequate to target

60 *See* FSB, 'Consumer Finance Protection with Particular Focus on Credit', (2011), <www.financialstabilityboard.org/wp-content/uploads/r_111026a.pdf>.

61 About the causes of the financial crisis in the U.S. *see* Financial Crisis Inquiry Commission, 'The Financial Crisis Inquiry Report', (2011), <www.gpo.gov/fdsys/pkg/GPO-FCIC/pdf/GPO-FCIC.pdf>. However, a recent study proves that the mortgage crisis has been mostly caused by prime mortgages instead of subprime ones: F. Ferreira and J. Gyourko, 'A New Look at the U.S. Foreclosure Crisis: Panel Data Evidence of Prime and Subprime Borrowers from 1997 to 2012', (2015) NBER Working Paper 21261, <www.nber.org/papers/w21261>.

62 *See* also Commission, 'Public Consultation on Responsible Lending and Borrowing in the EU', (2009), <http://ec.europa.eu/internal_market/consultations/docs/2009/responsible_lending/consultation_en.pdf>.

63 EBA, 'Final Report – Guidelines on Product Oversight and Governance Arrangements for Retail Banking Products', EBA/GL/2015/18.

64 Directive No. 2014/65/EU on markets in financial instruments (MiFID II) and Regulation (EU) No. 600/2014 on markets in financial instruments (MiFIR).

clients, also through adequate remuneration practices (recitals 71, 77 and Artt.16(3), 24(2), 24(10)).

Nonetheless, in the microfinance context such targeting is also required to fulfil social goals and deliver the expected social results, with social performance as an important risk-management technique.[65] The 2013 version of CPPs recommends to MFIs adequate product design and delivery, in order to avoid harm to clients and deliver suitable products for clients (*see* Chapters 3, §3.d; 8, §3.b).

b Diversification of products and activities in response to clients' needs and for resilience

The poor's needs are not always evident: for instance, some might not look for a banking account thinking of not needing it and relying instead on alternative and informal mechanisms (e.g. pawnshops, tontines, family support or even mattress), which might present some comparative advantages (timing and flexibility), despite being unsecure and often expensive. Others would need a banking account but might not trust mainstream financial operators (Chapter 1, §1).

Furthermore, products adequately targeting the poor might need to respond to specific requisites. Studies conducted on U.S. households have highlighted the interest of low-income families for short-term and flexible credit (often resorting to subprime credit cards, a quite expensive form of credit, or payday loans), with a tendency for technology-based tools (e.g. pre-paid debit cards, mobile apps, GPR cards, payday internet loans, payroll cards).[66] Moreover, low income might appreciate products that force and remind them to save, with disincentives to withdraw unless really needed.[67] Surveys conducted in the EU convey similar results. UK low-income consumers perceive bank personal loans as safe and acceptable but inflexible, impersonal, 'for rich' and entailing unfair charges and penalties. Instead, they value alternative informal means (such as payday loans, store card, home credit, friends/family loans, pawn shops) for the process speed, easy access/approval (also in consideration of an emergency/unexpected need), flexibility and, when applicable, friendly attitudes of agents.[68] A survey conducted in some Italian cities has identified different groups of preference among MFIs clients deserving offerings of distinct products. Anyway, the

65 S. Mullainathan and S. Krishnan, 'Psychology and Economics: What it Means for Microfinance', (2008), <www.iamfi.com/documents/PsychologyandEconomics.pdf>; D. Porteous, 'Consumer Protection in Credit Markets', (2009), FAI Policy Focus Note 2, 4, 5, <www.microfinancegateway.org/sites/default/files/mfg-en-paper-consumer-protection-in-credit-markets-jul-2009.pdf>.

66 *See* R. Levy and A. Schütte, '2011 Underbanked Seizing Market Study', (2011) CFSI, <www.cfsinnovation.com/Document-Library/2011-Underbanked-Market-Sizing-Study.aspx>; E. Wolkowitz, '2013 Underserved Market Size', (2014) CFSI, <www.cfsinnovation.com/Document-Library/2013-Financially-Underserved-Market-Size>.

67 *See* Morduch et al., 'An Invisible', 5, 8.

68 S. Worton et al., 'Consumer Credit Research: Low Income Consumers', (2014), 19–23, <www.fca.org.uk/your-fca/documents/research/consumer-credit-research-low-income>.

majority of the retail segment has showed a preference for short-term, small instalments, low interest rates, 'light' collateral, unconditioned use, fixed interest rate, with a fast procedure and professionals monitoring/support.[69] Payment accounts are often fundamental to pay bills and rents and receive salary and welfare support and can represent a first step towards further financial services.[70]

The first basic intuition behind microcredit has been offering the opportunity of receiving credit to the ones generally excluded. Nonetheless, it has become soon evident that low-income people also need mechanisms to save, in order to be prepared in case of negative events hitting their business (flood or other natural disaster) or family (need to pay for a funeral or health expenses). Similarly, they also need forms of insurance, payment instruments, also in the forms of remittances to family members located in other countries.[71] All this has led to the transformation from microcredit to microfinance (Chapter 2, §1)

Furthermore, MFIs and their supporters have realized that effective financial inclusion could not be achieved only through credit services. In fact, while not everyone needs or might be suited for credit (and a 100% credit coverage would not be optimal in terms of stability), a complete financial inclusion with reference to other services is instead desirable.[72] Moreover, savings are seen as a valuable source of funding for MFIs, also conferring more resilience[73] (*see* Chapter 5, §3.a about MFIs' funding options).[74] Activity diversification seems also to present advantages in terms of MFIs' risk management and stability (below §6.a).

Nonetheless, MFIs have encountered not only difficulties in market research and marketing among the poor but also regulatory obstacles.

6 Multiple services, non-bank entities and stability concerns in the era of fear for the shadow banking system

a Diversification of activities and structural reforms

Such expansion in MFIs services could not come without costs. Depending on countries' regulations, offering savings or payment services or other financial

69 *See* A. Andreoni et al., *Nuovi bisogni finanziari. La risposta del microcredito*, (Mulino 2013), ch. 4.

70 P. Muller et al., 'Consumer Protection Aspects of Financial Services – Study', (2014), <www.europarl.europa.eu/RegData/etudes/etudes/join/2014/507463/IPO L-IMCO_ET(2014)507463_EN.pdf>; Basel Committee on Payments and Market Infrastructures (BCPMI)-WB, *Payment Aspects of Financial Inclusion*, (BIS/WB 2016), 5–6.

71 *See* Demirgüç-Kunt et al., *Finance*, 129.

72 *See* Demirgüç-Kunt et al., *Finance*, x, 14, 17.

73 *See* A. Hannig and S. Jansen, 'Financial Inclusion and Financial Stability: Current Policy Issues', (2010) ADB Institute Working Paper 259, 3ff., <www.adbi.org/files/2010.12.21.wp259.financial.inclusion.stability.policy.issues.pdf>.

74 *See* A. Hannig and S. Jansen, 'Financial Inclusion and Financial Stability: Current Policy Issues', (2010) ADB Institute Working Paper 259, 3ff., <www.adbi.org/files/2010.12.21.wp259.financial.inclusion.stability.policy.issues.pdf>.

services can trigger the application of multiple and stringent regulations. Furthermore, there might be restrictions on permissible activities conducted by financial intermediaries to facilitate supervision, reduce conflicts of interests and ensure stability. In fact, despite some diversification advantages (e.g. economies of scale, reduction of idiosyncratic risk,[75] better information about clients and reputational capital),[76] the literature attests that diversification within and across business lines and, especially, increased reliance by banks on non-interest income (from activities other than loans, deposits, investments and trading such as securities, insurance and real estate) have not reduced earnings volatility or risk.[77] With special reference to small European banks, expansion to new business areas (especially for income from fee and commissions activities), in combination with competition, has been correlated with more risk, through increased volatility and leverage, as well as to reduced monitoring, with geographic concentration contributing to exposing all different activities to the same localized shocks.[78]

However, most studies correlate, at least with reference to banks and especially for small banks, restrictions on bank activities with lower GDPs and levels of efficiency as well as of stability,[79] but registering anyway a restrictions increase following the financial crisis.[80]

Nonetheless, the latter has led many countries to introduce structural limits on bank permissible activities (e.g. U.S. Volcker rule and UK Vickers reform) or separation of speculative activities from retail ones (French law 2013–672) to shield depositors' money from risky activities, reducing moral hazard and bank

75 In a Modigliani and Miller world, managers should not spend resources in internal diversification since investors are able to hedge risks through external diversification and thus do not price internal diversification. However, this might not stand for financial firms because, among others reasons, volatility, opaqueness, rating models and interests of other stakeholders: *see* K. Stiroh, 'Diversification in Banking', in A. Berger et al (eds), *The Oxford Handbook of Banking*, (1st edn, OUP 2012), 150–53.

76 *See* K. John et al., 'Universal Banking and Firm Risk Taking', (1994) 18 *J Bank Financ* 307; J. Barth et al., *Rethinking Bank Regulation. Till Angels Govern*, (CUP 2006), 47–49 and 108–109; Stiroh, 'Diversification', 149ff.

77 Among possible but speculative explanations, e.g., lack of parallel expansion in the customer base and motivations for diversification only in the empire building desire of managers: *see* R. De Young and C. Roland, 'Product Mix and Earnings Volatility at Commercial Banks: Evidence from a Degree of Total Leverage Model', (2001) 10(1) *J Financ Intermed* 54. For a literature review, Stiroh, 'Diversification', 149ff.

78 *See* S. Mercieca et al., 'Small European banks: Benefits from diversification?', (2007) 31(7) *J Bank Financ* 1975; A. Tarazi et al., 'Bank Income Structure and Risk: An Empirical Analysis of European Banks', (2008) 32(8) *J Bank Financ* 1452; V. Acharya et al., 'Should Banks Be Diversified? Evidence from Individual Bank Loan Portfolios', (2006) 79(3) *J Bus* 1355.

79 Barth, *Rethinking*, 106, 209, 215–17, 229–34; Mercieca, 'Small'.

80 J. Barth et al., 'Bank Regulation and Supervision in 180 Countries from 1999 to 2011', (2013) NBER Working Paper 18733, 14, <www.nber.org/papers/w18733>.

interconnectedness as well as facilitating supervision and re-directing bank attention to their core activities.[81] Also the Commission has proposed a structural reform (following the 2012 Liikanen High Level Expert Group Report),[82] preventing the largest banks and banking groups from engaging in the riskiest activities not included in the traditional area of banking (i.e. other than deposit taking, lending, payments, safe custody).[83] In particular, significant banks and banking groups[84] would not be allowed to engage in proprietary trading in financial instruments and commodities. Moreover, the competent authority (likely the ECB) would be granted the power to impose the separation of certain risky trading activities (namely, market-making, investment in/sponsoring of securitization and trading of certain derivatives) through the creation of a separated legal entity, when required by the goal of maintaining stability and based on certain harmonized metrics.

Anyway, such prospective reform targets large banks and speculative investment activities by banks, thus hardly touching MFIs, but gives us the sense of the growing fear worldwide for true universal banking and unlimited financial services offering. Furthermore, they have been partially criticized for the risk of leading to a 'too small to be viable' situation (*see* also Chapter 6, §2.c)[85] or inefficient government interference in financial markets entailing increased costs and concentration risks.[86] Finally, the above mentioned studies evidence that small banks should expand only in areas where they have competence and that Europe can better benefit from a banking sector with different specialized institutions than with only diversified/universal institutions.[87]

81 *See* M. Lehmann, 'Volcker Rule, Ring-Fencing or Separation of Bank Activities: Comparison of Structural Reform Acts around the World', (2014) LSE Working Paper 25, <www.lse.ac.uk/collections/law/wps/WPS2014-25_Lehmann.pdf>; J. Chow and J. Surti, 'Making Banks Safer: Can Volcker and Vickers Do It?', (2011) IMF Working Paper 11/236, <www.imf.org/external/pubs/ft/wp/2011/wp11236.pdf>; L. Gambacorta and A. van Rixtel, 'Structural Bank Regulation Initiatives: Approaches and Implications', (2013) BIS Working Papers 412, <www.bis.org/publ/work412.pdf>.

82 <http://ec.europa.eu/finance/bank/docs/high-level_expert_group/report_en.pdf>.

83 Commission, 'Proposal for a Regulation of the European Parliament and of the Council on Structural Measures Improving the Resilience of EU Credit Institutions', COM/2014/043 final.

84 Art. 3 of the proposed Regulation states that the requirements apply to banks of systemically global importance and, for three consecutive years, with total assets exceeding €30 billion and total trading assets and liabilities exceeding €70 billion or 10% of their total assets.

85 A. Mullineux, 'Financial Innovation and Social Welfare', (2010) 18(3) *JFR & C* 243, 253.

86 Such measures might cause an increase in transaction and operational costs as well as concentration risk: *see* J. Binder, 'To Ring-Fence or Not, and How? Strategic Questions for Post-Crisis Banking Reform in Europe' (2014), 18, <http://ssrn.com/abstract=2543860>; Lehmann, 'Volcker', 4ff.; C. Goodhart, 'The Vickers Report: An Assessment', (2012) 6 *Law and Fin Markets L Rev* 32.

87 Mercieca, 'Small'; Acharya, 'Should'.

b Savings mobilization and the European basic payment account

Restrictions on non-bank operators might be justified by the existence of activities reserved to other intermediaries and/or by the lighter regime for non-bank operators including simpler organizational and prudential requirements in combination with the need to ensure stability (*see* below about the shadow banking system).

In fact, in most countries, accepting repayable funds from the public represents an activity reserved to banks and entails the application of banking law, which imposes strict prudential requirements and safety nets to preserve depositors' trust and financial stability, avoiding depositors' run and the spread of a crisis in the entire sector (*see* Chapter 6). However, some countries encompass the existence of entities other than banks authorized to accept deposits. A recent survey conducted by the BCBS reports that this is the case in 50% of respondent countries but only 31% permit such Other Deposit Taking Institutions (ODTIs: generally, financial cooperatives and MFIs) to offer checking or current accounts (the types more subject to depositors' run).[88] Uganda, for example, in 2003/2004 created the category of deposit-taking MFIs, subject to prudential regulation (but tailored to microfinance activities) and supervision.[89]

The first form of saving mechanisms offered by MFIs has been 'compulsory savings', used also as a form of collateral. MFIs require the borrower to open a savings account (with the same or at a partner bank) and periodically deposit a certain sum, in order to promote a saving culture in clients but also allow the MFI to easily recover a part of the loan.[90] With the view of expanding financial access, some developing countries have introduced limited exceptions also for non-bank/non-ODTI MFIs, including compulsory savings among permitted services, especially under condition of depositing the money at a bank or investing it in low-risk securities.[91] Also the Basel Committee has recognized that the risks entailed by compulsory savings do not justify the application of prudential regulation and oversight. In fact, when the cash collateral is not intermediated (deposited at a bank or invested in low-risk securities) and the loan balance exceeds the amount

88 BCBS, *Range of Practice in the Regulation and Supervision of Institutions Relevant to Financial Inclusion*, (BIS 2015), 14–15. The survey covers 52 jurisdictions, evenly spread among high-income countries, upper-middle income, lower-middle income and lower-income.

89 *See* Microfinance Deposit-taking Institutions Act 2003 <www.bou.or.ug/bou/bou-downloads/acts/supervision_acts_regulations/MDI_Acts/MDIAct2003.pdf> and Microfinance deposit-taking Institutions Regulations 2004 <www.bou.or.ug/bou/bou-downloads/acts/supervision_acts_regulations/MDI_Regulations/MDIRegulatns2004.pdf>.

90 *See* Armendáriz and Morduch, *The Economics*, 172–73.

91 *See* T. Jansson, 'Microfinance Regulation Sweeping Latin America', (2002) 5 *Microenterprise Development Review* 1, 5. Zambia, since 2010, has instead considered compulsory savings as deposits and required MFIs deploying it to apply for a deposit taking or banking license: *see* C. Chiumya, 'The Regulation of Microfinance in Zambia', (2010), <www.microfinancegateway.org/sites/default/files/mfg-en-paper-the-regulation-of-microfinance-in-zambia-jan-2010.pdf>.

of compulsory savings, no significant risk is envisaged while in the temporary periods in which the cash collateral exceeds the loan balance, the size of supervisory costs would justify an exception anyway.[92] According to the above mentioned survey, 28% of respondent countries allow non-bank/non-ODTI MFIs and 85% financial cooperatives (other than deposit-taking ones) to collect compulsory savings.[93]

In Europe, we can find the most diversified range of services in countries where microfinance is offered by banks, savings banks or credit unions (Chapter 3, §5.a). Savings products appear offered by 20% of European MFIs but such share is amplified by the above-mentioned countries where microcredit is carried out only or primarily by banks/savings banks or credit unions (e.g. Spain where savings and checking accounts, in addition to micro-insurance, have also been widespread products).[94] In fact, non-bank financial institutions (NBFIs) and NGOs generally cannot accept deposits (also because of EU banking law restrictions: §c; Chapters 5, §2.a; 6, §§2–3, 5): for instance, NBFIs in Bulgaria and Romania have a quite wide range of financial activities permitted but the collection of savings is not among the same (while credit cooperatives can offer savings to their members).[95] Nonetheless, somewhere also not-for-profit are permitted to offer savings products.[96]

Anyway, offering savings services in the EU might appear a less urgent need than in developing countries because of the existence of alternative instruments such as savings banks (*see* Chapter 3, §5), postal services (e.g. Bulgaria, Lithuania, France, Luxembourg) and 'basic bank accounts'. In fact, a right to a bank account for basic financial services has been affirmed by law in few Member States (France, Belgium, Finland, Denmark and, only for deposits, Sweden) and, less effectively, through bank voluntary charters and agreements in another small group (Germany, Italy, Hungary, Portugal; through an agreement between the government and six major banks, in the Netherlands).[97] Also to reduce social and financial

92 BCBS, *Microfinance Activities and the Core Principles for Effective Banking Supervision*, (BIS 2010), 15.

93 BCBS, *Range*, 15.

94 Ibidem 15, 20; Bendig, 'Overview', 35.

95 Bendig, 'Overview', 59; K. Ganev et al., 'Microcrediting of SMEs in Bulgaria', in A. Szabó (ed.), 'Microfinance for SMEs in the BSEC Region', (conference, 12–15 November 2014, Bucharest), 68, <www.kas.de/wf/doc/kas_41327-1522-2-30.pdf?150513160755>. *See* the English version of the Bulgarian Law on Credit Institutions <www.bnb.bg/bnbweb/groups/public/documents/bnb_law/laws_creditinstitutions_en.pdf>. *See* also Art. 15(1)a of Romania Law 93/2009, <www.bnb.bg/bnbweb/groups/public/documents/bnb_law/regulations_financial_inst_en.pdf> (English version).

96 S. Lagoa and A. Suleman, 'Types of Financial Institution and their Supply of Financial Services: The Case of Microfinance in Europe', (2013) FESSUD Working paper 72, 23, <www.fessud.eu/wp-content/uploads/2013/04/Types-of-financial-institution-and-their-supply-of-financial-services-the-case-of-microfinance-in-Europe_WP-72.pdf>.

97 Commission, 'Study', 18; Commission, 'Impact Assessment Accompanying the Document "Commission Recommendation of 18 July 2011 on Access to a Basic Payment Account"', Staff Working Paper SEC(2011)906, 13.

exclusion and discriminatory access to benefits from the Single Market, the EU has, first, recommended, and, then, mandated to Member States to ensure the right of all consumers, irrespective of their financial circumstances, to access a payment account with certain basic features (e.g. to receive benefits/income, pay taxes, purchase goods, also using cards) for a reasonable fee (or even free of charge in case of vulnerable unbanked).[98] Member States might designate all credit institutions or, when justified on reasonable grounds (e.g. market share, size of territory, network coverage), without distortions or consumer stigmatization, a smaller part of providers (recital 38 and Art. 16(1) Dir. 2014/92).[99] After the Recommendation adoption, only Italy and the Netherlands had made a step forwards towards a right to a basic payment account,[100] convincing the Commission to adopt a Directive, which will need to be progressively implemented in all EU members. However, the right to basic payment accounts, despite improving financial access also opening up new chances for additional services, *per se* does not encourage a savings accumulation/culture nor ensure products responding to specific low-income clients' needs.

Furthermore, the access to other types of services might result anyway in being restricted.

c Other services, in particular lending activity. Shadow banking, post-crisis reforms and not-for-profit entities

As anticipated, countries are less restrictive with reference to services other than savings but new products and services entail more risk and might not be manageable by small and inexperienced institutions (§5.b; Chapter 6, §2). For instance, MFIs in Bosnia and Herzegovina, under competitive pressure, have engaged in new products without market tests nor staff training, consequently finding themselves in a severe repayment crisis.[101]

According to EU law, only banks can offer credit together with deposit services (Capital Requirement Directive–CRDIV No. 2013/36 and Capital Requirement Regulation–CRR No. 575/2013) but credit provision and, in general, NBFIs are not harmonized at EU level (save mortgage credit and, partially, consumer credit), although the Commission is currently consulting on further possible

98 Commission Recommendation 2011/442/EU of 18 July 2011 on access to a basic payment account, [2011] OJL190/87; Directive 2014/92/EU of the European Parliament and of the Council of 23 July 2014 on the comparability of fees related to payment accounts, payment account switching and access to payment accounts with basic features, [2014] OJL257/214.

99 The Recommendation, instead, required at least one payment service operator in charge, saved competition distortions (section II(2)).

100 Commission, 'National Measures and Practices as Regards Access to Basic Payment Accounts-Follow-up to the Recommendation of 18 July 2011 on Access to a Basic Payment Account', SWD(2012)249 final, 9–10, 13–14.

101 *See* G. Chen et al., 'Growth and Vulnerabilities in Microfinance', (2010) CGAP Focus Note 61, 11, <www.cgap.org/sites/default/files/CGAP-Focus-Note-Growth-and-Vulnerabilities-in-Microfinance-Feb-2010.pdf>.

harmonization in retail financial markets.[102] Consequently, multiple different national regimes co-exist, some more liberal while others more restrictive (subjecting the same to bank-like regulation) (Chapter 6, §§3–4). For instance, UK lending companies are not bound by prudential requirements (except for residential mortgage lenders) and only lightly regulated.[103] Instead, in Germany, Spain, Portugal and Serbia, banking monopoly has traditionally covered also credit provision with the consequence of forcing MFIs to collaborate with banks to operate, though often benefiting from governmental support (in the form of guarantee funds or credit lines for ensuring low interest rates), but with, as drawbacks, considerable costs or stricter selection of candidates (because of the bank partner and MFIs' moral guarantee) (Chapters 6, §5; 2, §2).[104] For example, German banking monopoly (Section 1(1) German Banking Act-*KWG*)[105] covers the mere credit activity conducted commercially or professionally (even in the form of guarantees or transmission of funds to the borrower through a bank), allowing MFIs only to handle credit applications and conduct monitoring under certain conditions (limiting outsourcing of core functions).[106] In Croatia, only banks and credit unions can offer loans and the latter have been subject since 2008 to what it is mostly considered an unfavourable regime (no depositor protection, mandatory deposit of funds at a bank but no preferential treatment in insolvency procedures, no external funding allowed, geographical limitations impeding scale and limiting even internal funding).[107]

Furthermore, more restrictive regimes have been introduced in the wake of the financial crisis, reflecting the post-crisis fear towards the 'shadow banking' sector,

102 *See* Commission, 'Green Paper on Retail Financial Services', COM(2015) 630 final, questions 29–32.

103 EBA, 'Report to the European Commission on Matters Relating to the Perimeter of Credit Institutions', (2014), 17–18, 89–91, <www.eba.europa.eu/documents/10180/534414/2014+11+27+-+EBA+Report+-+Credit+institutions.pdf>.

104 TrustLaw, 'Creating Jobs in Europe Legal and Regulatory Frameworks of Microenterprises and Microcredit in Europe', (2011), 61, <www.trust.org/contentAsset/raw-data/ac56cbae-2724-4226-bbfe-1903c01bb68b/file>; Bendig, 'Overview', 64, 76, 80.

105 For an English version: <www.bafin.de/SharedDocs/Downloads/EN/Aufsichtsrecht/dl_kwg_en.pdf?__blob=publicationFile>.

106 U. Reifner, 'Micro-Lending – A Case for Regulation', (2002), 52–3, <www.emnconference.org/archives/data/file/Micro-lending_-_A_case_for_Regulation.pdf>.

107 J. Borzic, 'Croatia', (2013) EMN Mapping Legislative Report 12/2013, <http://www.european-microfinance.org/index.php?rub=publications&pg=other-emn-publications&spg=emn-mapping-report-croatia> (no more than one credit union can exist per county; this needs at least €70,000 in funding capital collected from at least 30 members from the same county); Bendig, 'Overview', 61. For a different point of view, *see* M. Bateman and D. Sinković, 'Impact of Microfinance in Croatia', in M. Bateman (ed.), *Confronting Microfinance: Undermining Sustainable Development*, (Kumarian Press 2011), 103 (e.g. reporting that credit unions might avoid the geographical limitations when they can prove to serve a certain well-defined category of clients such as women). Members of credit unions must share employer/industry, occupation/profession, county residence or other aspects ensuring mutual interest: <www.hnb.hr/en/-/odobrenje-za-rad-kreditne-unije>.

ie forms of intermediation similar to banking but traditionally unregulated. Its problems can easily spread to the banking sector, too, thanks to existing interconnections (*see* Chapter 6, §4), as the financial crisis showed (although this point is highly debated).[108] Consequently, post-crisis reforms have expanded regulatory reach to sectors and operators previously not covered (*see* e.g. Regulations MIFIR and EMIR, Directives MiFID, AIFM, on Credit rating agencies, Money Market Mutual Funds and revisions to bank exposures towards shadow banking entities and accounting consolidation regimes).[109] As we will discuss later (Chapters 5, §3; 6, §4), European MFIs do not generally fall within the shadow banking category but might be affected anyway by such national regimes.

Italy, with the 141/2010 legislative decree, introduced a stricter regime for non-bank professional credit providers that partially reproduces banking regulation, but with lower minimum capital and other similar facilitations especially with reference to new requirements under CRDIV/CRR and simplifications in case of small providers (with volumes below €250 million). This new regime would have almost cancelled microcredit from the country if the same decree had not also created a special and favourable framework for microcredit providers (but also confidi and MAG, traditional mutual entities: Chapter 3, §5.a), subject to Banking Authority's supervision until the creation of a private/hybrid supervisor. However, microcredit providers' activity is restricted to microcredit, although both in its commercial and personal/social variations. For-profit MFIs, in particular, need to have a limited company or cooperative form, a minimum capital of five times an *s.p. a* (joint-stock company, therefore currently €250,000), fit and proper executives (also professional) and qualified shareholders, business programme and to offer primarily (51%) commercial microcredit (Artt. 111 *TUB*; 5–10 Decree 176/2014).

Other countries, like Belgium, do not have a specific microcredit regulation but do not excessively restrict loan offering by NBFIs and even on-lending (borrowing to lend: Chapter 5, §3).[110] Similarly, Poland has traditionally listed lending among permitted activities not only of banks and credit unions but also of almost unregulated entities such as limited liabilities companies, loan funds, associations and foundations.[111]

Romania and Bulgaria allow NBFIs to also offer mortgages, leasing and guarantees and are subject to simplified regulation and supervision (non-prudential). In particular, the Romanian Law 240/2005 created a special regime for Microfinance

108 Commission, 'Green Paper – Shadow Banking', COM(2012)102 final; P. Muller et al., *Non-bank Financial Institutions: Assessment of their Impact on the Stability of the Financial System*, (EC 2012).

109 *See* Commission, 'Communication'; M. Andenas and I. Chiu, *The Foundations and Future of Financial Regulation*, (Routledge 2013), 278; N. Moloney, 'The Legacy Effects of the Financial Crisis on Regulatory design in the EU', in E. Ferran et al. (eds), *The Regulatory Aftermath of the Global Financial Crisis*, (CUP 2012), 126, 171.

110 *See* TrustLaw, 'Creating', 25; Bendig, 'Overview', 56.

111 Bendig, 'Overview', 74; A. Szostek, 'The State of Microfinance in Poland', in B. Jayo-Carboni et al. (eds), *Handbook of Microcredit in Europe* (Edward Elgar 2010), 358.

Companies (MFCs), allowed to offer business microcredit (up to €25,000 for no more than 60 months) and, soon after, also individual and consumer loans (Government General Ordinance 28/2006). Nonetheless, a few years later, the special regime was revoked (Law No. 93/2009, anticipated in part by GO 28/2006) through the creation of the general NBFIs category, with permitted activities including microloans, larger loans, mortgages, consumer credit, leasing, factoring, guarantees and credit cards, subject only to registration (conditional to a €200,000 minimum capital, fit and proper owners and managers' and audit committee requirements) accounting, reporting (also about portfolio structure, other statistics and financial statements) and auditing requirements, consumer protection law and monitoring and inspection powers by the National Bank of Romania (Artt. 14ff. Law 93/2009).[112] However, large NBFIs are required to register in the 'Special Registry' and subject to bank-like requirements as regards capital requirements, large exposures, related party lending requirements, organization, risk-management, internal control and prudential surveillance by the National Bank (Art. 29 ff law 93/2009 and 58ff. ordinance 20/2009).[113] Art. 3a of the Bulgarian Law on Credit Institutions and Ordinance 26/2009 allow NBFIs to offer, through funds not collected from the public, loans, leasing, factoring, guarantees and money-transfer only subject to registration (when such activities represent at least 30% of total activities and conditional to minimum capital, managers' and owners' requirements) and simple own funds, organizational (internal structure and control) and reporting (financial statement) requirements as well as National Bank supervision (Art. 3ff. Ordinance).[114] A 2014 amendment raised the minimum capital to be paid in cash to BGN1,000,000 (€511,000) but allowed case-by-case exemptions from registration for activities conducted through funds provided for implementing EU programmes and projects (Artt. 4 and 2.a Ordinance).

The provision of loans, anyway, generally requires specific legal forms and structures (e.g. for-profit or mutual form) that should in principle help the financial authority supervise operators and ensure prompt corrective actions (*see* Chapter 5, §2). Therefore, non-profit entities are generally excluded from such sector (*see* in

112 C. Pop and P. Buys, 'Microfinance in Romania', (2015) 5 *Contemporary Legal & Economic Issues* 307, 312–13.

113 Large Romanian NBFIs are the ones with loan volume above RON 25 million (€11.5 million) and own resources and borrowed money above RON 50 million (€11 million): EMN, 'A Collection of Case Studies on the Legal and Regulatory Framework for Microfinance Provision', (2012) 12(2) electronic Bulletin, 16–18, <www.microfinancegateway.org/sites/default/files/mfg-en-case-study-a-collection-of-case-studies-on-the-legal-and-regulatory-framework-for-microfinance-provision-dec-2012.pdf>; M. Doiciu, 'The Importance of the Regulatory Framework for Development of the Microfinance Sector: The Romanian Experience', (2007) *MFC Microfinance Policy* Monitor 11, 6–8, <www.mfc.org.pl/sites/mfc.org.pl/files/PolMon11_2007_Eng.pdf>; TrustLaw, 'Creating', 125; M. Doiciu, 'Best Practice in Microfinance in Romania', in A. Szabó (ed.), 'Microfinance for SMEs in the BSEC Region', (conference, 12–15 November 2014, Bucharest), 104, <www.kas.de/wf/doc/kas_41327-1522-2-30.pdf?150513160755>.

114 Bendig, 'Overview', 59; Ganev, 'Microcrediting', 68–69.

Belgium[115]). For example, Romanian MFIs were forced by the 2005 microfinance law to convert into joint stock companies with at least €200,000 (€3 million in case of mortgages) of capital to offer microloans (Artt.6, 18 Law 93/2009 and 10 Regulation 20/2009).[116] Art. 3a of Bulgarian law on credit institutions requires joint stock company, limited liability company and association limited by shares forms to conduct lending as principal activity (but otherwise allows not-for-profit to lend as not-main-activity). In Italy, NGOs active in the microcredit sector prior to the 2010 reform, could only collaborate with banks (providing banks with candidates for micro-loans within their social network) despite running the risk of violating 'credit mediator/broker' regulation (requiring a specific licence: Chapter 6, §5). Nonetheless, the 2010 reform allows now both commercial firms and not-for-profit entities to provide microcredit under certain conditions. In particular, not-for-profit entities can provide only 'social' microcredit, need to be dedicated to microcredit or financial inclusion (not other charitable activities) and must set interest rates and other fees at such a level to only cover costs, and anyway below the market average rate for similar operations (*TEGM*) multiplied by 0.4 (by 0.8, instead, in case of social microcredit offered by commercial providers) (Artt. 111.3 *TUB*, 5.6, 11 Decree 176/2014: *see* also Chapter 8, §4).

The Hungarian Act No. CXII of 1996 on Credit Institutions and Financial Enterprises used to be interpreted in a way restricting the provision of loans to banks and financial enterprises, therefore requiring bank involvement in not-for-profit microcredit programmes (e.g. to open a separate account for the foundation-MFI, disburse the loan from such account, collect instalments), raising costs (banks requested a fee without being exposed to risks) and extending the procedure duration. After several commercial banks' withdrawals from microcredit programmes, the government decided in 1998 and 2003 to emend the Act, exempting the Local Enterprise Agencies(LEAs)/foundations operating within the National Microcredit Scheme from the Act and allowing them to provide microloans (section 2(1)h Act CXII, now section 2(1)f Act No. CCXXXVII of 2013).[117]

On the contrary, in the Netherlands, foundations and associations can provide microcredit (not savings) simply by registering with the Chamber of

115 Bendig, 'Overview', 56.

116 Pop and Buys, 'Microfinance', 313.

117 For an English version of the 1996 and 2013 Act, *see* respectively, <http://net.jogtar.hu/jr/gen/getdoc.cgi?docid=A1300237.tv&dbnum=62> and <http://gss.unicreditgroup.eu/sites/default/files/markets/documents/Act_on_Credit_Institutions.pdf>. EMN, 'A Collection', 7; I. Kovács, 'The Microlending Sector in Hungary: Microlending to SMEs', in Jayo-Carboni, *Handbook*, 206; T. Szekfu, 'Hungary', (2013) EMN Legislative Mapping Report 12/2013, <www.european-microfinance.org/docs/emn_publications/e_bulletins/Microfinance_MappingHungary.pdf>; Id., 'The Hungarian Microfinance Legislation', in J. Durán Navarro et al., *The Importance of a Microfinance Legislation for the Development of the Sector in Spain*, (Cromoimagen 2013), 51ff. Financial enterprises (subject to a prudential regime similar to banks') can be set also as foundations but this case can offer only guarantee and agency/financial intermediation services (section 9(4) Banking Act 2013).

Commerce.[118] Similarly, the UK allows CDFIs, also with a not-for-profit form, to offer microloans without being regulated or supervised by the FCA but only partially subject to consumer protection regulation (Chapter 8, §3.a).[119] In France, starting with Law 2001–420 of 15 May 2001 (*'Nouvelles Régulations Économiques'*), not-for-profit organizations (associations and foundations) have been able to provide loans, up to €12,000 for business loans and €5,000 for social/personal loans (Art. R518–61 *CMF*), to enterprises (less than five or seven-years young and with less than three employees), unemployed or financially-excluded/low-income people, for the creation or development of micro-enterprises or re-employment and social inclusion. They are supervised by the French Banking Authority (*ACPR*), which authorizes the same to start operations after evidence of competence and experience as well as a guarantee for debt. They must set up adequate internal controls, have their financial statements certified, submit an annual report about their lending activities and manage non-performing assets (through provisioning and a reserve fund for the part of micro-loans not covered by the mandatory guarantee fund, with own funds and similar resources always above 12% of microloans not covered by guarantees or provisioning) (*see* Art. L511–6(5) and R518–57ff. *code monétaire et financier-CMF*). Bulgaria also allows not-for-profit entities (as any private entity) to provide loans as long as it does not represent their principal activity or violate other laws (e.g. accepting deposits or distributing profits in violation, respectively, of banking and not-for-profit law).[120] Finally, Poland has traditionally allowed associations and foundations to set up loan funds coherent with their institutional objectives but a recent amendment (5 August 2015) to the 2011 Act on consumer credit now requires non-bank lenders providing consumer loans to operate as limited liability or joint-stock companies, with a minimum capital of PLN200,000 (about €46,000) and 'fit and proper' managers.[121] Consequently, the

118 Bendig, 'Overview', 73.

119 *See* Bendig, 'Overview', 84; EMN and EIF, 'Microfinance Market Studies in the framework of JEREMIE – Cross Country Study on Western Europe. United Kingdom, Spain, Germany, Italy', (2009), 72, 81, <www.emnconference.org/archives/data/file/EIF%20Study%20Microlending_Western%20Europe_March%202009.zip>; N. Goggin, K. Dayson and S. McGeehan, 'The Microcredit Sector in the United Kingdom: The Role of CDFIs', in Jayo-Carboni, ***Handbook***, 28; S. Lagoa, 'Financial Institutions and Supply of Financial Services in the European Microcredit Market: A Survey of Selected Countries' Experiences', (2014) FESSUD Working Paper 73, 26, <fessud.eu/wp-content/uploads/2013/04/Financial-institutions-supply-of-financial-services_European-microcredit-market_WP-73.pdf.>; *see* also <https://www.the-fca.org.uk/firms/apply-authorisation/banks-lending-alternatives>.

120 Ganev, 'Microcrediting', 68. *See* Art. 3 Bulgarian Law on credit institutions, Art. 13 ordinance 26/2009, Obligations and contracts Act and Art. 3 of Law of Not-profit Corporate bodies (all available here: www.lexadin.nl/wlg/legis/nofr/eur/lxwebul.htm).

121 J. Wisniewski, 'Important Changes in the Regulatory Landscape of the Consumer (Personal) Loans Market in Poland', (2016), <www.squirepattonboggs.com/~/media/files/insights/publications/2016/03/important-changes-in-the-regulatory-landscape-of-the-consumer-loans-market-in-poland/poland-loans-marketthought-leadership-(2).pdf>; Interview on 28 November 2016 with Izabela Norek, CoopEst Risk Manager.

law would limit to business loans not-for-profit entities' permissible lending but this might not affect such entities' activity since they have always traditionally offered only business micro-loans.[122]

Even within the perimeter of microcredit, countries might limit MFIs' activities. Regulatory definitions can in fact restrict microcredit to microloans for entrepreneurial activity or on the contrary expand the concept to microloans to socially excluded people in difficult conditions (*see* Chapter 3, §1). Alternatively, regulation can limit the types of products that can be offered by certain categories of providers. For example, in Italy, MFIs can offer only microcredit not assisted by collateral (Artt. 111.2 *TUB*; 6 Decree 176/2014) with a distinction between for profit and not-for-profit entities. In fact, as anticipated, for-profit MFIs can offer both commercial and social microcredit but with a mandatory predominance of the former (Artt. 111.3 *TUB*; 5.7 Decree 176/2014), while not-for-profit MFIs only social microcredit and with lower interest rates and other favourable conditions (Art. 111.4 *TUB*). Instead, in Bosnia-and-Herzegovina the microfinance market includes loans for energy efficiency, agriculture, vehicle registration, solar collectors and energy savers, fixed assets, working capital, consumption and seasonal[123] and in Bulgaria credit products in the permitted areas of MFIs in the form of NBFIs include consumer credit, guarantees, forfeiting, leasing and factoring.[124] MFIs in France offer commercial microcredit, social microcredit and '*prêts d'honneur*' (i.e. loans without guarantees, at zero interest rates, provided in conjunction with a bank loan to support it and promote clients' graduation to mainstream finance).[125]

d Residual services, in particular payment products

Most EU countries (85% of respondents) allow financial cooperatives to perform domestic remittances (65% when international) while the percentage drops to 38% in case of non-bank/non-ODTI MFIs (25% when international remittances).[126] Few MFIs report offering also insurance (9.3%), mortgages (9.3%), money transfers (8%) and checking accounts (7.3%).[127]

Money transfer services are dominated by savings banks and banks or government bodies.[128] In Croatia, credit unions can also offer payment, exchange services and collateral.[129]

In Europe, micro-insurance (not discussed in this book: *see* Introduction) is mainly offered by savings banks, NBFIs and NGOs/foundations.[130] Romanian MFIs focus mostly on microcredit (67% of MFIs do not offer other services) but

122 Interview with Izabela Norek.
123 Bendig, 'Overview', 58.
124 Ibidem 59.
125 *See* Lagoa, 'Financial', 9–12.
126 Lagoa and Suleman, 'Types', 23.
127 Bendig, 'Overview', 35.
128 Lagoa and Suleman, 'Types', 23–25.
129 Bendig, 'Overview', 61.
130 Lagoa and Suleman, 'Types', 23.

micro-insurance is rising (22%).[131] In France, guarantees and micro-insurance are also common microfinance products.[132]

On the other hand, it might be rather difficult for an European non-bank MFI to provide its clients with payment services. In fact, the Payment Service Directive – PSD (2007/64, now repealed by PDS2 2015/2366: *see* Chapter 7, §2.c) reserves the provision of payment services to credit institutions, postal offices, e-money institutions and payment institutions. It also recognizes to the latter an EU passport and excludes, under certain conditions (especially, safeguarding requirements: funds deposited at a bank and separate accounting of clients funds), the nature as deposits of the received funds (Art. 16(2) PSD, 1, 11, 18(3) PSD2). The Directive with the expression 'payment services' refers to all services listed in its annex, including the transfer of money from and to clients' accounts, remittances, and the operations to operate a payment account (e.g. placement and withdrawal of money) (Art. 1, 4 and 29 PSD, 4(2) PSD2). The same Directive subjects payment institutions (PIs) to a bank-like prudential regulation (e.g. authorization and own funds requirements, organizational and internal control requirements), although lighter in certain aspects (e.g. lower minimum capital requirements depending on the types of services offered; *see* recital 11 and Artt. 5ff. PSD, 5ff. PSD2), and to specific rules (e.g. safeguarding requirements – not applying deposit protection – and transparency rules). PIs can also conduct commercial activities at the same time ('hybrid' PIs, such as retailers and phone companies), respecting additional safeguarding requirements (Artt. 16(1)c, 9 PSD, 11(5), 18(1)c PSD2). However, they cannot accept deposits or other repayable funds and can offer credit only in very limited cases and under strict circumstances (ie the credit must be ancillary and granted in connection with a payment service, of short maturity and not using funds received to execute a payment service: Artt. 16(3)–(4) PSD, 18(4)–(5) PSD2). National authorities can exempt from the Directive application operators with payment volumes below €3 million per months (and without managers responsible for financial crimes) but these are excluded from the EU passport and can have their activity limited to payment services by national regulators (Artt. 26, 16 PSD; 32 PSD2). Consequently, a PI *per se* could not provide micro-loans, although some Member States (e.g. Italy) allow cumulative licences, as PI and lending provider. Anyway, applying for a PIs status might not be easy for a non-bank MFI because of the bank-like regulation, unless national authorities recognize a favourable regime for under-threshold providers.

However, considering the existence within the EU of the basic payment account obligation (§c), European low-income people might not need MFIs to be authorized to provide payment services. Nonetheless, the concrete effects of such reform are still to be seen since the Directive implementation deadline was September 2016. In addition, being able to manage all financial services at the same institution might provide customers with an added value as well as facilitate loan repayments. Furthermore, the ability to offer payment services by alternative providers might better serve low-income clients (e.g. with more targeted products, offered by

131 Ibidem 43.

132 Lagoa, 'Financial', 12.

providers other than traditional banks not considered trustworthy) and partially relieve traditional banks which hardly find it profitable to serve the poorest.[133]

e *The provision of non-financial services: BSD and support services*

One of the typical features associated with microfinance, especially in Western Europe, is the provision of accompanying services (with only 29% of respondent European MFIs not offering them, mostly located in Greece, Latvia, Austria, Croatia, Bosnia-and-Herzegovina) although not reaching all clients (only 26%).[134] These are non-financial services generally consisting in financial education (58%), entrepreneurship training (45%), business development (42%) and debt counselling (41%).[135] Such services not only enhance repayment chances[136] but also improve service's quality, more likely providing customers with services responding to their needs and with a friendly environment (Chapter 2).

Nonetheless, the provision of these services can rise frictions with financial law since banks or other financial intermediaries might not be allowed to provide non-financial services to simplify risk management and reduce conflicts of interest.[137] For instance, NBFI-MFIs in Romania can provide only financial services and have been forced to collaborate with NGOs to offer BDSs to their clients.[138]

Moreover, while accompanying services might be easily considered ancillary to the main financial activity and thus in most case permitted to regulated entities, financial authorities might then discourage the direct offering of such supportive services by the same for stability concerns (requiring at least the creation of a separate entity). For instance, the BCBS has recommended that non-financial

133 About the factors hindering the offering of basic payment accounts *see* BCPMI-WB, *Payment*, 6ff.

134 Bendig, 'Overview', 35–36. A 2002 survey reported that only 20% of clients were reached by a BDS (15% in case of sole proprietors): *see* S. Sheikh et al., 'Support Services for Micro, Small and Sole Proprietor's Businesses of the EC – Final Report', (2002), 58, <www.microfinancegateway.org/sites/default/files/mfg-en-paper-support-services-for-micro-small-and-sole-proprietors-businesses-2002_0.pdf>.

135 Bendig, 'Overview', 36.

136 But *see* M. Sievers and P. Vandenberg, 'Synergies through Linkages: Who Benefits from Linking Micro-Finance and Business Development Services?', (2007), 14, <www.ilo.org/wcmsp5/groups/public/@ed_emp/@emp_ent/@ifp_seed/documents/publication/wcms_143167.pdf> (affirming the unverified nature of such assertion).

137 BCBS, *Guidance*, 8.

138 Doiciu, 'Best Practice', 106. In Germany, instead, MFIs and business support centres are prohibited from bundling non-financial and financial services by consumer protection regulation, therefore being only allowed to recommend non-financial services provided by partner organisations: B. Maas and S. Lämmermann, 'Designing Microfinance Operations in the EU', (2013), 53, 115, <www.microfinancegateway.org/sites/default/files/mfg-en-toolkit-designing-microfinance-operations-in-the-eu-a-manual-on-how-to-build-and-implement-microfinance-support-programmes-using-the-esf-2013.pdf> (but I could not verify this examining German laws available in English).

services are conducted by deposit-taking MFIs 'in a separate entity and ring-fenced from the activities of the financial institution to minimise conflicts of interest and risk to the bank's or ODTI's safety and soundness'.[139] In fact, providing BDSs can be extremely costly and require competencies and structures not typical of a financial intermediary. For example, the French MFI ADIE estimates that the average cost for accompanying services provided to a single entrepreneur in a 22-month period amounts to €1,780.[140] Also for this reason, the sector has recently highlighted the need to channel EU funds to support accompanying services.[141]

Looking at existing business models, accompanying services are offered by the same MFIs or by an external operator (apparently the latter solution makes the client more willing to share her doubts with somebody other than the operator providing credit), by volunteers or professionals (the latter being more likely to provide an adequate and targeted service), upon request or mandatory.[142] In particular, they can be provided for free (subsidized at least in part by public authorities) or in exchange for a fee (although small). The existence of a fee might ensure that such services are needed, create an incentive for higher quality through competition and attract committed clients.[143] Existing studies are not able to demonstrate yet whether a model is the most efficient but targeting (e.g. services tailored to the types of client, business, business-cycle phase)[144] and marketing are important strategies also in this field as well as the separation of accounting, management and personnel between financial and non-financial services.[145] Such

139 BCBS, *Microfinance*, 15.

140 ADIE, 'Rapport Annuel 2011', 42, <www.adie.org/sites/default/files/links/Adie_Rapport_Annuel_2011_0.pdf>.

141 EMN, 'Policy Note on Sector Proposals to Increase the Impact of Microfinance in the EU', (2015), 6, <www.european-microfinance.org/docs/emn_publications/policy_notes/Policy2015_EMN_oct.pdf>.

142 *See* M. Lobbezoo, 'Lessons Learnt from the EMN Workshop: What Do We Really Know about BDS in Relation to Microfinance?' and 'Volunteer versus Paid Coaches Within Microfinance Initiatives: What So We Actually Know about Effectiveness?', (2012) (February) EMN eRB 2 and 8; S. Lämmermann and G. Ribbink, 'Microfinance and Business Development Services in Europe. What Can We Learn from the South?', (2011), 9ff., <www.european-microfinance.org/docs/emn_publications/em n_research_papers/4.af-bds-handbook-lowres2.pdf>. According to Sheikh, 'Support', in 2002, 20% of respondent MFIs offered BDS services on a mandatory basis, while another 20% only in certain cases mandated them. The 27% of respondent MFIs instead referred their clients to another organization. Mandatory services are effective only in a few cases (to provide very basic knowledge to inexperienced borrowers) while in most cases can represent unnecessary costs for borrowers and lead to low-quality services: Sievers and Vandenberg, 'Synergies', 18.

143 Sheikh, 'Support', 60; Lämmermann and Ribbink, 'Microfinance', 13.

144 At least until 2002, BSDs had no target group orientation (while more than 70% of entrepreneurs would prefer a service targeted to their sector, size class and phase of development) and 76% of micro and sole proprietor's businesses lack information about the availability of such services: *see* ibidem 15; Sheikh, 'Support', 19, 37, 58–59.

145 Lämmermann and Ribbink, 'Microfinance', 9ff.; Sievers and Vandenberg, 'Synergies'.

separation allows better monitoring and management without confusion between financial (more efficient and remunerative) and non-financial activities.

In Europe, in the majority of cases (42.5% of MFIs offering accompanying services), such services are offered directly by the MFI (only 28% for their clients) but the recourse to free services voluntarily provided by external subjects is also quite common (21.4%).[146] For example, in France such services are offered both directly by MFIs and by commercial chambers.[147] In Bulgaria, accompanying services are mostly provided by an agency for SMEs' promotion with the Minister of the Economy but also some NGOs and industry associations assist micro-entrepreneurs in this respect.[148] Similarly, in Poland SMEs can rely on multiple supporting services offered by national and regional development agencies, EU contact points and a network of a varied range of non-commercial organizations (e.g. local agencies, associations, chambers of commerce). In Spain, there are several public programmes to support SMEs but also MFIs assist, advise and monitor borrowers screened and assigned the loans by partner-banks.[149] In Italy, MFIs must now offer accompanying services directly or through external specialized organizations (Art. 3.2 Decree 176/2014) but BDSs have been traditionally provided by public institutions in combination with private actors such as chambers of commerce and business associations.[150] British micro-borrowers are assisted by enterprise agencies, CDFIs and NGOs.[151] More generally, supporting services in Europe are mostly supplied by public or semi-public providers (Bulgaria, Hungary, Romania), with a higher proportion of private actors in Germany, France, Portugal and the Netherlands but often heavily subsidized and free or at low cost.[152] In Germany, for instance, advisory services fees are financed, depending on the prior or post-start-up phase, by the *Länder* or the European Social Fund with *KfW* (German development bank).[153]

Furthermore, such non-financial services are mostly non-mandatory (only 11% MFIs describe them as mandatory and 8% as mandatory in certain cases).[154]

7 Principles and guidelines for regulators

From the analysis of this second dimension, the centrality of social perspective in microfinance emerges. Consequently, the measurement of social impact should become a priority for MFIs and at least gradually implemented in their processes. The first step consists of reporting the number and types of clients served (e.g.

146 Bendig, 'Overview', 35–36.
147 TrustLaw, 'Creating', 54. Lobbezzo, 'Volunteer', 8ff.
148 TrustLaw, 'Creating', 28.
149 Ibidem 137; Rico Garrido, 'Microcredit', 282ff.
150 TrustLaw, 'Creating', 83.
151 Ibidem 147.
152 Lämmermann and Ribbink, 'Microfinance', 13; TrustLaw, 'Creating', 28ff.
153 TrustLaw, 'Creating', 58.
154 *See* C. Lentz, 'Trends in the Microfinance Sector in Europe', in *Microfinance Barometer 2014*, 11, <www.citi.com/citi/microfinance/data/lebarometre.pdf>.

unbanked, low-income, unemployed, migrants, women) especially in connection with the MFI's social missions, which generally complement traditional or other alternative operators. Reporting of additional data (such as number of jobs created, number of clients 'graduated' and moved to banks, objective improvements in clients' lives) should be introduced shortly after. A more comprehensive social performance assessment should represent a subsequent step, especially for large MFIs, performed according to available harmonized tools. In this perspective, the social performance section of the European MFIs Code should be extended to all microfinance operators (while now limited to non-bank and unregulated ones) and the results of the assessment should be taken into account in supervisory decisions and financing applications. Moreover, MFIs should demonstrate to translate social mission and performance into corporate governance and processes, also through the insertion of specific clauses in articles of incorporation (e.g. dedicated body/official and specific liability) and investment contracts making more enforceable certain aspects.

As regards MFIs' activity, regulation should allow innovation through a certain degree of freedom in respect to non-complex products (especially types of loans) and services. Consequently, regulators should avoid strict and rigid definitions (Chapter 3, §1) and allow diversification in permitted activities, in the area of 'basic' services, in order to meet clients' demands and improve stability through lower concentration and sustainability.

Nonetheless, MFIs have to prove an organization and capacity (managers' expertise and resources) adequate to the kind of activities performed, as suggested by the BCBS.[155] Consequently, not-for-profit entities should be allowed to offer not only microcredit but also other basic services (e.g. payments) when showing adequate structures or relying on other providers. More complex services should entail escalating requirements as regards legal forms and organization (Chapter 6). MFIs should also be allowed to offer compulsory savings or savings accounts (not checking accounts) when the sums are deposited at a regulated institution. The use of technology should be promoted to reduce costs and meet clients' needs (Chapter 7).

Although mainly targeting low-income people, regulators should allow a partial diversification in the client base in order to allow cross-subsidization and make the MFI more sustainable.

Finally, as regards accompanying services, regulators should allow MFIs to decide whether providing them directly or through other operators and to receive public and private subsidies for the same. In any case, MFIs should also monitor the quality of accompanying services through client surveys and try to tailor them to clients' needs, especially when a fee is required.

155 BCBS, *Guidance on the Application of the Core Principles for Effective Banking Supervision to the Regulation and Supervision of Institutions Relevant to Financial Inclusion – Consultative Document*, (BIS 2015), 8.

5 Dimension III: Economic sustainability/effectiveness

1 Microfinance as a business venture and the obstacles to economic sustainability

The present chapter addresses the issues surrounding the objective of microfinance economic sustainability and ability to reach its goals.

Microfinance has been conceptualized as a business venture with a capitalistic model able, nonetheless, to reach the poor, despite mainstream banks' failure in this respect. Ideally, microfinance should attain its social goals without 'interference' (ie subsidies). However, experiences in both developing countries (DCs) and economically advanced ones (EACs) have showed that MFIs either are not able to reach the poorest, losing sight of their social goals, or need subsidies to fulfil their promises. International pressure towards financial sustainability and commercial forms in combination with the first MFI-IPOs and scandals about excessive interest rates and profits has put a strain on the 'double-bottom line' goal of microfinance (Chapter 4, §4 and below §§1.a, 2).

Obviously, corporate governance plays a fundamental role in an institution's economic effectiveness and 'double-bottom line' balance, both under the legal form adopted (not-for-profit, for-profit or new hybrids) and management rules perspectives (§2).

Furthermore, rules regarding MFIs' funding can significantly affect their activity. In fact, they can allow a diversified range of financing alternatives, supporting microfinance development. Alternatively, they might restrict funding to a few basic options, with the objective of protecting investors, creditors and the general financial system by limiting complex operations, risky products, and the spreading of trust, liquidity or financial crises to the mainstream sector (§3).

a Operational self-sufficiency and the trade-off between sustainability and social mission. The Compartamos case

One revolutionary assertion of microfinance has been to attain social goals through a commercial structure and therefore covering their costs through their activity. Moreover, we have recently witnessed, at international level, a shift in the microfinance context towards a new paradigm of operation based on self-sufficiency, commercialization and profit-orientation to attract investments, reach scale, increase efficiency and improve outreach (*see* Chapter 4, §4).

MFIs' self-sufficiency is often assessed through the operational self-sufficiency ratio (OSS) which measures the extent to which operating revenues (from interest rates, fees and investments) cover operating costs (including cost of capital, loan-loss provision expenses and operating expenses). A more effective measure is the financial self-sufficiency ratio (FSS) which also takes into account subsidies coming from donations and 'concessional' financing.[1] Other relevant ratios to measure MFIs' performance include: the return on assets (RoA, measuring how well an institution uses its assets to generate returns), portfolio at risk (PAR, calculating the value of outstanding loans with one or more instalments of principal overdue for more than 30 or 90 days) and portfolio yield (measuring revenues from the loan portfolio including income from the average interest rate charged).[2]

The 'European Code of Good Conduct for Microcredit Provision' (European MFIs Code) has identified the 'operational sustainability ratio' (OSR) as a priority clause and main measurement of MFIs' performance. Based on the most recent international practice, such ratio is calculated as operating expenses divided by financial expenses, loan-loss provision expenses, personnel expenses and administrative expenses (clause 4.1.16). However, also the financial sustainability ratio is recommended, which takes into account subsidy adjustments in order to improve comparability among institutions (clause 4.1.17).[3]

In fact, subsidies have represented a significant part of MFIs' funding considering the high operating costs linked to the labour-intensive business model (peculiar underwriting, relationship-banking and accompanying services) and the managing of a high number of small loans, as well as difficulties in finding affordable funding (Chapter 2 and below §3). A study reports that in 2007, 62% of worldwide MFIs

1 The cost of capital is often calculated (by MicroBanking Bulletin) based on the deposit rate but since only a few MFIs use deposits and such rate is low, a better measure is the prime interest rate (offered by banks to their best clients) plus extra percentage points to account for MFIs' higher risk and illiquidity of investments in MFIs: *see* B. Armendáriz and J. Morduch, *The Economics of Microfinance*, (MIT Press 2010), 243–47; MicroBanking Bulletin, 'Trend Lines', (2005) issue 10, 57; J. Ledgerwood (ed.), *Microfinance Handbook: An Institutional and Financial Perspective*, (1st edn, WB 1998), 217; R. Rosenberg, 'Measuring Results of Microfinance Institutions. Minimum Indicators That Donors and Investors Should Track – A Technical Guide', (2009), 9–10, <www.cgap.org/sites/default/files/CGAP-Technical-Guide-Measuring-Results-of-Microfinance-Institutions-Minimum-Indicators-That-Donors-and-Investors-Should-Track-Jul-2009.pdf>.

2 Ibidem.

3 Clause 4.1.17: 'There are two types of subsidy adjustments: subsidised costs of funds and in-kind subsidy. The subsidised cost-of-funds adjustment tries to account for the difference between an MFI's financial expense and financial expense it would pay if all funding were priced at market rates. It is commonly done by multiplying an MFI's average funding liabilities by some shadow price – market interest rate – then subtracting actual financial expense. The difference is the amount of adjustment and is treated as an expense.'

in the sample were self-sufficient.[4] However, a 2009 study[5] showed that many MFIs turned out not to produce profits, with only 57% of MFIs self-sufficient (serving 87% of all clients). This result was especially true for NGO-MFIs (capturing 61% of subsidies but serving only 51% of clients), while bank-MFIs showed better results (73% profitable). However, NGOs showed to be profitable in 54% of cases and to serve the poorest.[6] Anyway, reliance on subsidies is constantly declining because of pressure towards profitability (*see* §3.a).

Focusing now on Europe, 59% of responding MFIs in 2013 appeared self-sufficient (55% in 2012). The figures vary significantly among countries, with an average OSS of 88.4%, ranging from 143% (Lithuania) to 26% (Ireland).[7] Eastern MFIs present higher levels of self-sustainability. For instance, Romanian MFIs are almost completely self-sustainable (OSS 120%), since most international donors withdrew after the admission to the EU and the evidence of the sector sustainability.[8] Also Hungarian MFIs show good levels of self-sustainability (104%),[9] contrary to France (27.3%) and UK (57%).[10] However, Spanish microcredit

4 *See* A. Gonzalez, 'Sources of Revenue and Assets Allocation at MFIs', (2008) 17 *MicroBanking Bulletin* 18.

5 This study relies on a broader sample and uses the prime interest rate plus extra points as cost of capital instead of the deposit rate: R. Cull et al., 'Microfinance Meets the Market', (2009) 23(1) *J Econ Perspect* 167 (adding that a more realistic cost of capital would further shrink the class of profitable MFs). *See* also Armendáriz and Morduch, *The Economics*, 245–246.

6 *See* also Armendáriz and Morduch, *The Economics*, 317ff.; J. Morduch, 'The Role of Subsidies in Microfinance: Evidence from the Grameen Bank', (1999) 60(1) *J Dev Econ* 229; M. Tucker, 'Financial Performance of Selected Microfinance Institutions: Benchmarking Progress to Sustainability', (2001) 3 *J Microfinance* 107, 116; M. Hudon, 'Management of Microfinance Institutions: Do Subsidies Matter?', (2010) 22 (7) *J Int Dev* 890. *Contra*, V. Bogan, 'Microfinance Institutions: Does Capital Structure Matter?', (2008), <http://ssrn.com/abstract=1144762> (finding that subsidies bring down efficiency while not leading to better outreach). Others (A. Gonzalez and R. Rosenberg, 'The State of Microfinance – Outreach, Profitability, and Poverty: Findings from a Database of 2300 Microfinance Institution', (2006), <http://ssrn.com/abstract=1400253>) report that 44% (60% if considering only private organizations and so leaving out public banks) of micro-entrepreneur clients in their sample of 2,300 MFIs are served by profit-making MFIs.

7 *See* M. Bendig et al., 'Overview of the Microcredit Sector in the European Union – 2012/2013', (2014), 49, <www.european-microfinance.org/docs/emn_publications/emn_overview/Overview2012-2013_Nov2014.pdf>.

8 EMN-EIF, 'EIF Market Studies-Central and Eastern Europe', 116; Bendig, 'Overview', 49, 91; M. Doiciu and D. Bialus, 'Microcredit in Romania', in B. Jayo Carboni et al., *Handbook of Microcredit in Europe. Social Inclusion through Microenterprise Development*, (Edgar Elgar 2010), 324ff.; Pop and Buys, 'Microfinance', 319.

9 Bendig, 'Overview', 32, 49, 67–69; EMN, 'The Collection', 4–5; I. Kovács, 'The Microlending Sector in Hungary: Microlending to SMEs', in Jayo Carboni et al. (eds), *Handbook*, 190ff.

10 Bendig, 'Overview', 40–41, 46, 49; PwC, 'The Sustainability of Community Development Finance Institutions', (2015), <www.pwc.co.uk/assets/pdf/the-sustainability-of-community-development.pdf>.

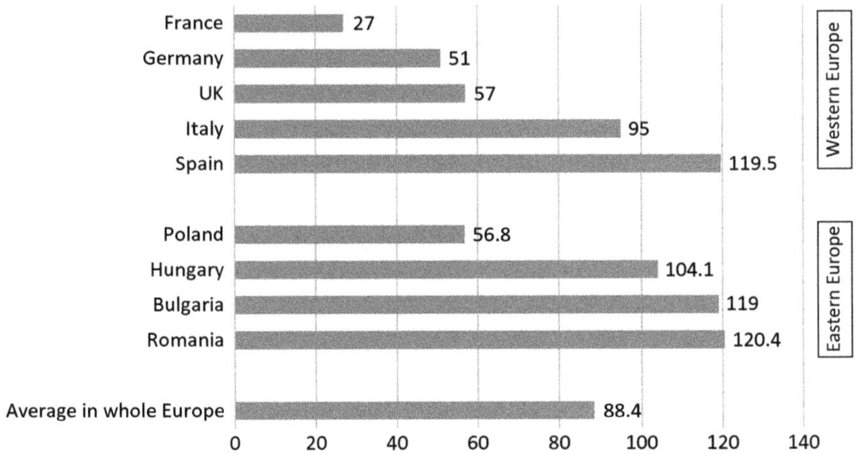

Figure 5.1 OSS ratio of European MFIs in the sample (%)
(Data from Bendig, 'Overview 2012/2013' (response rate 45%; no data available for Croatia)

(mostly provided by savings banks) has appeared self-sustainable (119.5%), at least until recently[11] (for additional comparisons, *see* Fig. 5.1).

Nonetheless, the response rate to the OSS question was, unfortunately, only 45% (43% in 2012) and we can presume lower OSSs for non-responding MFIs. The measurement of the sustainability ratio, as anticipated, is now required by the European MFIs Code but, as discussed, this Code is not compulsory and still receives a low level of application and enforcement (Chapter 3, §3.c). The above reported OSSs, in addition, do not provide a realistic picture of the sustainability of European MFIs, not taking into account subsidies. Actually, looking at the funding data, we can observe that 25% of European MFIs' funding in 2013 came from grants, with NGOs/foundations and microfinance associations heavily relying on grants (respectively, 41% and 56% of their funding).[12] Anyway, in the absence of subsidies, European MFIs would need to charge excessive interest rates, a result not acceptable by public opinion or under many anti-usury laws (Chapter 8, §4).[13]

Among financial reporting standards required by the European MFIs Code, we should also mention financial revenues (from loans and investments), operating revenues (from other services), personnel, administrative and financial expenses, PAR and write-offs (clause 4.1).

As expected, European MFIs' profitability is limited: the average RoA in 2013 was 4.5% but with significant differences among countries (7–10% in Germany,

11 Bendig, 'Overview', 25, 33.
12 Ibidem, 'Overview', 50–51.
13 *See* J. Evers et al., 'Status of Microfinance in Western Europe – An Academic Review', (2007), 26, <www.microfinancegateway.org/sites/default/files/mfg-en-paper-status-of-microfinance-in-western-europe-an-academic-review-2007.pdf>.

Romania and Hungary; 1–2% in France, Poland, UK and Italy).[14] The operating expense ratio was 23.7% on average but again with very different figures among countries (from 90% in Croatia to 48% in UK and Poland, 12–17% in Italy, Germany, Hungary, France and Romania and only 3% in Spain).[15] The average portfolio yield was 16.1% but the highest yields were found in Serbia, UK and Poland (around 25%) while below average (5–10%) in Italy, Spain, France and Germany (*see* Fig. 5.2 for more detailed data).

However, the above-mentioned pressure towards less subsidized and commercially viable microfinance has also revealed some downsides. We have in fact witnessed worldwide higher interest rates, a reduction in the number of the poorest and women served (with an increase in the number of wealthier clients) and, in general, fear of a mission drift, provoking the so-called 'microfinance schism' in the sector (*see* Chapter 4, §4) but also to exaggerations, such as denying the right to a profit when pursuing a social goal.[16]

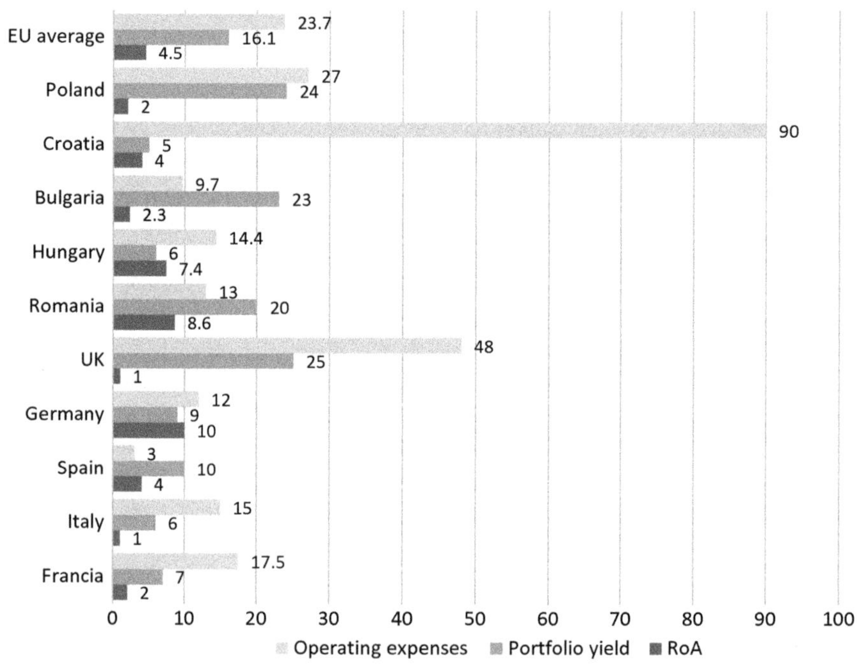

Figure 5.2 RoA, operating expenses and portfolio yields in sample countries in 2013 (%) (Data from Bendig et al., 'Overview 2012/2013')

14 Bendig, 'Overview', 46.

15 Ibidem.

16 *See* R. Rosenberg et al., 'Microcredit Interest Rates and Their Determinants – 2004–2011', (2013), 18, <www.cgap.org/sites/default/files/Forum-Microcredit%20Interest%20Rates%20and%20Their%20Determinants-June-2013.pdf>.

The discussion about mission drift received a peak in 2007 when the successful Mexican MFI Compartamos launched an IPO on its existing shares, 13-times oversubscribed. Compartamos had been funded in 1990 as NGO but created in 2000 a regulated financial institution (Financiera Compartamos) to tap commercial sources of funding and expand its client base. Such financial institution traded its bonds on the Mexican stock exchange in 2002, obtained a full banking licence in 2006 and reached 1.2 million clients in 2009 (from the original 60,000 in 2000).[17] Because of Comportamos' high profits, the IPO allowed existing shareholders (international organizations – IOs, NGOs, Development Financial Institutions – DFIs and private investors) to obtain extraordinary high proceeds from the sale with a small initial investment and benefiting from concessional loans.[18] Such profits seemed obtained at the poor's expense since Compartamos charged borrowers with rather high interest rates (even compared to other MFIs and competitors, although products and costs were not completely comparable), with an average interest yield of 86% in 2005. Nonetheless, a CGAP study has evidenced that the greatest part of interest income (88.3%) was to cover operating expenses (36.4%) and costs of funds (13.6%), with only 23.6% turned into profits. Therefore, reducing profits would not have considerably reduced interest rates, while potentially hindering growth and outreach (serving fewer poor), although there were likely other ways – more 'client-focused' but less appreciated by funders and managers – to cover costs (*see* §2).[19] The Compartamos case, therefore, has made more evident the 'microfinance schism' between reaching the poor through commercialization and the contribution of profit-driven investors or through socially responsible microfinance relying mostly on public funds and responsible investors.[20]

Such cases, in combination with scandals related to excessive interest rates, have further driven Western European microfinance towards social objective at the expense of sustainability.[21] However, the mission-drift risk also stands, at least in

17 Armendáriz and Morduch, *The Economics*, 241; R. Rosenberg, 'CGAP Reflections on the Compartamos Initial Public Offering: A Case Study on Microfinance Interest Rates and Profits', (2007), CGAP Focus Note 42, 2, 9, <www.cgap.org/sites/default/files/CGAP-Focus-Note-CGAP-Reflections-on-the-Compartamos-Initial-Public-Offering-A-Case-Study-on-Microfinance-Interest-Rates-and-Profits-Jun-2007.pdf>.

18 For example, the USD1 million USAID grant invested by Acción in Compartamos increased in value to USD300 million; the USD6 million invested in 2000 by International Finance Corporation (World Bank), Acción Gateway Fund, Profund, Compartamos NGO and some Mexican private investors was worth in 2007 USD2.2 billion: *see* Armendáriz and Morduch, *The Economics*, 239–40. *See* also Rosenberg, 'CGAP', 3 (reporting an internal rate of return on the selling of shareholders' original investment of around 100% a year compounded over eight years).

19 Ibidem 5.

20 *See* Armendáriz and Morduch, *The Economics*, 240. R. Rosenberg, 'Mohammed Yunus and Michael Chu Debate Commercialization', (*World Bank*, 14 October 2008), <http://blogs.worldbank.org/psd/mohammed-yunus-and-michael-chu-debate-commercialization>.

21 *See* B. Bruhn-Leon et al., 'Progress in Microfinance in Europe', (2012), EIF Working Paper 13, 26, <www.eif.org/news_centre/publications/eif_wp_2012_13_microfinance.pdf>.

part, for Europe.[22] In fact, the most self-sufficient MFIs are the ones with for-profit structure and more mature.[23] These MFIs are able to reach a larger number of people but they serve wealthier, less risky and less disadvantaged (e.g. lower number of women) customers than other MFIs,[24] especially when rushed to attain financial sustainability.[25] Other studies, however, prove that financial sustainability can coexist with outreach when managers focus on cost efficiency, providing alternative and socially responsible explanations to wealthier clients and larger loans.[26]

22 Lagoa ('Financial Institutions and Supply of Financial Services in the European Microcredit Market: A Survey of Selected Countries' Experiences'), 2014, FESSUD Working Paper 73, 47, <http://fessud.eu/wp-content/uploads/2013/04/Financial-institutions-supply-of-financial-services_European-microcredit-market_WP-73.pdf.>) reports that profit-orientation in Germany (but not in Romania) is associated with a smaller proportion of poor clients, while serving the poorest is associated with higher operational costs in France and the UK (but not in Romania).

23 These same MFIs represent only between 2% and 8% of MFIs but manage more than 90% of the sector's activities; their RoE (Return on Equity) index reaches 17.2% (while for most MFIs it is 4%): *see* R. Dieckmann, 'Microfinance: An Emerging Investment Opportunity', (2007), 6, 15, <www.dbresearch.com/PROD/DBR_INTERNET_DE-PROD/PROD0000000000219174/Microfinance%3A+An+emerging+investment+opportunity.pdf>. A study (S. Caudill et al., 'Which Microfinance Institutions are Becoming More Cost Effective with Time? Evidence from a Mixture Model', (2009) 41 *J Money Credit Bank* 651, 653) evidences that the most efficient MFIs are the ones receiving fewer subsidies, with a higher level of deposits as funding instrument and without network affiliation.

24 *See* N.Hermes et al., 'Outreach and Efficiency of Microfinance Institutions', (2008), 18ff., <http://som.eldoc.ub.rug.nl/FILES/reports/2008/08002/08002.pdf>; R. Cull et al., 'Financial Performance and Outreach: A Global Analysis of Leading Microbanks', (2007) 117 *Econ J* 107, 126ff. (attesting that the MFIs more experiencing mission drift are the biggest, oldest and offering individual loans).

25 *See* also B. Augsburg and C. Fouillet, 'Profit Empowerment: The Microfinance Institution's Mission Drift', (2010) 9(3/4) *PGDT* 327, 331, 336; G. Estapé-Dubreuil and C. Torreguitart-Mirada, 'Governance Mechanisms, Social Performance Disclosure and Performance in Microfinance: Does Legal Status Matter?', (2015) 86 *Annals of Public and Cooperative Economics* 137, 148–49.

26 E.g. greater availability of larger clients in the area or even a cross-subsidizing strategy (B. Armendáriz and A. Szafarz, 'On Mission Drift in Microfinance Institutions', (2011) MPRA Paper 31041, <https://mpra.ub.uni-muenchen.de/31041/1/MPRA_paper_31041.pdf>), natural growth, better economic conditions of clients, requests by poorer clients of larger loans (C. Frank, 'Stemming the Tide of Mission Drift: Microfinance Transformations and the Double Bottom Line', (2008) WWB Focus Note, 8ff., <www.microfinancegateway.org/sites/default/files/mfg-en-paper-stemming-the-tide-of-mission-drift-microfinance-transformations-and-the-double-bottom-line-apr-2008.pdf>). About the importance of good governance and cost-efficiency in reducing sustainability and outreach trade-off and avoiding mission drift, *see* A Nawaz, 'Issues in Subsidies and Sustainability of Microfinance: An Empirical Investigation', (2010) CEB Working Paper 10/2010; D. Gibbons and J. Meehan, 'The Microcredit Summit's Challenge: Working towards Institutional Financial Self-Sufficiency while Maintaining a Commitment to Serving the Poorest Families', (1999) 1(1) *J Microfinance* 131; T. Arena, 'Social Corporate Governance and the Problem of Mission Drift in Socially-Oriented Microfinance Institutions', (2008) 41(3) *Columbia J Law Soc P* 269.

All this might prove, anyway, that not-for profit, small and subsidized MFIs are still required to reach the poorest and most disadvantaged part of the population but also that the key to both financial sustainability (subsidy reduction) and outreach lies in inefficiencies reduction and good management. Subsidies can be justified from an economic point of view if they contribute to produce a socially beneficial outcome otherwise not achieved or at a higher cost (*see* also Chapter 3, §4 about EU State aid law). In this sense, subsidies might optimally support loans to very poor clients making them more likely to approach the financial sector in the future, or additional non-financial services of social impact (e.g. health and business education: Chapter 4, §6.e) or infrastructure investments (e.g. management information systems –MIS or incentives schemes).[27] However, instruments to ensure efficiency (through budget constraints) and efforts in innovative strategies or techniques need to be implemented.[28]

Consequently, an important step consists, once more, in achieving more transparency in the sector, also through common indicators, to allow comparisons among operators and an easy monitoring of the effectiveness of MFIs' operations both in terms of cost effectiveness and of attainment of social missions. Internationally, MIX Market has been collecting data about MFIs' financial and social performance, improving MFIs' comparability and monitoring, but presents some limitations (Chapter 3, §3.d). The European MFIs Code relies on similar common internationally-accepted indicators to improve transparency but at present it receives a limited application and enforcement (*see* Chapter 3, §3.c and 4, §3). Again, better transparency of financial indicators (such as operational and financial sustainability ratios, operating revenues and expenses with detailed indications of personnel and administrative costs as well as expenses for accompanying services) and the Code's enforcement would represent a way forward in the right direction. This might also allow MFIs' funders to design contractual obligations to attain certain levels of economic and social efficiency ('smart subsidies').[29] Anyway, the Code needs to take into account the likely differences with mainstream financial institutions indicator requirements (e.g. PAR-30 instead of PAR-45 or 90) and with specific indicators imposed by national governments, trying to reduce the risk of double burden especially for more mature NBFI-MFIs.

b Special challenges in transplanting microfinance in economically advanced countries

The transplant of microfinance in EACs has not been without challenges, losing on the way some of microfinance features (*see* Chapter 2, §2.a). Anyway, the

27 *See* also B. Blakenhol, 'Evaluating the Impact of European Microfinance – Business Models of Microfinance Institutions in Europe', (2015) Centre for Microfinance and Financial Inclusion, 5, <http://microfinance.ucd.ie/images/Reports/BusinessModel.pdf> (microfinance subsidies can be justified when they allow to save on fiscal resources); M. Hudon and D. Traca, 'On the Efficiency Effects of Subsidies in Microfinance: An Empirical Inquiry', (2011) 39(6) *World Dev* 966 ('small ("smart") subsidies allow MFIs to increase the productivity of their staff, but beyond a certain threshold, they lower productivity [...]').

28 *See* Armendáriz and Morduch, *The Economics*, 333–41.

29 *See* also in this respect Blakenhol, 'Evaluating', 10.

problem of sustainability is even more serious in such countries for various reasons.[30]

First, in EACs micro-entrepreneurs encounter more obstacles in setting up and running their businesses because of restrictive and complex regulations as well as bureaucracy. The EU has been trying to simplify SMEs' applicable regulation eliminating some of these burdens but the residual ones remain significant (*see* Chapters 6, 8).

Moreover, the preference for wage jobs (over self-employment)[31] and social security systems' rules in EACs create a considerable obstacle to self-employment. In fact, unemployed people often are forced to choose between setting up an enterprise or receiving welfare support, this creating a disincentive to entrepreneurial activity.[32] Consequently, Ireland, for instance, has recently reformed its welfare system providing for a gradual reduction in social subsidies after the start-up phase and the possibility to re-enter the welfare programme in case of business failure.[33] In France, unemployed people have been able since 2005 to allocate part of welfare benefits to the capital of a new enterprise and to resume the benefits in case of firm's failure.[34]

Moving to MFIs, these have to face in EACs the competition of several traditional financial providers specialized in low-income clients (cooperatives but also credit card providers) and therefore to justify the need for their existence (Chapter 3, §5.a).[35]

30 In general, *see* for the U.S.: M. Schreiner and J. Morduch, 'Opportunities and Challenges for Microfinance in the United States, in J. Carr, and Z. Yi Tong (eds), *Replicating Microfinance in the United States* (Woodrow Wilson Center Press 2002), 41–45 and other references in Chapter 2, §2.a. For Europe, *see* K. Dayson and P. Vik, 'Can MFIs in Western Europe be Sustainable?', (2009) 5 *EMN-Microfinance Europe* 10; M. Genet, 'Microfinance in Western Europe and Sustainability: Dream or Lack of Ambition?', ibidem, 16; Evers, 'Status', 23, 28; A. Andreoni et al., *Nuovi bisogni finanziari: la riposta del microcredito*, (Il Mulino 2013), 52–54.

31 In fact, many MFIs clients use micro-enterprises to supplement their existing wages: L. Servon, 'Microenterprise Programs in U.S. Inner Cities: Economic Development or Social Welfare?', (1997) 11(2) *Econ Dev Q* 166.

32 *See* M. Jung et al, 'EIF Market Studies on Micro Lending in the European Union: Capacity Building and Policy Recommendations', (2009), <www.emnconference.org/archives/data/file/EIF%20MF%Studies%20-%20Capacity%20Building%20final.pdf>; EMN and EIF, 'Microfinance Market Studies in the framework of JEREMIE – Cross-Country Study on Western Europe. United Kingdom, Spain, Germany, Italy', (2009), 17, <<www.emnconference.org/archives/data/file/EIF%20Study%20Microlending_Western%20Europe_March%202009.zip>.

33 *See* P. Guichandut, 'Europe Occidentale et reste du monde: parle-t-on des mêmes pratiques?', (2006) 25 *Finance & the Common Good/Bien Commun* 54, 56–57.

34 *See* ADIE, '20 Years of Microcredit in France the Knowledge Gained through Adie's Experience', (2008), 19, <www.microfinancegateway.org/sites/default/files/mfg-en-paper-20-years-of-microcredit-in-france-the-knowledge-gained-through-adies-experience-oct-2008.pdf>.

35 *See* A. Vanroose and B. D'Espallier, 'Do Microfinance Institutions Accomplish Their Mission? Evidence from the Relationship between Traditional Financial Sector Development and Microfinance Institutions' Outreach and Performance', (2013) 45(15)

The market for microfinance, moreover, is comparatively smaller because of the lower demand (less poor) and therefore scale of activities, while operating costs are higher because of regulation (e.g. complex microenterprise and environmental regulation) and accompanying services. Over-indebtedness, moreover, is widespread among clients.[36]

Furthermore, MFIs must cope with restrictive and pervasive regulations in the financial sector, sometimes even limiting the possibility to on-lend (obtaining loans to provide microcredit) (*see* below §5.c and Chapters 4, §6.c; 7, §3.b) as well as with the prevalent mentality conceiving microfinance more a social activity than a business. For instance, the Italian regulator, instead of recognizing the MFIs' higher operative costs and risks, has set ceilings for social microcredit interest rates well below market ones for similar transactions (with the difficulty of identifying 'similar' operations: *see* Chapter 8, §4).

Finally, some techniques distinctive of DCs' microfinance sector (e.g. group lending and progressive lending) have been unapplicable to EACs, forcing European MFIs to find new instruments to manage information, selection and monitoring problems and often leading to labour-intensive analyses and accompanying services (Chapters 2, §2.a–b; 6, §2.a).[37]

2 Corporate governance issues and legal forms

Corporate governance[38] becomes fundamental for ensuring social mission along with financial sustainability.

One first issue pertains to the legal form used to perform microfinance activities. The sector deploys various forms (e.g. holding, bank, NBFI, cooperative, NGOs, foundation, association, network), but each of them has special features that lead to different orders of priorities and to distinct structures and instruments to pursue such a dual objective. There are reasons to presume that some forms might be more effective in reaching financial efficiency while others in attaining social objectives but empirical studies cannot always confirm it (§§2.a–b).

Second, good governance might be able to improve financial efficiency without leading to mission drift or imposing certain legal forms. Rules on MFI management, board and internal control systems as well as special bodies/

Appl Econ 1965 (MFIs grow better in an environment with a low financial sector's development).

36 Evers, 'Status', 10, 32; Commission, 'Overcoming the Obstacles Faced by Dependent Employees Who Want to Become Self-employed and/or Start Their Own Business', (2004), <www.european-microfinance.org/data/file/second_career_final_reprt_expert_en.pdf>.

37 Andreoni, *Nuovi*, 53–54.

38 About existing multiple definitions of corporate governance, *see* J. Macey and M. O'Hara, 'The Corporate Governance of Banks', (2003) 9(1) *FRBNY Economic Policy Review* 91; P. Mülbert, 'Corporate Governance of Banks after the Financial Crisis – Theory, Evidence, Reforms', (2010) ECGI Law Working Paper 130/2009, 36ff., <http://ssrn.com/abstract=1448118>.

appointments can help respecting the double-bottom line (§§2.c–d). In this respect, it is also interesting to draw a parallel between the growing literature about corporate governance of banks (and relatively recent strict regulatory requirements) and the discussion about MFIs' governance, for the common relevance of stakeholders' interests besides shareholders' ones. However, microfinance double-bottom line creates specific governance issues, such as dealing with different types of shareholders' (e.g. socially responsible investors, DFIs, private investors, sometimes also employees and clients), mission drift risk in case of exit of certain funders and social performance planning and monitoring (§2.d; Chapter 4, §4).

a Legal form and regulatory requirements. Microfinance transformations

Although European banking law does not require any specific legal form for credit institutions (*see* recital 72 CRR), national regulators tend to require a for-profit and limited company (or at least financial cooperative) form to provide financial services, especially in the case of banking activity. Such restrictions exist because of the belief that certain organizational elements make some forms more suitable for balancing the different interests involved.

In fact, shareholders, companies' owners, have incentives to push managers towards companies' profitability as well as the power to monitor and influence the same, avoiding managers' extraction of private benefits. Instead, NGOs and foundations are ownerless, cannot be subject to takeovers (thus to market control) and their funders are generally too dispersed and disorganized to continuously monitor managers, who are basically self-controlling and self-perpetuating.[39] When a not-for-profit becomes more profitable, workers' interests and influence tend to prevail (but with limited effects due to competition effect and workers' altruistic motive) because of the governance weakness.[40] Again, for the lack of the profit-motive, not-for-profit managers might not have enough incentives to reduce costs and therefore might reach a lower level of efficiency and profitability (also because of capital constraints).[41] Furthermore, supervisory instruments and prudential measures can also be more effective in case of corporate form: capital calls, while representing an ordinary procedure for a company, might be not viable in case of NGOs, associations or foundations where donors and supporters might not be able or willing to promptly provide additional funds upon request. This is why the majority of worldwide regulators

39 *See* E. Rasmusen 'Stock Banks and Mutual Banks', (1988) 31 *J Law Econ* 395; E. Glaeser, 'The Governance of Not-for-Profit Firms', (2002) HIER Discussion Paper 1954, 2, 18–19, <http://scholar.harvard.edu/files/glaeser/files/the_governance_of_not-for-profit_firms.pdf?m=1360041717>; H. Hansmann, 'Ownership and Organizational Form', in R. Gibbons and J. Roberts (eds), *The Handbook of Organizational Economics*, (PUP 2012), 891ff.

40 *See* Glaeser, 'The Governance'.

41 H. Hansmann, 'The Role of Non Profit Enterprise', (1980) 89 *Yale L J* 835, 878.

require a corporate or cooperative form to be authorized to accept deposits and the BCBS discourages the use of the NGO-form to accept deposits (*see* Chapters 4, §6.b; 6, §6.f).[42]

Nonetheless, ownerless forms should not be struck out *per se* from the financial sector.[43] Contracting theories suggest that a not-for-profit form might even be more effective than a corporate one when service recipients are not able to complain or switch operator or the ones who pay cannot observe the quality of the service provided ('contractual failure'). In fact, in such a case, managers of a for-profit firm would have incentives to lower the service quality while charging high prices to divert most of the revenues to owners. This kind of incentive would not exist, instead, under a not-for-profit form because of the prohibition of revenue distribution.[44] In a microfinance context, micro-borrowers might not have alternatives or the ability to complain and funders might not monitor, making a not-for-profit form ideal to prevent MFIs' managers from charging exorbitant interest rates while lowering the service quality.

Moreover, not-for-profit firms seem not to be outperformed by for-profit ones in a case of strong competition (in capital or products), which acts as a substitute monitoring mechanism, making the organizational form irrelevant.[45] Empirical studies seem to find little difference in economic efficiency among different ownership structures.[46] However, diversion is possible and, therefore, legal constraints

42 BCBS, *Microfinance Activities and the Core Principles for Effective Banking Supervision*, (Aug. 2010), 36. *See* also 16–17: 'NGOs or other ownerless entities should not be allowed to operate as deposit taking institutions given their lack of shareholders to infuse new capital in the event that the institution's solvency is threatened.' Against the use of the NGO form in microfinance, *see* also R. Chavez and C. Gonzalez Vega, 'Principles of Regulation and Prudential Supervision: Should They be Different for Microenterprise Finance Organizations?', (1992), 44, <http://aede.ag.ohio-state.edu/programs/ruralfinance/pdf%20docs/Publications%20List/Papers/92P01.pdf>; S. Staschen, 'Regulatory Requirements for Microfinance: A Comparison of Legal Frameworks in 11 Countries Worldwide' (2003), 21, <www.izdihar-iraq.com/resources/mfsummit/ref_RegulatoryRequirementsInMicrofinance_GTZ.pdf>.

43 Many stock exchanges used to have a not-for-profit mutual form: C. Bradley, 'Demutualization of Financial Exchanges: Business as Usual', (2001) 21 *Nw J Int'l L & Bus* 657, 658.

44 Hansmann, 'The Role', 843ff.; Hansmann, 'Ownership'. *See* also D. Easley and M. O'Hara, 'The Economic Role of the Nonprofit Firm', (1983) 14(2) *Bell J Econ* 531; E. Glaeser and A. Shleifer, 'Not-for-profit Entrepreneurs', (2001) 81 *J Public Econ* 99 (specifying the relevance of the factor that the business is not particularly profitable and needs subsidies to move the balance towards not-for-profits).

45 *See* Ø. Bøhren and M. Josefsen, 'Stakeholder Rights and Economic Performance: The Profitability of Nonprofits', (2013) 37 *J Bank Financ* 4073 (studying the performance of not-for-profit, commercial and hybrid banks in Norway).

46 Y. Altunbas et al., 'Bank Ownership and Efficiency', (2001) 33(4) *J Money Credit Bank* 926; R. Crespi et al., 'Governance Mechanisms in Spanish Banks. Does Ownership Matter?', (2004) 28 *J Bank Financ* 2311; G. Iannotta et al., 'Ownership Structure, Risk and Performance in the European Banking Industry' (2007), <http://ssrn.com/abstract=1020306>.

and monitoring but also private regulation/enforcement[47] are fundamental to maintain not-for-profit form's advantages.

Literature focusing on microfinance resorts to additional arguments to discourage the use of not-for-profit forms, especially in case of deposits: not-for-profit board members often hold their office on a voluntarily basis, with no or low compensation (making it difficult to recruit financial sector experts or professionals)[48] and additional social or humanitarian activities conducted by NGOs might divert managers' attention or collected funds.[49] Furthermore, CEOs of NGO-MFIs show more discretion because of deficient monitoring by donors and difficult dual-mission balance, leading to higher performance variability (riskier decisions) when no stakeholder electives are on the board.[50]

All these arguments have been used to support NGOs transformation into regulated financial institutions, with the view also of expanding financing opportunities.[51] In fact, deposits are generally reserved to regulated entities, equity is limited to corporate forms and private investors appear less prone to provide credit to not-for-profit because of bad reputational effects in the case of credit enforcement and foreclosure.[52] However, studies present other factors able to counterbalance the above mentioned negative aspects. For example, the reputational effect on managers' behaviour seems to be stronger in not-for-profits[53] and risk can be reduced through regulation without transforming NGOs into regulated financial institutions.[54]

47 *See* Hansmann, 'The Role', 875–76; Glaeser, 'The Governance', 6.

48 *See* T. Jansson et al., 'Principles and Practices for Regulating and Supervising Microfinance', (2004), 22, <https://publications.iadb.org/handle/11319/5582?locale-attribute=en>; R. Rock et al., 'Principles and Practices of Microfinance Governance', (1998), ix, 21ff., <www.jointokyo.org/mfdl/readings/MFGovernance.pdf>; R. Mersland, 'The Governance of Not-For-Profit Institutions: Lessons From History', (2008), 132ff., <http://ssrn.com/abstract=1298613>.

49 *See* Jansson, 'Principles', 20ff. (with only reference to NGOs authorized to receive deposits, while suggesting not-deposit-taking NGOs to be only subject to private regulation through donors and creditors' monitoring); Rock, 'Principles', 18.

50 *See* R. Galema et al., 'Do Powerful CEOs Determine Microfinance Performance?', (2012) 49(4) *J Manage Stud* 718.

51 Advocating NGOs transformation: J. Ledgerwood and V. White, *Transforming Microfinance Institutions. Providing Full Financial Services to the Poor*, (WB 2006); V. White and A. Campion, 'Transformation – Journey from NGO to Regulated MFI', in D. Drake and E. Rhyne (eds), *The Commercialization of Microfinance* (Kumarian Press 2002), 2.

52 *See* Armendáriz and Morduch, *The Economics*, 251. *See* also Hansmann, 'The Role', 877.

53 F. Handy, 'Reputation as Collateral: An Economic Analysis of the Role of Trustees of Nonprofits', (1995) 24 *Nonprof Volunt Sec Q* 293; R. Mersland, 'The Cost of Ownership in Microfinance Organizations', (2009) 37 *World Devel* 469, 474; M. Labie, 'Corporate Governance in the Non-profit Sector: A Framework for Microfinance Organization', (2001) 39 *Manage Decis* 296.

54 *See* P. Morgan, 'Legal Form, Performance and Risk in the Microfinance Industry', (Master's Thesis, Utrecht University 2015), <http://dspace.library.uu.nl/bitstream/handle/1874/317523/MorganMasters2015.pdf?sequence=1>.

Furthermore, studies seem to prove the irrelevance of ownership structures in terms of performance (both financial and social) and efficiency.[55] In Europe, the highest MFIs' RoA in 2013 was experienced by NBFIs (12%), followed by NGOs and microfinance associations (5–6%) and, only eventually, banks and savings banks (1–2%). However, banks (except savings banks) show the lowest operating expense ratio (7%), while NGOs and other not-for profit MFIs (together with NBFIs) present rather high indicators also because of higher costs for smaller loans (16–25%; *see* Fig. 5.3).[56]

Pressure towards NGOs' transformation into for-profit forms have been significant, leading to numerous operations of this kind in microfinance.[57] In addition to the already mentioned reasons (international donors/investors' preference, expansion of financing options), transformations have also been determined by regulatory requirements in connection with the provision of deposit services (*see* K-Rep in Kenya) or MFIs' willingness to increase employees' or clients'

55 *See* R. Mersland and R. Strøm, 'Performance and Trade-offs in Microfinance Organizations – Does Ownership Matter?', (2008) 20 *J Int Dev* 598, 600; V. Hartarska, 'Governance and Performance of Microfinance Institutions in Central and Eastern Europe and the Newly Independent States', (2005) 33(10) *World Devel* 1627; R. Mersland and R. Strøm, 'Performance and Corporate Governance in Microfinance Institutions', (2009) 33 *J Bank Financ* 662, 663–64; Mersland, 'The Cost'; E. Périlleux et al., 'Productivity Surplus Distribution in Microfinance: Does Ownership Matter?', (2010) CEB Working Paper 10/036, <https://dipot.ulb.ac.be/dspace/bitstream/2013/60442/1/wp10036.pdf>; A. Beisland et al., 'The Association between Microfinance Rating Scores and Corporate Governance: A Global Survey', (2014) 35 *Int Rev Fin An* 268. *Contra* (to a limited extent and only with reference to certain indicators), H. Tchakoute-Tchuigoua, 'Is There a Difference in Performance by the Legal Status of Microfinance Institutions?', (2010) 50 *Q Rev Econ Financ* 436 (reporting a higher outreach and higher portfolio quality of privately owned MFIs compared to NGOs and cooperatives); R. Servin, 'Ownership and Technical Efficiency of Microfinance Institutions: Empirical Evidence from Latin America', (2012) 36 *J Bank Financ* 2136 (attesting that NBFI and bank-MFIs have better technology and are more technologically efficient than NGOs and cooperatives). Similar social performances between NGOs and banks might be explained by the fact that NGOs serve the poorest clients (providing smaller loans) and women but banks serve a higher number of clients. Moreover, NGOs present higher transaction costs because of the smaller size of their loans ($26 per $100 loan) and therefore need to charge higher interest rates (16%) than banks (which have a cost of $12 per $100 loan and 13% interest rate: *see* Armendáriz and Morduch, *Economics*, 249–250). Partially *contra see*, more recently, Estapé-Dubreuil and Torreguitart-Mirada, 'Governance', 148 (finding a better social performance and similar financial performance of NGOs compared to for-profit MFIs).

56 Bendig, 'Overview', 47.

57 One of the first cases of NGO-MFI transformations was BancoSol in 1992 in Bolivia, with many others following (K-Rep in Kenya, CARD Bank in Philippines, BRAC in Bangladesh, MiBanco in Peru, Finsol in Honduras and Compartamos in Mexico): *see* G. Hishigsuren, 'Transformation of Micro-finance Operations from NGO to Regulated MFI', (2006), 5, <www.microfinancegateway.org/sites/default/files/mfg-en-paper-transformation-of-micro-finance-operations-from-ngo-to-regulated-mfi-2006_0.pdf>.

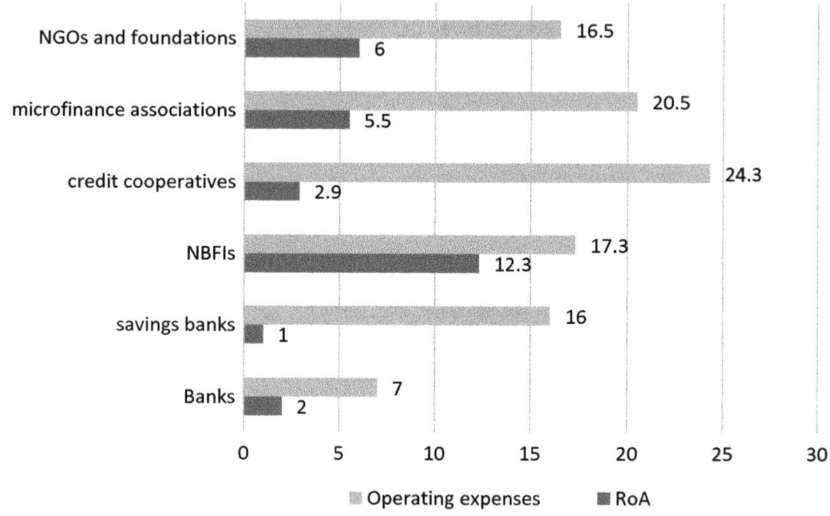

Figure 5.3 RoA and operating expenses per institutional type in Europe in 2013 (%) (Data from Bendig et al., 'Overview 2012/2013')

participation in decisions (*see* CARE and SHARE).[58] However, transformations, especially when imposed or speeded up without adequate planning, have led to additional issues. For instance, the original NGO often remains a main shareholder of the new entity but, considering its not-for-profit nature and structure, might not pass the 'fit and proper test' generally imposed on bank owners also because of lack of a prompt response to capital calls (*see* Chapter 6, §6.f). Moreover, the new entity will have to find ways to compose, in terms of governance, possible conflicts of views among original donors, NGOs and new private investors.[59] Furthermore, the staff might find it difficult to adjust to the new for-profit mission (*see* §d),[60]

58 K. Lauer, 'Transforming NGO MFIs: Critical Ownership Issues to Consider', (2008) CGAP Occasional Paper 13, 1, <www.cgap.org/sites/default/files/CGAP-Occasional-Paper-Transforming-NGO-MFIs-%20Critical-Ownership-Issues-to-Consider-Jun-2008.pdf>; Hishigsuren, 'Transformation', 6ff.; N. Fernando, *Micro Success Story? Transformation of Nongovernment Organizations into Regulated Financial Institutions*, (ADB 2004), 3ff.; C. Frank, 'Stemming the Tide of Mission Drift: Microfinance Transformations and the Double Bottom Line', (2008) WWB Focus Note, 2ff., <www.womensworldbanking.org/wp-content/uploads/imported/pdf/english/stemming_the_tide_of_mission_drift_microfinance_transformations_and_the_double_bottom_line.pdf>.

59 Fernando, *Micro*, 14 (about conflicts of interests between the original NGO and the new entity, leading to bankruptcy). About governance problems related to different types of shareholders: Lauer, 'Transforming', 10ff.; Labie, 'Corporate', 297ff.; C. Lapenu and D. Pierret, 'Handbook for the Analysis of the Governance of Microfinance Institutions', (2006), 43ff., <www.ifad.org/ruralfinance/pub/handbook.pdf>; Ledgerwood and White, 'Transforming', 200ff.

60 Hishigsuren, 'Transformation', 19, 26 (referring to MiBanco's experience).

managers to deal with new responsibilities and more complex operations[61] and exiting managers might try to resist the change and require 'golden parachutes'.[62]

In Romania, only joint-stock companies can register as NBFIs and offer financial services and similarly Bulgaria requires a joint stock company, limited liability company and association limited by shares form for NBFIs (Art. 3a of law on credit institutions). Instead, the UK allows CFDIs under different forms (also not-for-profit) to operate. Hungary, the Netherlands and Italy allow certain not-for-profit forms for credit/micro-credit provision (*see* Chapter 4, §6.c). Some caution towards not-for-profit forms can be recognized even in the French microfinance regime: while allowing microfinance association and foundations to lend since 2001, Article R518–62 *Code monétaire et financier* (*CMF*) has placed a €10,000 ceiling to their business loans (elevated by decree 2016–22 to €12,000 and, for personal loans, to €5,000), justified by 'prudence' and by the objective of keeping banks in the microfinance business.[63]

b MFIs as social enterprises. New hybrid corporate forms

The alleged superiority of for-profit forms in terms of efficiency and in attracting private capital but the existence of social objectives have suggested the creation of hybrid forms for social enterprises (including MFIs), especially when entailing tax advantages.[64] A social enterprise is in fact an operator providing goods and services for the market in an entrepreneurial and innovative way, whose main objective is having a social impact rather than making a profit for their owners or shareholders (using its profits primarily to achieve social objectives) and managed in a socially responsible way (with involvement of employees, consumers and stakeholders affected by its activities).[65] The use of a pure for-profit form would often obstruct grants from non-profit entities and the institutional objective of maximizing shareholders' value might prevent managers from fulfilling social objectives when not aligned with the latter.

Consequently, some regulators have created hybrid forms to conduct social businesses. In the U.S., many States have introduced the Low-Profit Limited

61 Hishigsuren, 'Transformation', 10ff.; Ledgerwood and White, 'Transforming', 68ff.

62 Council of Equity of Microfinance Equity Funds (CEMF), 'The Practice of Corporate Governance in Microfinance Institutions', (2012), 10, 30ff., <www.centerforfinancialinclusion.org/publications-a-resources/browse-publications/384-corporate-governance-in-microfinance-institutions-cmef>; P. Di Benedetta et al., 'Corporate Governance in Microfinance Institutions', (2015), 8ff., <https://openknowledge.worldbank.org/handle/10986/22059>.

63 *See* M. Brabant et al., 'Rapport – Le Microcrédit', (2009) Inspection Générale des Finances 2009-M-085–03, 4.

64 About the advantages of a corporate form to pursue social goals and rationales for extending to for-profit typical not-for-profit tax breaks, *see* A. Malani and E. Posner, 'The Case For For-Profit Charities', (2007) 93 *Va L Rev* 2017.

65 Commission, 'Social Business Initiative – Creating a Favourable Climate for Social Enterprises, Key Stakeholders in the Social Economy and Innovation', (Communication) COM(2011) 682 final.

Liability Company (L3C), allowing limited liability companies primarily pursuing social goals to receive both donations and investments, or benefit corporations (BCs) whose managers can prioritize environmental and social concerns in their decisions. In the UK, Community Interest Companies (CICs) aim at pursuing the community's interest rather than shareholders', are subject to private supervision, need to put in place mechanisms for stakeholders' input and annual shareholders' dividends are capped to a certain percentage of total distributable profits.[66]

Even the Italian system, traditionally characterized by the prohibition against using a corporate form for purposes other than profit-maximization, has created two new hybrid forms. The 'innovative start-up with social inspiration' (SIAVS) is a corporation offering products or services characterized by a high level of technological value and innovation, with a social objective among the ones indicated by the law (required to annually disclose its social impact) but able to tap capital markets (Art. 25.4 Legislative Decree 179/2012). This form basically presents only tax advantages for investors and a very limited scope (e.g. not including microfinance). Nonetheless, law 208/2015 (Artt. 1.376ff.) created, the first in Europe, the 'benefit corporation', inspired by the U.S. model, containing in its charter both for-profit objectives and social goals (even conflicting with the profit motive and consisting in realizing a positive impact or reducing negative effects on people, communities, environments etc.), with managers having the difficult task of balancing such dual vocation. Managers are liable only to shareholders for not achieving social goals, need to appoint a manager in charge of attaining the declared social goals and to annually report on social impact and performance. However, the company's drift from its social goals can be sanctioned under consumer law and misleading promotion regulation.

Hybrid forms are definitely fascinating but often criticized for failing to solve several problems.[67] First, when they entail tax advantages along with private investments, government money ends up benefiting private investors, although these might be justifiable on the grounds of the social welfare attained.[68] Moreover, although explicitly investing managers and the board with the double-bottom line mandate, hybrid forms do not help to solve the inherent conflict between profit and social goals, simply shifting the burden on executives and on dangerous *ex post* evaluations, complicated by difficult and not always standardized social measurements (*see* above Chapter 4, §3).[69] However, efficient hybrid forms should entail

66 *See* J. Horwitz, and R. Culley, 'Profits v. Purpose: Hybrid Companies and the Charitable Dollar', (2014) Law & Economics Working Paper 48, <http://repository.law.umich.edu/law_econ_current/art48>; A. Ebrahim et al., 'The Governance of Social Enterprises: Mission Drift and Accountability Challenges in Hybrid Organizations', (2014) 34 *Res Organ Behav* 81. *See* also D. Kleinberger, 'A Myth Deconstructed: The Emperor's New Clothes on the Low-Profit Limited Liability Company', (2010) 35 *Del J Corp L* 879; K. Westaway and D. Sampselle, 'The Benefit Corporation: An Economic Analysis with Recommendations to Courts, Boards, and Legislatures', (2013) 62 *Emory L J* 1002.

67 *See* Horwitz, 'Profits'.

68 *See* Malani and Posner, 'The Case'.

69 *See* also Ebrahim, 'The Governance'.

flexibility (e.g. allowing the creation of different classes of shares or special governance agreements or structures), not too strict caps on dividends or restrictions on sales (allowing free sales in case of financial need subject to a super-majority vote), disclosure and monitoring of social performance and tax advantages.

Anyway, the existence of multiple and conflicting goals is a complex issue, requiring the use of varied instruments in terms of governance.

c The importance of governance in microfinance for attaining efficiency

Corporate governance has appeared to investors, experts and networks as a priority for the sector since 2011, especially in a context of growing competition, complexity and over-indebtedness, even in Western Europe.[70] Doubts are in fact cast on the ability of MFIs' executives to manage risks and of boards to deal with new risks, technologies, complexity of new products and activities, market demand, competition and regulatory requirements.[71] Furthermore, MFIs' corporate governance needs to deal with dual mission (profit and social) issues (§d).

However, studies have not always been able to prove a positive impact of certain governance factors on MFIs' efficiency and outreach.[72] Since the board naturally plays a fundamental role in balancing different interests involved, some studies explore the effect of board composition on MFIs' activity: local members and informed by an internal auditor seem to improve MFIs' sustainability while members from the local economic environment, donors' representatives, female directors and CEO/Chairman duality improve outreach.[73] As evidenced in bank corporate governance literature[74] and contrary to mainstream corporate

70 *See* CSFI, *Microfinance Banana Skins 2014. Facing Reality*, (CSFI 2014).

71 Ibidem 34ff.

72 *See* Mersland and Strøm, 'Performance and Governance'; M. Pistelli et al., 'Measuring Governance in Microfinance: Initial Findings from a Pilot Project', (2012) 4 Micro-Banking Bulletin, <www.themix.org/publications/microbanking-bulletin/2012/04/measuring-governance-microfinance>; H. Tchakoute-Tchuigoua, 'Determinants of the Governance Quality of Microfinance Institutions', (2015) 58 *Q Rev Econ Financ* 32.

73 Hartarska, 'Governance'; Mersland and Strøm, 'Performance and Governance', 666 (international members of MFIs in DCs seems to be linked to inefficiency, presumably because of their culture of higher expenses). Estapé-Dubreuil and Torreguitart-Mirada, 'Governance', 149 found that female managers are negatively linked with fewer clients and lower depth of outreach.

74 *See* R. Adams and H. Mehran, 'Is Bank Holding Company Governance Different?', (2003) 9 *FRBNY Economic Policy Review* 123; P. de Andrés and E. Vallelado, 'Corporate Governance in Banking: The Role of the Board of Directors', (2008) 32(12) *J Bank Financ* 2570 (discussing the trade-off between the added value in terms of expertise and monitoring of a bigger board and the coordination, flexibility and excessive CEO power problems; the optimal board dimension also depends on the specific role – e.g. monitoring or counselling – of each member and its composition – e.g. insiders or outsiders); K. Hopt, 'Better Governance of Financial Institutions', (2013) ECGI Law Working Paper 207, 60, <http://ssrn.com/abstract=2212198>; G-30, *Toward Effective Governance of Financial Institutions*, (G-30 2012), 35.

governance results,[75] bigger boards (but only up to nine members) are linked to a higher level of efficiency, also thanks to the resulting diversified expertise, and a lower level of performance variability.[76] As opposed to mainstream banks,[77] MFIs with independent directors appear to reach better sustainability and poorer clients.[78] Similar results were achieved by MFIs with experienced or female managers and board members with financial skills.[79] Special board committees on social performance seem positively associated with both financial and social performance.[80] Finally, MFIs with insider board members and lack of CEO/Chairman separation are less efficient.[81]

Recent microfinance crises (e.g. in Nicaragua, Morocco, Pakistan and Bosnia and Herzegovina) have highlighted some governance deficiencies similar to the mainstream ones, such as inadequate risk management, defective compensation schemes (of loan officers and of resigning senior managers in case of transformations), unpreparedness for new services and products, concentration of power in a single person (CEO and Chairman), weak boards (uninformed and without needed skills) (*see* below §d and Chapter 8, §4).[82]

However, a recent survey (although likely capturing only the most virtuous MFIs)[83] seems to highlight a MFI's tendency to have well-structured and diversified boards (with on average seven board members,[84] increasing with the MFI's size, and many independent members), meeting regularly. Most have separated CEO and chairman functions (80%) and many (45%) have the board's oversight of

75 D. Yermack, 'Higher Valuation of Companies with Small Board of Directors', (1996) 40 *J Financ Econ* 185; T. Eisemberg et al., 'Large Board Size and Decreasing Firm Value in Small Firms', (1998) 48 *J Financ Econ* 35.

76 Galema, 'Do'; S. Cheng, 'Board Size and the Variability of Corporate Performance', (2008) 87(1) *J Financ Econ* 157. Estapé-Dubreuil and Torreguitart-Mirada ('Governance', 150) instead found no association between board size or diversity and RoA (only with social performance).

77 *See* Hopt, 'Better', 60 (banks with more independent directors performed worse during the crisis presumably because independence came at the price of less expertise). About data on corporate governance of European banks, *see* F. Arnaboldi and B. Casu, 'Corporate Governance in European Banking', in J. Barth et al. (eds), *Research Handbook on International Banking and Governance*, (Edward Elgar 2012), 588ff.

78 Hartarska, 'Governance and Performance', 1635.

79 Ibidem; Mersland and Strøm, 'Performance and Governance'; Tchakoute-Tchuigoua, 'Determinants'.

80 Estapé-Dubreuil and Torreguitart-Mirada, 'Governance', 148, 151.

81 Hartarska and Mersland, 'Which'.

82 *See* B. Marulanda et al., 'Failures in Microfinance: Lessons Learned', (2010), <www.calmeadow.com/pdf/failures.pdf>; Di Benedetta, 'Corporate', 19ff.; G. Chen et al., 'Growth and Vulnerabilities in Microfinance', (2010) CGAP Focus Note 61, <www.cgap.org/sites/default/files/CGAP-Focus-Note-Growth-and-Vulnerabilities-in-Microfinance-Feb-2010.pdf>.

83 Pistelli, 'Measuring' (the survey was conducted in 2011 among a sample of 162 MFIs across 57 countries, comprising the more active ones in reporting financial and social indicators, therefore likely entailing a self-selection bias).

84 The number of board members generally recommended is seven to nine, although it also depends on the MFI size: CMEF, 'The Practice', 14.

social performance (while only few respondents – 21% – have social performance committees in place). Examples of risk committees and risk managers are instead less widespread despite the evidenced need.[85] Good risk management appears nonetheless fundamental for MFIs and might justify relaxations in Basel requirements and extended range of activities (*see* Chapter 6, §§6–7).

The European MFIs Code, in addition to requiring a detailed business plan and operative manuals (2.1 priority clause; 2.37), mandates the presence of a board, with the majority of members independent (priority clauses) but of audit and supervisory committees (with independent and expert members) only for large MFIs (clauses 2.6–2.12). Expertise in finance, business, management, law and credit risk of board members is required only for large MFIs (clauses 2.24–2.25 and 2.29). The minimum number of board members is set at seven for large MFIs and five for others (2.11), while the minimum number of board meeting in a year at four (2.30). The Code also requires a succession plan for executive management to avoid jeopardizing the MFI's activity in case of a CEO's departure (2.34). It has also a dedicated section for risk management, mandating processes and procedures to identify and manage risks as well as a dedicated senior executive management for risk management (3.1–3.2 priority clauses) and one person responsible for internal audit (dedicated in medium and large providers: 3.20 priority clause), directly reporting to the board.

d Double-bottom line and governance. Corporate governance of banks in the aftermath of the financial crisis

Anglo-Saxon Corporate governance tradition puts shareholders' interest maximization as the fundamental board responsibility, able to solve agency problems ('shareholder primacy'). However, other European countries (e.g. Germany) instead traditionally identify a company's welfare as a whole, including stakeholders' interests, as its core mission and this perspective ('normative' approach) has been central to CSR and social enterprise theories.[86] Nonetheless, such an approach has been accused of conferring to the board excessive discretion, consequently reducing its accountability.[87] Expanding executives' duties beyond shareholders' interest maximization has been seen as risky, distracting them from traditional tasks, leading to excessive prudence and a shrinking job market (with adverse selection problems).[88]

85 *See* Pistelli, 'Measuring'; Di Benedetta, 'Corporate', 16ff.

86 *See* R. Freeman and S. Velamuri, 'A New Approach to CSR: Company Stakeholder Responsibility' in A. Akabades and M. Morsingn (eds), *Corporate Social Responsibility. Reconciling Aspiration with Application*, (Hampshire 2006); T. Donaldson and L. Preston, 'The Stakeholder Theory of the Corporation: Concepts, Evidence, Implications', (1995) 20 *Acad Manage Rev* 65.

87 K. Hopt, 'Comparative Corporate Governance: The State of the Art and International Regulation', (2011) 59(1) *Am J Comp L* 1, 28ff. *See* also R. Galema et al., 'Governance and Microfinance Institutions', in Barth, *Research*, 574.

88 *See* Arena, 'Social', 309. As regards the risks of executives' duties in the mainstream sector after the crisis, *see* Mülbert, 'Corporate'; J. Winter, 'The Financial Crisis: Does Good Corporate Governance Matter and How to Achieve it?', in E. Wymeersch et al.,

A particular and recent application of stakeholder approach can be found in the banking sector. Since banking regulation aims at maintaining the banking system's stability and soundness (*see* Chapter 6, §3), bank executives need either to take into account depositors' and other creditors' interests or to face supervisory response.[89] In fact, in the absence of regulation, bank executives and shareholders would tend to take excessive risks at the expenses of depositors and deposit insurance schemes, especially in non-widely held banks with powerful shareholders having invested only a low fraction of their personal wealth.[90] The importance of bank governance has become more prominent in the aftermath of the financial crisis, where the alignment of shareholders' and managers' interests has turned out to be detrimental,[91] although corporate governance failures are not deemed to be a direct cause of the crisis but only an aggravating factor.[92] Recent regulatory responses place depositors and stability concerns above shareholders' interests. The latter must now be disregarded to maintain stability and banking authorities have the power to interfere for stability's sake.

The CRD IV/CRR package (*see* Chapters 6; 3, §4.b) has in fact implemented a rather intrusive system of corporate governance (especially for banks of significant size, complexity and internal organization), targeting deficiencies highlighted by the financial crisis (e.g. risk management and monitoring, remuneration policies, board's experience and competence),[93] less respective of proportionality issues than EBA Guidelines based on Dir. 2006/48[94] saved remuneration (Chapter 6, §6.a). It entails, for example, the mandatory separation of CEO and Chair functions, the creation of special board committees of non-executive members (risk, nomination

Financial Regulation and Supervision, (OUP 2012), 385 (criticizing the shift in board non-executive directors' mandate, now focused on monitoring).

89 *See* Macey and O'Hara, 'The Corporate'; A. Mullineux, 'The Corporate Governance of Banks', (2006) 14 *JFR & C* 375; Mülbert, 'Corporate', 20ff.; D. Singh, *Banking Regulation of UK and US Financial Markets*, (2nd edn, Routledge 2012), 79ff.; K. Hopt, 'Better Governance of Financial Institutions', (2013) ECGI Law Working Paper 207, <http://ssrn.com/abstract=2212198>.

90 *See* L. Laeven, and R. Levine, 'Bank Governance, Regulation and Risk Taking', (2009) 93(2) *J Financ Econ* 259; L. White, 'Corporate Governance and Prudential Regulation of Banks: Is There Any Connection?', in Barth, *Research*, 344ff.

91 About the worse performance during the crisis of banks with better governance because of such alignment and consequent excessive risk taking, *see* A. Beltratti and R. Stulz, 'Why Did Some Banks Perform Better during the Credit Crisis? A Cross-Country Study of the Impact of Governance and Regulation', (2009) Fisher College of Business Working Paper 2009-03-012, <http://ssrn.com/abstract=1433502>.

92 *See* G. Ferrarini and M. Ungureanu, 'Economics, Politics, and the International Principles for Sound Compensation Practices: An Analysis of Executive Pay at European Banks', (2011) 62(2) *Vanderbilt L Rev* 431; Hopt, 'Better', 49.

93 *See* Hopt, 'Better', 11ff. and 49ff.; Winter, 'The Financial', 372ff.; P. Mülbert and A. Wilhelm, 'CRD IV Framework for Banks' Corporate Governance', in D. Busch and G. Ferrarini (eds), *European Banking Union*, (OUP 2015), 191ff.

94 EBA, 'Guidelines on Internal Governance', EBA/GL/2011/44. See, however, the recent EBA, 'Consultation Paper – Draft Guidelines on Internal Governance', EBA/CP/2016/16 (28 October 2016) assigning some relevance to the proportionality principle and setting criteria for the relevant size and complexity.

and remuneration committees, in addition to the audit one), 'fit and proper' requirements (i.e. knowledge, skills, experience and good repute) and diversity in qualities and competences for board members as well as their duty to dedicate sufficient time to their tasks and the prohibition of multiple appointments. Moreover, the board is responsible for the effectiveness of the overall governance system and vested with the tasks of implementing adequate risk governance and remuneration policies. When designing remuneration schemes, the remuneration committee and management must take into account 'the long-term interests of shareholders, investors and other stakeholders in the institution and the public interest', with a significant part of variable remuneration deferred over 3–5 years (at least 40%) and payed in non-cash instruments (at least 50%), with a 100% ratio ('bonus cap') between variable and fixed remuneration (Art. 94(1)(g), (l)-(m), 95(2) CRDIV).[95] Also the board's personal requirements seem to contradict the traditional shareholder primacy and limit executives' responsibility towards shareholders.[96] Supervisory and resolution authorities have relevant powers, including significant sanctioning powers (Artt. 104 CRDIV and 27–29 BRRD).

The new BCBS Guidelines on Bank Corporate Governance expressly declare: 'The primary objective of corporate governance should be safeguarding stakeholders' interest in conformity with public interest on a sustainable basis. Among stakeholders, particularly with respect to retail banks, shareholders' interest would be secondary to depositors' interest'.[97] Moreover, the board should hold senior managers accountable for their performance, including adherence to risk values and culture (*see* Chapter 4, §4),[98] in principle extending to non-financial aspects of executives' responsibility. Core governance information (e.g. structure, policies, remuneration, board selection) should be disclosed to the public.

The rationales for a special bank corporate governance reproduce the ones justifying special prudential regulation, which rarely apply to MFIs (Chapter 6, §3–4).[99] However, the financial crisis has signalled the relevance of stability and supervision in the whole financial system, therefore suggesting the need to extend governance principles and supervision (although not regulation) to the entire sector (including investment firms and insurance firms), although based on a proportionality principle.[100] MFIs (especially when not accepting deposits) tend not to entail systemic risk and present simple operations, therefore laying the grounds for a simplified governance framework for small institutions (Chapter 6). Furthermore, MFIs present more diversified legal structures and stages of development (from bank-MFIs to holding, big NBFIs and small NGOs), entailing different risks linked to

95 *See* also Artt. 92(2) and 94(1) CRD IV; FSF, 'FSF Principles for Sound Compensation Practices', (2009), <www.fsb.org/wp-content/uploads/r_0904b.pdf> and FSB, 'Implementing Standards', (2009), <www.fsb.org/wp-content/uploads/r_090925c.pdf>.

96 *See* Mülbert and Wilhelm, 'CRD IV', 199; Winter, 'The Financial', 385.

97 BCBS, *Guidelines. Corporate Governance for Banks*, (BIS 2015), 3.

98 Ibidem 12.

99 *See* Mülbert, 'Corporate'; White, 'Corporate'.

100 Hopt, 'Better', 63.

their sizes and types of activities and therefore with distinct needs in terms of governance (§§ 2.a, 3.a).[101]

Anyway, as suggested elsewhere (§c and Chapters 6, §2.a; 8, §3.b), many principles set by international authorities as a response to the crisis are relevant for microfinance too (risk-management and MIS, adequate remuneration incentives, board's experience and skills, compliance and performance monitoring) but should be implemented through less rigid rules, while recent CRDIV governance rules are rather rigid, with limited room for proportionality adjustments.[102]

Furthermore, as anticipated, we need varied instruments to address the double-bottom line dilemma. In addition to a legal form coherent with social goals, we would need to specify in the charter which goals managers should prioritize. Moreover, the charter needs also to specify the instruments used to find a correct balance between the conflicting goals and to compose conflicting views. Governance should in fact include an internal system to monitor not only financial but also social performance, information systems with the same objective and 'social' directors and other bodies in charge of certifying the coherence of the firm with social goals[103] (assigning separate tasks to solve specific agency problems in multi-task environments).[104] Moreover, shareholders agreements should indicate rules about votes (to balance different interests expressed by different types of shareholders with reference to certain decisions and managers' election), exits and transfer of shares (not to hinder social goals). Managers' compensation should take into account social performance also in the long-term.

The European MFIs Code falls short in this regard, not explicitly assigning to the board or other bodies the responsibility for monitoring social performance (not even in large MFIs), only requiring the board to assess MFIs mission fulfilment (i.e. target group reaching and financial performance) at least annually (clause 2.17), focusing more on traditional monitoring functions of financial performance (*see* clauses 2.15–2.18, 2.23 but *see* 2.22 on board approval and veto of pricing policies).

3 Policy concerns. The problem of funding *versus* stability and investor protection

MFIs need a significant amount of funds to cover high operative costs for managing many small loans and coaching services. However, the riskiness of their clients as well as of MFIs themselves shrinks funds' availability. In fact, MFIs replicate informational asymmetries and adverse selection problems typical of SMEs market and often do not have the institutional capacity or information management

101 About different board's characteristics depending on MFIs' maturity, *see* CEMF, 'The Practice', 11ff.; Di Benedetta, 'Corporate', 16ff.

102 *See* EBA, 'Opinion on the Application of the Principle of Proportionality to the Remuneration Provisions in Directive 2013/36/EU', EBA/Op/2015/25.

103 Arena, 'Social', 283ff.

104 *See* Galema, 'Governance', 574.

systems that private investors are looking for.[105] For the same reasons, some obstacles to sustainability consist of regulatory restrictions related to a varied range of policy concerns.

First, regulators might want to restrict MFIs sources of funding to facilitate authorities' monitoring and reduce balance sheet opacity or complexity of lightly regulated operators. However, they might also specifically aim at containing banks and mainstream financial institutions funding to MFIs in order to limit the interconnectedness between the two sectors. New prudential requirements introduced after the financial crisis to maintain systemic stability can further restrain banks and investment firms from providing financing to MFIs (e.g. new capital requirements discouraging banks' exposure to risky counterparts: *see* Chapter 6, §6.c). Deposits are generally reserved to banks, subject to extensive regulation and controls, in order to maintain stability and trust (*see* Chapters 4, §6.b; 6, §3). In some cases, special restrictions might derive from the legal form and intended use of the funds: for example, in countries with soviet-legal tradition not-for-profit organizations have not been generally allowed to borrow to lend (on-lend).[106] Similarly, until 2001 French associations could provide loans to their members but only using their own resources (Art. L511–6(1) *CMF*). The fifth paragraph of Art. 511–6 *CMF* introduced by Law420/2001 allowed, instead, not-for-profit (associations and, since law 77/2008, foundations) MFIs to lend – to certain categories (later expanded) – also money borrowed from banks (and, since 2008, also from individuals under certain conditions), but recently requiring the absence of maturity mismatch (Art. R518–62 *CMF*).[107] In Romania, credit unions cannot finance their lending activity through borrowed money.[108]

Second, regulators might want to restrict the access to such a risky market in order to protect investors (especially retail investors). In fact, the sector needs innovative instruments to reduce costs and enlarge the funding base but not at the expense of investors (*see* Chapter 7). This creates a relevant trade-off between SMEs and microfinance promotion, on one side, and investor protection, on the other (*see* below §§4–5). For example, French law previously prevented MFIs

105 M. Unterberg et al., *Study on the Imperfections in the Area of Microfinance and Options How to Address Them through an EU Financial Instrument–Final Progress Report*, (European Commission 2014); M. Jung et al., 'EIF Market Studies on Micro Lending in the European Union: Capacity Building and Policy Recommendations', (2009), <www.emnconference.org/archives/data/file/EIF%20MF%Studies%20-%20Capacity%20Building%20final.pdf>.

106 J. Reinke and K. Druschel, 'Finance for the Poor: Regulatory Challenges to Private Sector Investment', (2005) 7 *MFC Policy Monitor* 11.

107 P. Valentin et al., 'Le microcrédit', (2011) Rapport d'un groupe de travail du CNIS 125, 14ff., <www.unaf.fr/IMG/pdf/RAP_2011_125_microcredit.pdf>; ADIE, '20 years', 20.

108 Art. 3 Law 122/2009 on credit unions; interview on 21 November 2016 with Maria Doiciu, Senior Consultant Euratom Romania. Instead, credit cooperatives seem allowed to on-lend: *see* Art. 341 of emergency ordinance 99/2006 on credit institutions and capital adequacy (<www.bnr.ro/files/d/Legislatie/EN/E_OUG99_2006.pdf>).

from financing themselves through crowdfunding platforms (i.e. receiving loans from private citizens through an online platform),[109] not only because of the banking monopoly over the extension of loans but also to protect both borrowers and on-line lenders. However, the above mentioned Art. L511–6(5) was modified by the Law 737/2010 allowing MFIs to receive loans from individuals (and since 2015 also from legal persons) under the conditions of the absence of interest rates, a maturity of at least 2-years and risk warnings to lenders (even before the general 2014 crowdfunding law: *see* Chapter 7, §3.b).

Third, caps on interest rates imposed by anti-usury laws might prevent MFIs from covering an important part of their costs but aim at protecting an already vulnerable part of the population, creating another relevant trade-off (*see* Chapter 8, §4).

Finally, while subsidies are generally banned from the economic activity sector because of the distortion effect on competition and consequent EU state aid law, they might be required, especially in less mature markets such as Western Europe, to allow MFIs to reach the poorest and provide accompanying non-financial services (*see* above §1 and Chapters 4, §6.e; 8).[110]

a The range of MFIs financing options

Current methods of MFIs' financing are extremely varied and depend on the type and maturity of each institution.[111]

While representing a fundamental source of funds for MFIs in the past, grants have been fast decreasing, representing in 2013 only 12% of international commitments (cross-border funding) to the sector (almost a fifth of global commitments in debt).[112] In fact, the main source of financing is currently credit (57.5%

109 Such platforms, however, could facilitate loans to foreign MFIs since Law No. 2005–842 of 26 July 2005 introducing the sixth paragraph of Art. 511–6 CMF.

110 *See* also Jung, 'EIF Market', 16.

111 About MFIs' financing, *see* M. De Sousa-Shields and B. King, 'MFI Financing Strategies and the Transition to Private Capital', (2005) microREPORT 32, 1ff., <https://www.microlinks.org/sites/microlinks/files/resource/files/ML1776_mr8_financing_microfinance_institutions_1_.pdf>; J. Trant, 'Microfinance: Investing with an Impact. International Investment and Securities Review', (2009), 46 <www.microfinancegateway.org/sites/default/files/mfg-en-paper-microfinance-investing-with-an-impact-2009_0.pdf>; Dieckmann, 'Microfinance'; J. Ledgerwood (ed.), *The New Microfinance Handbook. A Financial Market System Perspective*, (WB 2013), Chapter 16.

112 *See* E. Lahaye and E. Dashi, 'Spotlight on International Funders' Commitments to Financial Inclusion', (2015), 2, <www.cgap.org/sites/default/files/Brief-Spotlight-on-International-Funders%27-Commitments-to-Financial-Inclusion-Mar-2015%20.pdf>; M. Soursourian and E. Dashi, 'Current Trends in International Funding for Financial Inclusion', (2015), <www.cgap.org/sites/default/files/Brief-Current-Trends-in-International-Funding-Dec-2015.pdf> (however, one third of projects have a grant component); C. Lützenkirchen and C. Weistroffer, 'Microfinance in Evolution. An industry between crisis and advancement', (2012) 7–8, <www.dbresea

of global commitments and – in 2011 – 28.8% of MFIs' funding):[113] from concessional loans by IOs and development banks (DBs – often also providing, alongside big foundations, guarantees) to commercial loans by international or local banks. Equity investments correspond to 15.4% of global commitments (in 2014) and 18.3% of MFIs' funding structure (in 2011).[114] Public financing represents 72% of global funding.[115]

As regards local sources of funding, these are mostly available in South Asia and Latin America (in Eastern Europe and Central Asia MFIs' funding is primarily coming from cross-border sources).[116] MFIs can rely on debt financing from financial institutions (in 2010, 38% of total debt financing) but mostly in mature markets (such as India). Loans to MFIs might entail high capital requirements for banks since the Basel Accord and CRR impose (under the standard approach) burdensome risk weights for exposures perceived as riskier, unless ratings or reliable guarantees are available (*see* Chapter 6, §6.c).

Government and other sources (e.g. foundations and individuals) also partially contribute to MFIs local funding.[117] Few MFIs are authorized to accept deposits but the number of bank-MFIs is increasing and deposits represent 47.56% of MFIs' funding structure, being a fundamental form of MFIs' financing especially in Latin America and Eastern Europe and Central Asia (about Europe, Chapter 6, §3.b).[118]

Generally speaking, investments (also in the form of foreign exchange protection) are comparatively limited but growing fast, mostly through Microfinance Investment Vehicles (MIVs – specialized investment entities),[119] mainly in the form of credit and guarantees for MFIs and only for a minor part equity (*see* §5). The sector has anyway also witnessed some bond issues and IPOs. The first bond issue was by Colombian MFI BancoSol in 1996 and 1997 for a total of USD5 million and backed by a 50% USAID guarantee (private placement).[120] IPOs are

rch.com/PROD/DBR_INTERNET_EN-PROD/PROD0000000000294314/Microfinance+in+evolution%3A+An+industry+between+crisis+and+advancement.pdf>.

113 *See* Lahaye and Dashi, 'Spotlight', 2. R. Sapundzhieva, 'Funding Microfinance. A Focus on Debt Financing', (2011), <www.themix.org/publications/microbanking-bulletin/2011/11/microfinance-funding-microfinance-debt-financing#ixzz3zKlnsaH9>.

114 Lahaye and Dashi, 'Spotlight', 2; Sapundzhieva, 'Funding'.

115 Lahaye and Dashi, 'Spotlight', 1.

116 Sapundzhieva, 'Funding', 4–5.

117 Ibidem (in 2010, 40% of debt financing was from cross-border investors, while the remaining 60% came from local lenders).

118 Sapundzhieva, 'Funding'.

119 Soursourian and Dashi, 'Current Trends'; M. El-Zoghbi et al., 'Cross-border Funding of Microfinance', (2011) CGAP Focus Note 70, 2, <www.cgap.org/sites/default/files/CGAP-Focus-Note-Cross-border-Funding-of-Microfinance-Apr-2011.pdf> (in 2009 almost half of investments in microfinance was channelled through MIVs).

120 MiBanco in Peru went through a public offering of its bonds in 2002 (raising around USD5.8 million) and Compartamos in Mexico in 2005 (USD19 million): Ledgerwood, *The New*, 400.

even scarcer.[121] There are anyway only few MFIs considered 'investible' from an investor's point of view in terms of professional structures and processes (e.g. sovereign risk, absence of capital flows or foreign investment restrictions, microfinance regulation, established MFIs), mostly concentrated in Eastern Europe and Central Asia as well as in Latin America.[122] In 2015, such MFIs were around 500, on the rise compared to the 250 figure in 2009.[123] Equity investments are anyway increasing because of the development of the MIVs sector, new socially responsible investors and EU programmes.[124]

Peer-to-peer lending platforms (P2P) are a recently successful instrument to obtain low-cost funding from the public (*see* Chapter 7, §3).

Anyway, such diversity in capital structure also reflects different levels of maturity and business cycles. In fact, many MFIs start as NGOs funded through donations or concessional loans by international financial institutions and donors while they move to private debt capital with restrictive clauses at more mature stages. Equity becomes available at the latest stages.[125] Debt is generally used to fund portfolio growth and refinance maturing debt while equity is generally required by regulators for prudential reasons or by private investors to secure other forms of financing.[126]

Looking now more closely at the EU, European MFIs find it even more difficult to access affordable funding because of information asymmetries, lack of institutional capacity (including technological infrastructures) and of suitable measurement of social and financial performance (with the creation of a vicious circle, the absence of investments also limiting organizational improvements).[127]

Recent estimations about non-bank MFIs' funding demand highlight their need to refinance the portfolio entirely through external funding (being operational revenues insufficient and having to cap interest rates), also considering a 5% (but 15–20% for riskier borrowers) default rate, with smaller MFIs presenting higher demand for funds because of the lack of economies of scale.[128]

121 Only three: Compartamos in Mexico (*see* §1.a), Equity Bank in Kenya and SKS in India: Ledgerwood, *The New*, 407.

122 *See* Symbiotics, 'Swiss Microfinance Investments. From Early Growth Stage to Maturity: History, Current Developments and New Challenges', (2011), 16, <www.eda.admin.ch/content/dam/deza/en/documents/themen/privatsektorentwicklung/212462-swiss-microfinance-investments_EN.pdf>.

123 *See* R. Etzensperger, 'Microfinance Market Outlook 2015. Growth Driven by Vast Market Potential', (2014), <www.responsability.com/funding/data/docs/es/10427/Microfinance-Market-Outlook-2015-DE.pdf>; Trant, 'Microfinance', 44–45; Dieckman, 'Microfinance'; FitchRatings, 'Microfinance – Testing its Resilience to the Global Financial Crisis', (2009), <www.fitchratings.com>.

124 Unterberg, 'Study', 28.

125 M. de Sousa-Shields and C. Frankiewicz, 'Financing Microfinance Institutions. The Context for Transitions to Private Capital', (2004) USAID microreport 8, <http://pdf.usaid.gov/pdf_docs/Pnadc887.pdf>; Bogan, 'Microfinance'.

126 Ledgerwood, *The New*, 382.

127 Unterberg, 'Study', 15–16, 28; Jung, 'EIF Market'.

128 Unterberg, 'Study', 20, 27–28.

Also in Europe, funding needs depend on the stage of development (Fig. 5.4):[129] new MFIs mostly rely on grants, donations and soft loans but soon need debt financing to expand their operations and products as well as to refinance their loan portfolio. Later on, equity or quasi-equity investments are needed (and possible thanks to increased profitability) to provide security or financial buffers for lending operations (also under lenders' and investors' pressure) and, likely, to transform into financial institutions. Bank-MFIs can rely on deposits as the main source of financing, making debt and equity less needed (but *see* current capital requirements: Chapter 6, §6.c). Guarantees might be needed to leverage private funds and cover high operational expenses without excessively rise interest rates. Operational expenses are particularly high in the case of accompanying services (particularly costly and therefore not covered by operational revenues: *see* Chapter 4, §6.e) but grants or concessional loans to finance them seem generally not available.[130] According to recent surveys,

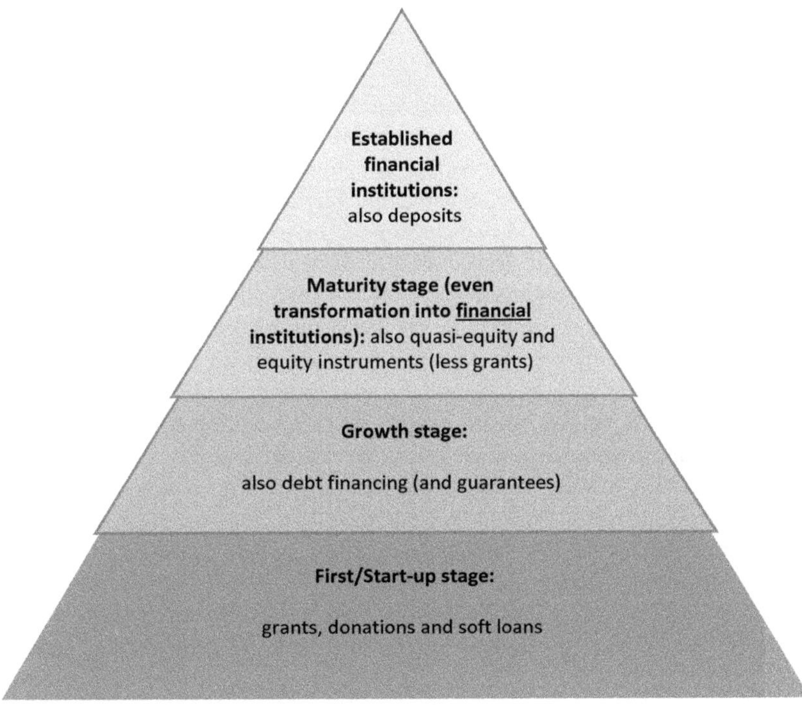

Figure 5.4 Typical evolution in MFIs' funding sources

129 *See* Jung, 'EIF Market', 13ff.; Unterberg, 'Study', 18–23.

130 Ibidem, 18–20, 23, 31, 44–45. *See* also EMN–MFC, 'Policy Note on Sector Proposals to Increase the Impact of Microfinance in the EU', (2015), <www.european-microfinance.org/docs/emn_publications/policy_notes/Policy2015_EMN_oct.pdf>.

MFIs also denounce a lack of resources to implement social performance measurement as requested by the European MFIs Code and EU programmes or to perform institutional reforms as suggested under technical assistance programmes.[131]

Comparing to the above mentioned figures referring to the global market, the EU market presents distinct patterns: the funding structure is led by equity (30.5%), followed, first, by other sources (e.g. earnings, deposits, donations) and grants and, only eventually, debt (*see* Fig. 5.5).[132] Only few MFIs rely on deposits as a source of funding, such as credit unions and bank-MFIs in Eastern, Central and Southern Europe (Chapter 6, §3.b).[133] Nonetheless, there are significant differences among countries: while in Romania, Poland and Serbia MFIs have a quite balanced structure among the above mentioned sources (with a low level of grants), in Switzerland (100%), Spain (73.5%), France (65%), Ireland (50%) and Italy (46.5%) the same mainly rely on grants. Instead, equity represents the dominant source of funding for MFIs in Belgium (66.2%), Germany, Bulgaria and Lithuania (respectively, 54.5%, 51.7%, 50%). Only Italy (Germany and UK to a considerably lower extent, respectively, 6.7% and 3.3%) presents a significant share of guarantee instruments (22.7%) (*see* Fig. 5.5).[134]

Looking at institutional types, bank-MFIs present a rather balanced funding structure with a predominance of deposits (48.6%), while MFIs in the form of associations, NGOs and foundations mostly rely on grants (41–58%). Also NBFIs have a balanced capital structure as banks but rely also on grants (3.1%) and, to a lower extent, on 'other' funds (including earnings and deposits – 32.5%).[135] Public funding (at national, regional and international level) in the forms of grants, concessional loans, equity and guarantees is still particularly important in Western Europe, where banks participation in the sector is still limited and in the framework of their CSR activities. In Central and Eastern Europe there is a higher availability of private funds because of the maturity and profit-orientation of the market and international organizations provide funds at commercial rates but they have been starting to retreat because of stricter regulations and recent losses in the area (*see* Bosnia-and-Herzegovina), and this might worsen because of new CRDIV requirements.[136]

European funds, centrally managed through programmes like Progress or nationally managed with resources coming from structural funds only partially respond to MFIs needs (in particular, guarantees for Western MFIs and debt finance for Central and Eastern ones) because of accessibility problems

131 Unterberg, 'Study', 25.
132 Bendig, 'Overview', 50.
133 Unterberg, 'Study', 20.
134 Bendig, 'Overview', 50.
135 Ibidem 51.
136 TrustLaw, 'Creating Jobs in Europe: Legal and Regulatory Frameworks of Microenterprises and Microcredit in Europe', (2011), 15, <www.adie.org/sites/default/files/links/AdieTrustlaw_2011.pdf>; Unterberg., 'Study', 16, 32.

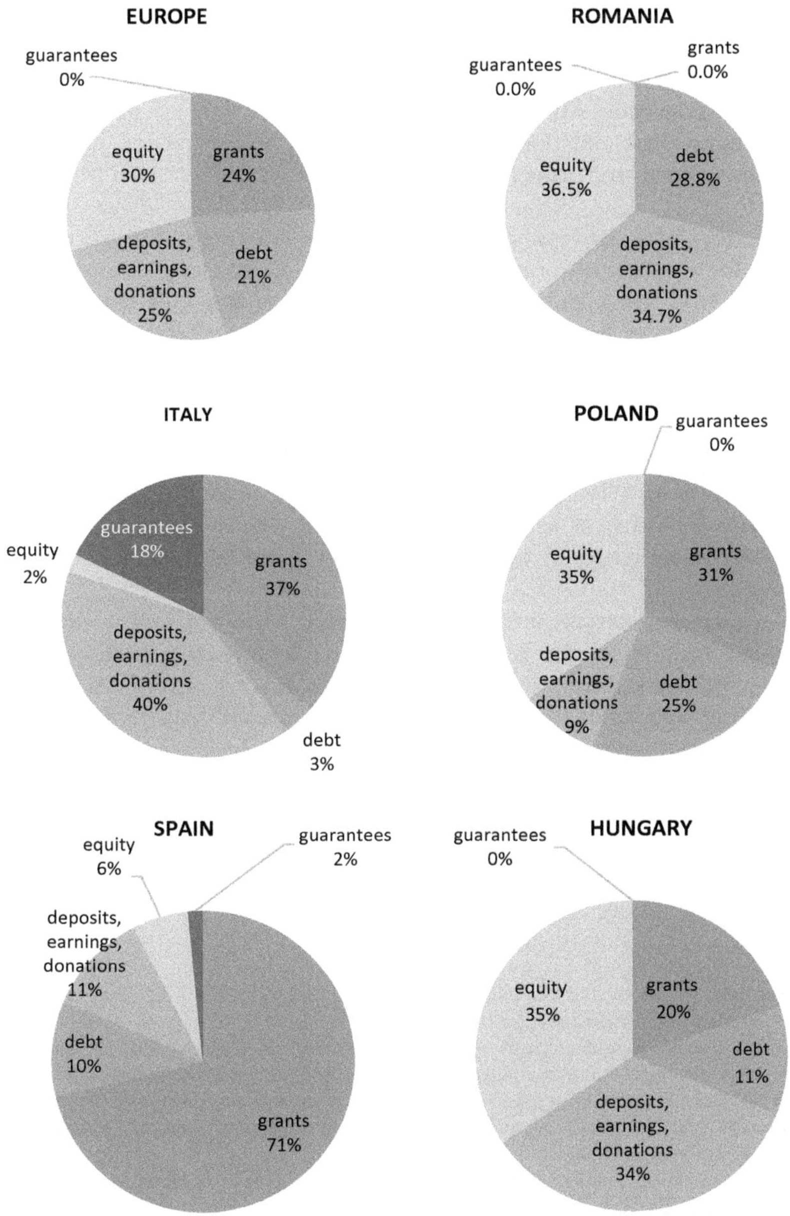

Figure 5.5 Funding structure of EU MFIs in 2013 (examples)
(Data from Bendig et al., 'Overview 2012/2013'

(especially for small MFIs presenting low leverage and high risk) and sometimes lack of flexibility.[137] Anyway, they offer quite varied instruments (e.g. subordinated loans and portfolio risk sharing loans for bank-MFIs, senior loans to mature non-bank MFI, equity/quasi-equity to start-up non-bank MFIs, guarantees to bank and non-bank MFIs)[138] and help attracting private funds, especially needed to counterbalance the negative effect from the financial crisis.[139]

However, from surveys conducted among European MFIs emerge the demand for a variety of forms of financing. First, senior long-term debt-finance with affordable rates and flexible terms for on-lending (all types of MFIs). Second, guarantees, with young and small MFIs from Western Europe reporting the need for guarantees in combination with equity and debt instruments from public actors, while many small MFIs from Eastern Europe seem not to desire guarantees having adequate risk control management in place.[140] Lastly, long-term equity investments, especially in the case of established MFIs both from Western and Eastern countries (with the latter hoping in some cases in forms of subordinated debt with bullet repayment because of restrictions on typical equity instruments linked to their legal status and ownership structure).

From such an overview, it emerges that especially start-up and small European MFIs (the majority in the EU) have problems in accessing funding since EU funding, MIVs and other investors favour large and established MFIs. For this reason, Adie International and Group Credit Cooperatif' have recently created a private placement investment fund (in the form of a Belgian Sicav) in combination with a technical assistance fund to provide socially responsible and sustainable start-up and small MFIs with long-term (ten years) funding ranging from €300,000 to €1.5 million, mainly in the forms of equity or quasi-equity (80%) and senior debt (20%).[141]

137 A recent report by the European Court of Auditors (ECA, *Is EU Financial Support Adequately Addressing the Needs of Micro-entrepreneurs?*, European Union 2015) has pointed at some inefficiencies within EU programmes for microfinance, especially as regards structural funds managed nationally: the instruments were not tailored to the needs lacking an *ex ante* specific needs assessment and there was not any investment strategy plan in place, adequate investment management systems, monitoring and reporting of performance.

138 About available products also depending on the types of MFIs, *see* Bruhn-Leon, 'Progress', 23.

139 Unterberg, 'Study', 30–31. However, the ECA (*Is Financial*, 18) has challenged this conclusion as regards structural funds managed nationally.

140 Unterberg, 'Study', 23–24.

141 *See* M. Nowak and P. Valentin, 'Helenos – Supporting, Financing and Strengthening Equity of Small and Start-up Microfinance Institutions. A Project for Europe and Neighbouring Countries', ('Workshop on Regulations and Laws for Microfinance in the EU', Bruxelles, 20 October 2015), <www.european-microfinance.org/docs/events/15-10-20_Helenos%20Presentation_1st%20EMD.pdf>.

4 Microfinance and investor protection. Special issue No. 1: securitization[142]

Access to capital markets might unlock considerable funds for MFIs (as evidenced by certain successful but disputed MFI-IPOs), although only for the most mature. Nonetheless, tapping retail investors' resources understandably raises relevant investor protection and stability issues (pertaining to the trust of investors in the financial sector and, consequently, to the flow of resources into the system), triggering a number of regulations aimed at protecting investors while enabling firms to access capital. For instance, Prospectus Directive (No. 2003/71 as amended by Directive No. 2010/73) requires issuers and offerors of financial instruments to provide investors with a document containing detailed information about the offer, the issuer and instruments to allow an informed investment decision. The Markets in Financial Instruments Directive (MiFID, No. 2004/39, now repealed by MiFID II, No. 2014/65), imposes a specific authorization (valid within the EU) and strict regime (with burdensome requirements as regards capital, organization and conduct) for firms offering financial services (including reception and transmission of orders, execution, underwriting, investment advice and portfolio management) pertaining financial instruments (including typical transferable securities such as shares and bonds).

Other forms of access to resources from the public used to be less regulated and therefore interesting also for less established operators, including MFIs with expanding operations and capital needs. The financial crisis, involving securitized products and operators from the shadow banking, has convinced regulators to close some loopholes and tighten the requirements for such alternative instruments.

a Securitization and microfinance

Securitization – in the true sale form most employed in the microfinance sector – is a transaction based on the transfer of a part of a portfolio of receivables from an originator to a, generally newly created, Special Purpose Vehicle (SPV or SPE) which, in exchange, will provide cash to the originator from another operation consisting of pooling the receivables and issuing securities to investors. In this way, the portfolio of receivables pass from the balance sheet of the originator to the SPV's one. The latter is a bankruptcy remote entity: consequently, investors can rely, in satisfying their claims, only on the SPV assets (but without the competition of the originator's creditors), and, therefore, primarily on the cash flow from the transferred portfolio.[143]

Securitization represents a viable option only for mature, medium/large MFIs, with demonstrated good operating capacities (in terms of financial track record,

142 For a deeper discussion, *see* E. Macchiavello, 'Securitisation in Microfinance and Global Financial Crisis: Innovation or Trojan Horse?', (2013) 28(3) *JIBLR* 109.

143 *See* S. Schwarcz, *Structured Finance* (3rd edn, Practicing Law Institute 2002); E. Iacobucci and R. Winter, 'Asset Securitization and Asymmetric Information', (2005) 34 *J Legal Stud* 161, 164–65; K. Kettering, 'Securitization and its Discontents: the Dynamics of Financial Product Development', (2008) 29 *Cardozo L Rev* 1553, 1556–1557.

governance, MIS, loan underwriting, managing and monitoring), standardized procedures, homogeneous but also large and diversified microcredit classes, as well as long-term funding plans.[144] Consequently, in the EU context, only some Eastern European MFIs might be eligible.

Observable microfinance securitization transactions can be organized under three different categories.[145] The first one and (up to some years ago) the most used[146] is the issuance of different tranches of securities (with different risk/return profiles) to investors backed by the loans extended to a group of MFIs. Under this scheme, the originator is an investment bank or an international structured fund which may or may not coincide with the SPV issuer ('indirect securitization' or 'multiple-MFI transactions'). The investors are generally DBs (and other IFIs) for the junior and riskier tranches and institutional and professional investors for the senior tranches.[147] The borrowers of transferred portfolio are the MFIs, typically located in different countries and sometimes with different stages of development, improving diversification.

The second type of securitization is a form of 'direct securitization' and 'single-MFI' transaction:[148] a mature and big MFI (originator) sells a relevant part of its microcredit portfolio (but often also of mortgage or consumer loans) to a SPV which issues securities to investors backed by the cash-flow coming from the transferred portfolio. This generally takes place in the local market and, due to the short maturity of microloans, shares some aspects of the securitization of credit card receivables (e.g. the revolving nature of the portfolio transferred).

144 *See* Dieckman, 'Microfinance'; De Sousa-Shields and King, 'MFI Financing'; H. Hüttenrauch and C. Schneider, 'Securitisation: A Funding Alternative for Microfinance Institutions', in J. Pischke and I. Matthäus-Maier (eds), *New Partnerships for Innovation in Microfinance*, (Springer 2009), 286–334.

145 For further information about the distinction, *see* J. De Vries Robbé, *Securitization Law and Practice in the Face of Credit Crunch* (Kluwer Law International 2008), 381ff.; E. Gretch and G. Kochubka, 'Methodology and Assumptions: Standard & Poor's Approach to Rating Microfinance Securitizations', (2008), <www.researchandmarkets.com/reports/3168154/archive-criteria-structured-finance-abs>; H. Byström, 'The Microfinance Collateralized Debt Obligation: A Modern Robin Hood?', (2008) 36(11) *World Dev* 2109, 2112–14; Z. Chen, 'Securitization Microcredit: The Implications of Securitisation for Microcredit Institutions' Human Rights Missions', (2008) 39 *Colum Hum Rts L Rev* 757, 778–81; A. Jobst, 'Mobilising Structured Finance for New Fields – Ready for New Applications?', (2007) KfW Financial Sector Development Symposium, available through researchgate.net; K. Fernandes, 'A Structured Finance Approach to Microfinance', in *Securitization and Structured Finance Handbook 2011/12* (Euromoney Yearbooks 2011), <www.ifmr.co.in/blog/wp-content/uploads/2011/08/Structured-finance-approach-to-Microfinance.pdf>.

146 E.g. BlueOrchard Microfinance Securities I 2004 (BOMS I); BlueOrchard Loans for Development 2006–1 (BOLD I); BlueOrchard Loans for Development 2007 (BOLD II); Deutsche Bank Microfinance-Invest Nr. 1.

147 DB Microfinance-Invest. Fund Nr. 1 by Deutsche Bank was open to wealthy private investors of the bank.

148 E.g. ProCredit Bank Bulgaria 2007; BRAC Microcredit Securitization Series I 2006; Equitas Micro Finance 2009.

The last and newest form of securitization is again a direct one but involving multiple MFIs, with the SPV pooling microloans originated by different (also geographically) MFIs.[149] These kind of deals might be problematic to build because the pool of microloans and relative documentation needs to be homogenous with standard characteristics in order to facilitate its risk evaluation and due diligence,[150] replicating an issue arising in the small business lending context, also characterized by the heterogeneity of terms and business models.[151]

Microfinance securitizations have generally been accompanied by varied forms of guarantees or credit enhancements which attract investors but might be burdensome for MFIs: cash collaterals, over-collateralization (the issuance face value is lower than the underlying portfolio value), substitution agreement (obligation to replenish the basket in case of delinquent loans or cash-flow below a certain threshold), excess in interest spread and guarantees by DFIs or even insurance.[152]

b Advantages and risks of securitization in microfinance

Most of the justifications for using securitization in microfinance are the same as explored in the mainstream sector.[153] Securitization would help MFIs

149 The first securitization of this type was IFMR Capital MOSEC I in 2010, pooling 42,000 microloans (USD6.5 million) from four Indian MFIs (across three Indian states and 23 districts). It involved a 13% cash collateral, in addition to the subscription by IFMR of the junior tranche: *see* IFMR Capital, 'IFMR Capital Structures the First Multi Originator Securitisation in Microfinance', (Press release, 18 January 2010), <www.ifmr.co.in/blog/wp-content/uploads/2010/01/Mosec_press_release.pdf>; A. Sahasranaman, 'Securitization in Microfinance', (2012), <www.vinodkothari.com/Session%204_Securitisation%20in%20Micro%20Finance%20sector_Mr.%20Anand%20Sahasranaman_IFMR.pdf>. Then, IFMR arranged an even larger (USD10.5 million) multi-originator securitization, gathering 49,881 microloans originated by seven Indian MFIs: *see* <www.microcapital.org/microcapital-brief-ifmr-capital-securitizes-15m-in-microloans-originated-by-indian-microfinance-institutions-mfis-asirvad-disha-grameen-koota-mimoza-satin-creditcare-suryoday-sv-creditline/>. *See* also Fernandes, 'Structured', 5.

150 *See* CGAP, 'Securitization. A Technical Guide', (2010), 4, <www.cgap.org/sites/default/files/CGAP-Technical-Guide-Securitization-Oct-2010.pdf>.

151 *See* I. Nassr and G. Wehinger, 'Unlocking SME Finance through Market-based Debt: Securitisation, Private Placements and Bonds', (2014) 2 *OECD Journal: Financial Market Trends* 89, 91, 99; Commission and GBRW, 'Study on Asset-backed Securities: Impact and Use of ABS on SME Finance-final Report', (2004), 42, <http://ec.europa.eu/DocsRoom/documents/3342/attachments/1/translations/en/renditions/pdf>.

152 About the use of these instrument in the BRAC securitization, *see* R. Rahman and S. Mohammed, 'BRAC Micro Credit Securitization Series I: Lessons from the World's First Micro-Credit Backed Security (MCBS)', (2007) MF Analytics, <www8.gsb.columbia.edu/sites/socialenterprise/files/BRAC_Micro_Credit_Securitization_MFA.pdf>; S. Zaman and S. Kairy, 'Building Domestic Capital Markets: BRAC's AAA Securitization', (2007) 14 *Micro-Banking Bulletin* 13; Macchiavello, 'Securitisation'.

153 Iacobucci, 'Asset', 166ff. Schwarcz, *Structured*; Kettering, 'Securitization'; BCBS–The Joint Forum, *Report on Asset Securitisation Incentives*, (BIS 2011), 9ff.

broadening their access to financing, increasing liquidity and diversifying funding.[154]

In particular, it is often claimed that the portfolio of microloans, by its separation from other MFI's assets, can obtain a higher rating and, therefore, cheaper funding from a diversified and broader range of investors (and lower costs and more flexible conditions for micro-borrowers).[155] In fact, tranching and rating reduce the 'lemon phenomenon' problem,[156] particularly severe in microfinance (*see* Chapter 1, §1). Another rationale, especially for regulated entities, is moving microloans off-balance and substituting them with liquidity, freeing up capital, consequently improving credit risk assessment (Chapter 6, §6.c). This would allow MFIs to extend more micro-loans, obtain, on the other hand, cheaper financing, spreading or transferring credit risk, and increase RoE.[157]

However, some traditional arguments in favour of securitization appear weak applied to microfinance. First, a microfinance portfolio, even if separated from the MFI's assets, is not transparent nor easily priced, making it unlikely securitization is able to improve the MFI's assets evaluation and eliminate the lemon phenomenon, unless, at least, the rating agency is a specialized one.[158] Similarly, transferred assets do not represent, generally, a separate and qualitatively different class of the MFI's assets, but often, on the contrary, a diversified range of the MFI's activities, not helping a more precise evaluation of the portfolio or, on the other hand, a deeper monitoring by shareholders over the residual assets and managers' efforts, especially since the MFI often plays also the role of the servicer (though through a formally separate entity and for a fee), keeping managing the transferred microloans.[159] Furthermore, some MFIs (e.g. NGOs) do not have shareholders or the owners are the same micro-borrowers (e.g. cooperatives), and are not in the

154 S. Basu, 'Securitization and the Challenges Faced in Micro Finance', (2005), 4ff., <http://ifmr.ac.in/cmf/publications/wp/2005/5_basu-Securitisation.pdf>; S. Stieber, 'Is Securitisation Right for Microfinance?', (2007) 2 *Innovations* 202, 205; Chen, 'Securitization', 781; D. Alarcón, 'Securitization in Microfinance. Creating Saving and Investments for the Poor', (2008) IDLOMicrofinance Research Paper, at 2.3.2, <www.idlo.int/microfinance/Documents/Publications/19E.pdf>; M. Mostowfi, 'Mobilising Structured Finance for Development – Added Value or Just More of the Same?', (2007), <www.kfw-entwicklungsbank.de/EN_Home/Sectors/Financial_system_development/Events/Pdf_documents_Symposium_2007/Session_4_Expert_Paper_-_Mehdi_Mostowfi.pdf>; Byström, 'The Microfinance', 2115.

155 Mostowfi, 'Mobilising', 5 and 7.

156 *See* Iacobucci, 'Asset', 180ff.; Byström, 'The Microfinance', 2115.

157 As regards the mainstream financial sector, studies evidence that banks tend to look at securitization to reduce funding costs and pursue economic efficiency rather than to exploit regulatory arbitrage: *see* BCBS–Joint Forum, 'Report', 40ff.

158 For a different opinion, Mostowfi, 'Mobilising', 5.

159 Also for this reason some believe that the rating of a securitization transaction cannot really be separated from the MFI's one: *see* FitchRatings, 'Indian Microfinance Securitizations Ratings Constrained by Unmitigated Risks', (2010), <https://asianbondsonline.adb.org/publications/external/2010/Indian_Microfinance_Securitisations_FR_16_Nov2010.pdf>.

best position to monitor. For similar reasons, the argument often used about the easier design of managers' performance-pay contracts also appears weak.

However, securitization can have beneficial effects also on the microfinance sector in general and on investors in particular. The reporting and disclosure systems required in order to engage in such operation would improve the MFI's transparency, management and understanding, filling a relevant and often mentioned gap (*see* §1.a; Chapter 3, §3.c). Moreover, securitization of microloans provides investors with short-term and double-bottom line securities, at least in part resilient to the events of the general sector, improving diversification (Chapter 6, §2.a).[160] Lastly, due to risk assessment standards set by Basel II, banks financing MFIs could actually better reduce risk exposure and be allowed to meet lower capital requirements through rated securitization than by extending loans (but *see* below §c, more recently, about post-crisis reforms targeting securitization; Chapter 6, §6.c).[161]

Some problematic aspects of microfinance securitizations relate to the sector infancy and the lack of adequate infrastructures and institutions in MFIs' countries, leading to considerable regulatory risk (e.g. incertitude on the true-sale effect, bankruptcy remoteness and priority among creditors, lack of sophisticated or adequate supervision).[162] Legal risk can be particularly severe in multi-originator transactions, involving different regulations and government interventions.[163] Instead, these aspects are less relevant in case of local, single-MFI securitizations where only local actors are involved (but likely averting foreign investors).

Also possible inexperience of MFIs officers in the type of transaction or frequent deficiencies of the reporting and credit history systems as well as the possible presence of pledges in previous financing contracts impeding the transaction (e.g. assigning to a certain creditor security interests on all MFI's assets) should not be ignored.[164] Moreover, the MFI's governance is central: the MFI's efficiency might depend on a certain manager being in charge (its departure endangering the operation success) while the legal form might present specific monitoring problems (*see* §2).[165] These difficulties apply to almost every microfinance funding transaction but are especially relevant for a complex operation like securitization.

Other problems derive from the securitization model but are exacerbated by certain microfinance features. For instance, the original form of true sale securitization involved an 'originate-to-distribute' (ODC) model: the originator creates new loans to immediately sell them to the SPV, therefore having few incentives to

160 Stieber, 'Is Securitisation', 207; Dieckmann, 'Microfinance'.

161 In this particular respect, *see* J. Andersen, 'Commercialization of Microfinance. Portfolio Aspects of Turning Banker to the Poor', (2009) Aarhus School of Business Thesis, 26ff., <http://theses.asb.dk/projekter/fbspretrieve/8073/THESIS_FINAL_CONTENTS.pdf>.

162 Mostowfi, 'Mobilising', 10.

163 *See* S. Schwarcz, 'Helping Microfinance Become Commercially Sustainable', (2010) 46(2) *Gonz L Rev* 495.

164 Basu, 'Securitization', 13; CGAP, 'Securitization', 5.

165 Lauer, 'Transforming', 10; Frank, 'Stemming'.

zealously select the borrowers and care about the quality of the portfolio. In a microfinance context, where repayments depend also on the close relationship between the MFI and its clients, the originator generally coincides with the servicer. Consequently, doubts can be cast on MFI's diligence in enforcing a credit it does not own anymore nor bear the risk.[166] This is, however, a critical point, since the quality of the portfolio heavily relies on the selection of the borrowers first and on the servicing work later. A number of techniques have been employed to reduce this moral hazard. For instance, the originator is left with a certain amount of the risk through the retention of a part/all equity tranche (i.e. minimum retention requirement) or through swap/replenishment deals or even maintaining some recourse against the originator.[167] These instruments, however, might, on the one hand, undermine the true sale structure of the deal[168] (partially eliminating the operation advantages), and, on the other hand, fail to completely address the moral hazard (and adverse selection) problem. In fact, the revolving nature of the portfolio sale (because of micro-loans short-term maturity and/or of the substitution/replenishing agreement) puts anyway the originator under pressure to continuously find new borrowers. As evidenced by the recent Indian case, this, combined with competition, can lead to lower lending standards with relevant negative effects on both portfolio quality and over-indebtedness (*see* Chapter 8).

Furthermore, the coincidence of the originator and servicer role aims also at maintaining progressive lending incentives to repay (Chapter 2, §1). This problem is magnified in case of MFI default, where borrowers are aware of both the MFI's and SPV's inability to provide further credit.[169] For the same reasons, in the few observed MFIs' defaults, creditors' recovery opportunities have been jeopardized by the absence of another entity, operating in the same area, with adequate structure and experience, able to collect the outstanding micro-loans in a short time and avoid borrowers' runs and the complete devaluation of the portfolio assets ('back-up service'). These problems are mitigated where borrowers are also

166 About the ODC model *see* among others, A. Berndt and A. Gupta, 'Moral Hazard and Adverse Selection in the Originate to Distribute Model of Bank Credit', (2009) 56 *J Monetary Econ* 725. But *see* U. Albertazzi et al., *Securitisation is Not That Evil After All*, (BIS 2011) (presenting evidence that, outside the U.S. subprime market, banks tend to securitize on average less risky loans than the ones they keep in their portfolios).

167 Alarcón ('Securitization', 2.4.1) suggests imposing requirements such as MFIs' legal structures facilitating recourse by interested parties' or managers' responsibility.

168 *See* Mostowfi, 'Mobilising', 8; Iacobucci, 'Asset', 192. *See* also for a different perspective, Schwarcz, 'The Future'.

169 *See* P. Bond and A. Rai, 'Borrower Runs', (2009) 88 *J Dev Econ* 185; D. Rozas, 'Throwing in the Towel: Lessons from MFI Liquidations', (2009), <www.microfinancegateway.org/sites/default/files/mfg-en-case-study-throwing-in-the-towel-lessons-from-mfi-liquidations-sep-2009_0.pdf>. Stieber ('Is Securitisation', 212) proposes the creation of a 'Microfinance secondary market agency' with the role of e.g. setting underwriting standards and servicing requirements, processing data from servicer and report to investors and monitoring servicers.

MFIs' depositors[170] but securitization is often suggested or needed as funding source for non-deposit-taking MFIs.[171]

As learnt from the subprime experience, monitoring incentives can be sub-optimal. Investors have generally no recourse against the originator except through the SPV and, when retail, no incentive to engage in monitoring. On the other hand, the SPV is a bankruptcy-remote and one-purpose vehicle, with the same receivables as the only assets at stake. Consequently, the multi-MFIs securitization represents a more reliable model since the SPV is often a fund linked with the originator, therefore with its reputation on the hooks.[172]

However, securitization also presents risks for MFIs. Such an operation, in fact, entails relevant costs not only in terms of legal fees, rating, credit enhancements, but also of expenses to implement adequate reporting systems and meet information requirements. The over-collateralization and the cash collateral can affect the MFI's RoE and liquidity (however improved through the operation itself),[173] all this making securitization only fit for mature MFIs.

Moreover, securitization, requiring a homogenous pool of loans for an effective evaluation and pooling, incentivizes the standardization of contracts, with a risk of mission and customized/person centred model drift. Furthermore and most importantly, through the portfolio sale, the MFI will lose control and management over the microloans transferred. Even retaining the role of servicer, the MFI will need the SPV's (and, indirectly, investors') authorization for renegotiating microloans, a relevant power in case of natural disasters or other contingencies, able to prevent the spread of delinquencies within the portfolio.[174] Complex securitizations tend to present the 'stickiness' feature: the existence of different rights of different tranches linked to the underlying assets (loans), create the need for standardization and immutability in the original terms.[175] Moreover, the MFI might be pressured to collect repayments of the securitized portfolio more promptly to ensure investors' returns, adopting stricter and more rigid criteria with some borrowers, leading to an unexpected and unequal treatment among borrowers of the same MFIs. Lastly, MFIs will have to disclose very sensitive aspects of their activity and business models, also to competitors' advantage.[176]

Finally, as regards the economic and business context, high repayment rates, friendly lending practices and resilience have been used to distinguish microfinance

170 Rozas, 'Throwing'.

171 *See* Hüttenrauch and Schneider, 'Securitisation'; Alarcón, 'Securitization', 2.3.2.

172 *See* e.g. BlueOrchard and Morgan Stanley in the BOLD II securitisation.

173 Mostowfi, 'Mobilising', 8 (reporting a 8 to 20% requirement); IFMR, 'IFMR Capital's Response to Fitch Ratings Report on Indian Microfinance Securitisations', (*IFMR*, 29 November 2010), <www.ifmr.co.in/blog/2010/11/> (reporting instead 10–14%, subject to an increase in case of a higher default rates); Jobst, 'Mobilising', 16 (referring to a 15 to 30% first equity tranche for MFIs compared to a 2 to 5% in mature markets).

174 Stieber, 'Is Securitisation', 208; Chen, 'Securitization', 788.

175 K. Judge, 'Fragmentation Nodes: A Study in Financial Innovation, Complexity, and Systemic Risk', (2012) 64 *Stan L Rev* 657, 701ff.

176 *See* CGAP, 'Securitisation', 3, 6–7.

from the subprime market.[177] Nonetheless, the financial crisis and increased competition in mature microfinance markets[178] have led to a rise in MFIs' failures, repayment crises, changes in MFIs business model (e.g. lower underwriting standards, increased exposure for individual and larger loans), decreased growth (fewer microloans with borrowers' running the risk)[179] and to lower resilience (Chapters 2, §2; 6, §2.a). However, the microfinance sector has reported good results counterbalancing such negative signs, especially when compared to the conventional sector (*see* Chapters 6–8) and microfinance securitizations have continued despite the crisis and post-crisis reforms.[180]

c Securitization and post-crisis reforms

The collateral damage caused by CDOs and the OTD model within the financial crisis have determined an unavoidable regulatory response targeting securitizations.

From the first years of the crisis, both international and regional regulators took measures to address securitization's shortcomings.[181] The BCBS modified the Accord amidst the crisis to respond promptly to such flaws: it increased risk weights for re-securitizations, required more careful credit analyses by banks of externally rated securitization exposures, prohibited the use of ratings in case of securitization exposures based on guarantees by the same bank, elevated credit

177 Chen, 'Securitization', 780 (note 193).

178 *See* S. Schwarcz, 'The Future of Securitization', (2009) 41 *Conn L Rev* 1313, 1319.

179 *See* FitchRatings, 'Microfinance'.

180 *See* D. Unnikrishnan, 'MFIs See Sharp Rise in Securitization Deals', *LiveMint* (Mumbai, 1 April 2012), <www.livemint.com/Politics/DAC3gIVnMJOUFi5KrE7prK/MFIs-see-sharp-rise-in-securitization-deals.html>; CRISIL, 'Performance of ABS & MBS Pools', (May 2011), 4ff., <www.crisil.com/Ratings/Commentary/CommentaryDocs/CRISIL-ratings_perf-of-ABS-MBS-pools_may11.pdf>.

181 *See* G20, 'The Leaders Statement. The Pittsburg Summit', (2009), points 11–12, <www.g20.utoronto.ca/2009/2009communique0925.html>; FSB, 'Improving Financial Regulation. Report of the Financial Stability Board to G20 Leaders', (2009), 2, 11ff., <www.fsb.org/wp-content/uploads/r_090925b.pdf?page_moved=1>; IOSCO Technical Committee, 'Unregulated Financial Markets and Products', (2009), <www.fsa.go.jp/inter/ios/20090911/02.pdf>; CEBS, 'Call for Technical Advice on the Effectiveness of a Minimum Retention Requirement for Securitisations', (2009), <www.eba.europa.eu/documents/Publications/Advice/2009/article-122a/Advice.aspx>; IMF, *Global Financial Stability Report. Navigating the Financial Challenges Ahead*, (IMF 2009), Chapter 2, 77ff., <www.imf.org/external/pubs/ft/gfsr/2009/02/pdf/text.pdf>; BCBS, 'Basel Committee's Response to the Financial Crisis: Report to the G20', (2010), 13ff., <www.bis.org/publ/bcbs179.pdf>. For U. S. reforms, *see* Department of the Treasury, 'Financial Regulatory Reform. A New Foundation: Rebuilding Financial Supervision and Regulation', (2009), 44ff., <www.treasury.gov/initiatives/Documents/FinalReport_web.pdf>; S. Schwarcz, 'Securitisation and Post-Crisis Financial Regulation', (2016) Duke Law School Public Law & Legal Theory Paper 2016–7, <http://ssrn.com/abstract=2701556>.

conversion factors for commitments of liquidity facilities to 50% for all maturities, increased risk management requirements and expanded securitization exposures disclosure.[182] In the EU context, in parallel with subsequent adjustments of the Basel framework (e.g. about capital requirements for market risk and trading book),[183] several measures have been adopted targeting securitization: a 5% retention requirement, due diligence requirements for banks investing in securitizations, extensive exposures disclosure, strict rules for originators to treat securitized assets as removed from balance sheet, higher capital charges for securitizations and re-securitizations and for exposures to off-balance sheet vehicles and limits on exposures to certain securitization vehicles (Articles 404ff. CRR).[184] In particular, banks can realize a risk transfer under capital requirement regulation only when certain conditions stand, including the absence of control over the transferred exposures, legal isolation of the same from the transferor and its creditors, lack of clauses allowing the transferor to alter the exposures to improve quality (unless through a third party) or to increase the level of its retained first-loss position or investors' yield in case of deterioration of the portfolio credit quality. Retaining loan servicing does not necessarily account as control of the exposures but the ability to repurchase the exposures and revolving facility coupled with an early amortization provision do.[185]

The European securitization market has shrunk because of such measures and the stigma consequent to the financial crisis, with the majority of issued transactions retained by issuers.[186] Acknowledging the ability of securitization to expand SMEs funds beyond bank credit and to deleverage banks and free-up capital to extend more credit, EU institutions (aligned with G-20, IOSCO and BCBS)[187]

182 BCBS, 'Enhancements to the Basel II Framework', (2009), <www.bis.org/publ/bcbs157.pdf> (so called 'Basel 2.5').

183 *See* BCBS, *Basel II Document. Revisions to the Basel Securitisation Framework*, (2014), <www.bis.org/bcbs/publ/d303.pdf>; Id., 'Fundamental Review of the Trading Book – Outstanding Issues', (2014), <www.bis.org/bcbs/publ/d305.htm>.

184 *See* Directives 2009/111/EC (CRD II) and 2010/76/EU (CRD III) and Regulation 575/2013/EU (CRR). *See* also Regulation 1060/2009 on credit rating agencies (CRA I) and Regulation (EU) 513/2011 (CRA II); Directive 2011/61/EU on Alternative Investment Fund Managers (AIFMD) and delegated acts.

185 *See* EBA, 'Guidelines on Significant Credit Risk Transfer relating to Articles 243 and Article 244 of Regulation 575/2013', (2014).

186 EBA, 'Report on Qualifying Securitisation', (2014), 10, <www.eba.europa.eu/documents/10180/950548/EBA+report+on+qualifying+securitisation.pdf>; Nassr and Wehinger, 'Unlocking', 114–115.

187 BCBS, *Criteria for Identifying Simple, Transparent and Comparable Securitisations*, (BIS 2015); Id., *Capital Treatment for "Simple, Transparent and Comparable" Securitisations – Consultative Document*, (BIS 2015). *See* also M. Segoviano et al., 'Securitization: The Road Ahead', (2015) IMF Staff Discussion Note 15/01, <www.imf.org/external/pubs/ft/sdn/2015/sdn1501.pdf>. For a comparison between EU STS securitisations and BCBS STC securitisations, *see* D. Lerario, 'The Basel Committee and the International Organization of Securities Commissions' "Criteria for Identifying Simple, Transparent and Comparable Securitisations": Not So Simple', (2016), <http://ssrn.com/abstract=2727772>.

have recently taken steps to incentivize simple, standardized and transparent (SST) securitizations, along with creating a uniform framework for all securitizations (as regards due diligence, retention and transparency).[188] Securitizations are simple when they imply a true sale and the underlying financial assets are homogenous, credit-worthy and not already securitized or including transferable securities (Art. 8 Proposal of Securitisation Regulation). The standardization requirement is met when interest rate and exchange rate risks are hedged, the retention requirement is satisfied, documentation clearly defines obligations, duties and responsibilities of the servicer, measures to ensure continuing servicing and liquidity as well as all asset performance remedies, payment priorities and systems to solve conflict of interests among different investor classes (Art. 9). Transparency is realized through access to historical default and loss performance data of similar exposures and a sample of exposures submitted to external verification (Art. 10). STS securitizations are subject to supervision and will receive reductions in capital requirements.[189]

Consequently, microfinance securitizations, while needing to pay attention to new requirements (in particular as regards risk transfer requirements, which might be compromised by repurchase or substitution clauses), could be eased up thanks to the new STS securitizations rules, although the financial assets homogeneity and credit-worthiness requirements might not be easily met.

d Conclusions on securitization in microfinance

Securitization appears a promising financing instrument for European MFIs but, considering its costs, MIS and organization requirements, it remains restricted to the most mature MFIs (especially in Eastern Europe). Furthermore, it presents relevant risks for investors and would benefit from adequate responses to certain critical issues.

First, the sector showed in the past the lack of a system ensuring liquidity. In the wake of the crisis, liquidity facilities have been created by multilateral agencies, development banks and private actors (*see* Chapter 6, §4), despite, sometimes, bad timing.[190] In Europe such role could be easily played by EU specialized institutions and funds.

188 *See* Commission, 'Proposal for a Regulation Amending Regulation (EU) No 575/2013 on Prudential Requirements for Credit Institutions and Investment Firms', COM/2015/0473 final; EBA, 'Report – Proposal for a Regulation of the European Parliament and of the Council Laying Down Common Rules on Securitisation and Creating a European Framework for Simple, Transparent and Standardised Securitisation', COM/2015/0472 final. *See* also the already implemented simplifications for qualified securitizations within the insurance framework and as regards liquidity requirements: Commission Delegated Regulation (EU) 2015/35 of 10 October 2014 supplementing Directive 2009/138/EC (Solvency II) ([2015] OJ L 12/1); Commission Delegated Regulation of 10 October 2014 to supplement Regulation (EU) 575/2013 with regard to liquidity coverage requirement for Credit Institutions ([2015]OJ L 11/1).

189 *See* Schwarcz, 'Securitization'; Nassr and Weinger, 'Unlocking', 131–132.

190 Based on MicroRate's opinion (a specialized credit rating of the sector), The 'Microfinance Enhancement Facility', because of poor timing, started disbursing funding

Second, it would be appropriate to identify as back-up servicer a MFI operating on the same territory as the originator/servicer and with similar organizational structures, from the same network or even among competitors with monitoring incentives (e.g. future financing).

Third, to address the predatory lending problem, investors should impose on the MFIs the implementation of the CGAP CPPs and social performance indicators internationally developed and partially included in the European MFIs Code (*see* Chapters 3, §3.c; 4; 7).

Fourth, to reduce collective action problems and negative effects on clients and loan portfolio, securitization agreements should allow flexibility and easy renegotiations with micro-borrowers.

Fifth, common financial indicators and definitions would also improve transparency and simplify securitization work (*see* §1.a).

Finally, credit rating agencies (CRAs) represent a fundamental part of the securitization problem: EU legislation has tried to address CRA issues introducing a registration requirement, reducing conflict of interests, making methodologies more rigorous and systematic, improving transparency (now also on fees charged on clients)[191] and supervision (*see* CRA I Directive). The recently proposed new rules[192] aim at further increasing transparency and comparability of ratings, improving independence (also through shareholding limitations and rotating obligations), reducing reliance on the same, making CRAs accountable for their ratings and encouraging the use of small CRAs. These rules might further affect the microfinance sector, where the landscape is already complicated by the lack of adequate specialized knowledge and of homogenous instruments to evaluate MFIs, with the risk of over-simplified models like in the subprime case. In fact, Standard & Poor's and FitchRating have tried to elaborate a specific rating model for MFIs[193] but, for instance, compliance with client protection guidelines is not a criterion. Also in this case, international agencies and organizations active in the microfinance field (and EU institutions) should organize their forces in this sense, maybe envisioning a multilateral (e.g. traditional financial actor and CGAP, Grameen bank) credit rating entity or specialized CRAs supervisor, although prospective limits on shareholding in CRAs may restrict in certain cases such option.

European securitization and CRAs rules might at the same obstruct the sector (because of costs) and benefit microfinance securitizations (rising trust). Anyway,

only in 2009 when the funding shortage had already vanished, therefore contributing to excessive liquidity: *see* MicroRate, 'State of Microfinance Investment – 2010 MicroRate MIV Survey', (2010), 7, <www.microrate.com/media/docs/archived/The-MicroRate-2010-MIV-Survey-Report.pdf>.

191 Commission Delegated Regulation 2015/1/EU supplementing Regulation (EC) No 1060/2009 with regard to regulatory technical standards for the periodic reporting on fees charged by credit rating agencies, [2015] OJ L 2/1.

192 Proposed Regulation 462/2013 and Proposed Directive 2013/14/EC.

193 Gretch and Kochubka, 'Methodology'; G. Buyske, 'Microfinance Ratings Market Assessment', (2014), <www19.iadb.org/intal/intalcdi/PE/2014/14412.pdf>.

it might be useful to introduce specific simplifications targeting SMEs and socially responsible securitizations and a mandatory data sharing about SMEs loans (*see* Chapter 8, §1.b).[194]

5 Special issue No. 2: MIVs

Investments in the microfinance sector can represent an advantage for both investors and MFIs. In fact, investors satisfy their expectations for financial return along with social impact while spreading investment risk among multiple institutions, potentially geographically dispersed, and in an alternative sector less correlated to mainstream economic shocks and therefore more resilient. MFIs can expand their access to finance through a variety of financial instruments. Nonetheless, microfinance also presents multiple risks, related to their activities with risky borrowers, often in countries with high political and sovereign risks (Chapter 6, §2.a). Moreover, MIVs tend to invest in countries and regions with mature sectors and established MFIs, leading to a concentration risk.

Consequently, regulators face once again the challenge to balance SMEs and financial inclusion promotion with investor protection.

a Sector overview

Intermediaries currently investing in microfinance are holding companies, non-specialized investment funds and microfinance investment vehicles.

In particular, MIVs represent a broad category of entities (as regards structure, regulatory framework, nature, investment objectives) investing more than 50% of their non-cash assets in MFIs (or other MIVs)[195] mostly in the form of credit (82.6% in 2014) but also through equity (14.7%)[196] or guarantees. Most MIVs (59%) invest in large MFIs (with total assets above USD100 million),[197] offering, in addition to business microcredit (with only 13% providing also social microcredit), voluntary deposits (58% of MFIs active borrowers) and non-financial services (57.9% of investees), while only in 25% of cases having undergone a Smart assessment (*see* Chapter 3, 3.d).[198] When investing in equity, the participation is generally (65% of MIVs) below 25% but representing 57.8% of their investees' board.[199]

194 Nassr and Wehinger, 'Unlocking', 154–155.

195 In 2014 MIVs invested around 80% of their assets in microfinance: *see* Symbiotics, '2015 Microfinance Investment Vehicles Survey', (2015), 16, <www.symbioticsgroup.com/media/79151/2015_09_symbiotics-2015-miv-survey.pdf> (the survey had 84 respondents out of 110 MIVs therefore 76% if the MIVs universe and corresponding to the 96% of the entire market size).

196 Direct equity investment reported a 109% growth rate between 2010 and 2014: ibidem 17.

197 35% of MIVs invest then in MFIs with total assets between USD10 million and USD100 million: ibidem 16.

198 Ibidem 24–25.

199 Ibidem 39.

The sector size in 2014 was estimated at USD10.4 billion.[200] Institutional investors are the main funders of MIVs (51%), followed by public sector investors (32%), except for mixed funds where retail investors prevail (52%).[201] It is a highly concentrated sector, with the top 5 MIVs with a 45% market share (total assets) and the top 20 MIVs with a 77% market share (microfinance portfolio).[202] The weighted average financial performance for 2014 ranged from above 4% for unlevered vehicles to around 2.5–3% for levered vehicles (issuing notes).[203]

b MIVs' regulation in Europe: from un-regulation to over-regulation?

MIVs have been either regulated entities or un-regulated ones and mostly based in Europe, especially in Switzerland (32% of assets) and the Netherlands (24%), where we can find regulatory simplifications and tax advantages for these kinds of intermediaries and investments. Luxembourg has been for years a preferred MIVs' domicile (with 52% of assets in 2013) but in 2014 hosted only 7% of MIVs' assets.[204] They can present varied legal structures: mutual funds, NGOs, cooperatives, structured funds (*see* §4 about securitization) and holding companies (e.g. Procredit and FINCA).[205]

Some funds, especially debt and hybrid MIVs, are open to retail investors[206] and set up as mutual funds, offering investors shares in the fund, which will provide (generally well established) MFIs with short- or medium-term loans (from two to five years) often in local currency (with hedge instrument to protect investors from foreign currency risk).[207] Equity MIVs are generally restricted to qualified investors, funded primarily in the long term by DFIs, international NGOs and, recently, HNWIs and institutional investors.[208]

Until a few years ago, MIVs could easily avoid burdensome regulation. In fact, EU law used only to regulate investment funds covered by the Undertakings for Collective Investment in Transferable Securities Directive-UCITS (2009/65 as modified by Directive 2014/91–UCITS IV), imposing a regime similar to MIFID

200 Ibidem 11.
201 Ibidem 9, 34.
202 Ibidem 14.
203 Ibidem 36.
204 Ibidem 15 and MicroRate, 'The State of Microfinance Investment 2013 – Survey and Analysis of MIVs', 10, <www.microrate.com/media/downloads/2013/11/MicroRa te-The-State-of-Microfinance-Investment-2013.pdf>. Reasons might be found in preferential tax treatment in the Netherlands and increased promotion of MIVs' programmes by Dutch authorities: Interview with Annemarie Arens, LuxFlag General Manger (30 May and 29 September 2016).
205 For an overview, *see* Ledgerwood, *The New*, 390ff.
206 52% of MIVs' mixed funds (which are the 17% of MIVs' assets) are funded by retail investors while in fixed income funds, which represent almost 75% of MIVs' assets, retail investors account only for the 4% of funders: Symbiotics, '2015 Microfinance', 9, 27, 34.
207 Ledgerwood, *The New*, 390.
208 Ibidem 392.

for investment firms[209] as a counterbalance to the European passport. Nonetheless, funds dedicated to microfinance could hardly fit into the UCTIS regime since the latter requires an open-ended structure (instruments redeemable at least bi-monthly), investments of at least 80% of assets in transferable securities traded on a regulated market or liquid financial instruments listed in Art. 50 (excluding loans), while investments in MFIs are mostly illiquid. Member States were free to subject non-UCTIS funds to lighter regulation (or no regulation), contributing to the development of some MIVs' markets (as in Luxembourg, Germany and the Netherlands).[210]

Consequently, the variety of MIVs' legal forms and place of formation along with the presence of different national regulations, prevented MIVs from being subjected to a uniform regulatory regime, especially as regards financial and social performance, hindering investors' choices and understanding of different offers.[211]

Nonetheless, the post-crisis fear towards the shadow banking system has determined EU regulators to adopt, after an intense debate, the Directive on Alternative Investment Fund Managers 2011/61/EU to improve investor protection and limit systemic risk in the collective investments sector. The Directive aims at regulating managers of collective investment undertakings from raising funds from investors with a view to investing in accordance with a defined investment policy for investors' benefit and not already subject to the UCITS Directive (Art. 4(1)a AIFMD), with the exception of holding companies and securitization vehicles (Art. 2(3)a) and g)).[212] The intended targets of the Directive are hedge funds and private equity funds but, due to its wide reach and residual scope, it can find application in case of MIVs.

AIFMD, contrary to UCTIS and MiFID, regulates the managers (AIFMs) and not the products, focusing on stability instead of consumer protection. AIFMs located within the EU are now subject to an authorization and adequate risk management requirement as well as to, e.g., extensive disclosure, depositary, remuneration, liquidity, leverage and capital adequacy requirements (although

209 Except for some special rules about depositary bank, conflict of interests, record-keeping and disclosure (e.g. KIID): *see* Moloney, *EU Securities*, 239ff.

210 R. Dominicé, *Microfinance Investments*, (Symbiotics 2012), 85

211 *See* P. Goodman, 'Microfinance Investment Funds: Objectives, Players, Potential', in I. Matthäus-Maier and J. von Pischke (eds), *Microfinance Investment Funds: Leveraging Private Capital for Economic Growth and Poverty Reduction*, (Springer 2005), 15–27; Dieckman, 'Microfinance', 15; R. Pouliot, 'Governance, Transparency, and Accountability in the Microfinance Investment Fund Industry', in Matthäus-Maier and von Pischke *Microfinance*, 148. For example, M. Kasala ('Labeling Microfinance as Socially Responsible Investing: What's the Risk?', 'The United Nations Principles for Responsible Investing conference', Copenaghen, 2010, 11) reports that many MIVs do not publish on their websites data about the importance given in their investment decisions to MFIs' client treatment, interest rate, lending techniques and how they evaluate MFIs' organizational model.

212 The Commission has adopted a number of delegated regulations complementing AIFMD: Delegated Regulation 694/2014, Implementing Regulation 447/2013, Implementing Regulation 448/2013, Delegated Regulation 231/2013. On the AIFMD regime *see* N. Moloney, *EU Securities*, 269ff.

with some calibrations and subject to the proportionality principle). Organizational requirements, business conduct and conflict of risks duties are similar to MiFID and UCITS ones.[213] AIFMs can benefit from a European passport, which, however, does not cover retail markets (Member States can decide whether to allow AIFMs to market their products to retails in their territories). Among the exemptions, we find a *de minimis* clause available to smaller funds (Art. 3(2)): AIF managers with assets under management (AUM) below €100 million or, if they do not employ leverage or do not have redemption rights for a period of 5 years, below €500 million are excluded from the Directive application and its passport (and subject to a registration-based light-touch regime: Art. 3(3)).

AIFs below the thresholds (or above but opting-in) can however qualify for the application of two other recent disciplines (currently under revision), adopted in the context of advancing the EU SME agenda and imposing lower requirements (about registration, portfolio allocation, marketing, simpler organizational and operational requirements such as own funds, conflict of interest, valuation and disclosure) while recognizing an EU passport (limited to marketing to professional investors).[214] The first one is Regulation 345/2013/EU on venture capital funds (EuVECA) covering funds investing mainly (70%) in small businesses[215] not admitted to trading on a regulated market or MTF. The second is Regulation 346/2013 on European social entrepreneurship funds (EuSEF), primarily (70%) investing in social businesses, ie firms trying to achieve social goals (e.g. sustainable or inclusive development) through the use of business techniques, with a regime replicating EuVECA's (with some special requirements as regards social impact and social return measurement as well as disclosure). Anyway, the marketing restriction (access limited to professional investors or entry ticket of €100,000) would limit the scope to private placement MIVs.

Consequently, MIVs face now relevant regulatory burden if they want to benefit from an EU passport and might need to restrict marketing to professional investors while they might still find some favourable national regulations (lighter regulation and retail access). However, an interesting legal framework for MIVs seems in principle be represented by the recent Regulation (EU) 2015/760 on European Long-Term Investment Funds (ELTIF) which allows AIF managers to set-up (and offer units of) collective investment vehicles providing long-term financing (including in the form of equity, quasi-equity and loans) to undertakings unlisted or listed but with a market capitalization below €500,000 ('qualifying undertakings' under Artt. 10–11) or even credit institutions financing exclusively qualifying undertakings. These funds benefit from an European passport and are open also to retail investors (who cannot generally invest more than 10% of their savings) and are therefore subject to certain conduct (including a suitability test) and diversification rules, leverage and derivatives limits, in addition to the Key Information

213 *See* Moloney, *EU Securities*, 283.
214 *See* Moloney, *EU Securities*, 311ff.
215 Employing fewer than 250 persons and annual turnover not above €50 million or annual total balance sheet not above €43 million (art. 3.d EuVECA Directive).

Document (KID) obligation (of Regulation 1286/2014 on PRIIPs – Packaged Retail and Insurance-based Investment Products). Nonetheless, ELTIF framework seems not to appeal much managers so far.

Anyway, in consideration of the differences in national regimes and investors protection, it is important to consider forms of private regulation (*see* Chapter 3, §§3.c–d) that have been trying to harmonize MIVs reporting requirements. CGAP issued in 2007 'MIV Disclosure Guidelines' with the objectives of improving competition among MIVs through disclosure, making different products offered more recognizable and therefore easily evaluable by investors, raising investors' interest and trust in the sector as well as providing less sophisticated MIVs' managers with useful instruments of analysis and reporting. However, they have not (at least yet) standardized the reporting currency or methods of calculation of many indicators nor mandate some fundamental information. For example, the Guidelines have mandated only since 2010 the disclosure of a benchmark (making easier to conceal losses behind social performance excuses),[216] MFIs foreign exchange risks exposure, hedging and rating. Moreover, MIVs need not to disclose mechanisms to prevent conflict of interests, suspicious operations, to ensure separation of assets and good governance (although all perceived as great risks especially in MIVs field).[217] Furthermore, the Guidelines lack indicators as regards exit strategies (thus, how the MFI is left – particularly relevant also in a socially responsible perspective – and how release an illiquid investment), political or legal risks, type of due diligence process[218] and systems to continuously monitor MFIs' risks and performance (as evidenced in the crises in Nicaragua and Morocco).

As regards social performance, the 2010 edition finally incorporated CPPs (*see* Chapter 3, §3.d) and other social performance indicators, with the effect of stimulating MIVs interested in showing a social mission to carefully select MFIs based on such indicators and implement consistent monitoring systems, reporting mechanisms and contractual clauses with the MFIs. The 2015 survey reports that almost all MIVs have currently endorsed CPP principles (98.9% of respondents).[219] Nonetheless, such social indicators are quite basic and do not reflect all results from other initiatives in the sector such as the SPTF work (not including eg possible non-financial services provided to MFIs by MIVs, the MFIs broader access to local markets thanks to the investment: Chapter 4, §3). M-CRIL and some other rating agencies adopt an aligned but much more detailed social assessment of MIVs, based on the best MIVs' social performance tools and the SPTF's (including indicators like investment outreach to MFIs and countries by

216 *See* Pouliot, 'Governance', 160.

217 *See* B. Mirchandani and H. Finkelstein, 'Microfinance Investment Vehicles: Best Practices and Lessons Learned', (2009) 13 *Microfinance Insights* 35; Pouliot, 'Governance', 171–172.

218 For example, directly managed or outsourced, based on inspections and on ground analyses or only on books and indirect sources: this can heavily influence the investment decision and the evaluation of MIV's expenses.

219 Symbiotics, '2015 Microfinance', 25.

level of their needs and development, imposition on MFIs of sustainable growth targets, investee feedback).

Another interesting initiative is the LuxFlag Microfinance Label created in 2006 to certify MIVs' microfinance focus and some limited features. Until 2011, in fact, such agency has only certified that MIVs (only the ones seeking a return and subject to EU or equivalent supervision) had a microfinance portfolio of at least 50% of total assets, 25% of such microfinance portfolio invested in MFIs rated by recognized specialized rating agencies and the occurrence of certain legal and governance requirements (e.g. distinct legal entity, segregation of functions, regular reporting and disclosure, diversification).[220] In 2011 LuxFlag also introduced social performance standards based on MIVs' adoption of some social performance objectives, of social indicators in the due diligence process, regular monitoring of portfolio's social performance and reporting to investors without imposing certain specific indicators. Such label, although in theory open to worldwide regulated MIVs, presently covers only 26 MIVs.[221]

In conclusion, MIVs represent a relevant source of funding for MFIs but mostly exclusively for larger and mature MFIs. In line with the current policy trend towards SME and social entrepreneurship support, we need partial regulatory simplifications for MIVs to lower costs and also facilitate smaller MFIs' financing and diversification, considering the common investor-type (professional/HNWIs and therefore with lower need of protection), although current reform proposals and the recent ELTIF Regulation might partially attain this goal.[222]

6 Principles and guidelines for regulators

Microfinance dual mission represents a problematic but fundamental issue. Efficiency is essential to reach social objectives and justify microfinance support but might also lead to mission drift. To balance both microfinance natures, we need multiple mechanisms.

First, implementing (even through private regulation) MFIs' transparency as regards FSR, operational expenses and outreach/social performance (following most widespread measurement instruments) can improve financial efficiency without endangering social missions and also allow not-for-profit MFIs to prove their both economic and social performance.

Second, in fact, corporate governance has a fundamental role in maintaining the double-bottom line and an MFI's efficient management. Regulators should not impose the only for-profit form to conduct financial activities (except for the collection of deposits), since ownerless forms might be justified some conditions standing. More generally, there is no evidence of significant diversity in efficiencies

220 <www.luxflag.org/documents/LuxFLAG_Application_Criteria.pdf>.

221 As of January 2016: <www.luxflag.org/labels/microfinance-label/labelled-mivs.html>.

222 *See* proposals at <http://ec.europa.eu/finance/investment/social_investment_funds/index_en.htm> (also a reduction in the entry ticket is envisaged, potentially expanding retail participation).

among different forms, making ownership forms irrelevant (often also in case of hybrid forms) and transformations can be detrimental when rushed or not adequately planned.

Instead, other corporate governance elements are fundamental to fulfil the dual mission. However, although mainstream banks and MFIs might present similarities (e.g. multi-task environment, certain opaqueness), also in governance failures, recent strict corporate governance requirements should not be simply extended to MFIs (unless they are large MFI-banks). The proportionality principle (Chapter 6, §6.a) should allow adjustments of governance requirements (e.g. number, diversity, expertise and dedication of executives, the structure for risk management) to the different structures and development stages of MFIs, especially when not accepting deposits, in consideration of the low systemic risk and simple products and activities but level 1 and 2 reforms might be needed considering CRDIV rigidity. Private regulation (e.g. best practices, codes of conduct and funders' monitoring and enforcement) and flexible governance rules should be able to attain an adequate balance between sustainability and social mission. Empirical studies are not able to evidence a significant correlation between many governance indicators and MFIs' efficiency but lay the grounds for suggesting the following elements, to be adapted to the complexity and variety of activities and structures of each MFI: a charter with a clear priority in the MFI's missions and managers' duties, separate directors/committees dedicated to risk assessment and management, on the one side, and social performance, on the other, internal clear mechanisms to compose conflicting interests among different classes of shareholders (e.g. in terms of vote, exit and transfer of shares), flexible medium size of the board (depending on the stage of development and types of activities), experienced board members, internal auditor referring directly to the board, CEO/chairman duality and compensations based on long-term financial and social performance.

Third, microfinance represents a risky (for the client-type and lack of traditional collateral) and expensive business (because of the small size of loans, labour-intensive model and accompanying services), finding it difficult to access affordable sources of funding (especially small and start-up MFIs). Regulators often further restrict available sources to facilitate supervision, counterbalance light regulation or for stability concerns. Nonetheless, they should allow a varied range of financing tools (including subsidies, crowdfunding and on-lending) in order to diversify MFIs' funding, reducing concentration risk, and facilitate their sustainability without mission drifts. European Union Institutions funding programmes appear particularly important when more targeted (in terms of types of instrument and other needs) and directed not only to established MFIs but also to smaller entities and for non-financial services and infrastructures.

Anyway, regulators should not ignore investor protection issues with special reference to innovative and alternative instruments. In fact, after the crisis, we have witnessed the adoption of burdensome regulations targeting securitizations (and CRAs) to eliminate pre-crisis perverse incentives and identified deficiencies in regulation, with the effect of reducing financing opportunities (also for MFIs) through this instrument. The most recent rules try to recalibrate regulation to re-open such a market but we would need a more specific regime for SMEs and socially responsible vehicles, although securitization might be appropriate only for certain mature MFIs, still entailing high costs and levels of standardization (not always desirable), along with MFIs' adequate structures and information systems. Moreover, we still need to redress some weaknesses within microfinance securitizations: forms of private regulation might succeed in implementing common social and financial performance indicators and definitions (to avoid mission drift and ensure monitoring), back-up services and liquidity facilities (*see* Chapters 3, §§3–4; 6, §4).

As regards MIVs, clarity about applicable regime is still lacking, discouraging investments. Consequently, the sector would benefit from a dedicated and improved regulation for MIVs and social investment funds, with simplifications/adaptations (in line with recent trends in EU law to favour SMEs, although sometimes limited to weak instruments) of AIFMD/EuSEF/EuVECA rules and tax advantages, to lower costs and allow investments also in smaller MFIs. Furthermore, private or hybrid regulation (e.g. conditions to receive tax or regulatory advantages) should achieve a higher level of harmonization in reporting financial and social performance.

6 Dimension IV: Microfinance as an alternative to traditional banking with 'peculiar' instruments. The fundamental problem of regulating microfinance

1 Introduction. Proportionate regulation of microfinance

The present chapter tackles the central topic of regulating microfinance within the context of financial regulation and, in particular, prudential regulation addressing the specific problems of the rationales of prudential regulation, the implications for microfinance and how the peculiar characters of the latter can impact regulatory requirements. It will in fact dissect the fourth dimension, namely the attitude of microfinance to pose as an alternative to mainstream banks and the differences between microfinance and traditional banking, highlighting different risks, weaknesses and strengths, as well as its closeness to the wide category of 'shadow banking'.

In fact, microfinance has often been presented as an alternative to mainstream banks but, especially in Europe, they cannot be completely assimilated since they generally do not accept deposits, do not intermediate resources and do not pose systemic risk. For this reason, the rationales for extending banking regulation to credit-only MFIs appear weak. This reasoning is in line with current proposals in putting forth a 'functional approach' to financial regulation and therefore calibrating regulatory responses to economic functions and activities performed by different actors.[1]

Nonetheless, some countries have concluded differently and a post-crisis policy trend extends also to non-bank operators most banking rules to maintain stability, preventing crises originated in the 'shadow banking' and their spreading to the banking sector. This chapter will therefore address whether we can consider European microfinance as shadow banking and apply its regime.

Furthermore, even when MFIs accept deposits, there might be reasons to adapt banking regulation to the specificities of microfinance. A part of the chapter will therefore compare MFIs with mainstream banks to discuss analogies and differences relevant for regulatory purposes.

The likely interaction between banks and microfinance will also be explored since commercial banks may directly provide microfinance or cooperate with MFIs. A paragraph discusses the related legal issues and the possible regulatory

1 About a 'functional approach' in financial regulation, *see* John Armour et al., *Principles of Financial Regulation*, (OUP 2016); Steven L. Schwarcz, 'Regulating Financial Change: A Functional Approach', (2016) 100 *Minnesota Law Review* 1441.

incentives for banks engaging in microfinance, as well as the reasonable differences in regimes between traditional banks offering microfinance and specialized institutions.

2 Mainstream banking *versus* microfinance: risks, borrower screening and the 'small *versus* large banks' debate

Microfinance has been often presented as a form of alternative banking. Anyway, whether it offers multiple services or only microcredit, it presents special characteristics compared to mainstream providers, therefore requiring a preliminary discussion of risks and regulatory implications of such special features.

In the next paragraph, I will then briefly describe typical banking risks in order to compare them with distinctive microfinance risks (§a). Second, I will focus on the differences between mainstream banks and MFIs in the loan process since credit risk represents the typical bank and microfinance main risk (§b). Third, I will discuss the 'small *versus* large banks' debate in the context of microfinance to assess whether it can bring new elements to the table (§c).

a Banking risks and MFIs specific risks

The feature characterizing the modern bank is its role in intermediating resources between savers who deposit money and borrowers who receive loans to realize their projects, thus moving resources to the most efficient users (§3). Consequently, the intermediating risk, consisting of being able to reimburse depositors even in the case of borrowers' default and of fluctuations in the interest paid to depositors and the one paid by borrowers, represents the main one.[2] The risk of 'depositor runs' is also typical and able to jeopardize the entire sector.[3]

However, credit risk (the risk of borrowers or guarantors' inability to repay) has traditionally focused banks' resources[4] and catered regulators' attention (*see* the 1988 Basel Accord), lending activity being the main one and the selection of borrowers the most challenging part. In order to maximize resources, banks have elaborated standardized methods to screen borrowers based on certain easily accessible and verifiable hard information (e.g. occupation, credit score, collateral). Moreover, they generally require borrowers to provide collateral to reduce moral hazard.

2 *See* H. Schooner and M. Taylor, *Global Bank Regulation. Principles and Policies*, (Academic Press/Elsevier 2010), 2ff.

3 Ibidem 35ff.

4 *See* H. Van Greuning and S. Brajovic Bratanovic, *Analyzing and Managing Banking Risk: A Framework for Assessing and Corporate Governance and Financial Risk*, (3rd edn, WB 2009), 9, 161; S. Gleeson, *International Regulation of Banking – Capital and Risk Requirements*, (OUP 2012), 6. In 2015, 83.1% of EU bank risk-weighted-assets stemmed for credit risk (operational risk 10% and market risk 6.4%): EBA, 'Report – 2015 EU-wide Transparency Exercise', (2015), 20, <www.eba.europa.eu/documents/10180/1280458/2015+EU-wide+Transparency+Exercise+Report+FINAL.pdf>.

Additional related risks are concentration risk (risk of large exposures to the same or related clients), related parties risk (risk of conflict of interest in case of financing to people able to influence the bank and related parties) and interest rate risk (risk of fluctuations of interest rates).[5] Furthermore, liquidity risk is the difficulty in meeting obligations because of the inability to find funds on the market or monetize assets.

Over time, banks have started engaging in diversified activities, often characterized by increased complexity and new risks (e.g. investment activities, derivatives and securitization), increasing opaqueness.[6] Generally, regulators and supervisors have also authorized such change depending on the bank's size and organization structure. In fact, besides credit risk, additional significant financial risks for banks are represented by market risk, which is the risk of changes in the prices of financial instruments, currencies and commodities. Counter-party risk is instead the risk of breach by the counter-party in a financial instrument's transaction.

From another point of view, operational risk should be considered and it consists of the risk of losses from inadequate or failed internal processes, human resources and systems and legal risk included. Among environmental risks, it is worth mentioning country and transfer risks (risk of losses due to events related to a particular country's macroeconomic, social and political environment). Strategic risk includes reputation and governance risks and external business factors (e.g. competition and macroeconomic trends).[7]

However, problems with a bank can have serious repercussions on the entire financial sector as well as on the real economy, as underlined by the financial crisis: 'systemic risk'[8] has become a main rationale for prudential regulation. Although there are many definitions, international financial authorities describe systemic risk as the 'risk of disruption to financial services that is (i) caused by an impairment of all or parts of the financial system and (ii) has the potential to have serious

5 In general about banking risks, *see* BCBS, *Basel II: International Convergence of Capital Measurement and Capital Standards: A Revised Framework*, (BIS 2004); Van Greuning and Brajovic Bratanovic, *Analyzing*, 3ff.; Schooner and Taylor, *Global*; Gleeson, *International*, 6ff.

6 *See* D. Llewellyn, 'Fifty Years in the Evolution of Bank Business Models', in M. Balling and E. Gnan, *50 Years of Money and Finance: Lessons and Challenges*, (Larcier 2013), ch. 9, 319ff.; L. Laeven et al., 'Bank Size and Systemic Risk', (2014) IMF Staff Discussion Note 14/04, <www.imf.org/external/pubs/ft/sdn/2014/sdn1404.pdf>.

7 *See* note 31.

8 Schwarcz defines it as the 'risk that (i) an economic shock such as market or institutional failure triggers (through a panic or otherwise) either (X) the failure of a chain of markets or institutions or (Y) a chain of significant losses to financial institutions, (ii) resulting in increases in the cost of capital or decreases in its availability, often evidenced by substantial financial- market price volatility': L. Schwarcz, 'Systemic Risk', (2008) 97 *Geo. L. J.* 193, 204. *See* also P. Smaga, 'The Concept of Systemic Risk', (2014) SRC Special Paper 5, <http://eprints.lse.ac.uk/61214/1/sp-5.pdf>.

negative consequences for the real economy'. It is generally evaluated based on the size, substitutability, interconnectedness of institutions/markets.[9]

What about microfinance and specifically MFIs?

MFIs are subject to specific risks or specific forms of traditional banking risks because of the nature and characteristics of microfinance.[10] The BCBS recognizes that operators targeting low-income people offer different services and products (generally simpler) from banks and therefore entail different risks.[11]

For instance, MFIs (and microcredit *per se*) are characterized by an intense credit risk. In fact, micro-borrowers generally operate small informal businesses, lack traditional forms of collateral and credit score/history. Moreover, the small loan size and limited borrower's resources prevent MFIs from rationally resorting to legal action in case of default.[12] Consequently, MFIs deploy particular techniques (e.g. progressive lending, group lending, frequent instalments, short maturity, coaching) to reduce typical market failures (Chapter 2). One of those, progressive lending, can nonetheless comport a form of 'contagion effect':[13] since a failing MFI cannot meet a micro-borrower's expectation of a new and bigger loan (which represents his/her main repayment incentive), most borrowers will likely stop repaying at the first sign of their MFI's troubles ('borrower run'), especially where no credit bureau exists.

9 *See* IMF, BIS and FSB, 'Guidance to Assess the Systemic Importance of Financial Institutions, Markets and Instruments: Initial Considerations', (2009), 2, <www.bis.org/publ/othp07.pdf>.

10 About microfinance risks, *see* S. Khan and A. Ashta, 'Managing Multi-Faceted Risks in Microfinance Operations', (2013) 22 *Strat. Change* 1; M. Goldberg and E. Palladini, *Managing Risk and Creating Value with Microfinance*, (WB 2010); BCBS, *Microfinance Activities and the Core Principles for Effective Banking Supervision*, (BIS 2010) 10–11; R. Christen et al., 'Microfinance Consensus Guidelines. A Guide to Regulation and Supervision of Microfinance', (2012), <www.cgap.org/sites/default/files/Consensus-Guideline-A-Guide-to-Regulation-and-Supervision-of-Microfinance-Oct-2012_0.pdf>; D. Kruijff and S. Hartenstein, 'Microfinance and the Global Financial Crisis. A Call for Basel', (2013), <www.ifc.org/wps/wcm/connect/afc335804294f279bf01bf0dc33b630b/Microfinance+and+Global+Financial+Crisis+BASEL+Report-Final.pdf?MOD=AJPERES>; N. Fernando, 'Managing Microfinance Risks: Some Observations and Suggestions', (2008), <www.microfinancegateway.org/sites/default/files/mfg-en-paper-managing-microfinance-risks-some-observations-and-suggestions-jul-2008.pdf>; T. Jansson et al., 'Principles and Practices for Regulating and Supervising Microfinance', (2004), <https://publications.iadb.org/bitstream/handle/11319/5582/Principle%20and%20Practices%20for%20Regulating%20%20and%20Supervising%20Microfinance.pdf?sequence=1>.

11 BCBS, *Range of Practice in the Regulation and Supervision of Institutions Relevant to Financial Inclusion*, (BIS 2015), 14.

12 *See* Jansson, 'Principles'; BCBS, *Microfinance*, 10ff.; Christen, 'Microfinance Consensus'.

13 P. Bond and A. Rai, 'Borrower Runs', (2009) 88 *J Dev Econ* 185; D. Rozas, 'Throwing in the Towel: Lessons from MFI Liquidations', (2009), <www.microfinancegateway.org/sites/default/files/mfg-en-case-study-throwing-in-the-towel-lessons-from-mfi-liquidations-sep-2009_0.pdf>.

Competition in most mature microfinance markets has recently contributed to portfolio quality deterioration through laxer underwriting standards and reduced fidelity,[14] inevitably increasing delinquencies (previously extremely low).[15] The 2014 Microfinance risk survey ranked over-indebtedness, credit risk in general and competition as the main risk factors of the sector.[16]

Moreover, in case of borrowers' default, MFIs are subject to a fast decapitalization risk because of their heavy reliance on high interest rates (and therefore on instalment repayment) to cover operative expenses.

Anyway, group-lending and progressive lending are less common in Europe, especially in Western countries, because of the lack of community identity among borrowers, longer maturities (leading to a new loan before the previous one has expired) and high mobility. Consequently, network systems, personal guarantees, 'references' from NGOs and assistance programmes as well as labour-intensive analyses of financing requests are deployed to compensate (§b; Chapters 2, §2; 5, §1.b).[17] For instance, PerMicro has recently moved from a system mainly based on letters from not-for-profit organizations introducing and assisting the applicant-borrower ('social' or 'reputational' guarantees, not enforceable) to co-obligation or formal personal guarantees from applicant's friends, family members or anyone willing to provide them (maybe not enforceable either for cost-reasons but effectively screening borrowers within a certain community).[18] Furthermore, competition is less intense in Western countries but in more mature markets such as in the Balkans, detrimental competition effects have already materialized and over-indebtedness is a widespread problem (*see* Bosnia-and-Herzegovina crisis).[19]

14 About the negative effects from competition (multiple borrowing, fraudulent transactions, costs for marketing and reduce the fluidity of staff, lower standards), *see* N. Srinivasan, 'Microfinance India. State of the Sector Report 2008', (2009) 86ff., <http://indiamicrofinance.com/wp-content/uploads/2009/08/state_of_the_sector_report_2008.pdf>; CFSI, *Microfinance Banana Skins 2009 – Confronting Crisis and Change*, (2009), 15, 24, <www.cgap.org/sites/default/files/CGAP-Microfinance-Banana-Skins-Jun-2009.pdf>; C. McIntosh and B. Wydick, 'Competition and Microfinance', (2005) 78(2) *J Dev Econ* 271.

15 *See* X. Reille et al., 'The Impact of the Financial Crisis on Microfinance and Their Clients. Results from CGAP's 2009 Opinion Survey', (2009) 3, <www.cgap.org/sites/default/files/CGAP-Brief-The-Impact-of-the-Financial-Crisis-on-Microfinance-Institutions-and-Their-Clients-May-2009.pdf>. About doubts on the reliability of MFIs delinquency data, R. Rosenberg, 'Measuring Microcredit Delinquency: Ratios Can Be Harmful to Your Health', (1999) CGAP Occasional Paper 3, <www.cgap.org/sites/default/files/CGAP-Occasional-Paper-Measuring-Microcredit-Delinquency-Ratios-Can-Be-Harmful-to-Your-Health-Jun-1999.pdf>.

16 CFSI, *Microfinance Banana Skins 2014 – Facing Reality*, (CFSI 2014).

17 *See* also experiments of different lending techniques at MicroBo (Italy): Andreoni et al., *Nuovi bisogni finanziari: la riposta del microcredito*, (Il Mulino 2013), 188ff.

18 Interview on 22 November 2016 with Andrea Limone (PerMicro CEO).

19 G. Chen et al., 'Growth and Vulnerabilities in Microfinance', (2010), CGAP Focus Note 61, <www.cgap.org/sites/default/files/CGAP-Focus-Note-Growth-and-Vulnerabilities-in-Microfinance-Feb-2010.pdf>.

The 2013 European microfinance survey shows an average PAR-30 of 13.1% (close to 2010/2011 figures) and 14.3% with specific reference to EU countries.[20] The highest ratios can be found in Spain (27.3%), Poland (21.8%), Italy (18%), Hungary and France (around 17%) while the most virtuous are Latvia (3%), Germany and Bulgaria (7.6–7.7%).[21] Such ratios seem high, especially compared to MFIs in developing countries but the current level of non-performing loans (NPLs) in the European banking sector is not reassuring either. Although the difference in indicators and respective measurement make data about microfinance and mainstream banking hardly comparable (*see* Fig. 6.1),[22] the 2015 EBA wide transparency exercise reports for 2014 an average aggregated NPE (i.e. non-performing exposure, mainly referred to 90-days past due) ratio of 5.2% (6.2% when only loans and advances) but of 10.7% when considering only non-financial corporations (mostly SMEs).[23] The 2015 ratio for small banks' loans and advances reached instead 18%.[24] Country-data reveal even closer figures between MFIs and mainstream banks especially in countries severely affected by NPL-issues (Fig. 6.1).[25] The average MFIs' write-off ratio in 2013 was 3.5% (with 84% of MFIs with a ratio below 5%), while in the European banking system it was 1.6%.[26] In Western Europe low repayment rates are sometimes reconnected to the charitable approach to microfinance (Chapter 2, §2.a) and to the large use of guarantee funds (often for up to 80% of the loan amounts), reducing incentives to careful selection and repayment collection.[27]

Anyway, European MFIs show a commitment to credit risk-management, with dedicated units and staff but, only less frequently, a formal loan collection service (*see* Chapter 5, §2.c). The European Code of Good Conduct for Microcredit Provision ('European MFIs Code', Chapter 3, §3.c) recommends a loan amount set within the client's repayment ability, sufficient loan duration to ensure affordable and frequent instalments and the use of non-traditional collateral (3.5.2–3.5.5), in

20 Bending, 'Overview', 42 (response rate for this question 63%, corresponding to 95 MFIs).
21 Ibidem 43.
22 According to EBA ITS on supervisory reporting and NPE (Commission Implementing Regulation EU 2015/227), 'non-performing exposures are those that satisfy any of the following criteria: (a) material exposures which are more than 90 days past due; (b) the debtor is assessed as unlikely to pay its credit obligations in full without realisation of collateral, regardless of the existence of any past due amount or of the number of days past due'. Therefore, PAR-30 ratio, being the value of loans outstanding with one or more instalments of principal past due more than 30 days is a more conservative indicator than the NPE ratio.
23 EBA, 'Report – 2015 EU-wide transparency', 26.
24 Ibidem 30.
25 Fig. 6.1 for Italy, Hungary and Spain: ibidem, 27; ECB, 'Financial Stability Review', (2014), 75.
26 Bending, 'Overview', 44 (the highest were in Switzerland 13%, Italy 6.3% and UK 5.5%); ECB, 'Financial Stability Review', (2013), 76–77.
27 For this reason, Art. 13.2 of the recent Italian Ministerial Decree 176/2014 forbids microcredit providers from using guarantee funds to cover credit risk above 80% of the loan.

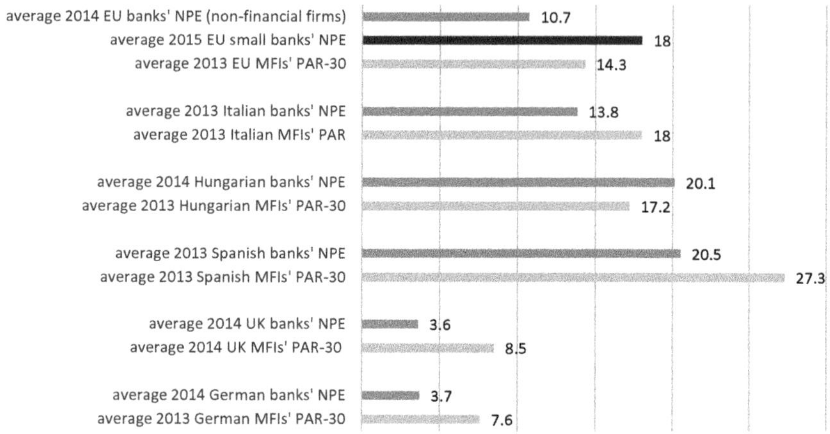

Figure 6.1 EU MFIs PAR-30 and EU bank NPLs (examples) (%)
(Data extracted from Bendig, 'Overview 2012/2013'; EBA '2015 EU-wide Transparency Exercise'; ECB, 'Financial Stability Review', 2014. PAR-30 and NPE are not comparable (and often not available for the same year) but the two sectors do not adopt the same indicators, restricting comparisons)

addition to the approval of the loan by at least two persons (to limit fraudulent and poor lending decisions: 3.6 priority clause).

MFIs provide small loans to a high number of borrowers and therefore are typically not exposed to concentration risk (large exposures). Nonetheless, they generally focus their activity on a certain geographic area and on a certain segment of population (the financially excluded, unbanked, low-income), this entailing, instead, a geographic and social concentration risk (*see* below §6.e).[28] Despite not unanimous views about diversification implications, geographic expansion (at least up to a certain distance, especially for small banks and because of agency/monitoring costs)[29] seems to improve risk-adjusted efficiency, particularly when expanding towards markets with different economic conditions.[30] Instead, product diversification increases volatility and risk (*see* Chapter 4, §5.b).

28 *See* Jansson, 'Principles', 22; T.Jansson and M. Wenner, 'Financial Regulation and Its Significance for Microfinance in Latin America and the Caribbean', (1997), 22ff., <http://ssrn.com/abstract=102523>; P. McGuire and J. Conroy, *The Role of Central Banks in Microfinance in Asia and the Pacific*, (ADB 2000), 43.

29 *See* A. Berger and R. DeYoung, 'The Effects of Geographic Expansion on Bank Efficiency', (2001) 19 *J Financ Serv Res* 163; C. Meslier-Crouzille et al., 'The Benefits of Geographic Diversification in Banking', (2015), <https://hal-unilim.archives-ouvertes.fr/hal-01155170>. Previously and partially *contra*, finding no significant impact on bank performance of local shocks and therefore denying significant advantages from geographic diversification for small banks: T. Yeager, 'The Demise of Community Banks? Local Economic Shocks are Not to Blame', (2004) 28 *J Bank Financ* 2135; W. Emmons et al., 'Reducing the Risk at Small Community Banks: Is it Size or Geographic Diversification that Matters?' (2004) 25(2/3) *J Financ Serv Res* 259.

30 *See* Meslier-Crouzille, 'The Benefits'.

Complexity does not generally belong to the microfinance model, but opaqueness might derive from difficulties in portfolio's evaluation because of borrowers' one and dependence on many factors such as loan agents' identity (*see* §§b, 6.f and Chapter 5, §4.b).

MFIs' liquidity can be puzzling: the short maturity of loans can suggest high liquidity but progressive lending, transforming short-term loans into long-term ones, nullifies such an effect (save in Europe where progressive lending is not much deployed).[31]

Because of the importance of personalized services and direct relationship with clients (for screening and monitoring purposes), MFIs generally adopt decentralized models of decision: this entails decentralization risks (therefore higher operational risk) requiring specific cautionary measures in staff selection and remuneration schemes (not linked to the number of loans but to long-term performance and client satisfaction: *see* Chapter 8, §§1.a, 3.b).[32] In Western Europe, MFIs often resort to voluntary workers to reduce operative costs (*see* in France, Italy and the UK),[33] therefore running the risk of lack of incentives and of technical skills. Nonetheless, the existence of a bulk of professional workers assisted by volunteers can temper such a problem.[34]

Furthermore, MFIs, operating in the field of social and financial inclusion and adopting high interest rates, can enter into frictions with political power (*see* in Morocco, Nicaragua and Andhra Pradesh where the entire sector has faced repayment crises originated from abusive practices by some MFIs and spread by political opposition: Chapter 8, §4).[35]

Reputational risk, as anticipated (Chapter 4, §§4–5), can be particularly severe for microfinance: borrower protection scandals can also lead to sudden stop in investments and liquidity, endangering the whole sector. Especially in Western Europe, where microfinance has a pronounced socially responsible connotation, a scandal could jeopardize the sector survival.

We have already discussed the specific risks related to organizational deficiencies and governance risks (both in terms of legal form/ownership and governance risks linked to the double-bottom line nature: Chapter 5, §2). Social mission *per se* might embody a risk to the safety and soundness of an institution: in fact, social

31 *See* BCBS, *Microfinance*, 11.
32 *See* J. Ledgerwood, *Microfinance Handbook: An Institutional and Financial Perspective*, (WB 1998), 30–31; BCBS, *Microfinance*, 11, 23–26.
33 F. Botti and M. Corsi, 'Measuring the Social Performance of Microfinance in Europe', (2011) CEB Working Paper 11/037, 10, <https://yoursri.com/users/59e6c00a724f29e873a6985cafb31f04/eb7a64112144493e6a8304f4ec293afb/@@download/fs/wp11037%5B1%5D.pdf> (while in Bulgaria, Hungary, Romania, Spain and Germany volunteers are almost absent).
34 Andreoni, *Nuovi*, 57.
35 *See* also Chen et al., 'Growth', 10ff.; E. Macchiavello, 'Microfinance Regulation and Supervision: A Multi-faced Prism of Structures, Levels and Issues, (2012) 9(1) *NYU J L & Bus* 125 and 'Private Regulation and Enforcement in Microfinance: A Multi-Layered and Polycentric Puzzle', in F. Cafaggi and G. Miller, *The Governance and Regulation of International Finance*, (Edward Elgar Publishing Ltd. 2013).

mission can push towards excessive lending or too low interest rates or unsustainable coaching services. For instance, Italian MFIs, despite the ineffectiveness of typical microcredit alternative techniques (i.e. group or progressive lending), hesitate in requiring other forms of alternative or traditional collateral, fearing that this could restrict access but at the expense of high default rates.[36] The same effect can result from the opposite mission-drift phenomenon: growth-pressure from investors and inadequate compensation incentives can lead to over-lending.

Instead, microfinance has traditionally showed a weaker connection with systemic risk than mainstream banks, especially at international level. Microfinance has long been considered resilient to macroeconomic events affecting the general financial system because of the mostly non-public ownership of MFIs, limited international exposure, short average loan maturity, low level of financial and operating leverage, their deep knowledge of borrowers.[37] Nonetheless, the recent financial crisis has showed that microfinance is not immune from global shocks and recent research has attested that the above mentioned factors are now weaker for several reasons. Among these: increased number of IPOs (and therefore public nature of some MFIs), deeper integration with the financial industry (in terms of commercial and cross-border funding as well as more 'formal' clients) and number of international transactions, higher level of MFIs' financial leverage, existence of fewer ties with borrowers (linked to standardization and scale of many MFIs operations) and, in general, risk of mission drift.[38] Anyway, although MFIs' operations are closely linked to a country's economy and their borrowers' economic activities and show more vulnerability (and similarities with the mainstream sector) in mature and high-growth markets, the sector still appears partially resilient. This is particularly true for Western Europe, where the size of the market compared to the mainstream financial sector and distance from the latter limits systemic risk.

Nonetheless, in some countries microfinance now represents an important part of the financial sector, in particular with reference to the most fragile and numerous part of the population, therefore triggering a 'too sensible to fail' public intervention (instead of 'too big to fail'). In fact, in case of a microfinance sector collapse, the most fragile and poorest part of the population is hit, pressing for government's intervention despite the small size of the sector and of MFIs.[39] For

36 *See* Andreoni, *Nuovi*, 175ff. and Chapter 3, §1.

37 N. Krauss and I. Walter, 'Can Microfinance Reduce Portfolio Volatility?', (2009) 58 (1) *Econ Dev Cult Change* 85; A. Gonzalez, 'Resilience of Microfinance Institutions to National Macroeconomic Events: An Econometric Analysis of MFI Asset Quality', (2010) *MI Exchange Research* 1, <http://ssrn.com/abstract=1004568>.

38 *See* Krauss and Walter, 'Can Microfinance'; G. Di Bella, 'The Impact of the Global Financial Crisis on Microfinance and Policy Implications', (2011) IMF Working Paper 175; C. Wagner and A. Winkler, 'The Vulnerability of Microfinance to Financial Turmoil. Evidence from the Global Financial Crisis', (2013) 51 *World Dev* 71; Kruijff and Hartenstein, 'Microfinance'.

39 *See* V. Kothari, 'Microfinance: Choose Schematic Regulation Now, or Face Sporadic Regulation', *Microfinance Focus* (23 Oct. 2010), <www.microfinancefocus.com/content/microfinance-choose-schematic-regulation-now-or-face-sporadic-regulation>.

example, in India, microfinance is an important part of the financial sector, and the Andhra Pradesh region represents one of the most penetrated areas, with 6.25 million micro-borrowers.[40] When a scandal concerning allegations of MFIs' abusive practices in Andhra Pradesh hit the sector and caused the local government to prohibit microfinance activities in the autumn of 2010, the whole Indian microfinance sector was at stake, with negative effects on the local economy and, possibly, even on the national financial system (in consideration also of the exposure of Indian commercial banks to MFIs).[41] Similarly, in the Eastern European area, some non-member countries have long showed incredible growth rates of microfinance, which represented a significant part of both national GDP and of the national financial sector (e.g. Kyrgyz Republic and Armenia).[42]

While the above mentioned peculiar risks are common to all MFIs, intermediating risk and bank runs can obviously affect only deposit-taking MFIs.

b Some characteristics of the microfinance model compared to mainstream banks: borrower screening. The future of new credit scoring and big data

Microfinance has also been developed as a response to the perceived inadequacy of bank models to address the poor's needs. The banking sector has in fact recently been affected by a trend towards standardization, automated procedures and increased distance between banks and customers linked to liberalization and deregulation streams, competition, pressure towards economies of scale, efficiency, profit-maximization and diversification among other factors, with a consequent abandonment of a relationship banking model and a decrease in loans to 'opaque' clients.[43]

40 One in every one hundred Indians is a microfinance borrower and one in fifty rural Indians or one in ten rural families is a MFI borrower: Kothari, 'Microfinance'.

41 In 2010, exposure of Indian commercial banks to MFIs in Andhra Pradesh appeared to reach about USD2.4 billion (USD4 billion with reference to the exposure to the whole Indian microfinance sector): *see*, for a discussion of such case and references, Macchiavello, 'Microfinance' and 'Private'.

42 Di Bella, 'The Impact', 3–4 (fig. 1).

43 *See* M. Petersen and R. Rajan, 'The Benefits of Lending Relationships: Evidence from Small Business Data', (1994) 49(1) *J Financ* 3; R. Cole et al., 'Cookie-Cutter versus Character: The Micro Structure of Small Business Lending by Large and Small Banks', (2004), 39(2) *J Financ Quant Anal* 227; R. DeYoung et al., 'The Past, Present and Probable Future for Community Banks', (2004) 25(2) *J Financ Serv Res* 85, 85–86, 92ff.; A. Berger et al., 'Does Market Size Structure Affect Competition? The Case of Small Business Lending', (2007) 31(1) *J Bank Financ* 11: these studies attest better credit availability for firms in less competitive banking environments thanks to relationship-lending. However, recent studies link only capital market competition (with investment banks and underwriters and instead of interbank competition) with relationship-banking reduction (although using a slightly different concept): *see* A. Boot and A. Thakor, 'Can Relationship Banking Survive Competition?', (2000) 55(2) *J Financ* 679; H. Degryse and S. Ongena, 'The Impact of Competition on Bank Orientation', (2007) 16(3) *J Financ Intermed* 399. About changes in banking business models, T. Gehrig, 'Changing Business Models in Banking and Systemic Risk', in H. Albach et al. (eds), *Management of Permanent Change*, (Springer 2015), 145ff.

In particular, it is a common belief that credit scoring, a technique based on algorithms and statistical data on lending (coming from credit bureaux and single bank's experience) greatly used within the banking industry to predict defaults, leaves out important 'soft' non-quantifiable information with reference to low-income people and their informal activities.[44] In fact, they typically appear opaque because of the lack, for instance, of credit records, financial statements and collateral,[45] preventing them from obtaining credit despite their creditworthiness. Indeed, large banks tend to finance larger, older and more financially safe and transparent firms,[46] with international regulation (e.g. Basel Accord) favouring statistical and quantifiable lending models over more judgmental ones.[47]After the financial crisis, there are recommendations to reconsider the incentives towards hard-information (e.g. financial statements, value of underlying assets) and standardization that have led to a departure from relationship-banking.[48]

Microfinance has supplemented the unavailability of credit scores and hard information with alternative techniques already discussed (e.g. group and progressive lending, frequent instalments and coaching services). Central for reducing asymmetric information and therefore credit risk has appeared the direct and personalized client-provider relationship. This implies, in the selection process, a careful evaluation of the candidate by the loan officer based on previous knowledge, field visits and analysis of other hard and soft data such as borrower's personality and business skills, family context in conjunction with bills and landlord's references.[49]

In this context, the microfinance model appears as a sort of re-discovery of banking services' origins rather than a revolution. In fact, MFIs' lending based on the careful evaluation of the client's personality, capabilities and business plan, without regard to the availability of traditional forms of collateral, used to

44 About the definition of lending technology and the distinction between hard (quantitative data easily transmitted and processed) and soft (more qualitative data) information, *see* A. Berger, 'Small Business Lending', in Berger et al., *The Oxford Handbook of Banking*, (OUP 2012), 531ff.

45 *See* E. Angelini, 'Italian Banks' Credit Approach Towards Low-Income Consumers and Microenterprises: Is There a Bias Against Some Segments of Customers?', in Anderloni et al., *New Frontiers in Banking Services. Emerging Needs and Tailored Products for Untapped Markets*, (Springer 2006), 299ff.; C. Freytag, 'Credit Scoring: Why Sceptisism is Justified', in I. Matthäus-Maier and J. Pischke, *New Partnerships for Innovation in Microfinance*, (Springer 2009), 233ff.

46 *See* Chapter 1, §1 and A. Berger et al., 'Does Function Follow Organizational Form? Evidence from the Lending Practices of Large and Small Banks', (2005) 76 *J Financ Econ* 237.

47 *See* J. Bessis, *Risk Management in Banking*, (Wiley 2011), 221; M. Sriram et al., 'Too Big to Fail versus Too Small to be Counted', (2012) BIS Paper 62, 94, <http://ssrn.com/abstract=2028905>.

48 *See* A. Mullineux, 'Financial Innovation and Social Welfare', (2010) 18 *JFR & C* 243, 252.

49 M. Schreiner and J. Morduch, 'Opportunities and Challenges for Microfinance in the United States', in J. Carr and Z. Yi Tong (eds), *Replicating Microfinance in the United States*, (Woodrow Wilson Center Press 2002), 26–27, 55.

correspond to the original banking model (based on a 'judgmental' model, rooted in the banker's personal experience and evaluation skills), before credit scores, credit bureaux and standard reviews requiring physical or personal collateral took over.[50] Similarly, this also partially corresponds to the way small banks cope with market failures in economically advanced countries (*see* §c).[51] On the other hand, it also shares many characteristics and evolutionary steps (e.g. mission-drift risk, commercialization, expanding activities, centrality of client–provider relationship), with the first not-for-profit or mutual banks and financial providers such as Irish funds or German Raiffeisen credit cooperatives (*see* Chapters 2, §2 and 3, §5a).

Anyway, some commercial banks have recently started adjusting credit scoring models to small businesses[52] and studies seem to link this to an increase in the availability of credit to SMEs, not otherwise served (but sometimes at the expense of pre-existing local markets), although at a higher price.[53] Nonetheless, the characteristics of low-income people (e.g. self-employed, no previous credit history or experience with banks) would require too much personalization (and therefore costs) as well as accumulation of data over time to be efficiently implemented by a bank. Moreover, it is difficult to predict whether and how much small business credit scoring would benefit the 'marginalized' borrowers.[54]

On the other hand, even some pioneer MFIs have introduced credit scoring in order to speed up and improve their underwriting models along with, in some cases, lowering costs. In fact, MFIs generally use credit scoring in combination with their traditional relationship-based techniques (therefore without reducing costs)[55] but this has resulted in an increase in loan officers' efficiency and loans.[56] Credit scoring might also be used by MFIs in economically advanced countries where other unconventional selection techniques (e.g. group-lending) have proved to be inadequate.[57] According to a recent survey (though with a small

50 *See* T. Durkin and G. Elliehausen, 'Consumer Lending', in Berger, *The Oxford*, 559–60.

51 *See* Barth, *Rethinking*, 22ff.; Demirgüç-Kunt, *Finance*, 114–123.

52 *See* Angelini, 'Italian', 308–10, 317–19.

53 Explanations for the increased SME credit are the reduction of costs (only when used alone) and of the risk of discrimination by loan officers as well as, in general, of information asymmetries: *See* W. Frame et al., 'Credit Scoring and the Availability of Small Business Credit in Low- and Moderate-Income Areas', (2004) 39(1) *Financ Rev* 35 (also warning against the risks from credit scoring models not representative of SMEs, especially in low-income areas); A. Berger et al. 'Credit Scoring and the Availability, Price, and Risk of Small Business Credit', (2005) 37(2) *J Money Credit Bank* 19 (reporting an increase in small business loan ratios, as well as in loan prices and loan risks suggesting a greater availability of credit to risky and otherwise not served SMEs willing to pay high prices).

54 *See* Angelini, 'Italian', 308–310, 317–319.

55 *See* G. Ivatury, 'Using Technology to Build Inclusive Financial Systems', in Matthäus-Maier and Pischke, *New Partnerships*, 159; M. Schreiner, 'Can Credit Scoring Help Attract Profit-Minded Investors to Microcredit?', ibidem, 207ff.

56 *See* V. Bumacov et al., 'The Use of Credit Scoring in Microfinance Institutions', (2014) 23 *Strat Change* 401.

57 *See* Schreiner and Morduch, 'Opportunities', 55.

sample), most European MFs started using credit scoring in 2008 (46.6% of respondents) or plan to use it within two years (a quarter of respondents), in order to screen or monitor clients (and reduce credit risk) and also to tailor products.[58] Anyway, MFIs tend to use credit scoring to screen applicants only in combination with loan officers' opinions and other hard data (e.g. credit bureau, financial data, credit history) (83.3%) or other soft data (e.g. personal information, peers' opinion) (75%), with only a few relying on the same as the sole screening tool (4.2%).[59] Credit scoring models employed have generally been specifically elaborated based on credit experts' experience (62%) and on a MFI's sample of past borrowers (46%) and rely on clients' credit history (92%), business financial data (80%), personal financial data and socio-economic factors (76%), in addition to credit bureaux reports (64%).[60]

Nonetheless, the lack of information about low-income borrowers and adequate MFI's internal structure to collect and elaborate information about clients, as well the peculiarities of microfinance models, reduce the availability of appropriate credit scoring, at least as the only method.[61] In particular, credit bureaus, more available in economically advanced countries than in developing ones, are not always useful to this end since they generally report only on formal loans (instead of also utilities bills or informal credit) and negative data (only bad loans) (Chapter 8, §1.b).[62]

However, an interesting new scenario has recently opened up for microfinance's credit scoring with internet-based technologies. We can in fact witness to the creation of 'net banks' and information-analysis platforms that use 'big data' (i.e. information about users' spending habits, payments, browsing history, messaging and call activity, collected through social networks, mobile providers, search engines and online commerce websites) and mobile phone payment history, often in combination with psychometric principles, to score loan applicants.[63] This would allow a fast and inexpensive screening with easily available data with

58 D. Forcella, 'European Microfinance Credit Risk Management and Credit Scoring. State of Art and Perspective', (2015) 15–18, 20, <www.european-microfinance.org/docs/emn_publications/other_emn_publications/EMN_RiskCredit%20v3C.pdf>.

59 Ibidem 19. For instance, the Italian MFI PerMicro use credit scoring (based on internal statistics) along with typical microcredit personal screening and a negative credit scoring does not necessarily impede loan disbursement but requires a executive committee decision: Interview on 22 November 2016 with Andrea Limone.

60 Ibidem 17.

61 Ibidem 11, 20 (reporting that the majority of MFIs not adopting credit scoring do so because they do not have the structure or access to data required to develop a credit scoring model or trusting more loan officers' judgment).

62 Ibidem 12; EMN Idea-Lab, 'Credit Scoring in the European (Micro)finance Sector', (2015), 8ff., <www.european-microfinance.org/docs/activities/think_tanks_idea_labs/SCORING_EMN2015_LINKS_2.pdf>.

63 Forcella, 'European', 12; EMN Idea-Lab, 'Credit', 15ff.; N. Packin and Y. Lev Aretz, 'Big Data and Social Netbanks: Are You Ready to Replace Your Bank?', (2015) Columbia Public Law Research Paper 14-460, <http://ssrn.com/abstract=2567135>.

reference also to low-income people. At present, it does not represent a widespread tool in microfinance (only 4% of respondent European MFIs),[64] but it has a relevant potential for the sector. Nonetheless, MFIs need to carefully adapt such a method since big data algorithms might lead to inaccurate (not encompassing other relevant data), unfair (denying credit to creditworthy subjects based on unrelated or private behaviours) or discriminatory results, with negative consequences also in terms of MFIs reputation and social impact.[65] Furthermore, EU and national regulations protect personal data[66] so that MFIs might not be able to legally use or share certain information, unless the client has been clearly informed and has truly understood the possible use of the data.[67] The recent Regulation on data protection (No. 2016/679/EU) might in fact restrain the use of big data for credit scoring: Art. 20 recognizes the right not to be subject to decisions based only on automated processes, including profiling, unless with his/her express consent and anyway 'to obtain human intervention on the part of the controller, to express his or her point of view and to contest the decision' (*see* also recital 71).

c Is 'small' beautiful? Lending models, diversification and SMEs development

MFIs are typically small and local and somewhere pressured to scale-up to reach economies of scale and therefore higher levels of efficiency and outreach, while others stay small, avoid mission-drift and serve the poorest ('microfinance schism': Chapter 4, §4 and Chapter 5, §§1–2). This recalls the large banks *versus* small banks debate in the mainstream literature.

In fact, studies, on the one hand, show the large banks' important role in spurring a country's economic development and their advantages over small banks. Advantages would consist, among others, in lower capital ratios due to the easy capital calls or stock issues, lower costs per transaction, investments in new

64 Forcella, 'European', 18.

65 *See* K. Judge, 'The Future of Direct Finance: The Diverging Paths of Peer-to-Peer Lending and Kickstarter', (2015), Columbia Law and Economics Working Paper 520, 120ff., <http://ssrn.com/abstract=2662697>; S. Lohr, 'Creditworthy? Let's Consider Capitalization', *The New York Times* (New York, 19 January 2015) A1; G. Chen and X. Faz, 'The Potential of Digital Data: How Far Can It Advance Financial Inclusion?', (2015) CGAP Focus Note 100, 9–10, <www.cgap.org/sites/default/files/Focus-Note-The-Potential-of-Digital-Data-Jan-2015.pdf>.

66 *See* the EU Data Protection Directive 95/46/EC (recently replaced by the General Data Protection Regulation 2016/679/EU) but also Directives on Electronic Communications and Privacy, on Unfair Commercial Practices, E-Commerce, on Unfair Contract Terms and on Distance Marketing of Financial Services. With particular reference to payment institutions and credit institutions' use of client data, Article 94 (2) PSD2 and 62 CRDIV and 172(1)(e)(iii) CRR: *see* EBA, 'Discussion Paper on Innovative Uses of Consumer Data by Financial Institutions' (2016), EBA/DP/2016/01, 11–12.

67 *See* also EBA, 'Discussion Paper', 23–26.

technologies, diversified activities and portfolios with lower risk, ability to offer larger loans and higher interest rates on deposits, increasing returns with scaling-up to a certain size.[68]

On the other hand, there is also evidence that larger scales imply larger and systemic risks[69] and that small banks (e.g. savings banks and cooperative banks) are able to promote more effectively SMEs' growth and the development of the poorest regions as well as SMEs' preference for small banks.[70] As just pointed out with specific reference to MFIs (above §b), small banks tend to rely more on the borrower's character and projects when evaluating his/her loan requests while large banks rely on hard information.[71] The former in fact appear better equipped to select among more 'opaque' borrowers, gathering 'soft' information about them through loan officers geographically, culturally and socially closer to the same, experienced in evaluating people, with more discretion as well as without such information having to travel up a long chain of command.[72]

Notwithstanding the current economic environment, research shows that small banks can survive and even grow more than big banks, exploiting their competitive advantages. These consist, in addition to particular borrowers' screening,

68 *See* P. McAllister and D. McManus, 'Resolving the Scale Efficiency Puzzle in Banking', (1993) 17(2/3) *J Bank Financ* 389; D. Wheelock and P. Wilson, 'New Evidence on Returns to Scale and Product Mix Among U.S. Commercial Banks', (2001) 47 *J Monetary Econ* 653 and Id., 'Do Large Banks have Lower Costs? New Estimates of Returns to Scale for US Banks', (2012) 44(1) *J Money Credit Bank* 171.

69 *See* J. Hughes et al., 'Are Scale Economies in Banking Elusive or Illusive? Evidence Obtained by Incorporating Capital Structure and Risk-Taking into Models of Bank Production', (2001) 25 *J Bank Financ* 2169; Laeven, 'Bank Size'.

70 *See* L. Nakamura, 'Small Borrowers and the Survival of the Small Bank: Is Mouse Bank Mighty or Mickey?', (1994) *FRBP Economic Review Recent* 3; Cole, 'Cookie-Cutter'; H. Hakenes et al., 'Small Banks and Local Economic Development', (2009), <http://ssrn.com/abstract=1343048>.

71 *See* L. Whiteman, 'Small Banks Say One-on-One Beats Credit Scoring Models', (1998) 163(193) *American Banker* 13; Cole, 'Cookie-Cutter'; Berger et al., 'Does Market Size'; Berger, 'Small Business Lending', 534. However, Berger et al. ('The Surprising Use of Credit Scoring in Small Business Lending by Community Banks and the Attendant Effects on Credit Availability and Risk', (2011) 39 *J Financ Serv Res* 1) found that 46% of US Community Banks surveyed in 2005 were using some form of credit scoring too and, in particular, that 86% of them adopted exclusively consumer credit scoring models with reference to small businesses' owners (instead of the more comprehensive small business credit scoring) but coupled with more traditional lending techniques (e.g. relationship lending); this was associated with greater credit availability to small businesses without changes in the portfolio's quality.

72 *See* A. Berger and G. Udell, 'Small Business Credit Availability and Relationship Lending: The Importance of Bank Organisational Structure', (2002) 112 (477) *Econ J* F32, F40–41; C. Stein, 'Information Production and Capital Allocation: Decentralized versus Hierarchical Firms', (2002) 57(5) *J Financ* 1891; Whiteman, 'Small Banks'; Cole, 'Cookie-Cutter'; Berger, 'Does Function'. Nonetheless, Berger et al. ('Does Market Size') do not find a net disadvantage of large banks in financing small firms/opaque borrowers thanks to the use of different transactional lending techniques (e.g. leasing, asset-based lending and small business credit scoring).

in certain organizational structures, (lending) specialization, flexibility and decentralization of loan decisions[73] (most common also among MFIs).

In particular, literature assigns central importance to the relationship-banking[74] character of small banks, whose main elements are: the long duration of the relationship, its intensity in terms of predominance of credit from the same bank to the firm and number of services, as well as the organizational procedures and structures in terms of lending technologies and contracts, types of information and proximity. Nonetheless, drawbacks are possible hold-up problems (bank extracting rents from superior private information) and soft-budget constraint (bank's inability to commit *ex-ante* to a certain behaviour because of the *ex post* inefficiency coming from the termination of credit in case of borrower's default, with consequent borrower's incentive *ex ante* to default) with perverse incentives.[75]

Anyway, the small banks analysis mainly apply to European MFIs only when banks (or accepting deposits), otherwise lacking the competitive advantage of the deep knowledge from borrowers' checking accounts (although having other sources of information and monitoring devices)[76] and the main and most stable source of funding. Furthermore, unless MFIs serve a partially different market sector from small traditional banks, competition among small lenders can reduce such advantages (Chapter 3, §5.a).[77] In fact, studies seem to show that competition can benefit relationship-banking only with adaptation to different markets.[78] Finally, MFIs are specialized institutions, focusing on a limited number of services, targeting a limited category of clients, therefore with limited diversification advantages. A limited expansion in MFIs' permitted activities would therefore contribute to improving microfinance (Chapter 4, §6).

Furthermore, these results can also support the argument that financial systems need not only large banks but also small banks and MFIs to cover all market sectors.[79] Furthermore, they suggest that MFIs should maintain their comparative

73 *See* DeYoung et al., 'The Past', 104ff.; A. Akhigbe and J. McNulty, 'The Profit Efficiency of Small US Commercial Banks', (2003) 27 *J Bank Financ* 307 (keys to higher profit-efficiency are relationship banking and lower competition in small banking markets).

74 About relationship lending, E. Elyasiani and L. Goldberg, 'Relationship Lending: A Survey of the Literature', (2004) 56(4) *J Econ Bus* 315; Petersen and Rajan, 'The Benefits', 5ff.; Berger and Udell, 'Small'; Stein, 'Information'; DeYoung et al., 'The Past', 104ff.; Berger, 'Small', 535–537.

75 *See* F. Allen and E. Carletti, 'The Roles of Banks in Financial Systems', in Berger, *The Oxford*, 52–3.

76 *See* Petersen and Rajan, 'The Benefits'; L. Mester, L. Nakamura and M. Renault, 'Checking Accounts and Bank Monitoring', (2002), Wharton Financial Institutions Center Working Paper 99–02C, <http://fic.wharton.upenn.edu/fic/papers/99/9902.pdf>.

77 *See* Akhigbe and McNulty, 'The Profit'; DeYoung et al., 'The Past'; Berger, 'Small', 540.

78 A. Boot and A. Thakor, 'The Accelerating Integration of Banks and Markets and its Implications for Regulation', in Berger, *The Oxford*, 64–65.

79 *See* L. Zingales, 'Leave Room for Growth', (*Economist*, 11 July 2009) Lin roundtable <www.economist.com/blogs/freeexchange/2009/07/the_devastation_produced_

advantage of relationship-banking and lending specialization. In fact, research attests that 'the optimal industrial organization of a banking sector might be one that comprises several focused or specialized banks instead of a large number of diversified banks, an outcome that may also be attractive from a systemic risk standpoint'.[80]

Furthermore, since MFIs have somewhere showed patterns similar to large banks as they mature and grow (e.g. competition, standardization, activities expansion, excessive growth, multiple borrowing and over-indebtedness, deterioration of underwriting criteria, overstretched MFI systems and controls) (see §a),[81] arguments might be advanced to limit MFIs' size or activities. This recalls post-crisis about large banks' excessive risks and proposals to limit their organizational and operational complexity.[82]

In particular, bank-size caps have been proposed to contain costs and perverse incentives of bail-outs,[83] but objections are identified in the lack of credit-risk diversification, loss of high-skilled jobs and, anyway, persistent systemic risk in case of multiple small banks facing liquidity or solvency problems simultaneously.[84] Furthermore, identifying an optimal size is rather impossible, persuading international regulators to focus large-banks' regimes on capital surcharges, activities limitations (Chapter 4, §6.a on structural reforms), corporate governance and better resolutions (Chapter 5, §2; 3, §4.b; below §6.f).

by_th>; R. Levine, 'Function, Not Form', (*Economist*, 11 July 2009) Lin roundtable, <www.economist.com/blogs/freeexchange/2009/07/ross_levine_is_james_and> (underlining different competitive advantages between small and large banks); A. Schoar, 'Scale Matters', (*Economist*, 11 July 2009) Lin roundtable, <www.economist.com/blogs/freeexchange/2009/07/antoinette_schoar_is_michael_k> (tiny banks are not able to allow small business to grow not having the scale to offer large loans or to finance riskier and new projects being exposed to local shocks); T. Moss, 'The Value of Stock Markets', (2009) Lin roundtable (*Economist*, 11 July 2009), <www.economist.com/blogs/freeexchange/2009/07/todd_moss_is_senior_fellow>; M. Thoma, 'Small Banks Need Help', (*Economist*, 11 July 2009) Lin roundtable, <www.economist.com/blogs/freeexchange/2009/07/lin_roundtable_small_banks_nee> (underlining the important role of small banks in gathering information about their communities and partnering with large banks to share such information and offering more sophisticated products to their costumers).

80 Acharya, 'Should Banks'.

81 *See* Kruijff and Hartnestein, 'Microfinance', 11ff.

82 Laeven et al., 'Bank Size'.

83 *See* M. King, Speech, (Lord Mayor's Banquet for Bankers and Merchants of the City of London, 17 June 2009), <www.bankofengland.co.uk/archive/Documents/historicpubs/speeches/2009/speech394.pdf>; M. Goldstein and N. Véron, 'Too Big to Fail: The Transatlantic Debate,' (2011) Bruegel Working Paper 2011/3, <http://bruegel.org/wp-content/uploads/imported/publications/Nicolas_Veron_WP_Too_big_to_fail_2011_03.pdf>.

84 *See* J. Dermine and D. Schoenmaker, 'In Banking: Is Small Beautiful?', (2009) DSF Policy Paper 2, <http://ssrn.com/abstract=1476764>; J. Barth and A. Prabha, 'Breaking (Banks) Up is Hard to Do: New Perspective on Too Big To Fail', (2012) Wharton Financial Institutions Center Working Paper 12–16, <http://fic.wharton.upenn.edu/fic/papers/12/12-16.pdf>.

Setting an optimal size for MFIs would be particularly complex because of wide difference in business models and of existing evidence of large scale-social mission coexistence (Chapters 4 and 5). Consequently, once more, better social and financial disclosure and governance combined with a tiered proportional regulation that becomes more stringent in case of more complex activities can instead have positive effects without endangering the sector (§3).

3 Rationales for prudential regulation. Microfinance as a banking activity?

a The specialty of banks and banking regulation

Banks are traditionally identified as the undertakings conducting both the activity of accepting deposits and of granting loans,[85] as also reflected in the EU definition of 'credit institution'.[86]

The qualification as bank entails the application of banking regulation, a special and complex bulk of rules and principles, characterized by a predominance of prudential regulation (i.e. need of an authorization, rigid and strict rules focusing on risks and pervasive supervisory powers) and public interest considerations (such as protecting stability and depositor trust), prevailing over the rights of firms, shareholders and subordinated creditors (Chapter 3, §2).

The rationales for creating a special regime for banks, with a reserve of activity counterbalanced by strict regulation, are obviously linked to the above mentioned definition of bank. The fact of being authorized to receive deposits and other repayable funds from the public and to on-lend a fraction of these sums to other clients – that will perpetuate the chain through the deposit of the funds received at another (or the same) bank – allows banks to participate in the creation of liquidity and to the transmission of central banks' monetary policy.[87] Furthermore, for the same reasons, banks bear the risk of maturity transformation (accepting deposits often for an indeterminate time, therefore also on demand, and lending for a short or long time) and, consequently, of depositor run. In fact, when a bank seems unable to repay the deposits at a client's request, all other clients rush to call back their funds, with tragic consequences for the bank, which, by definition, is not able to repay all deposits at once having lent most of them ('fractional

85 *See* R. Carnell et al., *The Law of Banking and Financial Institutions*, (4th edn, Aspen Publisher 2009), 48ff.; R. Cranston, *Principles of Banking Law*, (2nd edn, OUP 2002), 4.

86 Article 4(1)1 Regulation 575/2013 (CRR): '"credit institution" means an undertaking the business of which is to take deposits or other repayable funds from the public and to grant credits for its own account'.

87 *See* Carnell, *The Law*, 48ff.; Cranston, *Principles*, 65ff.; M. Duwatripont and J. Tirole, *The Prudential Regulation of Banks*, (MIT Press 1993), (critical towards some of the justification commonly presented in favour of special rules for banks and recognizing deposits protection as the only real justification for banking regulation); L. Dragomir, *European Prudential Banking Regulation and Supervision: The Legal Dimension*, (Routledge 2010), 26ff. and 39–47.

reserves'). Furthermore, suspicion towards a bank can easily transform into a general distrust towards the banking system or at least interconnected banks, leading to a financial crisis which is likely to affect the entire economic system, heavily relying on bank funding especially in Europe. Systems of deposit guarantee have been created to mitigate such effect, generally leaving unprotected only big depositors (currently in the EU, above €100,000 per depositor per bank), considered able to monitor bank managers and therefore reducing bank moral hazard. Moreover, prudential regulation (and now new rules about bank resolutions) aims at forcing banks to contain risks despite the existence of deposit insurance. In fact, deposit insurance and government back-up (bail-out) in case of systemic banks have also led banks to high leverage levels and risky behaviours.[88] Additional traditional arguments for a special bank regulation relate to the opaqueness of banks' balance sheets and quick shifts in risk profile (because of activities' complexity) and their centrality in payment systems.[89]

Although such rationales for a special banking regulation have been extensively criticized,[90] the main arguments imposing banking regulation in case of deposits still stand.

b Microfinance and the deposit-taking business. Non-deposit-taking MFIs

It appears logical to derive from the above discussed reasoning the extension of banking regulation to deposit-taking MFIs, while considering outside of such a perimeter credit-only MFIs, the majority in Western Europe. Even the BCBS in evaluating microfinance specificities in the light of its 'Core Principles for Effective Banking Supervision' considers relevant and covered by its scope only banks and other non-bank institutions accepting deposits.[91] Non-deposit taking non-bank financial institutions might be required to register (instead of having a licence) with the financial authority in order to allow corrective actions in case of unsafe or unsound practices able to jeopardize the banking system.[92] The BCBS also reports that the majority of countries participating in its survey restrict MFIs' permitted activities and impose on non-bank MFIs accepting deposits the same rules as for

88 Carnell et al., *The Law*, 46ff., 251ff. and 309ff.; Cranston, *Principles*, 76ff.; J. Barth et al., *Rethinking Banking Regulation. Till Angels Govern*, (CUP 2008), 57ff.

89 Ibidem; C. Goodhart et al., *Financial Regulation. Why, How and Where Now?*, (Routledge 1998), 10–12.

90 *See* R. Aspinwall, 'On the "Specialness" of Banking', (1983) 7 *Issues in Bank Reg* 16; Carnell, *The Law*, 60ff.; Duwatripont and Tirole, *The Prudential*, 5, 29ff.; G. Ferrarini, 'Introduction', in G. Ferrarini (ed.), *Prudential Regulation of Banks and Securities Firms*, (Springer 1995), 10ff.

91 BCBS, *Microfinance*; BCBS, *Guidance on the Application of the Core Principles for Effective Banking Supervision to the Regulation and Supervision of Institutions Relevant to Financial Inclusion – Consultative Document*, (BIS 2015), 5 (note 24) (in addition acknowledging that in some countries deposit-taking non-bank institutions might be subject to lighter or different regulation unless representing a significant part of the country's deposits or, when numerous, small and dispersed, even only to monitoring).

92 BCBS, *Guidance*, 5 (text and note 25).

banks, with some exclusions or exceptions to banking regulation for small institutions.[93] Similarly, the Commission in its 2007 Initiative confirms the need of a banking licence only for MFIs simultaneously accepting deposits and extending loans and recommends, when Member States apply prudential requirements to non-bank MFIs to build a proportionate regime in consideration of costs and risks (*see* Chapter 3, §4.c).

Currently, only 20% of European MFIs offer micro-savings and are mainly bank-MFIs located in Eastern Europe.[94] In the West, traditional savings banks (Spain) or credit unions/CDFIs (UK) offer deposits and a broader set of products, although this phenomenon is still limited (Chapter 4, §6).

Nonetheless, countries might decide to extend a banking licence requirement or banking regulation to other types of activities, including lending, as recently verified by the EBA.[95] Previous Banking Directives, in fact, allowed Member States to adopt a wider definition of credit institution. Instead, the CRR, being a maximum harmonization tool, prohibits Member States from including in the 'credit institution' scope operators not conducting both reception of deposits and provision of loans.[96] However, European countries are still free to liberalize credit-only services (UK) or reserve them to banks (Germany, Portugal) or to extend banking regulation to non-bank entities, also in reaction to the financial crisis (e.g. Italy, France, Romania) (*see* Chapter 4, §6.c).[97] This leads us to consider whether there might be other and more recent rationales to apply prudential regulation to credit-only MFIs, as a reaction to the expansion of the shadow banking system.

4 Rationales for prudential regulation of non-bank intermediaries in the crisis era: microfinance and shadow banking

The European definition of credit institutions leaves all non-deposit-taking operators outside of the perimeter of banking regulation, many of which are not included either in the purview of securities or insurance regulators and are consequently prudentially unregulated. This has allowed the creation of a 'grey' market called 'shadow banking', conducting bank-like activities and currently under the scrutiny of public authorities for stability's sake (*see* Chapter 4, §6). With 'shadow banking' we can in fact refer to 'a system of intermediaries, instruments, entities or financial contracts generating a combination of bank-like functions but outside of the regulatory perimeter or under a regulatory regime that is either

93 BCBS, *Microfinance*, 2, 5.

94 M. Bending et al., 'Overview of Microcredit Sector in the European Union – 2012–2013', (2014), 35, 50, <www.european-microfinance.org/docs/emn_publications/emn_overview/Overview2012-2013_Nov2014.pdf>.

95 EBA, 'Report to the European Commission on Matters Relating to the Perimeter of Credit Institutions', (2014), <www.eba.europa.eu/documents/10180/534414/2014+11+27+-+EBA+Report+-+Credit+institutions.pdf> (suggesting in its Opinion 2014/12 to adopt a clearer and harmonized definition at EU level).

96 EBA, 'Report', 16.

97 EBA, 'Report', 17–18.

light or addresses issues other than systemic risks, and without guaranteed access to central bank liquidity facility or public sector credit guarantees'.[98] Such a sector includes entities transforming maturities or liquidity and transferring credit risk (e.g. Special Purpose Vehicles – SPVs – in securitizations), reception of funds from the public with deposit-like instruments (e.g. money-market mutual funds), use of financial leverage (e.g. exchange traded funds, hedge funds and private equity funds or reinsurance firms).[99]

UK has the second largest shadow banking system in the world (11%) with USD4.3 trillion, while euro-countries have a 23% share.[100] However, shadow banking borders remain unclear: based on a broad definition ('MUNFI', including insurance, investment and pension funds), shadow banking accounts for USD137 trillion and 40% of the global financial system, while adopting a narrower definition ('other financial intermediaries – OFIs', excluding funds and insurance), it reaches USD80 trillion and 24% of the global financial system.[101] A recent methodology adopted by FSB further restricts the sector to credit intermediaries with certain economic functions in order to cover only operators entailing systemic risk, this leading to a shadow banking's size of USD36 trillion, accounting for 12% of the global financial system.

In fact, the FSB defines shadow banking as 'credit intermediation involving entities and activities outside of the regular banking system' and aims at identifying the same for stability and systemic risk concerns.[102] It recognizes the main features/risks of such a phenomenon in the functions of maturity or liquidity transformation, leverage creation and imperfect credit risk transfer. The above mentioned approach based on five economic functions includes, besides the management of collective investment vehicles with maturity/liquidity transformation or leverage and so susceptible to runs (economic function 1), securitization-based credit intermediation and funding of financial entities (economic function 5), also simple loan provision that is dependent on short-term funding (economic function 2, corresponding to 7% of the shadow banking), intermediation of market activities that is dependent on short-term funding or on secured funding of client assets (economic function 3, 11%) and the facilitation of credit creation (economic

98 *See* European Parliament, 'Resolution of 20 November 2012 on Shadow Banking', 2012/2115(INI) and FSB, 'Shadow Banking: Strengthening Oversight and Regulation-Recommendations of the Financial Stability Board', (2011), <www.financialstabilityboard.org>. For a description of the shadow banking sector and critics about such terminology, E. Wymeersh, 'Shadow Banking and the Functioning of Financial Markets', in D. Busch and G. Ferrarini (eds), *Regulation of EU Financial Markets: MiFID II and MiFIR*, (OUP 2017), ch. 22, 613ff., 617ff.

99 *See* Commission, 'Shadow Banking – Addressing New Sources of Risk in the Financial Sector', (Communication) COM/2013/0614 final, 3.

100 FSB, 'Global Shadow Banking Monitoring Report 2015', (2015), 11, <www.fsb.org/wp-content/uploads/global-shadow-banking-monitoring-report-2015.pdf> (participating euro-countries were France, Germany, Ireland, Italy, Netherlands and Spain).

101 Ibidem 2.

102 Ibidem 1.

function 4, 0.3%).[103] Consequently, the economic function 2 category, which includes finance companies, leasing companies and consumer credit companies, could also well fit MFIs in the case of short-term funding.

Similarly, the Commission's attention on shadow banking is justified by its potential systemic risk in consideration of its size and interconnectedness with the banking sector. The characteristics of such intermediaries are again identified in maturity/liquidity transformation, leverage, credit transfer, in addition to deposit-like funding,[104] and not already subject to Banking Directive (CRDIV 2013/36/EU) and Regulation (CRR 575/2013), MiFID, UCTIS, AIFMD/EuVECA/EuSEF (when limited leverage), Electronic Money and Payment Services Directives or occupational pension funds and insurance Directives.[105]

EU regulatory approach to shadow banking has been limited, however, to disclosure or appropriate self-imposed limits in banking exposures to shadow banking entities (as regards risk factors for capital adequacy calculations and risk concentration measures towards shadow banking entities), with specific regimes for securitization, AIFMs, OTC derivatives and securities financing transactions (*see* Chapter 5, §4.c). It has not come to envision prudential regulation extension to non-bank intermediaries (except for AIFMs) yet.

Anyway, European credit-only MFIs do not generally engage in credit risk transfer, deposit-like or liquidity transformation activities. Leverage risk has internationally increased because of higher profits and consequent rise in credit availability (*see* microfinance crises in Morocco, Nicaragua, Pakistan and Bosnia and Herzegovina).[106] Nonetheless, the average debt-to-equity ratio of European MFIs in 2013 was 100.2% (with loans equal to their capital), therefore rather high for non-banks, but the results vary significantly among countries. The highest ratios can be found in Hungary (340%), France (193%) and Italy (183%), while the lowest are in the Netherlands (1%), the UK (4%) and Croatia (5%). The remaining group presents ratios between 45% and 65% (Germany, Poland, Spain, Lithuania and Romania).[107] Such a high debt-to-equity ratio can be explained by the current growth phase but parallel restricted access to equity funding, making loans (in addition to grants) the main source of financing, with mid-size MFIs presenting the highest ratios (*see* Chapter 5, §3.a). However, this is lower than banks and shadow banking's levels (especially during the financial crisis)[108] and

103 Ibidem 14.

104 Commission, 'Shadow Banking', 3–4.

105 Ibidem 16–17; EBA, 'Guidelines. Limits on Exposures to Shadow Banking Entities Which Carry out Banking Activities Outside a Regulated Framework Under Article 395(2) of Regulation (EU) No. 575/2013', EBA/GL/2015/20.

106 *See* Chen, 'Growth', 3.

107 *See* Bending, 'Overview', 51–52 (institutions reporting data on this aspect corresponded to the 30% of responding MFIs; the Netherlands, UK and Croatia low ratios could not be validated since they may result from different methods of calculations).

108 Some banks during the crisis had exposures above 40 times their capital (40:1 instead of 1:1 as here): <http://europa.eu/rapid/press-release_MEMO-14-580_en.htm>. Similarly for some U.S. shadow banking broker-dealers: <www.bloomberg.com/news/articles/2014-03-20/shadow-banking-deals-prompt-sec-plan-to-cap-levera

such debt-financing is provided by professional or institutional investors engaged in monitoring MFIs.

In fact, as evidenced by FSB classifications, the source and type of funding is particularly relevant in this context and MFIs do not heavily rely on short-term funding (*see* Chapter 5, §§3–5). Recourse to crowdfunding is in fact still limited and the policy issues raised by such funding sources can be addressed through other mechanisms (*see* Chapter 7, §3). Moreover, according to an eminent scholar, shadow banking should be subject to prudential regulation only when involving deposit-like funds or short-term funding (as also suggested by FSB and EU positions), while other intermediaries should be only targeted by improved transparency and data collection requirements, also depending on their funding sources.[109] In particular, shadow banking appears less troublesome when it receives its main bulk of funding long-term from large institutions with a reputation to defend (such as banks and pension funds), assuming they carefully scrutinize.[110] This what happens with MFIs, which are mostly funded through grants and public resources, bank loans, international organizations' concessional loans or MIVs.[111]

In conclusion, European MFIs can hardly be considered shadow banking entities based on international and European standards (unless they accept deposits or continuously issue bonds) and, anyway, do not seem to present such risks justifying prudential regulation but, at most, improved transparency (as regards financing, financial and social performance as well as governance: *see* Chapters 3–5). Then, obviously, national MFIs regulation should consider the regime applying to other credit-only intermediaries but its double-bottom line nature, limited size and particular funding might allow a differentiated treatment.

Consequently, MFIs might be subject to lighter regulation compared to banks and shadow banking operators, and with rules more focused on transparency and business conduct, in addition to, at least, a registration requirement in order to allow a financial authority's intervention for the protection of financial stability and the functioning of the financial system.[112] Such registration should present reasonable conditions such as adequate resources for the kind of activities conducted, a low minimum capital or a professional insurance, fit and proper managers and

ge-for-brokers>. The aggregated leverage ratio of European banks (calculated as tier 1 capital/exposures) in 2014 was 4.9% (corresponding to the actual 50% on average of European MFIs); Basel III minimum leverage ratio is 3%, allowing banks to have assets up to 33 times their tier 1 capital (versus the registered 2 times of MFIs on average).

109 *See* E. Wymeersh, 'How Far Should Financial Regulation Go? Shadow Banking and Related Phenomena', (International Working Group on MIFID II conference, Amsterdam, 28–29 January 2016).

110 Ibidem.

111 About differences in incentives based on the capital structure of financial institutions, *see* Barth et al., *Research Handbook on International Banking and Governance*, (Edward Elgar 2012), 344ff.; R. Galema et al, 'Do Powerful CEOs Determine Microfinance Performance?', (2012) 49(4) *J Manage Stud* 718.

112 BCBS, *Guidance*, 5 (with reference to Core Principle 1, ECs 2, 6, 7).

owners, feasible business plan and back-up/continuity plan. As discussed in other parts of this book, additional rules should address risk management and governance, with flexible and principles-based requirements, tailored to the size and types of activities, and disclosure of funding and financial/social performance as well as business conduct (*see* Chapters 4–5, 8). Furthermore, regulation should allow a diverse range of financing options but with a capital structure adequate to the type of business (Chapter 5). In fact, the activities and products should be simple and target clients' needs, more complex services requiring a more 'mainstream' regime.[113] Liquidity and back-stop facilities provided by local or regional or transnational networks managing common funds and enforcing living wills might be required considering recent microfinance crises also in Eastern Europe (*see* Chapters 3, §3.d; 5, §4).[114] Finally, while in principle subject to financial authorities' supervision, in case of a high number of MFIs, a partial delegation to a highly respected, hybrid and diversified private organization might be acceptable (Chapter 3).

5 Banks–MFIs interaction. Regulatory implications

Mainstream banks and MFIs should not always be conceived as rivals and opposed models. Also in everyday life, traditional banks and MFIs often cooperate (so called 'linkage model'). In fact, as observed in Chapter 2, §2.a, there are many ways in which commercial European banks are involved in microfinance[115] and even the European MFIs Code recommends to non-bank MFIs a bank partner to reduce the risk of cash handling (clause 3.17).

The reason for commercial banks' involvement in the sector might be linked to corporate social responsibility (CSR) or even strategic economic objectives when microcredit programmes allow them to reach a new segment of clients in a convenient way (thanks to not-for-profit organizations' screening work or public support and guarantees) or to cross-sell other bank products and services.[116]

113 BCBS, *Guidance*, 9–10.

114 *See* the 'Emergency Liquidity Facility', an investment fund administered by IADB and funded by many private investors designed to provide pre-qualified MFIs in Latin America and Caribbean with liquidity to face credit crises or shocks: *see* P. Bate, 'In Case of Emergency: Break Glass: ELF, an Innovative Fund That Helps MFIs Respond to All Kind of Disasters', (2007), <www.iadb.org/micamericas/section/detail.cfm?id=4241&sectionID=SPCAL>; R. Moro Visconti, 'Global Recession and Microfinance in Developing Countries: Threats And Opportunities', (2012), 27, <http://ssrn.com/abstract=1318581>. Furthermore, the 'Microfinance Enhancement Facility' was announced in late 2008 as an investment fund promoted by IFC and KfW and co-managed by BlueOrchard, with the aim to enhance liquidity support of MFIs to overcome the credit crisis: *see* <www.ifc.org/ifcext/spiwebsite1.nsf/ProjectDisplay/SPI_DP27827> and <www.mef-fund.com/>.

115 *See* A. Cozarenco, 'Microfinance Institutions and Banks in Europe: The Story to Date', (2015), <www.european-microfinance.org/docs/emn_publications/emn_research_papers/research_3.pdf>.

116 *See* European Banking Federation, 'Microfinance within the EU Banking Industry: Policy and Practice', (2010), 8, <www.ebf-fbe.eu/uploads/D1093k%20Microfinance%20EU%20banking%20industry.pdf>; Cozarenco, 'Microfinance', 11.

Moving now to examples of existing models of European banks' involvement in microfinance, the lowest level of involvement (and the most common) consists in simply financing MFIs through loans (e.g. BNL/BNP Paribas with PerMicro and Adie),[117] equity investments (e.g. BNL holding 23.2% of PerMicro equity) or subsidies (e.g. Adie). Second, banks might provide MFIs with access to their infrastructures, such as offices, ATMs and IT (*see* BNL with PerMicro), also in exchange for cross-selling opportunities.

Under other partnerships, banks might refer 'unbankable' candidates to specific microcredit providers depending on different applicants' needs and MFIs' capacities (see partnerships between Crédit Mutuel and Adie and BNL and Permicro).[118] A referral partnership is also common between UK banks and MFIs.[119]

A more active role sees banks directly disbursing micro-loans, working with microfinance organizations which introduce prospective borrowers to the bank, provide them with coaching services and monitor developments (*see* in Germany, Spain and some cases in Italy). Both actors need the other: banks need not-for-profit organizations to reduce asymmetric information (the organizations sponsor people they have known during their socially responsible activities and within their network) and to monitor and support borrowers (through coaching services). The organizations need the bank to disburse loans (when they are not authorized credit providers), taking advantage of bank experience, widespread branches and clientele, with opportunities to cross-subsidize poorer clients.[120] MFIs' clients can build a trustful relationship with banks and 'graduate', i.e. moving from micro-finance to mainstream banking, with access to a broader set of services and network.[121]

Public programmes are often also involved: for instance, microcredit in Spain has been traditionally a joint work of public institutions (making available guarantees), savings banks and Social Microcredit Supporting Organizations (providing

117 The French law No. 737/2010 has required banks to disclose the amount and number of loans provided to MFIs under a public guarantee scheme (Art. L511–4-1 *Code monétaire et financier*).

118 BNL (of BNP Paribas Group), in addition to holding the majority of PerMicro shares, it also hosts 5 out of 14 selling points of the Italian MFI, provides technical support through volunteers and in 2015 referred more than 20% of PerMicro clients. BNP Paribas Group, more generally, invests 82% of its microfinance portfolio (reaching overall €213 million) in direct funding (21% in domestic markets – especially Italy, France, Luxembourg and Belgium – and 55% abroad), of which only 2% in grants and 4% in equity investments in MFIs, the remaining being debt financing (each loan ranging from €0.50 to €10 million): *see* interview on 27 July 2016 with Claudia Belli, Head Social Enterprises and Microfinance at BNP Paribas and BNP, 'BNP Committee to Microfinance', (2016), 4, 7, 9, <http://rse2016.bnpparibas.com/microfinance-csr-booklet/#/pageNumber=1>. *See* also C. Fökehrer, 'Gaining Scale in Micro-credit. Can Banks Make it Happen?', (2007) *EMN Bi-annual Magazine* 2, 8.

119 Bending, 'Overview', 84.

120 A. Cozarenco and A. Szafarz, 'Microcredit in Developed Countries: Unexpected Consequences of Loan Ceilings', (2013), <http://ssrn.com/abstract=2269022>.

121 Cozarenco, 'Microfinance', 13.

accompanying services and monitoring).[122] Similarly, in Germany, when micro-loans are not directly disbursed through public programmes, private banks supply microcredit in cooperation with microfinance associations and relying on public guarantees (if not even public funds).[123] The original bank–MFI linkage model in Italy has entailed the participation of microfinance associations, partner banks and public entities or charity funds providing guarantee funds (Chapter 2, §2.a).

Sometimes banks and MFIs co-finance risky loan (e.g. Créa-Sol) to share the burden and their respective knowledge and techniques (but with the risk for MFIs to be subject to uneven terms).[124]

Alternatively, there are cases where banks have their own microfinance programme through an internal unit or department (*see* 'Parcours confiance' in France created by the *Fédération Nationale des Caisses d'Épargne*) or through a separate entity. Sometimes such a separate entity sees also the participation of not-for-profit actors and the government. In Spain, La Caixa group has created a separate but 100%-owned corporation, MicroBank, specializing in microloans for individuals not served by mainstream providers, which can take advantage of La Caixa multiple branches in the country.[125] 'Down-scaling' models run the risk of replicating mainstream models, keeping untouched internal procedures and systems. Nonetheless, to have an authentic and effective microcredit programme we need at least some of the following adjustments: short-term loans, frequent instalments, decentralized decisions, fast loan approval and disbursement, screening based on cash flow and business plan's analysis as well as varied soft information also through on-site visits and talks with friends and associates (*see* §2.b; Chapters 2; 3, §1).[126] Based on a recent analysis of Italian banks involvement in microfinance,[127] large banks tend to adopt specific structures and procedures for microfinance, while medium and small banks, with a business model closer to microfinance, to adapt existing products and services. Screening procedures for microloans differ from other loans from the same bank: they mainly rely on information provided by the same client (about financial needs and situation as well as credit history and business plan or family unit; more rarely, about his/her relationship network) double-checked with other sources and microfinance associations' reports while microcredit scoring only complements such an evaluation (in 50–60% of sample banks). They mostly require personal collateral, pledge or guarantees from public institutions or mutual funds.[128]

122 Bending, 'Overview', 82–83.
123 Ibidem 64–65.
124 Cozarenco, 'Microfinance', 8.
125 Fökehrer, 'Gaining', 10.
126 *See* B. Maas and S. Lämmermann, 'Designing Microfinance Operations in the EU', (2013), 41, <www.microfinancegateway.org/sites/default/files/mfg-en-toolkit-designing-microfinance-operations-in-the-eu-a-manual-on-how-to-build-and-implement-microfinance-support-programmes-using-the-esf-2013.pdf>.
127 Andreoni, *Nuovi*, 97ff. (using a sample of 15 Italian banks representing 66% of national bank branches and attesting that the large majority of the banks in the sample, corresponding to 66% of national bank branches, reported providing at least a microfinance service).
128 Ibidem.

Other banks, within the cooperative or mutualistic tradition, might instead find it natural to expand their products to such area (*see* savings banks in Germany and, before the recent sector's crisis, in Spain; Chapter 3, §5.a).

In France, partnerships between banks and microfinance associations have been incentivized by the regulatory ceilings set on the size of loans disbursed by the latter, introduced for 'prudence' and to keep banks engaged with SMEs (*see* Chapters 4, §6.c; 5, §2.a). In fact, loan ceilings are believed to address competition issues between banks and alternative providers, forcing the latter to focus on the poorest while benefiting from public subsidies and leaving to the former the less-poor segment, although simultaneously reducing the access to financing of larger projects and cross-subsidization opportunities.[129] Nonetheless, in France it has had the unexpected effect of pushing MFIs to co-finance larger loans with banks, free-riding on the bank screening process, and thus to a partial mission drift.[130] Therefore, it seems more appropriate to set a high maximum level for the definition of microloan for both banks and MFIs along with other conditions, while tailoring favourable treatments based on different factors (e.g. borrower's income; *see* Chapter 3, §1).

The regulatory framework might complicate the picture in other ways: for example, in Italy, MFIs' work as facilitators of the loans from the banks to the borrowers could be categorized as 'credit mediation', subject to a specific regulation and licence, which does not allow not-for-profit entities conducting a wide range of activities to engage in such service (Art. 128-*sexies* ff TUB).[131]

Furthermore, traditional banks' involvement in microfinance might entail regulatory implications. For instance, too much reliance in the loan process on the non-bank partner can raise issues within the prudential regulation framework: in fact, a part of the loan process appears outsourced to entities that fall outside of the radar of the banking supervisor (e.g. NGOs), not bearing the consequences of borrowers' defaults and by nature prone to favour borrowers' needs over financial sustainability. Despite the absence of EU harmonization on bank outsourcing, CEBS and BCBS guidelines set important principles. A bank cannot outsource core activities (including lending) requiring a licence unless to an institution having an equivalent authorization. Anyway, '[t]he ultimate responsibility for the proper management of the risks associated with outsourcing or the outsourced activities lies with an outsourcing institution's senior management', who must also retain adequate core competences to be able to resume control *in extremis.*[132] Therefore, even when borrower selection is seen as only a part, although fundamental, of the lending activity generally not necessitating *per se* an

129 Christen, 'Microfinance Consensus', 12.

130 *See* A. Cozarenco and A. Szafarz, 'Microcredit in Developed Countries: Unexpected Consequences of Loan Ceilings', (2014), CEB Working Paper 14/015, <www.iap-socent.be/sites/default/files/SOCENT%20Pub%202014-05%20(wp14015).pdf>.

131 *See* S. Di Castri, 'The Microcredit Sector in Italy: Small Initiatives in a Dynamic Scenario', in B. Jayo Carboni et al. (eds), *Handbook of Microcredit in Europe*, (Edward Elgar Publishing 2010), 91–92.

132 CEBS, 'Guidelines on Outsourcing', (2006), guidelines 4 and 2, <www.eba.europa.eu/documents/10180/104404/GL02OutsourcingGuidelines.pdf.pdf>.

authorization, bank executives are required to continuously monitor partner organizations. Due diligence must be exercised in the provider's selection, which must have adequate resources and competence and be able to meet institution's regulatory objectives.[133]

Anyway, different models entail different levels of risk. In fact, only cooperating with a microfinance partner generally involves a lower level of risk and costs than a dedicated unit, but this also depends on the specific type of cooperation (funding to MFIs or shared microloan backed by guarantees or only office host). Furthermore, microfinance programmes at commercial banks tend to represent only a small part of the bank's balance sheet compared to specialized microfinance banks, providing diversification without jeopardizing its stability. All this inevitably has an impact in terms of regulatory requirements. The fact of not being specialized in microfinance, while reducing concentration risk, might also weaken the arguments in favour of regulatory advantages. However, it cannot exclude them when there is evidence of social outcomes and performance, allowing facilitations based on the level of involvement. For instance, exposures towards MFIs and micro-borrowers might receive a preferential treatment under Basel rules when public guarantees or effective risk-management rules are in place at the MFI. In case of MFIs' participation to the lending process, simplifications might be introduced in terms of supervisory review process and disclosure/documentation requirements.

6 Microfinance characteristics and specific prudential requirements

a Rationales for simplifications and adjustments to prudential requirements for bank-MFIs. The proportionality principle

Once the application of banking regulation to deposit-taking MFIs has been affirmed, we still need to assess whether 'adaptations' might be needed. In fact, adjustments to prudential regulation applicable to bank-MFIs and deposit-taking MFIs (or NBFIs subject to bank-like regulation despite what is recommended above) can be desirable on two separate grounds. First, microfinance presents specific risks and characteristics that might cause traditional prudential tools to be ineffective (unable to prevent crises or excessively burdensome: §2). Second, simplifications can be justified by MFIs' social goals or limited size and systemic risk involved.

In fact, post-crisis regulation has become increasingly complex and mostly conceived to address risks posed by large and complex systemic institutions, raising at the same time concerns about the likely negative impact on small banks.[134]

133 BCBS, 'Outsourcing in Financial Services', (2005), 15ff., <www.bis.org/publ/joint12.pdf>.

134 D. Tarullo, 'Rethinking the Aims of Prudential Regulation', (Federal Reserve Bank of Chicago 'Bank Structure' Conference, Chicago, 8 May 2014), <www.federalreserve.gov/newsevents/speech/tarullo20140508a.pdf>; Id., 'Tailoring Community Bank Regulation and Supervision', (Independent Community Bankers of America Policy Summit, Washington, 30 April 2015), <www.federalreserve.gov/newsevents/speech/tarullo20150430a.pdf>; EBA-Banking Stakeholder Group, 'Proportionality in Bank

Regulatory burden can in fact disproportionally affect small banks since they are less able to spread fixed costs over a large set of activities (*see* §2.c and Chapter 3, §2) and, especially in consideration of their role in contributing to SMEs' growth and financial inclusion, a partial burden relief has been proposed for small banks.

A proportionate approach has been recognized also in the revised 2012 Basel Core Principles on effective banking supervision, requiring competent authorities to tailor supervision and supervisory resources to the risk profile and systemic importance of banks.[135] The BCBS further acknowledges that

> in countries where non-bank financial institutions provide deposit and lending services similar to those of banks, many of the [Core] Principles would also be appropriate to such non-bank financial institutions [but] [...] also that some of these categories of institutions may be regulated differently from banks as long as they do not hold, collectively, a significant proportion of deposits in a financial system.[136]

Moreover, 'in countries where these non-bank deposit-taking institutions are numerous, very small, and geographically remote, supervision may be limited to monitoring',[137] since in allocating resources supervisors have to take into account the risk profile and systemic importance of individual institutions and groups.[138]

Although some specific requirements targets only large banks (e.g. some additional capital requirements, organizational requirements such as certain board committees), most CRDIV/CRR apply to all banks to ensure a level playing-field, while Basel III, targeting internationally active banks, would have allowed some differentiations.[139] Nonetheless, not only the proportionality principle has partially inspired such documents (and should direct implementing measures),[140] but the Commission is even

Regulation', (2015), 23–24, <www.eba.europa.eu/documents/10180/807776/European+Banking+Authority+Banking+Stakeholder+Group-+Position+paper+on+proportionality.pdf>; S. Hoskins and M. Labonte, 'An Analysis of the Regulatory Burden on Small Banks', (2015) Congressional Research Service Report, 30, <www.fas.org/sgp/crs/misc/R43999.pdf>.

135 *See* BCBS, *Core Principles for Effective Banking Supervision*, (2012 BIS), principle 8: 'Supervisory approach – An effective system of banking supervision requires the supervisor to develop and maintain a forward-looking assessment of the risk profile of individual banks and banking groups, proportionate to their systemic importance.'; principle 9: 'Supervisory techniques and tools – The supervisor uses an appropriate range of techniques and tools to implement the supervisory approach and deploys supervisory resources on a proportionate basis, taking into account the risk profile and systemic importance of banks.' *See* also BCBS, *Guidance*, 6.

136 BCBS, *Core*, 13 (note 12).

137 BCBS, *Guidance*, 5 (note 24).

138 *See* Principle 2, essential criterion 8, 2012 *Core Principles.*

139 *See* DG-FISMA, 'Consultation Paper on the Possible Impact of the CRR and CRD IV on Bank Financing of the Economy', (2015), 7–8, <http://ec.europa.eu/finance/consultations/2015/long-term-finance/docs/consultation-document_en.pdf>.

140 *See* recital 46 CRR: 'The provisions of this Regulation respect the principle of proportionality, having regard in particular to the diversity in size and scale of operations

evaluating the possibility of revising the CRR/CRDIV package also to take into account differences in size, scale, business model and range of activities of banks, with simplifications for small local banks.[141] Complexity and size might be measured by varied indicators such as total balance sheet, cross-border activities, systemic relevance (including deposits and payment system), organizational complexity, business profile and funding.[142]

The scope for adjustments by Member States, competent authorities or Commission/EBA to reflect the proportionality principle has been explicitly recognized within the CRR/CRDIV framework in certain areas such as supervisory review and evaluation process (SREP) of institutions' compliance (Art. 97 CRDIV), own funds reporting (recital 127 and Art. 99(5) CRR),[143] governance (recital 54, Articles 76(5), 91(3) CRDIV), strategies for liquidity risk (Art. 86(2)–(3) CRDIV), qualified holdings, EU freedoms, remuneration and recovery and resolution plans (recitals 66, 92(2) and Articles 23, 74(4) CRDIV), leverage (recital 95 and Art. 511(2)–(3) CRR).[144] However, its relevance is limited to certain specific aspects (e.g. in the governance area, only risk-management function, number of directorships of each management body's member), leaving out many relevant others for which a level 1 reform would be needed considering CRDIV/CRR inflexibility. For instance, the EBA itself recognizes the need of a CRDIV reform to make the proportionality principle effective in the remuneration area (Art. 92(2)), 'excluding certain small, non-complex institutions from the requirements to

and to the range of activities of institutions. … Member States should ensure that the requirements laid down in this Regulation apply in a manner proportionate to the nature, scale and complexity of the risks associated with an institution's business model and activities. The Commission should ensure that delegated and implementing acts, regulatory technical standards and implementing technical standards are consistent with the principle of proportionality, so as to guarantee that this Regulation is applied in a proportionate manner. EBA should therefore ensure that all regulatory and implementing technical standards are drafted in such a way that they are consistent with and uphold the principle of proportionality.' *See* also recitals 43, 127–28 CRR and recitals 66 and 92 of CRDIV.

141 DG FISMA, 'Consultation', 7–8; ECB, 'The Impact of the CRR and CRD IV on Bank Financing. Eurosystem Response to the DG FISMA Consultation Paper', (2015), 18, <www.ecb.europa.eu/pub/pdf/other/impact_of_the_crr_and_crd_iv_on_bank_financing.en.pdf?88c21ee4d8283b0cbd89a25700b32cda>.

142 *See* Commission, 'Summary of the Responses to the Public Consultation on the Potential Impact of CRR and CRD IV on the Financing of the Economy', (2015), 21–22, <http://ec.europa.eu/finance/consultations/2015/long-term-finance/docs/summary-of-responses_en.pdf>. *See* also criteria in EBA, 'Guidelines on the Application of Simplified Obligations under Article 4(5) of Directive 2014/59/EU', EBA/GL/2015/16, §25ff.

143 *See* Commission Implementing Regulation (EU) No 680/2014 ('EBA ITS on own funds reporting', with different thresholds triggering reporting).

144 Further relevance to the proportionality principle can be found in Art. 73 (credit institutions shall maintain proportionate internal capital adequacy procedures), 74 (governance and remuneration arrangements proportionate to risk scale, nature and complexity) and Art. 77(1)–(3) CRDIV (competent authorities shall encourage institutions to adopt proportionate internal approaches for calculating own funds requirements).

apply the remuneration principles regarding deferral and payment in instruments for variable remuneration' (but not the 'bonus cap'), because of their high fixed costs and limited availability of instruments in case of cooperative/savings banks.[145] EBA SREP Guidelines, although recommending different supervisory engagement models as regards depth, intensity and frequency for different categories of institutions based on systemic and cross-border relevance (with reference to activities' size, nature, scope, complexity and structure), then adopt undifferentiated guidelines except for limited aspects (update and engagement frequency).[146]

Furthermore, some responses to the Commission's consultation highlighted the opportunity to intervene also as regards minimum requirement for eligible liabilities (MREL) under BRRD (Bank Resolution and Recovery Directive 2014/59/EU) and the definition of default.[147] BRRD allows competent authorities to simplify the content and details of recovery/resolution plans (and their updating), reporting requirements and resolvability assessment to, for example, the size, interconnectedness and complexity (cross-country, OTC-derivatives, deposits) of certain institutions' activities, even waiving relevant obligations in case of credit institutions exempted from prudential regulation affiliated to a central body or members of a institutional protection scheme *ex* Art. 10 CRR (recitals 14, 21, 25 and Articles 1(1), 4 BRRD).[148] Furthermore, resolution authorities can lower MRELs for 'more resolvable banks', particularly the small ones mainly funded through deposits and that can be liquidated under normal insolvency procedures (and through contributions of the deposit guarantee scheme).[149]

As anticipated, exemptions and simplifications in favour of small banks can also be grounded on the ability of such banks to fill important market voids and the

145 EBA, 'Opinion on the Application of the Principle of Proportionality to the Remuneration Provisions in Directive 2013/36/EU', EBA/Op/2015/25, 4ff. More recently *see*, EBA, 'Review of the Application of the Principle of Proportionality to the Remuneration Provisions in Directive 2013/36/EU', EBA/Op/2016/20.

146 EBA, 'Guidelines on Common Procedures and Methodologies for the Supervisory Review and Evaluation Process (SREP)', EBA/GL/2014/13, §§ 16ff. (with category 2 of domestic or non-significant cross-border operations, limited business lines, offering predominantly credit products to retail and corporate customers; category 1 with all other small non-complex domestic institutions, i.e. with limited activities and market share).

147 Commission, 'Summary', 21–23. About the disproportionate effect on small banks of reporting, leverage, remuneration and MREL requirements, *see* also Commission, 'Summary of Contributions to the "Call for Evidence EU Regulatory Framework for Financial Services"', (2016), 12, <http://ec.europa.eu/finance/consultations/2015/financial-regulatory-framework-review/docs/summary-of-responses_en.pdf>.

148 EBA, 'Guidelines on Simplified Obligations'.

149 *See* Commission Delegated Regulation (EU) 2016/1450 supplementing Directive 2014/59/EU ('EBA RTS Specifying the Criteria Relating to the Methodology for Setting the Minimum Requirement for Own Funds and Eligible Liabilities – MREL', EBA/RTS/2015/05), Art. 4; A. Enria, 'Opening Remarks by the Chairperson of the EBA', (EBA proportionality workshop, London, 3 July 2015), 5–6, <www.eba.europa.eu/documents/10180/1044289/Opening+remarks,%20Andrea+Enria,%20EBA+proportionality+workshop+-3+July+2015.pdf>.

consequent public benefit (arguments applicable to microfinance, too),[150] but this rationale finds recognition in EU banking Directives only for historical mutual operators (*see* below).

The prevailing idea in the international specialized literature is to adapt the existing prudential regulatory framework to the characteristics and specific risks of the microfinance business by looking mainly at activities rather than at institutional forms, for the creation of a level playing-field and flexibility for innovation, exempting in some cases small institutions.[151] Avoiding 'special windows' for microfinance or special legal statuses (unless existing requirements would impede the activity itself)[152] contain a segregation effect with reference to financial services for low-income people (with an excuse for mainstream banks to ignore such part of the population), limiting their chances to move to the mainstream sector ('graduating').[153] On the other hand, applying the same regulation on social and for-profit operators would destroy incentives for socially responsible services, perpetuating the exclusion of non-remunerative clients (*see* Chapter 3, §2).

However, while in developing countries MFIs are generally sustainable, compete with the mainstream sector and face a simple regulation often oriented to financial inclusion, in (especially Western) Europe, MFIs strives to reach sustainability and deal with multiple obstacles (*see* Chapters 2, §2; 5, §1). Consequently, the creation of special regimes and special windows for microfinance or even socially responsible financial operators can be reasonable. Differentiated regimes can be envisaged and based on the different levels of risks (including systemic) posed by their respective activities and products, allowing operators offering basic services to comply with simpler requirements while moving up to a higher regulatory regime in case of more complex operations and larger scale (*see* §§b and 4).[154]

Some European countries (e.g. Italy and, recently reformed, Romania) have adopted specific microfinance regulations while others have recurred to special exemptions (France and Hungary) or to already existing regimes for operators with social mission (*see* British CDFIs) (Chapter 4, §6),[155] but savings collection is generally precluded to non-bank operators, unless they are credit unions or

150 Hoskins and Labonte, 'An Analysis', 30–31; Tarullo, 'Tailoring'.

151 *See* R. Chavez and C. Gonzalez Vega, 'Principles of Regulation and Prudential Supervision: Should They Be Different for Microenterprise Finance Organizations?', (1992), <http://pdf.usaid.gov/pdf_docs/PNABM578.pdf>; R. Christen and R. Rosenberg, 'The Rush to Regulate: Legal Frameworks for Microfinance', (2000) CGAP Occasional Paper 4, <www.cgap.org/sites/default/files/CGAP-Occasional-Paper-The-Rush-to-Regulate-Legal-Frameworks-for-Microfinance-Apr-2000.pdf>; Christen, 'Microfinance Consensus'.

152 Christen, 'Microfinance Consensus', 9ff., 15, 23; Jansson, 'Principles', 6; Christen and Rosenberg, 'The Rush', 13ff.; BCBS, *Microfinance*, 6–7, 37–42; Ledgerwood, *The New*, 419ff.

153 *See* R. Rajan, 'Separate and Unequal', (2006) 43(1) *Finan Dev* 58, 56–57.

154 *See* BCBS, *Guidance*, 9–10.

155 *See* B. Bruhn-Leon et al., 'Progress for Microfinance', (2012) EIF Working Paper 2012/13, 9, <www.eif.org/news_centre/publications/eif_wp_2012_13_microfinance.pdf>.

financial cooperatives (e.g. Croatia, Bulgaria, UK). In fact, such traditional operators have even received express special exemptions from CRDIV because of their historic role in serving members-only, social inspiration, limited activities, sometimes external funding limitations and therefore difficulties in meeting capital requirements, subject to special national regimes (*see* Ireland Art. 2(5)8; Portugal Art. 2 (5)19; UK Art. (2(5)23; Lithuania Art. 2(5)14 CRDIV).

In the next sections, I will analyse some typical prudential regulatory requirements that might raise critical issues when applied to microfinance-banks (or NBFIs subject to the same requirements) and in consequence might need adaptation. The Commission has pleaded against exemptions of bank-MFIs from prudential requirements for banks – but in favour of adaptations in reason of the small size as allowed under the proportionality principle – since, despite the low systemic risk entailed, the failure of a microcredit provider can affect the credibility of other bank-MFIs.[156]

b In particular, authorization, minimum initial capital and corporate governance

Principle 4 of the Basel 'Core Principles for effective supervision' establishes that '[a]t a minimum, the licensing process consists of an assessment of the ownership structure and governance (including the fitness and propriety of Board members and senior management) of the bank and its wider group, and its strategic and operating plan, internal controls, risk management and projected financial condition (including capital base) [...]'. The BCBS accepts that supervisors might establish different licensing criteria and procedures for different institutions reflecting a proportionate approach and therefore different levels of risks in activities, services and products, graduating supervisory resources to the systemic importance and risks posed by different operators.[157]

Under EU law, the commencement of banking activity has to be preceded by an authorization by competent authorities (Art. 8 CRDIV) subject to certain requirements (economic needs of the market excluded: Art. 11 CRDIV) and a safe and sound evaluation of the same. Among these requirements, CRDIV imposes the presentation of a programme of operations, minimum initial capital of €5 million (Art. 12 CRDIV) and 'fit and proper' test for qualifying shareholders and managers as well as professionality requirements for managers (Articles 13, 14, 91(1) CRDIV).

Such requirements do not generally represent an obstacle for setting up a microfinance bank, unless, for instance, the professional experience required for managers is set too high or the limits to cumulative appointments and time commitment are too restrictive (Art. 91(1)–(3) CRDIV) in consideration of the smaller and less attractive (because of lower returns) job market. Instead, imposing the

156 Commission, 'Report on the application of Directive 2006/48/EC to Microcredit', (Report) COM(2012) 769 final, 10.

157 BCBS, *Guidance*, 9.

presence of private investors or development and international organizations among bank owners might reinforce private monitoring.[158]

The minimum capital requirement, established to signal the seriousness of the business venture and support the initial infrastructure, could represent instead a critical issue. Nonetheless, Art. 12(2) CRDIV allows Member States to set lower levels (equal or above €1 million) if they can reasonably justify their choice before the Commission and EBA, with financial inclusion objectives used in the past as partial justification for cooperative-banks.

The above mentioned proportionality principle can support a lower initial capital as well as less strict executives' requirements based on the simplest nature and range of the activities (only basic financial services for low-income clients) and limited size of the business. Similarly, based on the proportionality principle, we might defend more flexible rules about corporate governance instead of the new rigid requirements for (especially large) banks already examined.[159] Anyway, good corporate governance is fundamental for microfinance and can counterbalance simplified prudential requirements (Chapter 5, §2).

c Own funds requirements and the impact of Basel III. Non-performing loans

Since the 1988 Basel Accord (Basel I), internationally active credit institutions have been required to have own funds proportionate to the riskiness of their credit exposures, in order to contain managers' moral hazard and maintain a cushion against sudden losses.[160] Subsequent reforms have tried to address shortcomings that have surfaced over time and reinforce its main structure. For instance, the 2004 Basel II reform expanded its reach to banking risks (operative and market risks) other than credit risk but the latter remains the fundamental one. Furthermore, although maintaining the own funds requirement as the central pillar, Basel II added two other pillars to better contain risks through the combined action of capital requirements, supervisory review and market discipline (public disclosure).

Basel I prescribed only one method to calculate the value of risk-based assets (Standardized Approach – SA): first, banks had to sort their assets into certain risk-weight categories identified by the Accord and based on the expected riskiness depending on the counterparty type (e.g. sovereign, retail, residential property, corporate) and collateral; then had to multiply the value of each asset for the risk-weight corresponding to a risk category and again assigned by the Accord (e.g. certain development banks 0%, OECD banks 20%, corporate and other assets 100%, etc.). Off-balance sheet items had preliminarily to be converted in a credit-equivalent value by multiplying the face amount per a credit conversion factor.

158 Jansson, 'Principles', 53–55.

159 *See* EBA, 'Guidelines on Internal Governance' and 'Guidelines on the Assessment of the Suitability of Members of the Management Body and Key Function Holders', EBA/GL/2012/06.

160 About the Accord and the reasons leading to it, *see* D. Tarullo, *Banking on Basel: The Future of International Financial Regulation*, (Institute for International Economics 2008), 210–11; Barth, *Rethinking*, 64–65.

However, Basel II, on the one hand, assigned relevance to credit rating agencies' evaluations to identify risk-weights under the SA and introduced more diversified and risk-sensitive categorizations (e.g. different risk-weights for corporate exposures depending on the existence of a rating and its grade). On the other hand, it added two other methods of calculation, allowing banks meeting certain parameters to use their internal risk parameters to calculate the regulatory capital required (Internal Ratings-Based approach – IRB). Different degrees of bank discretion were recognized, with the 'Foundation' IRB allowing discretion only in the calculation of the probability of default and the 'Advanced' IRB, almost entirely based on the bank internal estimates. Especially the latter was conceived to allow large banks with sophisticated internal capital allocation processes to better calculate risks, improving also risk management.

Nonetheless, the main ground-breaking reform has taken place after the financial crisis, when Basel III has introduced quality requirements for capital and new buffers to reduce Basel II weaknesses.[161] The ratio between capital and risk-based assets still needs to be at least 8% (total capital ratio: Art. 92(1)c CRR) but now, additionally, banks must have a capital composed exclusively of high quality instruments at their complete disposal (common equity tier-1 capital – CET1) corresponding to at least 4.5% of risk-based assets (Art. 92(1)a CRR). CET1 is composed of instruments issued by the same bank, fully paid-in, subordinated, with fully discretionary noncumulative dividends or coupons and have neither a maturity date nor an incentive to redeem. These are typically common shares, stock surplus, retained earnings and reserves (*see* Articles 26–28 CRR).[162] Additional tier 1 instruments are instead instruments that are subordinated, with distribution restricted and perpetual but, instead of CET1 instruments, they can be called, redeemed or repurchased under certain conditions at the issuer's discretion not before 5 years and can be written down or converted in case of certain trigger-events (Articles 53–54 CRR). These should contribute with CET1 to account for tier-1 minimum capital requirement of 6% of risk-based assets (Art. 92(1)b CRR).

However, Basel III also introduced additional capital buffers: the capital conservation buffer (2.5% of risk-based assets and composed of CET1) to be built outside of stress periods and protect against these, and the countercyclical capital buffer, to hedge from downturns after periods of excessive credit growth (a national ratio is set between 0% and 2.5% of risk-based assets by competent authorities depending on credit market growth). Tougher capital requirements have been set for capital market, trading business and securitizations exposures as well as additional requirements introduced for Systemically Important Financial Institutions (SIFIs).

161 About Basel II weaknesses, *see* Tarullo, *Banking*, 178ff.; BCBS, 'Basel Committee's Response to the Financial Crisis: Report to the G20', (2010), 8ff., <www.bis.org/publ/bcbs179.pdf>; Cranston, *Principles*, 90–91; Carnell, *The Law*, 272ff.; G. Miller and G. Rosenfeld, 'Intellectual Hazard: How Conceptual Biases in Complex Organizations Contributed to the Crisis of 2008', (2010) 33 *Harvard J Law and Publ P* 807, 830ff.

162 BCBS, *Basel III: A Global Regulatory Framework for More Resilient Banks and Banking Systems*, (2011, revised December 2011), 2, 14.

The Basel Accord represents soft-law and within a restricted group of countries but has been adopted worldwide by most countries to signal the robustness of their banking systems or imposed as conditions for financing from International Organizations.[163] As anticipated, it was conceived for internationally active banks since the objective was to create a level-playing field among cross-border banks but many countries (and in particular the EU) have decided to make Basel requirements mandatory for all banks (*see* previous banking Directives and CRDIV-CRR).

This fact has raised issues about the likely negative impact of the new capital requirements (especially the conservation buffer) on small banks (because of the comparatively higher regulatory burden: *see* above §§4.c and 6.a) and, more generally, on SME-lending. In fact, although Modigliani-Miller theory suggests that better capitalized banks can recapitalize issuing cheaper equity without shrinking lending, studies evidence that tighter capital requirements lead banks to reduce lending (at least in the short term) because of asymmetric information in the equity market and agency costs with bank management.[164] Moreover, such a reduction hits mostly the perceived riskiest borrowers, including SMEs,[165] especially when there are the same capital requirement rules to treat SMEs as risky. In fact, SMEs have a more fragile financial structure, statistically lower profitability and activity ratio, lower ability to pay interest rates and higher probability of default although counter-balanced by higher granularity, lower concentration and systematic risk.[166] Under the SA, SMEs are likely to be assigned a 100% risk-weight because they are generally unrated while large firms can receive a risk-weight ranging from 20% to 150% depending on the credit agencies' assessment (Art. 122 CRR). Nonetheless, CRR allows banks to consider SMEs as retail exposures subject to a 75% risk-weight for loans below €1 million when sharing similar characteristics with a significant number of exposures (Art. 123 CRR). The risk-weight can be as low as 35% (but up to 150%) when loans are secured by residential mortgage and 50% (up to 150%) when secured by commercial real estate (Art. 124–126 CRR). Consequently, the Commission has also considered the implementation of new and favourable risk-weights for SME-lending.[167]

163 Tarullo, *Banking*, 206; Barth, *Rethinking*, 71.

164 *See* H. Fraisse et al., 'The Real Effect of Bank Capital Requirements', (2015) ACPR-Banque de France Débats économiques et financiers N° 8, <http://acpr.banque-france.fr/fileadmin/user_upload/acp/publications/Debats_economiques_et_financiers/20130802-The-Real-Effects-of-Bank-Capital-Requirements.pdf> (1% increase in capital requirements leads to a reduction in lending by approximately 10%).

165 *See* U. Albertazzi and D. Marchetti, 'Credit Supply, Flight to Quality and Evergreening: An Analysis of Bank–Firm Relationships after Lehman', (2010) Banca d'Italia Working Paper 756, <www.bancaditalia.it/pubblicazioni/temi-discussione/2010/2010-0756/en_tema_756.pdf?language_id=1> (less capitalized larger banks present such 'flight to quality' more than smaller, less capitalized banks).

166 EBA, 'Assessment of SME Proposals for CRD IV/CRR', (2012), 8, <www.eba.europa.eu/documents/10180/16148/EBA-SME-Report.pdf>.

167 EBA, 'Assessment', 8ff.; EBA, 'Report on SMEs and SMEs Supporting Factor', EBA/Op/2016/04, 28ff., <www.eba.europa.eu/documents/10180/1359456/EBA-Op-2016-04++Report+on+SMEs+and+SME+supporting+factor.pdf>.

However, to foster SME-lending and counterbalance the negative effects of the crisis and the perspective introduction of the conservation buffer, Article 501 CRR has already introduced a SME Supporting Factor (SME-SF), which applies a deduction of 0.7691 on the capital requirement for exposures to SMEs below €1.5 million. The EBA has however estimated that the SME-SF, although entailing a reduction in capital requirements (increase of 0.21% in CET1 for credit risk of large banks using IRBA method)[168] sometimes above the corresponding systemic risk,[169] has not led to more SME credit (but also recognizing that some effects might show up later and the likely influence on the results of other factors).[170]

Current proposals at Basel level consider assigning a 85% risk-weight to SMEs in the corporate class (maintaining the 75% in the retail one) under the SA, justified by the frequent existence of non-eligible collateral (e.g. in terms of listed categories, liquidity, enforceability: Articles 194ff. CRR) and lower correlation.[171]

The treatment of SME-lending is a fundamental issue for small banks since SMEs are generally their main clients. Small banks tend to use SA, not generally having the scale (in terms of number of observations and therefore statistical relevance and resources) to develop an IRB.[172] Current proposals envisage the creation of an intermediate method of calculation (between the SA and the IRB) to avoid the negative effects for small banks of the allegedly excessively strict SA risk-weights.[173]

Analogous considerations can be applied to bank-MFIs. The consequences of excessive rigidity in SME-lending treatment under SA approach are even more severe for bank-MFIs since alternative forms of collateral used in microfinance generally do not qualify as eligible collateral under the Basel Accord and SME-lending

168 The EBA Report relies only on data provided by large banks from the euro area reporting to the ECB, for which the capital relief is limited (except for banks in Italy, France and Spain where almost 59% of the capital relief is concentrated because of the large SME-lending sector). However, we can presume that the bulk of SME-lending is supplied by small European banks (§2.b–c) for which no reliable and comparable data are available. Nonetheless, e.g. in Italy the capital relief for small banks is estimated at 0.50 percentage points while at large banks at 0.22: EBA, 'Report', 71ff.

169 EBA study shows that the lower risk-weights for SME-lending consequent to the application of the SME-SF are consistent with the lower level of systematic risk for all exposures under the SA and for corporate exposures under the IRBA while they are not for retail exposures under IRBA (where capital requirements are lower than systematic risk): EBA, 'Report', 88ff.

170 EBA evidences that SME not qualifying for the SME-SP would have represented a better control group than large firms but information about these data were not available at EU level: EBA, 'Report', 11 (note 8), 68ff.

171 BCBS, *Revisions to the Standardised Approach for Credit Risk – Standards. Second Consultative Document*, (BIS 2015).

172 About the difficulties in elaborating a specific IRB for MFIs because of the lack of sufficient statistical data, *see* P. Brown et al., 'Microfinance Sector Transformation – Making Sense of the Basel II Capital Accord', (2008), 6, <www.citifoundation.com/citi/microfinance/data/news080602a.pdf>.

173 EBA-Banking Stakeholder Group, 'Proportionality', 35.

tends not only to be the main exposure but also the only one.[174] However, microloans might be riskier than SME or retail loans because of the contagion effect and risk of fast de-capitalization as well as of typical geographic concentration and borrowers' interdependency (although such factors are less severe in Europe: §2.a).[175] These specificities have made some authors propose a specific risk category ('private development finance') for forms of financing directed to low income people and small businesses with development goals.[176]

Microloans are generally classified in Europe as SME retail exposures, subject to the 75% risk-weight.[177] Nonetheless, as already evidenced, in Europe public authorities, international organizations and other subjects provide support to the sector, also through guarantees that partially cover the amount of microloans. Consequently, bank-MFIs, under both SA and IRBA can apply to the part of the micro-loan covered by the guarantee the risk-weight applicable to the guarantor (Art. 235–236 CRR), which might even be, in case of a public authority of a Member State (or an EU institution or development bank), 0% or 20% (otherwise from 0% to 150% depending on the rating evaluation: Art. 114–118 CRR), significantly reducing capital requirements.[178] Private guarantees (frequent in Hungary and Spain) by the same guarantor might violate the 25% large exposures limit (Articles 387ff. and 395 CRR), while public ones are exempted.[179]

However, large European bank-MFIs from international networks might be able to elaborate, based on the network experience in developing countries, specialized IRB methods, although adapted to the different context and procedures.

Additional hurdles can originate from the strict conditions to qualify as CET1, considering the limited availability of investors (*see* Chapter 5, §3). For instance, preferred shares, often used by MFIs to fund themselves without losing control over the business and its social orientation, can account to CET1 only if, in addition to other conditions, there is not an obligation to pay dividends nor

174 In favour of lower CARs or risk-weights for microloans because of high capital levels or low leverage, *see* Brown, 'Microfinance', 5; K. Imboden, 'Basel II and Microfinance: Exercising National Prerogatives', (2005), 11ff., <www.microfinancegateway.org/sites/default/files/mfg-en-paper-basel-ii-and-microfinance-exercising-national-prerogatives-2005.pdf>.

175 *See* Christen, 'Microfinance Consensus', 19; McGuire and Conroy, *The Role*, 43ff.; Jansson., 'Principles', 22; Jansson and Wenner, 'Financial Regulation', 22ff.; BCBS, *Microfinance*, 19–20; BCBS, *Guidance*, 22. For instance, in Pakistan Microfinance Banks (MFBs) have had to reach a 15% CAR as opposed to the usual 8% (but 10% starting 2009) for commercial banks: *see* State Bank of Pakistan, 'Annual Report 2008–2009', 45 and 'Capital Adequacy Framework for MFBs – Amendment in the Prudential Regulation (R-1) issued vide BPRD Circular No. 10 of June 3, 2015', <www.sbp.org.pk/bprd/2015/C10-Revised-PR-R-1-Annex-A.pdf>.

176 *See* E. Avgouelas, 'Access to Finance, Microfinance, and International Capital Adequacy Standards for Banks: A New Approach to Development', (2007) 4 *Manchester J Int'l Econ L* 7, 44ff.

177 Commission, 'Report', 8.

178 *See* Commission, 'Report', 8–9.

179 Ibidem 9.

preferential distribution treatment regarding the order of payments (Art. 28(1)h CRR), likely diminishing part of investors' interest.[180]

Rules about capital requirements for credit risk obviously take into account exposures in default and of general and specific applied risk adjustments (Articles 62, 110–111, 127ff. CRR). In fact, the Core Principles require competent authorities to ensure that banks have 'adequate policies and processes for the early identification and management of problem assets, and the maintenance of adequate provisions and reserves' (Principle 18), including the ongoing oversight of problem assets, the early identification of deteriorating assets, the value of risk mitigants and adequate classification of loans and loan provisioning. In particular, banks are generally required to create a general reserve for NPE (as a percentage of the total value of loans and which can account as tier 2 capital: Art. 62 and 110 CRR) and an additional one with provisions based on specific risks of loans (depending eg on the existence of collaterals, credit history, arrears). Strictly applying typical loan-loss provisions of commercial banks to bank-MFIs would result in excessively burdensome requirements since micro-loans might be classified as risky, in the absence of traditional forms of collateral or credit history. For this reason, supervisors should adapt their requirements to alternative forms of collateral and credit-worthiness checks.[181] The 'MFIs European Code' simply requires MFIs to disclose and periodically review loan-loss provisioning methodology (clauses 3.10–3.11).

On the other hand, because of the short maturity, contagion effect and fast de-capitalization in microfinance (*see* §4), 'past due loans should move to riskier categories with higher provisioning and be classified as nonaccrual more quickly than other types of loans' (especially when re-scheduled).[182] Consequently, supervisors could impose reporting and reserve obligations in presence of a few days or a certain number of instalments delay (instead of weeks/months).[183] This should be complemented with risk-management requirements entailing

180 According to EBA CET1 list (updated September 2016, <www.eba.europa.eu/-/eba-updates-its-cet1-list>), Croatian, Belgian and Romanian preferential shares are CET1 instruments but cannot fully account as such under Art. 28.

181 BCBS, *Guidance*, 25.

182 BCBS, *Guidance*, 24.

183 *See* J. Rosengard, 'Oversight is a Many-Splendored Thing: Choice and Proportionality in Regulating and Supervising Microfinance Institutions', in M. Labie and B. Armendariz (eds), *The Handbook of Microfinance*, (World Scientific Publishing 2011), 165. For example, in Pakistan a credit is considered sub-standard after 180–364 days delay for commercial banks (requiring a provision of 20% of net delinquent principal) while after 30–89 days for MFBs (triggering a 25% provision). MFBs loans become loss (requiring a 100% provision and written-off after a month) at the 180th day (while after two years for commercial banks). Reporting obligations are various and with different timing but, generally, more frequent for MFBs: *see* Bank of Pakistan, 'Annual Report 2008–2009', 44ff. Similarly, Nigerian Microfinance banks have to maintain a 20% of assets liquid (while commercial banks 40% and community banks 30–35%): *see* D. Porteous et al., 'Prudential Regulation in Microfinance', (2010) FAI Policy Framing Note 3, 11ff., <www.microfinancegateway.org/sites/default/files/mfg-en-paper-prudential-regulation-in-microfinance-jan-2010.pdf>.

monitoring of loans and early warning systems to promptly respond to problems (*see* Chapter 5, §2.c).

In the EU, NPLs now represent an acute problem, with European banks' portfolios, especially in some countries (e.g. Italy, Greece, Spain, Slovenia) filled with NPLs.[184] Non-performing assets are currently defined (after verifying the existence of wide variations in the definitions among countries) as '(a) material exposures which are more than 90 days past due' or for which '(b) the debtor is assessed as unlikely to pay its credit obligations in full without realisation of collateral, regardless of the existence of any past due amount or of the number of days past due'.[185]

Bank-MFIs are required to report NPLs but, as evidenced above, would need an adjusted definition, since 90-days represents a too large period and would not allow prompt measures in response to NPLs.

d Liquidity and leverage requirements

Microcredit is typically short-term and, consequently, should not entail high liquidity problems but progressive lending extends the maturity, without MFIs generally having the opportunity to rely on central bank liquidity facilities. In Europe, where progressive lending is rare, micro-loans however typically present longer maturities (§2.a). Furthermore, MFIs can rely on a quite restricted number of funding resources, not necessarily able to provide prompt responses to liquidity needs, this aggravating liquidity risk.[186]

Basel III, after the liquidity crises experienced in 2007/2008 (*see* Northern Rock and Bearn Sterns cases), imposes on banks also liquidity requirements and related reporting requirements. In particular, the Liquidity Coverage Ratio (LCR) measures short-term resilience to liquidity problems and aims at ensuring that banks have 'an adequate stock of unencumbered high-quality liquid assets (HQLA) that can be converted easily and immediately in private markets into cash to meet their liquidity needs for a 30 calendar day liquidity stress scenario' (and are low risk, of easy evaluation, low volatility and low correlation with risky assets).[187] The Net Stable Funding Ratio (NSFR) targets instead long-term (over 1-year) liquidity and limits over-reliance on short-term wholesale funding (*see* also Articles 411ff. CRR).[188] Basel III and the CRDIV/CRR package make such

184 *See* ECB, 'Financial Stability Review', (2015).

185 *See* ITS 29(145) Commission Implementing Regulation (EU) 2015/227 amending Implementing Regulation (EU) 680/2014 laying down implementing technical standards with regard to supervisory reporting of institutions according to Regulation (EU) No 575/2013, [2015] OJ L 48/1.

186 *See* BCBS, *Guidance*, 25–27.

187 The ratio between highly illiquid assets and net cash outflows over 30 days must be at least 100%: BCBS, *Basel III: The Liquidity Coverage Ratio and Liquidity Risk Monitoring Tool*, (BIS 2013).

188 The ratio between available stable funding (capital and liabilities reliable in a one-year time horizon considering maturities and propensity of funding providers to withdraw) and required stable funding (determined based on the liquidity characteristics and

ratios fully mandatory only in 2018 (the LCR was introduced already in 2015 but set at 60% and then gradually risen). Again, Basel III mandates liquidity requirements only for internationally active banks but CRR applies the same to all banks and the EBA has not identified significant differences among banks of different sizes while studying the impact of NSFR introduction. EBA, however, does not exclude future lower reporting requirements for small banks.[189]

For the reasons highlighted above (longer maturities and limited funding), abiding to such requirements might be troublesome for European MFIs but a recent study seems to attest MFIs' low liquidity risk and adequate liquidity coverage.[190] However, small bank-MFIs should be subject anyway to simplified rules but ensuring the presence of certain unencumbered liquid assets against a percentage of micro-deposits and limit the concentration from a single funding source.[191]

Basel III and CRR also introduced a non-risk based leverage requirement to complement capital requirements and that will be fully in force starting 2018 (although public reporting started in 2015). The ratio between tier 1 capital and exposures (leverage) must be at least equal to 3%, meaning that banks' exposures can account for up to 33 times of their tier 1 capital (*see* also Articles 429–430 CRR).[192] As with liquidity, despite the reference to the proportionality principle for establishing reporting requirements (Articles 414, 99(5) CRR), the single rulebook does not distinguish among different bank types and sizes. However, as evidenced above (§4 and note 107), European MFIs show an average leverage ratio below the one reported by European banks.

e Concentration risk and disclosure

MFIs typically extend small loans to a high number of clients, therefore generally not triggering the application of large exposures rules (but see above §c about exposures to private guarantors of microloans). The Core principles (principle 19, AD 1) and CRR (Articles 392, 395 CRR) in fact require banks to limit exposures of more than 10% of their capital to the same client or group of connected clients to maximum 25% of their capital.

MFIs concentrate their activity on certain types of clients and certain geographic areas (*see* §2.a) but 'large exposure' obligations are interpreted quite strictly (related to specific control relationships or economic dependencies such

residual maturities of assets) must be at least 100%: BCBS, *Basel III: The Net Stable Funding Ratio*, (BIS 2014). *See* also Commission Delegated Regulation (EU) 2015/61 to supplement Regulation (EU) No 575/2013 with regard to liquidity coverage requirement for Credit Institutions, [2015] OJ L 11/1.

189 EBA, 'Report on Net Stable Funding Requirements under Article 510 of the CRR', EBA/Op/2015/22, 141–155, <www.eba.europa.eu/documents/10180/983359/EBA-Op-2015-22+NSFR+Report.pdf>.

190 T. Gietzen, 'The Exposure of Microfinance Institutions to Financial Risk', (2015) University of St. Gallen School of Finance Research Paper 2015/06, <http://ssrn.com/abstract=2590058>.

191 BCBS, *Microfinance*, 24.

192 BCBS, *Basel III Leverage Ratio Framework and Disclosure Requirements*, (BIS 2014).

that, were one of the counterparties to fail, all of the counterparties would very likely fail), generally not involving sectoral or geographic concentration.[193] Nonetheless, such concentrations are relevant too and Art. 81 CRDIV (as well as the Core Principles) requires competent authorities to ensure that also concentration risks from exposures to each counterparty or group of interconnected counterparties, in same industries or geographic region are addressed and controlled,[194] balancing such risk with the benefits coming from specialization and local knowledge.[195] EBA Guidelines on SREP (§ 146) require authorities to evaluate sectorial, geographic, product and guarantee concentration. The 'MFIs European Code' recommends limiting geographic, sector and types of clients concentrations, although recognizing vulnerable groups as main targets (clause 3.7).

Finally, as reaffirmed several times in this book, transparency is fundamental and good information systems and monitoring needed, these measures counterbalancing and justifying regulatory simplifications but some CRDIV/CRR obligations such as stress tests, supervisory review, frequency and documentation required might result excessively burdensome in consideration of MFIs' simpler structures and activities.[196]

f Prudential supervisory and resolution instruments

Supervising numerous and varied (in terms of processes, structures, contracts, products) institutions relying on relationship-based models can be extremely costly and in contrast with the proportionality and maximization of resources principles, therefore somewhere justifying forms of private or hybrid supervision (*see* Chapter 3, §3.c–d). However, when MFIs are able to reach such a scale to become banks, they likely recur to more standardized, closer to commercial banks' models (e.g. legal form, products, documentation and internal processes). Consequently, supervision of bank-MFIs or large NBFI-MFIs might be less complex and costly. Anyway, supervisors need to get familiar with peculiar microfinance products and procedures.[197]

Supervisory tools might require adaptations too: in fact, typical stop-lending orders (e.g. Art. 104(1)e–f) might jeopardize MFI's ability to continue its operations (*see* §2.a). Depending on MFIs' ownership, capital calls might remain unanswered in the short period because of the difficulties experienced by foundations, social investors, public actors and NGOs in promptly providing capital (*see* Chapter 5, §2.a).

193 BCBS, *Standards Supervisory Framework for Measuring and Controlling Large Exposures*, (BIS 2014), 3–4.
194 BCBS, *Microfinance*, 22.
195 CEBS, 'Guidelines on the Management of Concentration Risk under the Supervisory Review Process (GL31)', (2010), guideline 21, 27, <www.eba.europa.eu/documents/10180/16094/Concentration.pdf/75fb2eca-955d-4c8e-a730-b491eef93188>.
196 *See* Christen, 'Microfinance', 21; Jansson, 'Principles', 31ff.; BCBS, *Microfinance*, 4–5, 7–8, 21–22, 30.
197 *See* BCBS, *Guidance*, 11–12

Furthermore, banking regulation traditionally includes special rules and procedures for managing banking crises and winding up in order to protect depositors and their trust, with an increasingly wider use of non-liquidating procedures for the maximization of bank assets and depositors rights. Post-crisis intense integration process in Europe has led to the adoption of a single rulebook also as regards bank crises (Chapter 3, §4.b). The BRRD has in fact harmonized the tools available to supervisory and resolution authorities in case of bank difficulties with the objective of promptly and effectively managing bank crises without resorting to bail-outs at the expenses of public resources. Such instruments range from recovery and resolution plans (to establish in advance measures to be taken in case of a crisis: Articles 4ff. BRRD), to early intervention measures (e.g. managers removal and substitution, capital calls, request of reduction of certain risks, prohibition of certain activities: Articles 27ff.), to resolution tools (sale of assets, bridge-bank, bail-in, bad bank: Articles 37ff.) to avoid inefficient bank liquidations (contrary to depositor interest and systemic risk considerations). These rules are of particular importance for SIFIs but apply also to small banks.

Nonetheless, in case of microfinance, the use of such tools might be problematic and ineffective. For instance, the sale or transfer of the portfolio as well as manager's substitution might result in a portfolio deterioration because of relevance of MFI identity for ensuring clients' repayment or of certain and experienced managers in the MFI's functioning (*see* Chapter 5, §2 and §4.b).[198] Many recent MFIs crises have showed that the combination of the contagion effect and the lack of a prompt substitute for the failing MFIs for the collection of loans contribute to the rapid loss of asset value and permanent failure of the MFI.[199] Recovery and resolution plans entailing arrangements with partners and within a microfinance network therefore become fundamental.

7 Principles and guidelines for regulators

Microfinance shares with banking (especially small banks) some characteristics and risks but also presents many relevant specific features (e.g. business model, lending techniques, borrower evaluation, etc.) that necessarily influence the assessment of how to regulate microfinance.

Traditional arguments for banking regulation justify the restriction of prudential regulation's scope to financial institutions offering both loans and deposits. Therefore, European MFIs would generally escape prudential rules since only a small and mature part of the sector provides savings products.

Nonetheless, the financial crisis had paved the way for the extension of prudential requirements to entities formally outside of the banking area but

198 *See* BCBS, *Guidance*, 16; BCBS, *Microfinance*, 30–31; Rozas, 'Throwing'; D. Rozas and V. Kothari, 'Preparing for Failure: Strategies for Challenging Times in Microfinance', (7 Nov. 2010), <www.danielrozas.com/2010/11/08/preparing-for-failure-strategies-for-challenging-times/>; Meagher, *Microfinance*, 14; Christen and Rosenberg, 'The Rush', 4–5; Christen et al., 'Microfinance Consensus', 25–26.

199 *See* Rozas, 'Throwing'.

performing similar functions (shadow banking system). However, after analysing the main rationales and limits for subjecting shadow banking entities to the reach of prudential regulation and in line with a functional approach in financial regulation, European MFIs tend to fall outside of such prudential perimeter, since they generally do not present systemic risk, do not engage in credit risk transfer, maturity or liquidity transformation or leverage creation as well as mostly rely on long-term financing from institutional and professional actors (as opposed to short-term retail financing). Consequently, there are grounds to propose a lighter regulation based on a registration requirement subject to simple and conventional conditions (e.g. fit and proper executives and owners, adequate resources and business plan) and on disclosure, business conduct and flexible governance requirements, with some (although limited) space for private regulation and supervision to save public resources.

As regards deposit-taking MFIs, they are naturally subject to banking regulation but the peculiar characteristics and risks of microfinance impose an adaptation of mainstream requirements (even for NBFI-MFIs subject to bank-like regulation despite the above mentioned contrary recommendations). As regards simplifications, the CRDIV/CRR package and the BRRD embed the proportionality principle, which can justify a different treatment in consideration of size, risks, types of activities. Such a position is reinforced by the existence of objective difficulties and obstacles to microfinance development in Europe, despite its relevant role in filling a market gap. Regimes closer to banks' should be applied in case of larger scale and complexity. Other adaptations are needed to adequately respond to microfinance characteristics and needs. For instance, Basel risk-weights might not represent an issue, especially in the presence of guarantees by public entities, but CET1 quality requirement can. Also loan-loss provisioning framework should recognize the existence of alternative collateral and risk-management instruments, on the one hand, and the risk of faster deterioration, on the other (therefore referring to shorter periods or number of defaulted instalments in the definition of NPLs in microfinance and faster provisioning). Similarly, liquidity, reporting and supervisory review requirements need to be simplified as suggested for small banks, although ensuring a good level of transparency.

There are also arguments for introducing a favourable treatment for commercial banks' involvement in microfinance, tailored to the type and size of the same. For instance, simplifications in terms of Basel requirements are justified for commercial banks providing funding to MFIs and in terms of SREP and reporting for banks with a MFI lending-partner.

The use of guarantee funds, although fundamental, should be limited to a certain percentage of each loan amount (no more than 80%) to contain moral hazard.

7 Dimension V: Microfinance as an innovative chameleon: the ability to take advantage of new technologies

1 Microfinance as financial innovation and the 'regulatory dialectic'. The new subprime?

Microfinance has presented itself as a new way of delivering financial services to the poor in a sustainable way and, therefore, as a financial innovation, such as in the past banking checks, derivatives, certain credit screening techniques and internet banking.[1]

In fact, financial innovation can be defined as a '1) "new" or "better" way of providing the fundamental financial services of the financial sector, which increases the opportunity set of the sector participants and lower transaction costs; and 2) [...] new instrumentalities and processes that facilitate the delivery of the fundamental services of the financial sector'.[2] Consequently, microfinance (especially microcredit) can be considered *per se* financial innovation representing a new product/service or new production process or organizational form,[3] using new combination of existing instruments to go back to banking origins (*see* relationship-banking and business plan's evaluation: Chapters 2; 6, §2.b).

1 About financial innovation, *see* E. Kane, 'Impact of Regulation on Economic Behavior. Accelerating Inflation, Technological Innovation, and the Decreasing Effectiveness of Banking Regulation', (1981) 36(2) *J Financ* 355; D. Llewellyn, 'Financial Innovation: A Basic Analysis', in H.Cavanna (ed.), *Financial Innovation*, (Routledge 1992), 14ff.; W. Scott Frame and L White, 'Technological Change, Financial Innovation, and Diffusion in Banking', in Berger et al., *The Oxford Handbook of Banking*, (1st edn, OUP 2012); J. Ackerman, 'Financial Innovations: Balancing Private and Public Interests', in M. Haliassos (ed.), *Financial Innovation: Too Much or Too Little?*, (MIT Press 2013).

2 C. Pouncy, 'Contemporary Financial Innovation: Orthodoxy and Alternatives', (1998) 51 *SMUL Rev* 505, 518. Financial innovation generally consists of different bundles of standard products already offered but dormant and with zero supply until something happens: *see* BIS, 'Recent Innovations in International Banking', (1986), 169, <www.bis.org/publ/ecsc01a.pdf>; P. Molyneux and N. Shamroukh, *Financial Innovation*, (Wiley 1999), 60–61, 78.

3 Frame and White ('Technological', 488) group financial innovation 'as new products (e.g., subprime mortgages) or services (e.g., Internet banking); new production processes (e.g., credit scoring); or new organizational forms (e.g., Internet-only banks)'. *See* also Ackerman, 'Financial', 214.

As such, it differs from other types of innovation for low research costs, lack of patent and the influence of regulation in the creation and features of financial innovations (*see* below).[4] First movers bear all the risk for failure but once they succeed, newcomers can easily copy their model without sharing the research and investment costs (the first-movers dilemmas/free-rider problem).[5]

As with other financial innovations, microfinance contributes to achieving a higher level of the financial sector's efficiency (reducing costs or filling a market gap: *see* Chapters 4–5)[6] and democratization.[7] Forces behind financial innovation might be in fact the search for increased competiveness and efficiency in response to market changes, including lowering costs, responding to customers' needs (e. g. the poor financial needs for adequate products and services, *see* Chapter 4), new technologies (mobile-banking and finger-print ATMs) and avoiding or taking advantages of regulation (e.g. banking regulation restrictions).[8]

Financial innovations typically increase the integration of markets:[9] in this sense, microfinance, on the one hand, might be conducive of a deeper integration of mainstream financial and microfinance sectors (i.e. 'graduating' clients) but instead also of a sharp separation of the mainstream financial sector from the low-income clients one (Chapters 3; 6).

Microfinance, more importantly, also participates in the 'regulatory dialectic' between innovation and regulation:[10] the latter acknowledges the benefits coming from the former, on the one side, but also its risks, related instability for the system and asymmetric information from the regulatory side[11] (e.g. difficult evaluation because of peculiar models and functioning), on the other. Financial innovation, similarly, might be prevented or destroyed by regulation but welcomes the latter when favourable, being able to spur its development. The resulting scheme is a sort of passionate tango, an '*odi et amo*' dance between financial innovation and regulation, with moments of magnificent coordination and others of abrupt interruption.

The financial crisis has evidenced the risks linked to unregulated financial innovations. Some authors distinguish financial innovation designed to circumvent regulation from the one aiming at reducing transaction costs and optimizing risk

4 *See* Llewellyn, 'Financial', 16; Molyneux and Shamroukh, *Financial*, 7, 194–95. R. Harrington ('Financial Innovation and International Banking', in Cavanna, *Financial*, 58 and 65) argues that the highly regulated (but not suffocating) nature of the banking sector and the variety of the characteristics of financial transactions and products are proximate causes of financial innovation.

5 *See* Molyneux and Shamroukh, *Financial*, 195.

6 *See* Molyneux and Shamroukh, *Financial*, 61.

7 Haliassos, *Financial*, 5–6; Llewellyn, 'Financial', 49.

8 BIS, 'Recent', 7ff., 169ff.; Llewellyn, 'Financial', 25–31; Harrington, 'Financial', 56–58: Ackerman, 'Financial Innovations', 215ff.

9 Llewellyn, 'Financial', 16, 49.

10 *See* Kane, 'Impact', 355; Pouncy, 'Contemporary', 546.

11 *See* J. Mason, 'Regulating for Financial System Development, Financial Institutions Stability, and Financial Innovation', (2009), <http://ssrn.com/abstract=2101731>; Llewellyn, 'Financial', 47.

management, only the first deserving a strict regulatory response.[12] Furthermore, the most dangerous characteristics of financial innovations (as also responsible for contributing to cause the financial crisis) have been traced back to complexity and uncertainty (asymmetric information).[13] Consequently, post-crisis proposals have advanced an *ex ante* control process of certain financial innovations based on the U.S. Food and Drugs Authority model in order to prevent the entry of excessively dangerous products.[14] However, applying such a type of proposal to all financial products might turn out to be excessively restrictive and stifle innovation, in particular in the socially responsible financial sector. Current regulatory trends in Europe aim at reducing financial innovations with a speculative character through product governance obligations on intermediaries (ensuring the manufacturing and delivering of adequate products: e.g. Art. 16(3) Directive No. 2014/65–MiFID II) and the attribution to financial authorities (ESMA or national authorities) of product intervention powers (Articles 39–42 EMIR).[15] The latter entails monitoring markets and assessing the social utility of specific financial innovations raising financial stability and consumer protection concerns, with the ability to prohibit or restrict the marketing, distribution or sale of certain financial instruments or type of financial activity or practice, towards more simplification (*see* also Chapters 4, §5.a; 5, §4; 8, §2).[16]

Microfinance has been compared, because of its intense and rapid success in some regions, consequent significant international investments and first scandals, to other financial innovations recently become unpopular such as subprime loans and securitizations (*see* also Chapters 4, §5.a; 8, §2–3.a). Similar features have been identified in making the financial sector more inclusive in an efficient way

12 A. Mullineux, 'Financial Innovation and Social Welfare', (2010) 18 *JFR & C* 243 (qualifying microfinance as innovation improving social welfare).

13 *See* Mason, 'Regulating'; D. Llwellyn, 'Financial Innovation and a New Economics of Banking: Lessons from the Financial Crisis', (2010), <http://frank-oertel-math.de/Financial_crisis_and_new_economics_of_banking_Aug_2009.pdf>. About complexity's role in the financial crisis, *see* G. Miller and G. Rosenfeld, 'Intellectual Hazard: How Conceptual Biases in Complex Organizations Contributed to the Crisis of 2008', (2010) 33 *Harv. JL & Pub Pol'y* 807, 813–15 and 821ff.; S. Schwarcz, 'Regulating Complexity in Financial Markets', (2009) 87(2) *Wash U L Rev* 211; K. Judge, 'Fragmentation Nodes: A Study in Financial Innovation, Complexity, and Systemic Risk', (2012) 64 *Stan L Rev* 657.

14 E. Posner and E. Wey, 'An FDA for Financial Innovation: Applying the Insurable Interest Doctrine to 21st-Century Financial Markets', (2012), <http://ssrn.com/abstract=2010606> (with reference to financial derivatives). Similarly, for complex financial products, S. Omarova, 'License To Deal: Mandatory Approval of New Complex Financial Products', (2012) 90 *Wash U L Rev* 63, 116.

15 *See* N. Moloney, 'The Legacy Effects of the Financial Crisis on Regulatory Design in the EU', in E. Ferran et al. (eds), *The Regulatory Aftermath of the Global Financial Crisis*, (CUP 2012), 186–202; M. Andenas and I. Chiu, *The Foundations and Future of Financial Regulation*, (Routledge 2013), 244–245, 272–273.

16 *See* Moloney, 'The Legacy', 127ff. *See* also on criteria for product intervention Art. 19 Commission delegated Regulation of 18 May 2016 supplementing Regulation EU/600/2014 with regard to definitions, transparency, portfolio compression and supervisory measures on product intervention and positions, C(2016) 2860 final.

while being at risk of bubbles and lacking transparency. In fact, many MFIs have been unable to deal with incredible growth-rates, changes in funding schemes and needed adaptations of structures and operating systems (Chapters 4–5). Products in the most mature markets are not as simple as they used to be, presenting more standardization, less attention to clients' education and lower levels of transparency about interest rates and fees.[17] Moreover, both microloans and subprime loans tend to be subject to political and populist pressure, also because of high interest rates (Chapter 8, §4) and favourable public policies.[18] Some additional problematic aspects such as inadequate compensation programmes, over-reliance on credit ratings, strong demand for loans and foreign investments were present in both the subprime case and in some microfinance experiences.[19]

However, the microfinance sector has overall reported good results (in terms of repayment rates, good practices, standards, growth and profits) notwithstanding the crisis, especially if compared to the conventional sector, and operations are in any case simpler than in the subprime market, even in the securitizations context (*see* Chapter 5, §4).[20] In fact, especially in Europe, products and services remain simple, client-focused and relationship-based, in line with the above-mentioned simplification and anti-speculative trend (*see* also Chapter 8, §3.a).

Some considerations flow from qualifying microfinance as a financial innovation, also upholding reflections in previous chapters. First, microfinance is a continuously evolving process, able in principle to increase efficiency and access (Chapter 4). Microfinance would likely pass an anti-speculative test (being able to expand financial access) but an *ex-ante* and bureaucratic control over business models and new products might stifle innovation. Consequently, we need a kind of regulation not too rigid nor based on strict categories, reflecting the evolving nature of the poor's needs. However, favourable rules are justified only in case of proved financial access or other social performance effects, including simplicity (*see* Chapters 3–4).

Second, the difficult evaluation of the activity by the authority justifies partial forms of private regulation and supervision (*see* Chapter 3).

17 *See* K. Gokhale, 'A Global Surge in Tiny Loans Spurs Credit Bubble in a Slum', *Wall St. J.*, (New York, 13 Aug. 2009) A1; FitchRatings, 'The Microfinance Sector: its Success Could be its Biggest Risk', (2008), 14ff., <www.microfinancegateway.org/sites/default/files/mfg-en-paper-the-microfinance-sector-its-success-could-be-its-biggest-risk-jun-2008.pdf>; P. Das, 'Avoiding a Subprime-like Crises in Microfinance: Lessons from the Mexican and Bolivian Experience', (2009) 15 *Law & Bus Rev Am* 819, 840.

18 *See* S. Schwarcz, 'Disintermediating Avarice: A Legal Framework for Commercially Sustainable Microfinance', (2011) 4 *U Illinois L Rev* 1165, 1178, 1181 and 1199.

19 As regards the subprime sector, BCBS–Joint Forum, 'Report on Asset Securitisation Incentive', (2011), <www.bis.org/publ/joint26.pdf>; P. Bolton et al., 'The Credit Ratings Game', (2012) 67(1) *J Financ* 85.

20 *See* A. Yee, 'Buzz around India's Maturing Microfinance Sector Quietens', *Financial Times* (London, 23 March 2009), 8; E. Rhyne, 'Toward a Distributed Global Banking Grid', *The New York Times* (New York, 27 January 2009).

Finally, a differentiated and tiered regime of access (stricter with increasing variety, complexity and size of activities) might reduce the first-movers dilemma (*see* Chapters 4–6).

2 Microfinance and its use of new technologies. In particular, mobile banking

a Microfinance and FinTechs: an even more complicated dance

Microfinance has often recurred to other financial innovations and new technologies with the objective of reducing costs, expanding the potential reach of clients as well as of financers and responding to clients' needs. For instance, MFIs in developing countries have deployed ATMs responsive to finger prints to reduce the risk of identification instruments' loss or theft or to respond to illiteracy issues.

The following paragraphs will focus on two types of financial innovations often deployed by MFIs, crowdfunding (in particular, peer-to-peer lending – P2P-) and mobile banking (M-banking). These innovations exploit new technologies to reduce costs and expand the audience/client base.

Technology has always been at the service of the financial sector but recently FinTechs (i.e. start-ups resorting to new technologies to more efficiently offer financial services/products) have entered the sector, challenging traditional operators' business models.[21] This phenomenon necessarily raises the regulator's concern. First, such new entrants contribute to further enlarging the worrisome group of shadow banking entities (*see* Chapters 4, §5; 6, §4). Furthermore, the FinTech industry is growing particularly fast, running the risk of directly moving from 'too small to care' to 'too big to fail', skipping the 'too large to ignore' intermediate step.[22] Second, they do not only pose consumer protection and systemic risk issues but also competition concerns since they often offer services similar to mainstream operators without being subject to comparable regulation, further increasing incentives to move to less-regulated markets.[23]

Finally, new technologies, creating the opportunity for new structures and business models, challenge traditional legal categories and regulatory instruments, often making it difficult for regulators to force them inside existing legal boxes. In fact, big data and new credit analytics (*see* Chapter 6, §2.b), forms of collaborative economy, online services, robot-advice, mobile services, virtual currencies and blockchains are changing the financial sector landscape also through

21 *See* D. Arner et al., 'The Evolution of Fintech: A New Post-Crisis Paradigm?', (2015) University of Hong Kong Faculty of Law Research Paper 2015/047, 6ff., <http://ssrn.com/abstract=2676553>.

22 Arner, 'The Evolution', 34.

23 *See* EBA, 'Consumer Trends Report 2016', (2016), 17ff.; Commission, 'Green Paper on Retail Financial Services. Better Products, More Choice, and Greater Opportunities for Consumers and Businesses', COM(2015) 630 final, 10–11; Judge, 'Fragmentation', 667.

disintermediation and more blurred lines between providers and consumers, challenging the validity of current regulatory approaches.[24]

Consequently, microfinance use of FinTech further complicates the applicable legal framework and transforms the above mentioned tango into a complicated collective dance where a common rhythm might be difficult to find.

b In particular, microfinance and mobile banking. Advantages and risks

M-banking consists of the offering of financial services (especially payment and money transfers but also eg bank inquiries, deposits, withdrawals, remittances) through mobile devices, thanks to technologies related to SIM cards, POS and applications. Although currently widespread also in the mainstream banking sector, it represents for MFIs a particularly valuable instrument since it permits, especially in developing countries, a high number of low-income people to be reached at lower costs,[25] also in consideration of the dispersed nature of the population in these countries but the constantly increasing high diffusion of mobile and smart-phones also among low-income people.

Consequently, it has somewhere represented (e.g. in Brazil, South Africa and Kenya) a revolutionary instrument to improve financial inclusion,[26] while in other cases client illiteracy or unease with technologies or lack of a reliable connection in some remote areas or IT partners with adequate technology have limited such impact.[27]

M-banking might however make less easily understandable microfinance pricing, adding new fees and costs. Furthermore, MFIs must be prepared to fulfil

24 *See* C. Brummer and D. Gorfine, 'FinTech: Building a 21st Century Regulatory Toolkit', (2014) Milken Institute Report, <www.milkeninstitute.org/publications/view/665>; C. Brummer, 'Disruptive Technology and Securities Regulation', (2015) 84(3) *Fordham Law Rev* 977. S. Schwarcz ('Regulating Financial Change: A Functional Approach', 2015, Duke Law School Public Law & Legal Theory Series Paper, <http://ssrn.com/abstract=2469467>) proposes, to more generally react to financial change, to move to a functional approach in financial regulation since, while financial institutions and structures change, economic functions do not. About regulation and collaborative economy *see* Commission, 'A European Agenda for the Collaborative Economy', (Communication) COM(2016) 356 final.

25 Some studies attest, however, that branchless banking (m-banking and banking agents) saves on average only 19% of costs (but 54% for e.g. long-term savings, utilities payment, especially where the amount of the transactions is low) and that only 10% of branchless banking clients would be otherwise unserved clients: *see* C. McKay and M. Pickens, 'Branchless Banking 2010: Who's Served? At What Price? What's Next?', (2010) CGAP Focus Note 66, 3ff., <www.cgap.org/sites/default/files/CGAP-Focus-Note-Branchless-Banking-2010-Who-Is-Served-At-What-Price-What-Is-Next-Sep-2010.pdf>.

26 M. Pickens et al., 'Scenarios for Branchless Banking in 2020', (2009) CGAP Focus Note 57, 2, <www.cgap.org/sites/default/files/CGAP-Focus-Note-Scenarios-for-Branchless-Banking-in-2020-Oct-2009.pdf>.

27 *See* G. Ivatury, 'Using Technology to Build Inclusive Financial Systems', in I. Matthäus-Maier and J. von Pischke (eds), *New Partnerships for Innovation in Microfinance*, (Springer 2009), 159–160.

client requests since a malfunctioning can hinder clients' trust and lead to a contagion crisis (*see* Chapter 6). Other significant risks to manage are security and privacy issues[28] as well as compliance with quite burdensome anti-money laundering (AML) and counter-financing terrorism (CFT) regulations.[29]

Nonetheless, m-banking models seem somehow to be incompatible with microfinance's supposed essential characteristics (*see* Chapters 2–3), entailing a looser and more indirect relationship between MFIs and costumers, therefore limiting risk-monitoring as well as financial education and coaching opportunities. For such reasons, some MFIs have decided to exclude credit repayment from m-banking services or anyway maintain periodic meetings.[30] However, some MFIs have proved to be able to manage this new risk and even used m-banking to originate loans and related due diligence, grounding their evaluations on transaction histories and mobile data usage (*see* also Chapter 6, §2.b).[31] Anyway, m-banking is less tempting for European MFIs also because of the higher penetration rate of bank branches and internet coverage (where therefore internet banking is preferred).[32] Furthermore, m-banking usage in Europe, although now on the rise, still appear low (compared to the U.S.) because of consumers concerns about security.[33] Nonetheless, it still represents an interesting way to reach some rural areas or better meet clients' needs and save costs[34] (also considering the increased importance of remittances flow).[35]

28 For instance, G-Cash (Philippines) used to employ a system based on text commands through SMS which could entail human errors (clients not remembering or not correctly writing the commands) or third parties finding other's personal codes among sent SMS. Consequently, G-Cash, under the authority's pressure, adopted an interactive menu and commands encrypting access codes: *see* Barton et. al., 'Client-focused MFI Technologies Case Study', (2007) USAID MicroReport 77, 26, <http://pdf.usaid.gov/pdf_docs/Pnadn418.pdf>.

29 About m-banking risks, *see* J. Ledgerwood (ed.), *The New Microfinance Handbook. A Financial Market System Perspective*, (WB 2013), 41ff.; T. Lyman et al., 'Regulating Transformational Branchless Banking: Mobile Phones and Other Technology to Increase Access to Finance', (2008), 9ff., <www.cgap.org/sites/default/files/CGAP-Focus-Note-Regulating-Transformational-Branchless-Banking-Mobile-Phones-and-Other-Technology-to-Increase-Access-to-Finance-Jan-2008.pdf>; Barton, 'Client-focused', 26; Pickens, 'Scenarios', 6; K. Kumar et al., 'Microfinance and Mobile Banking: The Story So Far', (2010) CGAP Focus Note 62, 7ff., <www.cgap.org/sites/default/files/CGAP-Focus-Note-Microfinance-and-Mobile-Banking-The-Story-So-Far-Jul-2010.pdf>.

30 *See* Kumar, 'Microfinance', 7–8. Based on a recent survey, MFIs seem to use m-banking most for loan repayment and savings mobilization: M. Hanouch and S. Rotman, 'Microfinance and Mobile Banking. Blurring the Lines', (2013) CGAP Focus Note 88, <www.cgap.org/sites/default/files/Focus-Note-Microfinance-and-Mobile-Banking-August-2013.pdf>.

31 Hanouch and Rotman, 'Microfinance'.

32 KPMG, 'Mobile Banking 2015', 12–13, <https://assets.kpmg.com/content/dam/kpmg/pdf/2015/08/mobile-banking-report-2015.pdf>.

33 Commission, *Cyber Security. Special Eurobarometer 423*, (EU 2015), 4, 23ff.

34 A. Cozarenco, 'Microfinance Institutions and Banks in Europe: The Story to Date', (2015), 18, <www.european-microfinance.org/docs/emn_publications/emn_research_papers/research_3.pdf>.

35 *See* K. Lubambu, *The Impacts of Remittances on Developing Countries* (EU 2014).

c Legal issues and regulatory approaches

When m-banking is offered directly by banks, not many legal issues arise (except in terms of bank duty to ensure the security and timely delivery of payment operations and of level of outsourced activities). Nonetheless, the real m-banking revolution has been represented by the opportunity of non-bank providers to directly offer m-banking services, especially MFIs in partnerships with mobile operators (MOs) or MOs alone. This can in principle clash with those banking laws reserving payment services and emission of e-money to banks in addition to the reception of repayable funds from the public.[36]

The Basel Committee, while generally denying the qualification of such funds as deposit under banking law, underlines the need for a separate licence and financial authority supervision for the provision of m-banking services by non-bank operators.[37]

Some developing countries have allowed only m-banking provided by banks (collaborating with MOs but retaining the control), prohibiting the same by non-bank operators unless they are divisions of a bank (e.g. Wizzit Bank in South Africa).[38] Some other countries allow m-banking by non-bank providers (even non-financial MOs) and only require the sums collected to be deposited at a bank (to benefit from deposit guarantee schemes) (*see* G-Cash in the Philippines),[39] while others impose a broader range of requirements (e.g. minimum capital, certain liquidity level, prudent investments, maximum number of transactions) (*see* M-PESA in Kenya).[40]

36 *See* D. Porteous et al., 'Prudential Regulation in Microfinance', (2010) FAI Policy Framing Note 3 (2010), 18ff., <www.microfinancegateway.org/sites/default/files/mfg-en-paper-prudential-regulation-in-microfinance-jan-2010.pdf>; Lyman, 'Regulating', 3ff., 12ff.

37 BCBS, *Guidance on the Application of the Core Principles for Effective Banking Supervision to the Regulation and Supervision of Institutions Relevant to Financial Inclusion – Consultative Document*, (BIS 2015), 8.

38 *See* Barton, 'Client-focused', 27–29; Kumar, 'Microfinance', 12.

39 M-banking in the country had been unregulated for years and then disciplined by a special e-money regulation. The banking authority, however, set since the beginning a ceiling to the number of daily and monthly transactions, the total number of clients and imposed monthly reporting: *see* Porteous, 'Prudential', 21; Barton, 'Client-focused', 24–26; Lyman, 'Regulating', 13; Kumar, 'Microfinance', 12.

40 *See* M-PESA in Kenya, operating as a non-bank but offering deposits and payments services – although deposits are so structured not to trigger banking regulation – under a special authorization by the Central Bank. In 2014 the National Payment Regulation has allowed banks, PIs and e-MIs (also MOs through separate divisions) to offer m-banking, subject to money segregation and adequate governance obligations and prohibition to lend or invest such money, in addition to consumer protection rules (redress, disclosure and privacy): *see* Lyman, 'Regulating', 9; B. Muthiora, 'Enabling Mobile Money Policies in Kenya Fostering a Digital Financial Revolution', (2015) Bill & Melinda Gates Foundation-GSMA, <www.itu.int/en/ITU-T/focusgroups/dfs/Documents/2015_MMU_Enabling-Mobile-Money-Policies-in-Kenya.pdf>.

In Europe, where bank branches are generally well distributed and close to low-income clients, providers interested in offering m-banking must deal not only with banking law restrictions but also with e-money (Directive 2009/110/EC, e-MD) and payment service (PSD, recently repealed by Directive 2015/2366/EU -PSD2: Chapter 4, §6.d) Directives. In fact, e-money is defined as money 'electronically, including magnetically, stored monetary value as represented by a claim on the issuer which is issued on receipt of funds for the purpose of making payment transactions [...] and which is accepted by a natural or legal person other than the electronic money issuer' (Art. 2(2) e-money Directive). At the same time, PSD covers all payment services listed in its Annex, including the transfer of money to and from clients' accounts, remittances, and the operations to operate a payment account. EU framework allows banks and specifically authorized providers (payment institutions – PIs and e-money institutions – eMIs) to offer such services. These are subject to prudential requirements similar (e.g. authorization, programme of operations and business plan, minimum capital, segregation of funds and duty to deposit funds with a bank, prohibition to use client funds for lending, minimum own funds, fit and proper requirements of owners and executives) but simplified to bank ones especially in terms of transparency and capital (depending on the type of services). National authorities can exempt operators with volumes below a certain amount per month, but these are excluded from EU passport and can be limited in the services by national regulators (Artt. 26, 16 PSD; Art. 32 PSD2; Art. 9 e-MD). Moreover, PIs and eMIs are in principle allowed to provide credit only in limited cases in connection with payment and e-money activities, lying then with national regulators the choice of linking IP/eMIs authorization to nationally-pre-existing NBFI ones (e.g. Italy).

Finally, telecom operators used to be exempted not only in case of small networks but also when allowing the use of client digital credit to buy services/goods that can be used through telecom devices (Art. 3(l) PSD and Art. 1(5) e-MD). The recent PSD2 has, on the one hand, expanded its reach to cover technical service providers (at the same time helping the same access the market receiving mandatory account information from banks) previously excluded (e.g. payment initiation services and account information services subject to light national regulation), and, on the other, introduced stricter customer identification and security requirements as well as internal complaints mechanisms duties (significantly increasing compliance costs). Furthermore, telecom operators are generally now subject to the Directive unless they facilitate the sale of digital content or tickets or for charitable activity below certain thresholds (Art. 3(l) PSD2).

Such reform can, on the one hand, help European MFIs, through expanding consumer trust in m-banking thanks to enhanced security and increasing competition in the sector also favouring payment account data sharing and the entrance of new low-cost providers. On the other, it might inhibit the same to develop their own m-banking services or collaborating with specialized providers because of the costs increase.

3 Microfinance and crowdfunding[41]

a Peer-to-peer lending features, business models, advantages and risks

Crowdfunding allows users of an internet platform to provide financing to firms or consumers in the form of donations (donation-based crowdfunding), advancements in exchange for some future non-financial reward (such as product previews or prototype sale or simply credits), loans (lending-based crowdfunding or P2P) or investments (equity or other forms of investment: investment-based crowdfunding).[42] It represents a booming phenomenon,[43] fuelled by the distrust towards mainstream financial operators consequent to the financial crisis and grown as a reaction to banks' restricted lending trend (*see* Fig. 7.1). The lending-based segment represents the main one, with €274.6 million (113% growth rate – GR) collected in the form of loans to consumers (P2P strictly speaking) in 2014 by EU platforms (UK excluded) and €93.1 million (272 % GR) for loans to businesses (P2B).[44] The leading European market is however the UK (in 2014, P2P £749 million with a 99% GR and P2B £250 million with a 66% GR) (Figs 7.1 and 7.2).[45]

The emergence of P2P lending is historically linked to microfinance: one of the first P2P platforms has been the U.S.-based Kiva, channelling small funds from internet users to small business owners in developing countries based on their profiles and project presentation.[46] Through Kiva (which covers its costs thanks to donations), people can lend, without expecting returns, as little as $25 to MFIs

41 The following paragraphs draws from some previous works of mine, especially E. Macchiavello, 'Peer-to-peer Lending and the "Democratization" of Credit Markets: Another Financial Innovation Puzzling Regulators', (2015) 21(3) *Colum J Eur L* 521, to which I refer for a deeper discussion and further details.

42 *See* E. Kirby and S. Worner, 'Crowdfunding: An Infant Industry Growing Fast', OICV-IOSCO Staff Working Paper 3/2014, <www.iosco.org/research/pdf/swp/Crowd-funding-An-Infant-Industry-Growing-Fast.pdf>; Commission, 'Unleashing the Potential of Crowdfunding in the European Union', (Communication) COM(2014) 172 final. The EBA provides the following working definition of lending-based crowdfunding: 'open calls to the wider public by fund seekers through a third party, typically an on-line platform, to raise funds for a project or for personal purposes, in the form of a loan agreement, with a promise to repay with (or in certain cases without) interest. The fund raisers may include individuals, start-up companies or existing SMEs that are seeking an alternative means of funding, rather than the traditional credit market': EBA, 'Opinion on Lending-based Crowdfunding,' EBA/Op/2015/03.

43 The global crowdfunding industry reached in 2014 $16.2 billion (with a 167% GR compared to 2013) and $34.4 billion in 2015: MasSolution, '2015CF: 2015 Crowdfunding Industry Report', (2014).

44 B. Zhang et al., 'Moving Mainstream – The European Alternative Finance Benchmarking Report 2015', (2015), 9 and 17–19, <www.jbs.cam.ac.uk/fileadmin/user_upload/research/centres/alternative-finance/downloads/2015-uk-alternative-finance-benchmarking-report.pdf>.

45 B. Zhang et al., 'Pushing Boundaries. The 2015 UK Alternative Finance Industry Report', (2016), 37, 39, <www.nesta.org.uk/sites/default/files/pushing_boundaries_0.pdf>.

46 *See* C. Bradford, 'Crowdfunding and the Federal Securities Laws', (2012) *Col Bus L Rev* 1, 8, 27–29; K. Davis and A. Gelpern, 'Peer-to-Peer Lending for Development: Regulating the Intermediaries', (2010) 42 *NYU J Int'l L & Pol* 1209.

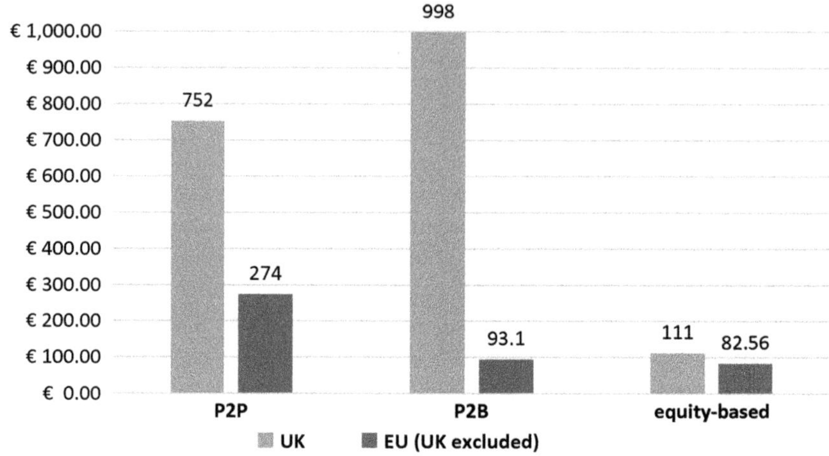

Figure 7.1 Financial-return crowdfunding – EU market – 2014 (million €) (data extracted from Zhang et al., 'Moving Mainstream', 2015)

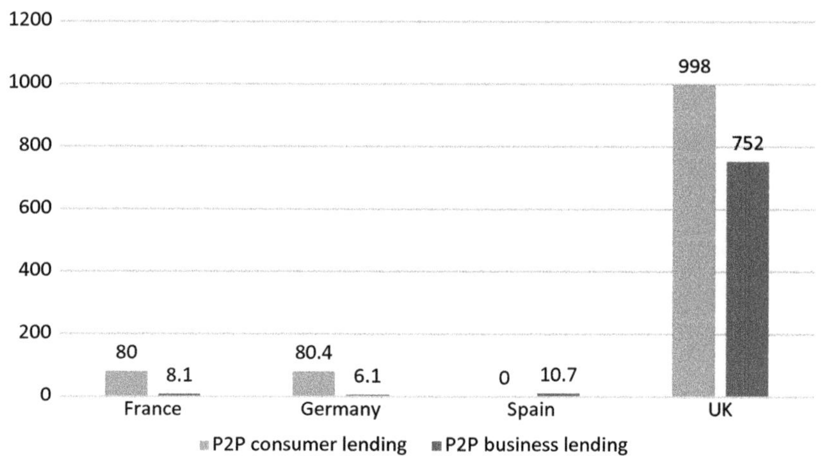

Figure 7.2 P2P lending in selected EU countries – 2014 (million €) (data extracted from Zhang et al, 'Moving Mainstream', 2015

which screen borrower applications and provide micro-loans (charging instead interest rates) to entrepreneurs succeeding the approval process and chosen by Kiva-users based on their web-profiles.[47] Kiva has recently added, with reference

47 These passages and features were not so clearly stated on the Kiva website. In fact, Kiva used to market the loans as directly supplied by crowd-lenders to micro-entrepreneurs, but was then forced to reveal that the sums dispensed at 0% interest rates by Internet users in theory assigned to specific projects were typically used by Kiva to fund different projects, or to reimburse local microfinance institutions (MFIs) for having already financed the very same

only to the U.S. market, the possibility of providing direct loans to entrepreneurs (without the intermediate step of the MFIs' field partners), warning of their intrinsic riskiness (not having a MFI following up the loan and collecting repayments: *see* below).[48]

The French MicroWorld and Babyloan platforms follow the original Kiva model, with MFIs' micro-loans funded through the platform by its registered users (singularly providing as little as €20).[49]

Consequently, P2P platforms allow MFIs to access a new form of financing, of anti-cyclical nature (not based on typical bank or government considerations), at a relatively low price, without losing control over their activity (as opposed to private investments), diversifying their funding and reducing their exclusive reliance on bank financing or donations (*see* Chapter 5; Table 7.1).[50]

The indirect character of the micro-loan, with a MFI field-partner selecting, following-up and coaching final borrowers, permits the reduction of the well-known asymmetric information, adverse selection and moral hazard problems (particularly intense when borrowers are located in developing countries while lenders are private citizens in industrialized countries).

Nonetheless, the most-widespread P2P lending model (outside the microfinance area) involves the direct provision of loans by internet users to consumers or firms, with significant information asymmetries and risk of fraud, and a commission fee for the platform. Considering the flexible definition of microcredit (*see* Chapter 3, §1), many consider crowdfunding loans *per se* a form of microcredit, because of their generally limited amount and objective of expanding financial access. Somewhere, banks have started collaborating with platforms (similarly to what was experimented in microfinance: Chapter 6, §5), deferring unbankable applicants.[51] However, such assimilation needs to be assessed on a case-by-case basis, also considering existing legal definitions, since other microcredit features

projects (anyway charging an interest). It turned out that only 4.3% of the loans listed on Kiva had yet to be disbursed: *see* D. Roodman, 'Kiva Is Not Quite What It Seems', (2 October 2009), <www.cgdev.org/blog/kiva-not-quite-what-it-seems>; S. Strom, 'Confusion On Where Money Lent via Kiva Goes', *The New York Times* (New York, 9 November 2009); Davis and Gelpern, 'Peer-to-peer'.

48 <www.kiva.org/about/how>.

49 <www.microworld.org/en/about-microworld/how-it-works#what-is-platform>.

50 *See* D. Burand, 'Microfinance Managers Consider Online Funding: Is It Finance, Marketing, or Something Else Entirely?', (2009) CGAP Focus Note 54, <www.cgap.org/sites/default/files/CGAP-Focus-Note-Microfinance-Managers-Consider-Online-Funding-Is-It-Finance-Marketing-or-Something-Else-Entirely-Apr-2009.pdf>; Davis and Gelpern, 'Peer-to-peer'.

51 *See* M. Aspan, 'LendingClub Courts Small Banks as Personal-Loan Partners', *American Banker* (New York, 11 December 2013); FinAlternatives, 'After Breakout Year, Peer-To-Peer Lending Still Evolving', (23 January 2014), <www.finalternatives.com/node/25928>; N. Athwal, 'The Disappearence of Peer-To-Peer Lending', *Forbes* (Jersey City, 14 October 2014), <www.forbes.com/sites/groupthink/2014/10/14/the-disappearance-of-peer-to-peer-lending/>; M. Scully, 'Banks Heat Up Bidding for Peer-to-Peer Loans', *American Banker* (New York, 10 Oct. 2014); K. Judge, 'The Future of Direct Finance: The Diverging Paths of Peer-to-Peer Lending and

Table 7.1 Benefits and risks of P2P lending

Benefits	Risks
For lenders/investors: • Higher returns (if interest rate) • Diversification across types of investments and resilience (if interest rate) • Non-financial returns: 'direct' finance, sense of involvement, expanded network	For investors: • Capital loss • Illiquidity and concentration • Lack of clarity about costs, risks, checks, etc.; misleading advertisements • Retail inexperience and influence of persuasive narratives
For MFIs: • Diversification of funding, < dependence on bank financing • anti-cyclical and affordable source of funding • fast process	For MFIs: • Subject to unpredictable shifts in preference/fashions (if the main source) and FX-risk (if in foreign currency) • Costly disclosure and monitoring obligations • Collection problems in micro-loan renegotiation
For receivers: • > access to finance and < transaction costs • Market test/Marketing tool/ Suggestions • Lower psychological pressure than family or bank loans (if direct model)	For receivers: • Risk of discriminatory selection, unfair terms and abusive collection practices • Privacy issues/Disclosure of corporate information and unprotected innovative processes
For the system: • Increased competition in financing • Innovation stimulator	For the system: • Fraud, money-laundering, financing terrorism, cyber-crimes • Very low systemic risk (but now > interconnectedness)

might be lacking, not all platforms significantly limit the size of loans and might adopt selection criteria restricting access only to the 'prime' applicants. In fact, the vast majority of P2P loans on the two major U.S. platforms go to middle-to-upper income borrowers,[52] which are generally 'prime' or 'near-prime' borrowers (above-640 FICO score being an eligibility requirement).[53] Moreover, studies attest crowd-lenders' tendency to consider less reliable (and therefore to disregard or provide smaller loans or demand higher interest rates) very young, elderly and

Kickstarter', (2015) Columbia Law and Economics Working Paper 520, 111–13, <http://ssrn.com/abstract=2662697>.

52 A. Morse, 'Peer-to-Peer Crowdfunding: Information and the Potential for Disruption in Consumer Lending', (2015), 18, <http://ssrn.com/abstract=2551272>; *see* also Y. Komarova Loureiro and L. Gonzalez, 'Competition against Common Sense: Insights on Peer-to-Peer Lending as a Tool to Allay Financial Exclusion', (2015) forthcoming IJBM (special issue on financial exclusion), 24, <http://ssrn.com/abstract=2533520>.

53 Judge ('The Future', 113, 116) also reports that the percentage of Prosper subprime borrowers moved from 25% in 2006 to 8% in 2008.

certain ethnic minorities borrowers,[54] which also correspond to the most financially excluded categories (*see* Chapter 1).

Anyway, in the event of direct loans, platforms' information verifications and checks appear fundamental,[55] although studies attest some ability of the 'crowd' to correctly infer borrowers' risk profiles both from standard information (e.g. number of delinquencies, of credit inquiries, and debt-to-income ratio) and from 'soft' personal information (e.g. interest rate that the borrower is willing to pay). Also the relevance of social networks backed by financial commitments (in the form of early financing) in determining a campaign success as well as in reducing information asymmetries has been attested.[56]

However, the business models adopted by P2P platforms are very diverse and some platforms provide little information about single projects, with little crowd-lenders' freedom of choice, splitting each lender's contribution across a large number of projects based on pre-established matching criteria or algorithms (e.g. RateSetter, Zopa UK, Smartika)[57] but always presenting themselves simply as marketplaces. In other cases, the platform is explicitly an intermediary, collecting funds from users and then resorting to a partner bank for loan origination, with the platform issuing a note to the lenders/investors for the value corresponding to each contribution (e.g. Prosper).[58]

The success of P2P-lending can be explained not only by the advantages for borrowers but also by the social-return for crowd-lenders (the opportunity to help somebody), directly choosing the beneficiary even based on criteria generally ignored or disregarded (such as ethnicity, religion, and self-presentation),[59] as

54 *See* about Prosper lenders' discrimination against Hispanic or Asian borrowers, J. Duarte et al., 'Do Individual Investors Form Rational Expectations? Evidence from Peer-to-Peer Lending', (2014), <http://ssrn.com/abstract=2473240>; about higher interest rates charges on black and elderly borrowers, D. Pope and J. Sydnor, 'What's in the Picture? Evidence of Discrimination from Prosper.com', (2011) 46(1) *J Hum Resour* 53 (however also reporting higher default rates of black borrowers).

55 According to a survey conducted by the Commission, 'Between 80 percent and 90 percent [of the platforms responding to the consultation] perform the following tasks: preliminary screening of projects (legality, compliance with platform's conditions), informing project owners and contributors of applicable fees, checking identity of project owners, facilitating the communication between contributors and project owners, informing contributors of risks': Commission, 'Summary – Responses to the Public Consultation on Crowdfunding in the EU', (2014), 4, <http://ec.europa.eu/internal_market/consultations/2013/crowdfunding/docs/summary-of-responses_en.pdf>.

56 *See* literature in Macchiavello, 'Peer-to-peer', 525 (note 19), 577 (note 283).

57 Automatic matching and diversification is reported as the prevailing model in Judge, 'The Future'.

58 For an overview of many different P2P-models *see* Kirby and Worner, 'Crowdfunding', 16 and Macchiavello, 'Peer-to-peer', 525ff.

59 *See* Davis and Gelpern, 'Peer-to-peer'; Kirby and Worner, 'Crowdfunding', 44; Commission, 'Unleashing', 5; Commission, 'Summary', 3.

well as, in case of financial-return crowdfunding, interesting returns and diversification opportunity.[60]

Nonetheless, such a phenomenon also presents significant risks (again, Table 7.1). First, crowd-lenders might not completely understand the whole range of risks (including illiquidity and concentration) and costs involved as well as be primarily influenced by persuasive narratives. In fact, they can lose their money either because of borrowers' defaults[61] (platforms generally denying any responsibility for such an event, although some mature for-profit platforms have recently implemented guarantee funds)[62] or the platform's failure (when being the only counterparty or in absence of a back-up collection agent). They might rely on the information published on the platform but many platforms check only a small part of the information provided by borrowers. For instance, Prosper and LendingClub used to verify only employment and income information and only for, respectively, 40% and 60% of their loans,[63] while Kiva improved its due diligence process only after critiques on this topic.[64] Additional risks, for investors and the system, are cyber-crimes, money-laundering and financing terrorism issues, while systemic risk is not yet an issue because of the still limited size of such sector. However, the increasing involvement of banks as originators or lenders/investors in the sector or even platforms' creators might cause some hurdles.[65]

60 Kirby and Worner, 'Crowdfunding', 4, 21ff.

61 The industry reached a peak 30% default-rate in 2009 but after a much-needed review of best practices, the default rate now ranges around 0.2–7%: Kirby and Worner, 'Crowdfunding', 5, 23.

62 *See* Macchiavello, 'Peer-to-peer', 529, 541.

63 *See* A. Vernstein, 'The Misregulation of Person-to-Person Lending', (2011) 45(2) *UC Davis L Rev* 445, 467–70.

64 *See* M. Flannery, 'Kiva at Four', ***Innovations*** (special edition for Skoll World Forum 2009), 35ff., <http://media.kiva.org/INNOV-SKOLL-2009_flannery.pdf>. Kiva now assigns, through a many-step procedure, a rating to its MFI-partners measuring their perspective restitution capacity, based on the following factors: recent audited financial statements, portfolio reports, résumés of board and management members, organizational manuals, projections and ratings, on-site due diligence about governance, management, capital, liquidity, transparency, management information system, and internal controls. The evaluation of borrowers' repayment capacity instead is conducted by the MFI-partners (which examine e.g. past loan history, village or group reputation, loan purpose): *see* <www.kiva.org/about/due-diligence>.

65 The 80% and 90% of the total capital invested on the two major U.S. platforms comes from professional investors (including banks) while in the UK institutions account for one third of Funding Circle loans: *see* FinAlternatives, 'After'; Athwal, 'The Disappearence'; J. Gapper, 'The Lenders of the Revolution Look Familiar', ***Financial Times*** (London, 18 June 2015); Judge, 'The Future', 111. *See* also A. Milne and P. Parboteeah, 'The Business Models and Economics of Peer-to-Peer Lending', (2016) ECRI Research Report 17, 22, <www.ceps.eu/system/files/ECRI%20RR17%20P2P%20Lending.pdf>: 'Financial stability could instead be undermined by P2P lending if a large share of institutional investment came from domestic or international banks investing in illiquid P2P loan portfolios re-financing their positions using short-term money market borrowing.'

Instead, borrowers might be victims of abusive collection practice, unfair terms and discriminatory selection criteria (online lenders not being subject to consumer protection regulation unlike professional lenders), violation of privacy and intellectual property (disclosing relevant information on the website).[66]

Crowdfunding might be risky also for MFIs: using crowdfunding as main source of funding, MFIs make their activity subject to unpredictable shift in the crowd's funding patterns.[67] Furthermore, receiving funds in foreign currency increases MFIs' foreign exchange (FX) risk[68] and disclosure and monitoring obligations might be more costly than expected.[69] Prompt renegotiations of MFIs' loans or even resolution plans might be impeded by collective action problems due to the high number of crowd-lenders, unless the platform acts as trustee having adequate resources to perform such delicate role.

The EIF looks also at investment-based crowdfunding to inject capital in MFIs, although cautioning about increased platforms' risk profile.[70]

b Regulatory issues and approaches in Europe

The highlighted risks have traditionally been addressed by regulators through different types of regulations, from banking to financial markets and services, payment services and consumer protection laws. Depending on the business model and the interpretation adopted by national authorities of basic concepts such as public offer, financial product, financial instruments, investment service, bank, P2P platforms are potentially subject to one or, more likely, multiple regulations, with relevant implications in terms of compliance costs, consumer and investor protection as well as competition within the financial market and authority's powers. In fact, providing financing through money collected from the public may recall banking activity or at least credit services. Some business models bring instead to mind payment services or even investment services, also in consideration of the language used by some platforms (which, despite their presentation as simple facilitators of loans between private citizens, refer to crowd-lenders as 'investors' or to loans as 'investments').

66 Commission, 'Unleashing', 6; Burand, 'Microfinance', 9; Davis and Gelpern, 'Peer-to-peer', 1232, 1264.

67 Kiva in fact prevents MFIs partners from funding more than 30% of their portfolio through the platform: *see* Burand, 'Microfinance', 6; Flannery, 'Kiva', 31–32.

68 *See* Flannery, 'Kiva', 32. Since June 2009, Kiva MFI-partners have the possibility to enter into FX-risk sharing agreement, shifting FX-risk on the crowd-lender when local currency depreciation exceeds 20%: *see* G.A.O., 'Person-to-Person Lending. New Regulatory Challenges Could Emerge as the Industry Grows', (2011), 39, <www.gao.gov/new.items/d11613.pdf>.

69 Burand, 'Microfinance', 3ff.; Davis and Gelpern, 'Peer-to-Peer', 1231.

70 *See* B. Bruhn-Leon et al., 'Progress for Microfinance in Europe', (2012) EIF Working Paper 2012/13, 29, <www.eif.org/news_centre/publications/eif_wp_2012_13_microfinance.pdf>. About a discussion of the legal issues related to investment-based crowdfunding, *see* G. Ferrarini and E. Macchiavello, 'Investment-based Crowdfunding: Is MiFID II Enough?', in D. Busch and G. Ferrarini (eds), *Regulation of EU Financial Markets: MiFID II and MiFIR*, (OUP 2017) ch. 23, 659ff.

Platforms facilitating interest-free loans are generally subject to a light regulation since they are not directly providing financing and some jurisdictions do not qualify such products as loans (*see* in France where loans have an onerous component by definition[71]). French supervisors have looked favourably on P2P lending, permitting platform operations under certain conditions (i.e. lack of remuneration, loans to MFIs, no expenses or commissions charged on MFIs, disclosure of specific risks to users) also to facilitate microcredit by non-for-profit organizations.[72] In fact, since 2010, French MFIs have also been allowed to finance themselves through platforms (previously allowed to operate only through their own resources and, only more recently to on-lend: Chapter 5, §3), which used instead to facilitate only loans from private people to foreign MFIs.[73] Consequently, payment services regulation might at most apply (*see* in France, Spain and UK), since transferring money from an account to another generally constitutes a payment service.[74]

Instead, approaches in case of P2P with expectation of profits are varied. For instance, the UK has left the sector unregulated for years (imposing at most a licence as debt-collector/administrator) while it has recently adopted an approach closer to consumer protection and investment activities regulation. French and Italian financial authorities have instead tended to identify violations of banking law by P2P platforms for, respectively, facilitating the illegal activity consisting of providing loans without a banking licence (which also used to cover in France loans between private citizens: Art. L511–5 *CMF*) or receiving reimbursable funds without a banking authorization (by the platform, when the platform and clients' funds were not clearly separated originating an obligation to repay and users' options regarding the use of reimbursed funds were so broad as to qualify the contract as an on-demand deposit; by the recipients, in the case of standardized terms and absence of private negotiations between crowd-borrowers and crowd-lenders).

Crowdfunding loans are instead qualified as securities in the U.S. when they have a for-profit component, therefore often requiring at least a broker licence, securities

71 *See* Art. L313–3 *CMF*; AMF-ACP, 'Crowdfunding: A Guide for Funding Platforms and Project Owners', (2013), 4, <http://acpr.banque-france.fr/fileadmin/user_upload/acp/Communication/Communiques%20de%20presse/20130514-guide-professionnel-crowdfunding.pdf>.

72 *See* J. Perron, 'Dans le cadre de la Social Business Initiative de la Commission européenne: Lever les freins au développement du Peer to Peer de microcrédit solidaire en Europe', (2012), 2–3, <http://ec.europa.eu/internal_market/social_business/docs/expert-group/geces/perron_fr.pdf>.

73 *See* Law of 1st July 2010 No. 737 and Art. L511–16 *CMF*. *See* also P. Valentin et al., 'Le Microcrédit: Rapport d'un group de travaille du CNIS', (2011), <www.cnis.fr/files/content/sites/Cnis/files/Fichiers/publications/rapports/2011/RAP_2011_125_microcredit.PDF>. Furthermore, other secondary EU provisions might apply to lending-based crowdfunding (for profit or not, depending on different scopes of application), such as Directives 2000/31/EC on e-commerce, 2006/114/EC on misleading and comparative advertisements and 2005/29/EC on unfair commercial practices.

74 *See* Art. 2(1) PSD2. Art. 3(1)d PSD2 exempts '(d) payment transactions consisting of the non-professional cash collection and delivery within the framework of a non-profit or charitable activity' but the activity of a crowdfunding platform cannot be considered 'non-professional' because of the organization and continuity features.

registration and prospectus.[75] In Europe, the qualification of crowdfunding products as financial instruments (based on their, in case, 'negotiability on the capital market' and therefore freely transferable character) might entail the application of the Prospectus Directive (Dir. No. 2003/71 currently under revision) and MiFID (Dir. No. 2004/39 recently repealed by MiFID II) but the scope of such regulations varies a lot among Member States (extending it to investment products in, eg, Italy and Germany) and, consequently, their applicability to crowdfunding platforms as well. For instance, Germany and Austria have recently decided to assimilate crowdfunding subordinated loans and profit-participation loans to investment products, exempting them at the same time from Prospectus requirements under certain conditions and imposing a very light investment service licence under a MiFID-exempted regime.[76]

However, in different ways, all existing financial sector regulations applied to crowdfunding without adaptations end up leaving unanswered some of the above mentioned critical issues: for instance, banking regulation, with its main objectives of stability and safe and sound management, depositor protection, deploys burdensome and invasive measures (*see* Chapter 3, §2) that appear excessive considering the low systemic risk of platforms and might kill the sector. Instead, prospectus and investment services regulations, while similarly burdensome (especially for borrowers considered issuers) but more focusing on transparency,[77] do not consider the particularity of crowdfunding and might result in information overload, being conceived for traditional investments often assisted by professional operators (instead of focusing disclosure on the most relevant elements to crowd-funders). The payment institutions regime, on the other hand, although the preferred qualification for EBA, might protect lenders from cyber-crimes or delays and ensure segregation of funds, but do not impose sufficient disclosure and due diligence obligations on platforms and ignores borrowers' protection issues. This is also because payment service qualification focuses only on a limited part of platforms' activity, leaving aside the most important activities (i.e. screening borrowers or matching borrowers and lenders).[78]

Consequently, many EU countries have recently adopted specific crowdfunding regulations, some also targeting specifically a lending-based one (France, UK, Spain and Portugal). The tendency has been to subject to regulation only financial-return crowdfunding (UK and Spain but not in France or Portugal), allowing also (in addition to mainstream operators: *see* France and UK) or only (Spain) new operators specialized in facilitating loans between private people and disciplined by a simplified regime but limited in the kind of operations and products allowed as well as in the sums involved, often with limitations to the amount provided by each (retail) lender for a single loan (France, Spain, Portugal), to the total amount invested through the platform by each (retail) lender (Spain, Portugal) and to the total financing obtainable by each borrower (France, Spain, Portugal). The regime often entails a

75 *See* Macchiavello, 'Peer-to-peer'; Commission, 'Crowdfunding in the EU Capital Markets Union', SWD(2016) 154 final.

76 Macchiavello, 'Peer-to-peer' and Ferrarini and Macchiavello, 'Investment-based'.

77 About the traditional importance of disclosure in securities and markets regulation in contrast to post-crisis reflections, *see* Chapter 3, §3.d (text and footnotes 100–104).

78 Macchiavello, 'Peer-to-peer', 545ff.

registration/authorization (subordinated to the usual requirements except for minimum capital in France where there is instead a professional insurance requirement), back-up plans/continuity arrangements in case of failure, extensive disclosure requirements (towards investors about risks, checks, special status, costs and to the public about governance and statistical data) including special warnings, client-money safeguards, simplified IP regime, AML-CFT regulations, supervision by financial authority (UK, Spain) or professional organization (France), information and warnings to borrowers (otherwise generally not applicable, e.g. Directive 2008/48/EU, for the absence of a "professional lender" or a "consumer", see Chapter 8; in UK also creditworthiness assessment obligation based on consumer credit regulation). Sometimes additional rights are recognized to consumer/investors such as withdrawal and redress rights (UK) or require platforms to perform simplified forms of adequacy test on crowd-lenders (France, Spain) and proportionate conflict of interest policy in place (UK, Spain and Portugal). The presence of such regulations is beneficial for local platforms but the relevant difference among countries hinders cross-border operations, at present quite limited,[79] lead to unequal treatment of European investor and create limitations to EU freedoms.

Consequently, I have already elsewhere[80] proposed the adoption, in the short-term, of local national crowdfunding regulations with common requirements and, in the long-term, of a harmonized EU-regime, both drawing from existing EU law but simplified and adapted to crowdfunding features and risks (in line with existing national crowdfunding regulations). Such regimes would impose very light obligations based on the exempted PSD one (for volumes below €3 million) for not-for-profit platforms (unless using another payment service provider), although integrated by disclosure and check obligations towards lenders and borrowers. Instead, the new regime for for-profit lending-based platforms offering simple products would almost disregard prudential measures (because of the low systemic risk), focusing mostly on registration (with managers professionalism/good standing and insurance/adequate resources requirements), client-money separation, back-up plans/continuity arrangements, incentives for private based risk-mitigations instruments (e.g. forums/feed-backs, co-investing with professional investors, lending groups) and, in case of retail/consumers, withdrawal rights, special warnings and maximum thresholds as regards the total amount invested by single crowd-lenders and for each project to limit the risks posed by this sector and to each lender. Lenders must in fact be aware of the 'alternative' and therefore risky, without traditional safeguards, of this sector and as a result be prepared to suffer losses (limited through thresholds for protective and stability/trust reasons). For the same reasons, banks and investment firms interested in entering the sectors might be required to create a separate entity and limit

79 Only 38% of European crowdfunding platforms (equity or lending-based) are cross-border, but most of them (48%) explain this fact by reporting scarce clarity about applicable rules, as well as excessive diversity among national rules and declaring their interest in expanding their operations cross-border and are in favour of forms of harmonization at EU level: *see* Commission, 'Summary', 9–10.

80 Macchiavello, 'Peer-to-peer' and Ferrarini and Macchiavello, 'Investment-based'.

their investment in crowdfunding in order to contain systemic risk and loss of trust in the mainstream sector.

4 Principles and guidelines for regulators

The qualification of microfinance as financial innovation confirms the need for a flexible regulation and for regulatory facilitations in presence of an effective social objective (and therefore anti-speculative character), with the power of authorities to intervene once the activity presents effects not coherent with the social objective and dangerous for the system or clients/investors (*see* also Chapter 4).

From the same qualification, as well as from the difficult evaluation of a microfinance portfolio, we can draw justifications for partial forms of private regulation and supervision (*see* Chapter 3).

Furthermore, in consideration of the first mover dilemma typical of financial innovation, we can defend the need for a progressive regime with stricter rules in case of more complex and varied activities (*see* also Chapters 4–6).

The use of FinTech in the context of microfinance adds considerable legal issues and contributes to challenging traditional legal categories and regulatory schemes, underlying the need for new solutions and approaches. Consequently, in order to facilitate microfinance, regulators might need also to address additional financial innovations as important ways to deliver services or to finance themselves.

As regards m-banking, in the EU context the recently approved PSD2 might reinforce trust and therefore spur the use of such less costly way of providing services but obviously entail additional costs, requiring in consequence the use of low-volume exemptions to balance different objectives and still present lending-limitations.

Crowdfunding does not receive a clear and harmonized regulatory response in Europe and might therefore entail significant legal and reputational risks for MFIs but the use of not-for-profit platforms and possible future favourable reforms might also benefit the microfinance sector and its clients.

8 Dimension VI: Microfinance as a responsible activity: client protection without curtailing access

1 Microfinance and client protection issues. Consumer protection and stability

a The importance of consumer protection in a post-crisis world

The financial crisis has proved the relevance of consumer protection and client monitoring also to ensure the stability and efficiency of financial institutions and of the system.[1] Among the global crisis' multiple causes, inadequate underwriting and marketing strategies, unfair practices taking advantage of clients' cognitive biases, complex and not intelligible contract terms by clients, poorly designed staff remuneration policies, credit-risk transfer instruments coupled with competition have been frequently listed (*see* Chapters 4, 6–7). Consequently, the European Union, with the aim of reinforcing stability and rebuilding the confidence of investors, consumers and SMEs, laid down in 2009 a plan of intervention including measures of responsible lending.[2]

The link between client protection and stability is particularly evident in the microfinance industry where financing and regulatory simplifications heavily depend on MFIs' social performance (*see* Chapters 4–6): erroneous or hurried client evaluations and inadequate collection practices or internal monitoring systems can cause clients' defaults, contagion effect, political reaction and social revolts as well as liquidity problems (also as a consequence of socially responsible investors cutting-off their investments). Such events have materialized in the last

1 *See* L. Dragomir, *European Prudential Banking Regulation and Supervision: The Legal Dimension*, (Routledge 2010), 120–121; FSB, 'Consumer Finance Protection with Particular Focus on Credit', (2011), 10, 19–20, <www.fsb.org/wp-content/uploads/r_111026a.pdf>; G-20, 'High-level Principles on Financial Consumer Protection', (2011), <www.oecd.org/g20/topics/financial-sector-reform/48892010.pdf>; BCBS, *Guidance on the Application of the Core Principles for Effective Banking Supervision to the Regulation and Supervision of Institutions Relevant to Financial Inclusion – Consultative Document*, (BIS 2015), 34.

2 Commission, 'Driving European Recovery, Volume 1', (Communication) COM (2009)114 final; Commission, 'Public Consultation on Responsible Lending and Borrowing in the EU', (2009), <http://ec.europa.eu/internal_market/consultations/docs/2009/responsible_lending/consultation_en.pdf>.

years, when some MFIs (in India, Bosnia-and-Herzegovina, Morocco and Nicaragua), while purportedly pursuing their social objectives, have nonetheless endangered clients' situations through exorbitant interest rates, unfair terms or abusive collection practices. The causes of such practices have been reconnected, among others, to increased competition, which led to over-indebtedness (micro-borrowers being able to borrow larger loans from different MFIs) and worsening underwriting criteria as well as to perverse incentives in staff behaviour (with wages linked to the number of loans extended instead of their performance).[3]

Anyway, client protection measures entail costs, a sensible topic in microfinance (*see* Chapters 3, 5–6), and, consequently, a risk of restricted access, thus urging regulators to find a difficult balance between economic sustainability and access to finance, on the one hand, and client protection, on the other.

b Over-indebtedness and the role of credit bureaux

Over-indebtedness is also a common problem in industrialized countries and specifically in Europe, therefore listed as one of the main problems to address in the EU post-crisis action-plan.[4] Among the typical responses, in addition to the measures discussed in the next paragraph, we can find credit bureaux/registries, ie public or private agencies that collect credit information (number and amount of outstanding or defaulted loan for each person) and then share the aggregated data with credit institutions upon request.

Consultation of credit registries is a common procedure in Europe but generally not mandatory under national laws (nor by Consumer Credit Directive 2008/48 or Mortgage Credit Directive 2014/17,[5] where it figures only as one possible way of verifying consumer information: *see* §2).[6] Furthermore, the features of such databases vary considerably among Member States: they can be only public (e.g. Belgium) or only private (e.g. UK, Croatia, Hungary) or, in some countries, both types can coexist (e.g. Italy, Bulgaria, Germany, Spain) and the majority are private and for-profit. Most credit agencies collect information about the original amount of credit, its outstanding amount and its duration but fewer about interest rate, on-time payments, rejected cheques, missed payments, number of days past-due and special payments terms in case of difficulty.[7]

3 *See* among others, G. Chen et al., 'Growth and Vulnerabilities in Microfinance', (2010) CGAP Focus Note 61, <www.cgap.org/sites/default/files/CGAP-Focus-Note-Growth-and-Vulnerabilities-in-Microfinance-Feb-2010.pdf>.

4 *See* note 2.

5 Directive 'on credit agreements for consumers relating to residential immovable property'.

6 Ibidem, 23 (sharing of data is voluntary in 52% of cases and required by law in 29%; consulting the database is required by law only in 33% of cases and recommended in 14%).

7 *See* ACCIS, 'ACCIS 2012 Survey of Members – An Analysis of Credit Bureaus in Europe', (2013), 7, 17–18, <www.accis.eu/fileadmin/filestore/newsflash/50923786_2_UKMATTERS_accis_2012_survey_of_members_.pdf>. *See* also Commission, 'Report of the Expert Group on Credit Histories', (2009), <http://ec.

According to data protection Directive 95/46/EC, borrowers have to give their consent for the use and sharing of data and have the right to access the information about them and to demand a rectification in case of error.[8] The Directive has just been repealed by the new Regulation on data protection 679/2016,[9] which has fortified the right to access data and 'to be forgotten' and introduced the right to data portability (*see* also Chapter 6, §2.b). Some of these new rules have raised concerns within the credit information industry.[10] In particular, an individual might be able to delete all his/her credit history data at a certain point in time, depending on the interpretation of the expression 'the personal data are no longer necessary in relation to the purposes for which they were collected or otherwise processed' (Art. 17). Furthermore, credit bureaux might be required to transfer all data about a borrower, collected through long, complex and expensive processes, to another database (Art. 20). While the practical implications of such new rules highly depend on their interpretations, the Regulation will entail new costs for credit bureaux, which might further hinder MFIs access to the same.

As evidenced in Chapter 6, §2.b, MFIs might only partially benefit from credit bureaux reports when information is provided or can be accessed only by banks[11] or does not cover all types of loans. For instance, non-bank MFIs in Spain and Croatia have no access to the central risk information centre, while in Romania only large NBFI-MFIs registered in the Special Register do (NBR Regulation No. 2 of 9 January 2012). Similarly, in Hungary only banks and financial enterprises can have access to the Central Credit Information System (CCIS) set up with CXXII of 2011 (while the majority of MFIs are not-for-profit entities).[12] In Poland, only

europa.eu/internal_market/consultations/docs/2009/credit_histories/egch_report_en.pdf>.

8 Ibidem and ACCIS, '2012 Survey', 21–24.

9 Regulation (EU) 2016/279 on the protection of natural persons with regard to the processing of personal data and on the free movement of such data (General Data Protection Regulation), [2016] OJ L 119/1.

10 *See* ACCIS, 'Proposal for Amendments to the Proposed Review of the EU's Data Protection Legal Framework', (2012), <www.accis.eu/fileadmin/filestore/position_papers/ACCIS_Position_Paper_on_Proposed_Data_Protection_Regulation_May_2012.pdf>.

11 The Mortgage Credit Directive now requires (recital 60 and Art. 21) Member States to allow all types of credit providers to have access to credit registries.

12 EMN, 'A Collection of Case Studies on the Legal and Regulatory Framework for Microfinance Provision', (2012) 12(2) electronic Bulletin 2, <www.microfinancegateway.org/sites/default/files/mfg-en-case-study-a-collection-of-case-studies-on-the-legal-and-regulatory-framework-for-microfinance-provision-dec-2012.pdf>. Some commentators believe, however, that adequate access and sharing of client data is ensured in Romania through private agencies: M. Doiciu and D. Bialus, 'Microcredit in Romania', in B. Jayo Carboni et al. (eds), *Handbook of Microcredit in Europe* (Edward Elgar 2010), 323; TrustLaw, 'Creating Jobs in Europe: Legal and Regulatory Frameworks of Microenterprises and Microcredit in Europe', (2011), 74–75, <www.adie.org/sites/default/files/links/AdieTrustlaw_2011.pdf>. About Croatia, S. Rutledge (ed.), *Croatia – Diagnostic Review of Consumer Protection and Financial Literacy. Volume I – Key Findings and Recommendations*, (WB 2010), 17 (a private credit bureau was created in 2006 by 20 banks and only accessible by banks).

banks and credit unions (Art. 105(4) Banking Act of 1997)[13] can access the major credit bureaux (BIG InfoMonitor and BIK) but many private credit information systems exist (e.g. ERIF, KBIG, Credit Check) and a 2015 amendment extended access to lending companies. Similarly, in Germany, the Bundesbank Bureau is required by law to collect information only for loans above €1 million[14] but private databases (e.g. Schufa and CEG) grant access to credit information also to non-bank MFIs when they are participating entities and the borrower's counterparty or through a partner bank.[15] Instead, in Bulgaria, MFIs participation to the Credit Bureau is mandatory since 2012. In France, since 2001 non-bank MFIs have the duty to report and the right to access two public credit databases ('*Fichier central des chèques impayés*' – FCC and '*Fichier des incidents des crédits aux particuliers*' – FICP) collecting negative data (while only PIs and banks can directly access FIBEN, a database and credit scoring for enterprises).[16] The UK, relying until recently on a competitive system of private credit reference agencies (CRAs) based on closed-groups and reciprocity principle (with lenders often able to obtain information only with reference to the products/line of business they offer and from a CRA to which they participate providing similar data), has recently expanded credit data sharing. The 2015 Small Business, Enterprise and Employment Bill, in order to improve SMEs' access to finance and new and alternative providers access to the market, empowers the Treasury to mandate designated banks to share information about SMEs with certain CRAs and these with requesting lenders, where there is the consent of the business and the lender shares data with the CRA (Part I, section 4). Moreover, when a designated bank rejects a loan request, it refers, with the applicant's consent, to designated online platforms with whom it has to share its available data on the applicant ('Bank Referral Scheme') and which will help the borrower to make contact with alternative providers (Part I, section 5).[17]

Furthermore, in a few countries (e.g. the UK, the Netherlands and Poland) credit bureaux collect information about utilities and telecommunication payments or from government departments, Courts or tax authorities,[18] which represent

13 Available in English at <www.nbp.pl/en/aktyprawne/thebankingact.pdf>.
14 Nonetheless, it seems to collect data voluntarily also on loans below such threshold: interview on 5 December 2016 with Professor U. Reifner.
15 TrustLaw, 'Creating', 62.
16 M. Bendig et al., 'Overview of the Microcredit Sector in the European Union – 2012/2013', (2014), 59, <www.european-microfinance.org/docs/emn_publications/emn_overview/Overview2012-2013_Nov2014.pdf>; TrustLaw, 'Creating', 18, 30, 56.
17 For the text of the Bill: <www.legislation.gov.uk/ukpga/2015/26/contents>; for the Treasury Regulation draft: <www.gov.uk/government/uploads/system/uploads/attachment_data/file/389204/DraftRegulations_12_12_14_1111__2_.pdf>. The British Treasury has identified so far nine of the biggest UK banks as designated providers of data and three neutral online platforms as receivers (Funding Options, Funding Xchange and Business Finance Compared): <http://british-business-bank.co.uk/participating-banks/> and <http://british-business-bank.co.uk/finance-platform-referrals-designated-platforms/>.
18 ACCIS, '2012 Survey', 7–11.

particularly relevant data in case of low-income customers without an official credit history (*see* Chapter 6, §2.b).[19]

The 'European Code of Good Conduct for Microcredit Provision' ('European MFIs Code': *see* Chapter 3, §4.a) recognizes the right of clients to have their credit history accumulated with MFIs reported to national credit bureaux and databases when existing (but not considering the case where national law does not grant MFIs' access) (clause 1.9).

Consequently, credit bureaux have a great potential for addressing microfinance over-indebtdness and credit risk management but existing national systems only partially respond to MFIs and low-income clients' needs and reflect a very fragmented picture, which EU institutions have not been able to compose yet, despite their efforts (also for diversity and costs reasons).[20] A step forward might anyway be represented by the recent AnaCredit regulation for the collection of granular credit and credit risk data within the European System of Central Banks,[21] forcing Euro-area countries to adjust their banks' IT systems.

Mandatory sharing of data about SMEs and low-income would also improve competition among providers (to the benefit of new entrants and alternative operators) and investments (e.g. through securitizations: *see* Chapter 5, §4).[22]

2 The protection of the consumer of financial services in Europe. The recent trend towards more paternalistic and intrusive measures

European law includes a number of rules aimed at protecting consumers, in order to respond to relevant market failures related to power concentration on the supply side (consumers have weaker bargaining power), asymmetric information on the demand side (lack of resources and incentives for information search) and, more recently, limited rationality of consumers (lower level of sophistication and cognitive biases). Retail clients, in fact, are generally low-volume customers who cannot learn from experience, face high costs for acquiring information, are not able to assign a correct price to financial products and rely on the provider's advice.[23]

This need of protection appears particularly acute within the financial sector, where innovation has led to complex and difficult to understand contractual terms,

19 *See* EMN Idea-Lab, 'Credit Scoring in the European (Micro)finance Sector', (2015), 14, <www.european-microfinance.org/docs/activities/think_tanks_idea_labs/SCORING_EMN2015_LINKS_2.pdf>.

20 *See* Commission, 'Report'.

21 Regulation ECB/2016/13 and <www.ecb.europa.eu/stats/money/aggregates/anacredit/html/index.en.html>.

22 *See* I. Nassr and G. Wehinger, 'Unlocking SME Finance through Market-based Debt: Securitisation, Private Placements and Bonds', (2014) 2 *OECD Journal: Financial Market Trends* 89, 154–55.

23 *See* C. Goodhart et al., *Financial Regulation. Why, How and Where Now?*, (Routledge 1998), 7–8.

often designed to take advantage of consumer cognitive biases.[24] For instance, subprime mortgage contracts and credit card contracts have often presented small down-payments but escalating disbursements (with 'balloon' interest rates or teaser rates) based on complex calculations (linked to certain indexes), prepayment penalties and numerous fees to confuse and attract consumers affected by optimism, myopia, information over-load and framing effect.[25] Low-income customers might represent the most unprepared and subject to biases part of the population, generally having few or no alternatives and scarce financial education.[26]

Despite this, consumer protection used to be traditionally seen as a secondary objective in the banking field, with depositor protection instrumental to financial stability and consumer protection to competition. However, the financial crisis has highlighted the negative effects consumer issues can have on stability and blurred the line between the two areas, with an increase in the importance of disclosure and consumer protection in the banking sector.[27] Consequently, a financial operator's customer is likely to find protection under several Directives either generally protecting consumers or specifically targeting financial operations. Within the first category, for example, the Directives Unfair Commercial Practices No. 2005/29/EC (transparency and fair marketing practices), the Unfair Contract Terms No. 93/13/EEC (good faith obligation, clear terms) and the Consumer Rights No. 2011/83/EU (transparency especially about total price and 14-days withdrawal right in case of distance contracts). As regards the latter, Directives No. 2014/92/EU on payment accounts (PSD2: access to basic payment account, transparency, comparability of fees, switching in payment accounts), Consumer Credit No. 2008/48/EC (pre-contractual information in a standardized form, Annual Percentage Rate – APR – disclosure including all costs for ensuring comparability, withdrawal right within 14-days, right of early repayment and even consumer creditworthiness assessment obligation).

Anyway, regulators have also implemented over time more protective and sometimes 'paternalistic' measures, especially in the investment services area (*see* product governance and intervention MiFID II provisions, Chapter 7, §1) but also in important segments of bank lending, both at European and national levels. For instance, the EBA has been assigned (and taken seriously) a consumer protection remit, issuing guidelines, opinions and trend analysis in this area. Consequently, the authority, acknowledging the potential negative effects of poor remuneration

24 *See* J. Campbell et al., 'Consumer Financial Protection', (2011) 25(1) *J Econ Perspect* 91, 92–94; I. Ramsay, *Consumer Law and Policy: Text and Materials on Regulating Consumer Markets*, (3rd edn, Hart 2012), ch. 2.

25 O. Bar-Gill, 'The Law, Economics and Psychology of Subprime Mortgage Contracts' (2009) 94 *Cornell L Rev* 1073.

26 *See* V. Mak and J. Braspenning, '*Errare humanum est*: Financial Literacy in European Consumer Credit Law', (2012) 35 *J Consum Policy* 307; BCBS, *Guidance*, 34.

27 *See* M. Andenas and I. Chiu, *The Foundations and Future of Financial Regulation*, (Routledge 2013), 18ff., 277ff.; H. Hu, 'Disclosure Universes and Modes of Information: Banks, Innovation, and Divergent Regulatory Quests', (2014) 31 *Yale J on Reg* 565, 569, 573; N. Moloney, 'The Legacy Effects of the Financial Crisis on Regulatory Design in the EU', in E. Ferran et al. (eds), *The Regulatory Aftermath of the Global Financial Crisis*, (CUP 2012), 122–123.

policies of sales staff not only on clients (ending up with inadequate, unsustainable or unnecessary products) but also on financial institutions' reputations and resources, has recently issued its draft guidelines on remuneration policies applicable to a wide range of financial institutions (including PIs, eMIs and finance companies) and products (also personal loans and payment services).[28] The Draft requires providers, in designing remuneration schemes, to take into account consumer's rights and interests, preventing conflict of interest, to avoid linking remuneration to quantitative targets and creating incentives for certain products over others and to document remuneration policies and practices. It also asserts the management body's responsibility and imposes an independent evaluation about guidelines compliance as well as a periodic review. Similarly, the EBA, in line with the Commission's goal of responsible lending,[29] has also adopted guidelines on product governance for retail banking products to ensure that consumers are reached by products corresponding to their needs and characteristics (*see* Chapter 4, §5.a).

Furthermore, in addition to traditional measures (e.g. transparency, fair treatment, accessible redress mechanisms and, sometimes, withdrawal rights), the European regulator has recently introduced in certain areas more incisive and intrusive measures,[30] under the post-crisis belief that transparency might be useless or ineffective (when too much and complex information is channelled to clients) and consumers tend to be irrationally optimistic about disclosed negative events because of human cognitive limitations (*see* above). For instance, the recent Mortgage Credit Directive has introduced the obligation of financial intermediaries to assess a client's creditworthiness and ability to repay (conditioning loan disbursement), also verifying available information from the consumer or external sources (recital 55 and Artt. 1, 18, 20). Furthermore, to ensure that consumers make an informed choice, considering alternatives on the market and implications (Art. 14) and receive the right product, the intermediary shall provide, through competent and prepared staff, personalized pre-contractual information (Art. 14(1)), clear and comprehensible (Art. 13), adequate explanations about the information and effects on consumer (Art. 16) and for services adapted to his/her needs and financial situation (Art. 16(1)). Moreover, the Directive prohibits the remuneration of the staff (conducting the credit evaluation) based on the number or percentage of accepted applications (Art. 7) and tying practices (Art. 12) (*see* Chapter 4, §5.a).[31] Finally, the Directive requires Member States to adopt measures to make creditors react proactively to borrower's difficulties (early detection of problems and explanation of implications and solutions) and exercise reasonable forbearance through the use of alternative instruments to foreclosures (recital 28

28 EBA, 'Draft Guidelines on Remuneration Policies and Practices Related to the Sale and Provision of Retail Banking Products and Services', EBA/CP/2015/29.

29 *See* Commission, 'Public Consultation', 6–8 (about suitability in product design and distribution).

30 About post-crisis reforms in the consumer credit area, *see* FSB, 'Consumer'.

31 Additional protective measures: the right of withdrawal and of early repayment, prohibition to base creditworthiness evaluation only on the value of the immovable property (recital 59 and Art. 18).

and Art. 27), such as term extension, payment deferral, interest rate or type of mortgage change.[32]

Even the UK, a typical example of a liberal and non-paternalistic approach, has recently introduced forms of responsible lending in the area of consumer credit, with a duty to explain the credit agreement's key features and assess clients' creditworthiness, to provide borrowers in arrears with notice and information sheets directing to impartial debt advice, to warn about the risks and refinancing consequences in high-cost short-term credit (in addition to a 2 maximum limit of roll-overs) or when the loan is secured against the borrower's home as well as product intervention powers.[33] Some Member States impose a duty to provide the most suitable products to customers' needs (e.g. Belgium, Finland and Ireland) and loan-to-income ratios (e.g. Hungary and Romania).[34] Poland introduced in August 2015 (effective in April 2016) a ban on mis-selling, ie offering financial services to consumers not corresponding to their needs or in a manner inappropriate to the service design. The Consumer Protection and Competition Authority (UOKiK) is entrusted with the power to detect and prohibit such abusive clauses and products.[35]

Consequently, while in developing countries microfinance providers have been advocating for client protection rules to reassure investors and forestall public intervention, MFIs in Europe have to deal with multiple consumer protection rules and, in case, advocate for lighter regimes.

3 The European notion of 'consumer' and micro-entrepreneur protection while ensuring access

a Micro-entrepreneurs as consumers?

Micro-entrepreneurs can hardly be considered consumers since the definition of 'consumer' under EU law (although not universal being inserted in several EU texts in very different areas) generally refers to a natural person, who is acting outside of the scope of an economic activity (*see* for instance Art. 3(1)a Consumer Credit Directive). The European Court of Justice has held that the European notion of consumer cannot extend to legal persons (even when not having a business character such as not-for-profit organizations) but Member States remain free to adopt wider definitions in case of minimum harmonization Directives.[36]

32 *See* EBA, 'Guidelines on Arrears and Foreclosure', (2015) EBA/GL/2015/11, 14, guideline 4.

33 *See* FCA, 'Detailed Rules for the FCA Regime for Consumer Credit', (2014) PS14/3.

34 U. Reifner et al, 'Study on Interest Rate Restrictions in the EU – Final Report for the EU Commission DG Internal Market and Services', (2010), 117–118 <http://ec.europa.eu/internal_market/finservices-retail/docs/credit/irr_report_en.pdf>.

35 *See* <https://uokik.gov.pl/news.php?news_id=11827&news_page=13>.

36 *See* Cases C-464/01 *Johann Gruber v Bay Wa AG* [2005] ECR I-439; C-361/89 *Di Pinto* [1991] ECR I-1189; C-89/91 *Shearson Lehmann Hutton v TVB* [1993] ECR I-139; C-269/95 *Benincasa v Dentalkit* [1997] ECR I-3767.

Certain recent European instruments explicitly admit under national law the treatment of micro-enterprises as consumers (*see* recital 53 and Articles 38, 61 PSD2; recital 13 Consumer Rights Directive; recital 29 Distance Marketing of Consumer Financial services No. 2002/65; EBA guidelines on remunerations of sale staff and product governance). For instance, France applies misleading practices provisions of the Unfair Commercial Practices Directive to micro-enterprises and the UK has extended most consumer credit protections as well as the right to switch bank accounts without charge and in seven days to micro-loan business customers.[37] In Germany, consumer credit provisions also protect natural persons founders of new businesses (start-up and self-employment) but only in case of loans not exceeding €75,000 (section 512 BGB).[38]

Even the Commission, in reviewing the European consumer acquis, has raised the question whether individual entrepreneurs and small businesses, sometimes 'in a similar situation as consumers when they buy certain goods or services [...], should benefit to a certain extent from the same protection provided for to consumers'.[39]

In fact, especially micro-entrepreneurs can present the same unsophistication, lack of expertise and weak bargaining power as consumers, also due to lack of alternatives and scarce financial education.[40] An interesting application of behavioural studies to microfinance is bundling of MFIs' financial products: bundling a microloan with an insurance coverage can be socially beneficial[41] since clients tend to underestimate negative events affecting their activity and therefore to omit putting aside savings for these occasions.[42] However, in some countries MFIs agents have been accused of pushing clients too hard, even leading to suicides as an escape from debt, whose repayment to the MFI had been conveniently secured through a mandatory insurance (Chapter 4, §3). Furthermore, even when bundling is voluntary, clients receiving information about multiple products might not clearly understand the characteristics and implications (including costs) or feel

37 The Consumer Credit Act applies to credit facilities (even if interest-free) to individuals and partnerships, also when entrepreneurs, with the exceptions of loans for business purposes above £25,000: *see* A. Fletcher, 'Small Businesses As Consumers: Are They Sufficiently Well Protected?', (2014), 23, <http://competitionpolicy.ac.uk/documents/8158338/8264594/fsb+project_small_businesses_as-consumers.pdf/f1ed4da5-14cf-4b80-a1d8-ff76a0781def>.

38 For an English of the German Civil Code: <www.gesetze-im-internet.de/englisch_bgb/englisch_bgb.html#p1876>.

39 Commission, 'Green Paper on the Review of the Consumer Acquis', COM(2006)744 final, 13.

40 *See* R. Mazer, 'Applying Behavioral Insights in Consumer Protection Policy' (2014) CGAP Focus Note 95, <www.cgap.org/sites/default/files/Focus-Note-Applying-Behavioral-Insights-in-Consumer-Protection-Policy-Jun-2014.pdf>.

41 About the social optimality of bundling, with some distributive concerns, *see* O. Bar-Gill, 'Bundling and Consumer Misperception', (2006) 73 *U Chicago Law Rev* 33.

42 *See* S. Mullainathan and S. Krishnan, 'Psychology and Economics: What it Means for Microfinance', (2008), 10–11, <www.microfinancegateway.org/sites/default/files/mfg-en-paper-psychology-and-economics-what-it-means-for-microfinance-apr-2008.pdf>.

pressured to buy additional products in order to obtain the loan. Some studies in fact attest that a significant part of microfinance clients were willing to give up a microloan to avoid a bundled health insurance (with negative effects for financial inclusion or MFI-client relationship).[43] However, there is also evidence that well-designed and fair-priced bundled products can benefit both MFIs and clients, especially when voluntary, affordable and offered in conjunction with financial education services and post-sale support.[44] Similarly, compulsory savings can optimally force clients to save money for rainy days but, on the other hand, can be used by the MFI as collateral, and retained or sized even when the savings balance is higher than debt.

Opt-out clauses might not be an answer to such problems since consumers tend to accept and retain what they are offered.[45] Disclosure of costs and fees in the form of total cost of credit (TCC) and repayment schedule might appear more effective than APR in low-income contexts since the former are expressed in more concrete terms (e.g. value in euros instead of an interest rate expressed in percentage).[46]

On the other hand, the application of consumer protection measures to business microloans entail an increase in costs for European MFIs,[47] already striving for sustainability, therefore endangering their ability to serve the poor. Furthermore, micro-loan contracts tend to present simple terms and easily understandable language as well as financial education services and, in the absence of collateral, entail a careful evaluation of repayment capacity. In fact, the Italian regulator has therefore decided to exclude the application of consumer credit rules to micro-loans with interest rates below market prices or market prices but more favourable conditions (Art. 122.1(n) *TUB*).

Public authorities and socially responsible investors have both incentives and means to impose and monitor reporting and disclosure of social performance, therefore avoiding the imposition of other burdensome consumer protection measures (*see* Chapters 3; 4, §§2–3). Therefore, excluding the automatic extension of consumer regulation to micro-loans, we should design a regime striking a balance between the need of micro-entrepreneurs protection and financial access objective. For instance, we might want to impose written form, consumer credit pre-contractual information duties, as well as minimum contractual content

43 *See* E. Zimmerman et al., 'Responsible Bundling of Microfinance Services. A Mixed Method Evaluation of the Impact of Timing, Pressure, and Information' (2015), <www.cgap.org/sites/default/files/Working-Paper-Responsi ble-Bundling-of-Microfinance-Services-Mar-2016.pdf>.

44 Ibidem.

45 *See* C. Camerer et al., 'Regulation for Conservatives: Behavioral Economics and the Case for "Asymmetric Paternalism", (2003) 151 *U Penn Law Rev* 1211, 1227ff.

46 *See* J. Chien, 'Designing Disclosure Regimes for Responsible Financial Inclusion', (2012) CGAP Focus Note 78, 3, <www.cgap.org/sites/default/files/Focus-Note-Designing-Disclosure-Regimes-for-Responsible-Financial-Inclusion-Mar-2012.pdf>.

47 About the side effects of expanding the scope of consumer protection laws, *see* Mak and Braspenning, '*Errare*', 310; P. Rott, 'Consumer Credit', in H.-W. Micklitz et al. (eds), *Understanding EU Consumer Law*, (Hart 2009), 177ff.

requirements tailored to microfinance clients (e.g. a short and clear form with amount and characteristics of financing, number, amount and maturity of instalments; annual interest rate including costs and fees, expressed as a percentage – APR- and in euros – TCC, main contractual terms with consequences of rom breach), pre-payment rights and evaluation of client's creditworthiness duty. Instead, a withdrawal right should not be recognized (unless motivated) since MFIs would incur in high costs for choosing possible clients, carrying out an in-depth evaluation of the client's profile, financial situation and business project as well as financial and business education services to then lose the client.

b Initiatives to protect microfinance clients

Microfinance has recently witnessed a large number of different initiatives in the area of consumer protection, originated both by public authorities and private actors (*see* Chapter 3, §3), also as a response to the already mentioned scandals in some mature markets.[48] Focusing on European microfinance, some forms of private regulation are particularly important, especially the transnational ones.

For instance, the 'Client Protection Principles' (CPPs) campaign launched in 2009 by CGAP and many other organizations (in particular, Acción) involves the endorsement and application by worldwide MFIs of CPPs, initially consisting of six quite general directives based on the avoidance of over-indebtedness, transparent pricing, appropriate collection practices, ethical staff behaviour, mechanisms for redress of grievances and privacy of client data. Such principles have been updated over time and the 2013 version includes not only prevention of over-indebtedness, transparency, fair and respectful treatment of clients, privacy of client data and mechanisms for complaint resolution, but also appropriate product design and delivery (also reflecting recent trends in the mainstream financial sector: *see* §2; Chapter 4, §5.a) and responsible pricing.[49] Therefore, CPPs recommend MFIs to offer simple, easily understandable and comparable products, minimizing the use of bundled products and avoiding bullet or balloon payment requirements.[50] Contracts should use simple terms and provide complete and understandable information about all costs (also through the use of total cost of credit – TCC– and annual percentage rate – APR- formats). Remuneration policies should incentivize good staff–client relationships while stuctures should ensure client feedback and easily accessible complaints. As regards staff remunerations, in order to align loan officers' interest with MFI's dual mission, bonuses could be for

48 *See* E. Macchiavello, 'Private Regulation and Enforcement in Microfinance: A Multi-Layered and Polycentric Puzzle', in F. Cafaggi and G. Miller (eds), *The Governance and Regulation of International Finance*, (Edward Elgar 2013).

49 *See* <www.smartcampaign.org/storage/documents/smart_campaign_cpps.pdf> and SmartCampaign, 'Putting the Principles to Work: Detailed Guidance on the Client Protection Principles – Version 2.0, (2011), <www.smartcampaign.org/storage/documents/20110916_SC_Principles_Guidance_Draft_Final.pdf>.

50 SmartCampaign, 'Putting', 3, 10ff.

instance based not only on the number of clients but also on high repayments and to year-to-year performance.[51]

Such CPPs are now widely endorsed and might be enforced through the inclusion into the MFI network or association articles, MIVs guidelines, investors' due diligence process and financing contracts (although doubts remain on the dissemination and effectiveness of such practices). A certification process has been recently implemented and currently involves 55 MFIs (Chapter 3, §4.a).

The 'European MFIs Code' aims to set industry standards (especially for non-bank MFIs, not already regulated) also as regards: pre-contractual information to clients, clients' rights, assessment of client's indebtedness and repayment capability, redress mechanisms, adequate collection and collateral practices and consumer data protection. In particular, the Code basically extends to microfinance clients many protective measures included in European instruments for certain loan contracts: MFIs must take adequate measures to ensure that clients understand products, to assess client's repayment ability, to recognize clients' right to early repayment and withdrawal within 14 days, to set up redress mechanisms and, in addition, to avoid discrimination and to periodically appraise staff behaviour. Also from a risk-management perspective, the Code requires loan conditions (amount, maturity and frequency of instalments) for affordable repayment and staff incentives also linked to portfolio quality (clauses 3.5.2–3.5.4 and 3.8: *see* Chapter 5, §2.c).

Such a private sector initiative represents a good opportunity to ensure a tailored-approach to the protection of MFIs' clients without imposing on European MFIs unbearable costs but needs to be made effective through a more incisive endorsement and quasi-enforcement by European Institutions and agencies (*see* Chapters 3, §3.c; 4).

4 A topical issue: interest rates in microfinance. Usury laws in Europe after the crisis

In order to prevent lenders from imposing excessive interest rates on borrowers taking advantage of their weak bargaining power and financial needs, many countries have adopted anti-usury laws, also entailing maximum caps on interest rates charged. Such caps are generally determined by the authority (typically, Central Bank/Banking Authority, Ministry of Finance or Courts) also based on the type and average market price of comparable operations as well as duration and amount.[52] Coefficients applied to the average market price to calculate the

51 B. Armendáriz and J. Morduch, *The Economics of Microfinance*, (MIT Press 2010), 354.

52 *See* the comparative analysis in S. Munzele Maimbo and C. Henriquez Gallegos, 'Interest Rate Caps around the World. Still Popular, but a Blunt Instrument', (2014) WB Policy Research Working Paper 7070, 4, <www-wds.worldbank.org/external/default/WDSContentServer/WDSP/IB/2014/10/17/000158349_20141017143420/Rendered/PDF/WPS7070.pdf>; Reifner, 'Study'. In Germany, the interest rate cap has been set only by case law at double or 12% market rate (based

maximum rate significantly vary among Member States (ranging from 1.3 to 3).[53] In some countries, instead, disproportionate rates are sanctioned on a case-by-case basis by Courts (Hungary and Spain). Interest rate caps in some countries cover all loans (e.g. Italy and Poland) but in most countries only loans to consumers (e.g. Portugal, France and Croatia).[54] Sanctions range from civil ones (including the restitution obligation limited only to the capital part of the loan or with the interest rate reduced to the statutory one) to criminal and administrative ones (authorization cancellation).[55] Sometimes, national laws cap interest rates only or more strictly with reference to not-for-profit operators or 'social' lending: for instance, the UK imposes interest caps only on credit unions' loans[56], and, since 2015, on short-term loans (total cost capped at 100%).

Usury laws have been conceived to react to market failures and protect unsophisticated customers, although sometimes also finding their roots in certain religious beliefs (see usury prohibition in Islamic and Catholic traditions).[57]

Modern interest rate restrictions often aims specifically at protecting low-income people.[58] Nonetheless, such measures are widely debated since they might limit access to credit, distort the market (including higher interest rates for lower-risk borrowers to compensate for imposed lower rates to higher-risk ones), cause the offering of inadequate products (not covered by usury laws), and create adverse selection problems and informal markets development.[59] In fact, some countries have over time partially removed interest rate caps with the objective of reducing barriers to growth and SMEs development.[60] For instance, France decided in 2003 (Art. 32 law of 1 August 2003 No. 721) to liberalize loans to

on section 138 of the German civil code) but there is an ongoing discussion on the validity nowadays of such threshold: *see* J. Evers and S. Lahn, 'Status of Microlending in Germany: An Empirical Survey of Programmes in 2006', in Jayo-Carboni, *Handbook*, 183; interview with Reifner.

53 Reifner, 'Study', 68, 78–79.

54 *See* Munzele Maimbo, 'Interest Rate', 19; Reifner, 'Study', 27, 157; H. Vidan, 'Amendments to the Consumer Loans Act', (*Lexology*, 23 August 2013), <www.lexology.com/library/detail.aspx?g=54381349-08f8-40c0-b3d3-804f2d85b740; Croatian National Bank, 'Interest Rates', (2015), <www.hnb.hr/en/-/kamate>.

55 Reifner, 'Study', 79–80.

56 Reifner, 'Study', 63ff.

57 C. Blitz and M. Long, 'The Economics of Usury Regulation', (1965) 73(6) *J Polit Econ* 608; G. Cavalier, 'Is the Economic Crisis Driving Western Laws Closer to Islamic Laws on Interest Rate Prohibition?', (2013) 7(2) *IJEP* 47.

58 G. Ramsay, 'Regulation of Consumer Credit', in G. Howells et al., *Handbook of Research on International Consumer Law*, (Edward Elgar 2010), 397ff.; Reifner, 'Study', 28.

59 About anti-usury laws, interest rate caps and its effects, *see* R. Carnell et al., *The Law of Banking and Financial Institutions,* (4th edn, Aspen Publisher 2009), 335ff.; A. Ashta, 'Another "French Paradox": Explaining why Interest Rates to Microenterprises did not Increase with the Change in French Usury Legislation', (2015) 40 *Eur J Law Econ* 479; D. Gabrielli, 'Les incidences de la réforme de l'usure sur les modalités de financement des PME', (2007) *Bulletin de la Banque de France* 157; Blitz and Long, 'The Economics'; Munzele Maimbo, 'Interest', 4; Reifner, 'Study', 158ff.

60 *See* Ashta, 'Another', 485–486; Munzele Maimbo, 'Interest', 1.

corporations and in 2005 (Art. 7 law of 2 August 2005 No. 32) to individual entrepreneurs (save for overdrafts), hoping in an increase in bank lending to SMEs.[61] Nonetheless, the financial crisis has determined a return – although contained – of interest rate controls for consumer protection.[62]

EU Directives mostly focus on disclosure and do not address credit pricing issues, leaving this aspect to national regulators. In particular, the 2008 Consumer Credit Directive introduced the APR as a harmonized indicator, referring to the 'total cost of the credit to the consumer, expressed as an annual percentage of the total amount of credit', all costs and fees included (Art. 3(1)I and 19). In addition, both Consumer Credit and Mortgage Credit Directives only require providers to disclose all costs, bundled services included (for which the price should be included in the APR or, where not possible in advance, clearly communicated to clients), leaving national regulators free to prohibit or limit bundling. Furthermore, the Directives on unfair contract terms (Art. 4(2)) and on consumer rights (recital 14) are without prejudice to national laws on excessive or extortionate prices and state that the assessment of the fairness does not relate to the adequacy of the price, although a limited relevance of a disproportionate price is recognized under Art. 14(3) in the event of the exercise of the client's withdrawal right (and the duty to remunerate what has been provided until then).

Interest rate levels is a very sensitive issue in microfinance: microfinance has often flourished both in developing countries and in economically advanced ones thanks to interest rate cap exemptions for MFIs,[63] with the Commission also suggesting higher interest rate caps for European MFIs (Chapter 3, §4.c).[64] Nonetheless, recently MFIs' interest rates have been regarded as excessive[65] and

61 Actually, expectation not completely fulfilled: *see* Gabrielli, 'Les incidences'; Ashta, 'Another', 486ff.; L. Attuèl-Mendes and A. Ashta, 'French Legislation and the Development of Credit Availability for Microenterprise', (2008) 2(2) *GJBR* 123 (attesting an expanded availability of credit to the riskier borrowers but no increase in interest rates).

62 Munzele Maimbo, 'Interest', 3.

63 *See* the Colombian case in J. Trigo Loubière et al., 'Supervising & Regulating Microfinance in the Context of Financial Liberalization. Lessons from Bolivia, Colombia and Mexico', (2004), 15ff., <www.microfinancegateway.org/sites/default/files/mfg-en-paper-supervising-and-regulating-microfinance-in-the-context-of-financial-sector-liberalization-lessons-from-bolivia-colombia-and-mexico-aug-2004.pdf>; D. Porteous et al., 'Interest Rate Policy', (2010) Financial Access Initiative Policy Framing Note 4, 15ff., 29, <www.microfinancegateway.org/sites/default/files/mfg-en-paper-interest-rate-policy-jan-2010.pdf>.

64 Commission, 'A European Initiative for the Development of Micro-credit in Support of Growth and Employment', (Communication) COM(2007)708 final.

65 In Nigeria or Mexico interest rates can be as high as 100% (in the latter, on average 70%): *see* P. Das, 'Avoiding a Subprime-like Crisis in Microfinance: Lessons from the Mexican an Bolivian Experience', (2009) 15 *Law & Bus Rev Am* 819, 830; A. Campion et al., 'Interest Rates and Implications for Microfinance in Latin America and the Caribbean', (2010) IDB Working Paper 177, 14, <http://idbdocs.iadb.org/wsdocs/getdocument.aspx?docnum=35121757>.

somewhere triggered population, governments and social investors' reactions.[66] Microfinance clients have long been considered less sensitive to interest rate increases due to the lack of alternatives,[67] but recent studies evidence the risk of moral hazard and adverse selection (MFIs raising interest rates attract 'bad' clients), demand elasticity (loss of clients for MFIs raising interest rates compared to MFIs with stable ones) and a correlation between high interest rates and the number of defaults.[68]

Anyway, interest rate calculation worldwide and among MFIs (even within the same country) is generally not uniform, making comparison difficult due also to the relevant differences in cost of capital and social/economic contexts among countries. In fact, interest rates can be high to compensate for low performance or low efficiency of the MFI or managers/investors' greed but might also be justified by the higher costs and risks in extending credit to otherwise unserved people. Interest rates above commercial banks' rates might be in fact reasonable considering the costs incurred for the evaluation of client applications and credit recovery (lacking court enforcement) in the case of small loans, labour-intensive model and higher-risk borrowers.[69] For instance, the recent rise in microfinance interest rates has also been linked to a general rise in the costs of funds, loan losses and steadily high operating expenses.[70]

66 For example, in Nicaragua caps on interest rates had been already introduced in 2001 but the possibility since 2004 to charge clients with fees and commissions made unclear and not transparent the real price of the microloan, leading to several clients' defaults, aggressive recovering practices by MFIs and the 'no pago' movement revolt. The government consequently adopted a general moratorium on microloans, a strict consumer protection regulation and interest rates caps, triggering a microfinance crisis in the country: *see* Campion, 'Interest', 5ff.; other references in E. Macchiavello, 'Microfinance Regulation and Supervision: A Multi-Faced Prism of Structures, Levels and Issues', (2012) 9(1) *NYU J L & Bus* 125, 143 (footnote 44).

67 D. Porteous, 'Competition and Microcredit Interest Rates', (2006) CGAP Focus Note 33, <www.cgap.org/sites/default/files/CGAP-Focus-Note-Competition-and-Microcredit-Interest-Rates-Feb-2006.pdf>.

68 R. Cull et al., 'Microfinance Tradeoffs. Regulation, Competition, and Financing', (2009), WB Policy Research Working Paper 5086, 3ff., <https://openknowledge.worldbank.org/bitstream/handle/10986/4278/WPS5086.pdf?sequence=1&isAllowed=y>; R. Dehejia et al., 'Do Interest Rates Matter? Credit Demand in the Dhaka Slums', (2012) 97(2) *J Dev Econ* 437; D. Karlan and J. Zinman, 'Credit Elasticities in Less-Developed Economies: Implications for Microfinance', (2008) 98 *Am Econ Rev* 1040; Porteous, 'Interest', 5ff.

69 *See* B. Helms and X. Reille, 'Interest Rate Ceilings and Microfinance: The Story So Far', (2004) CGAP Occasional Paper 9, <www.cgap.org/sites/default/files/CGAP-Occasional-Paper-Interest-Rate-Ceilings-and-Microfinance-The-Story-So-Far-Sep-2004.pdf>; N. Fernando, 'Understanding and Dealing with High Interest Rates on Microcredit', (2006), 2–3, <www.microfinancegateway.org/sites/default/files/mfg-en-paper-understanding-and-dealing-with-high-interest-rates-on-microcredit-a-note-to-policy-makers-in-the-asia-and-pacific-region-2006_0.pdf>.

70 R. Rosenberg et al., 'Microcredit Interest Rates and Their Determinants – 2004–2011', (2013), 21ff., <www.cgap.org/sites/default/files/Forum-Microcredit%20Interest%20Rates%20and%20Their%20Determinants-June-2013.pdf>.

On the other hand, capping interest rates might increase the risk of MFIs' mission drift, trying to cover costs, and consequently restrict access to credit.[71] Studies list among the negative effects in some countries also a lower level of transparency and clarity (operators added fees and commissions to cover costs but circumventing interest rates limits) and less variety of products for low-income clients.[72]

A first needed step would consist in the standardization of interest rate and cost of capital calculation method, in combination with forms of financial and social performance disclosure, with the effect of improving private monitoring by investors and international organizations. Up to now, Microfinance Information eXchange (the MIX: Chapter 3, §3.c) has been collecting from worldwide MFIs several data about their operations (e.g. target market, legal status and nature, age, scale, financial and social indicators) but interest rates are not included. Interest yield (expressing all income from loans as a percentage of lender's GLP and generally lower than APR) disclosure was introduced only in 2010.[73] Specifically targeting pricing was MFTransparency, a programme set up in 2008, after the debate originated by the Compartamos case (*see* Chapter 5, §1.a), to promote transparency on interest rates and other loan costs, providing guidelines about methods of microloans pricing, publication of data about costs and pricing imposed by MFIs.[74] However, after facing low compliance[75] and technical difficulties in collecting data, the project shut down, denouncing MFIs' reluctance in sharing their pricing data (fearing to become vulnerable to competitors and public criticism) and international networks and funders' inability to attain MFIs compliance.[76] Nonetheless, the financial crisis and some microfinance crises have focused the sector's attention on 'responsible pricing' issues (§3.b), raising the number of networks and investors including responsible pricing and transparency among their due diligence and affiliation criteria.[77]

Within the European microfinance market, interest rates (only, not including all other costs)[78] range from 3% (for Austrian business microloans; below 5% Italian

71 Fernando, 'Understanding', 6; Armendáriz and Morduch, *The Economics*, 250.

72 Munzele Maimbo, 'Interest', 11; Helms and Reille, 'Interest', 6–7.

73 *See* C. Waterfield, 'Responsible Pricing – Where There is no Will, There is no Way', (2015), 12, <www.mftransparency.org/responsible-pricing-where-there-is-no- will-there-is-no-way/>; Rosenberg, 'Microcredit Interest' (interest yield does not give a complete idea of borrower's costs since it does not account for the effects created by compulsory savings, delinquent loans and differences in types of loans).

74 *See* Waterfield, 'Responsible', 6ff.

75 The *Microfinance Transparency Initiative* website (www.mftransparency.org/data/countries/, now inactive) listed in July 2010 as participating only 10 MFIs in Azerbaijan, 14 in Bosnia-Herzegovina, 24 in Bolivia, 32 in Ecuador and 26 in Kenya, although other countries were at the time under evaluation.

76 *See* <www.mftransparency.org/homeslide/mftransparency-dead-mean-pricing- transparency/> and Waterfield, 'Responsible', 20ff., 73, 121ff. (describing MFIs' reluctance with the expression 'suffer if I do, safe if I don't').

77 *See* Waterfield, 'Responsible'.

78 Bendig ('Overview', 33) reports that 27% of surveyed MFIs charge additional fees but are mostly located in non-EU countries (e.g. Bosnia and Herzegovina).

and French microloans) to 42% (for UK personal microloans, followed by 31% in Bulgaria), with expected peaks in countries without interest rate ceilings (e.g. UK, Romania and Bulgaria where portfolio yield is also high while operating expenses are relevant only in the first).[79] In Romania, only government-supported loans have negotiated caps on interest rates as well as credit unions but the obligation to fully disclose interest rates and other expenses is supposed to restrain NBFIs from charging excessive IRs.[80] In Hungary, no interest rate cap exists but Articles 201–202 of the Civil Code make null and void disproportionate/unfair clauses and contracts.[81] Since 2006, Poland has had a general cap on interest rates for all loans (Art. 359 Civil Code) at four times the Lombard rate set by the National Bank but fees and other costs of the loan were not included.[82] Two amendments (5 August and 9 October 2015) not only changed the method of calculation of the maximum interest rate on capital (now two times the statutory rate which corresponds to the sum of the NBP reference rate plus 3.5 percentage points),[83] but also introduced a cap on the non-interest cost of credit for consumer loans[84] and on the interest on delay.[85]

In some of the above mentioned low-interest rates Member States microfinance interest rates are lower than the ones in the mainstream sector for similar (in terms of maturity and size) operations but this is not always the case (e.g. Germany) and data are not comparable (*see* Fig. 8.1 for a rough comparison of interest rates

79 In the UK in 2013 the annual interest rate was 27% for business micro-loans and 42% for personal loans although with significant variations among different organizations (portfolio yield 25% and operating expenses 47%), in Bulgaria, respectively, 21% and 31% (portfolio yield 23%, operating expenses 9%), in Romania 18% and 17% (portfolio yield 20%, operating expenses 13%). Bulgaria introduced in 2014 an interest rate ceiling only on consumer loans (annual interest rate capped at five times the legal rate set by the Cabinet for overdue payments – in 2014 at 50.5%): Art. 19(4) Consumer Loans Act (in English: <http://psc.egov.bg/documents/10180/249779/CONSUMER+LOANS+ACT_8.pdf>) and <http://sofiaglobe.com/2014/07/22/bulgarias-new-rules-on-consumer-loans-come-into-effect-on-july-22/>.

80 EMN, 'A Collection', 17; M. Doiciu and D. Bialus, 'Microcredit in Romania', in Jayo Carboni, *Handbook*, 319, 323.

81 TrustLaw, 'Creating', 73.

82 In 2014 the maximum limit was 16% (Lombard rate 4%) and MFIs' interest rates ranged from the reference rate to such maximum regulatory limit, on average 8% for business loans: Bendig, 'Overview', 32–33, 47–49, 75; Goggin, 'The Microcredit', 26; EMN-EIF, 'Microfinance', 83.

83 *See* R. Kuchta, 'Changes in Maximum and Statutory Interest Rates', (2016), <www.codozasady.pl/en/changes-in-maximum-and-statutory-interest-rates/>. As of November 2016 the reference rate is 1.5% and therefore the maximum interest rate 10%: <https://uokik.gov.pl/news.php?news_id=12256&news_page=8> and <www.nbp.pl/homen.aspx?f=/en/dzienne/stopy.htm>; interview with Izabela Norek.

84 Corresponding per annum to the sum of 25% of the total amount of the credit plus 30% of the variable amount and anyway per the entire loan term to 100% of the total amount of the credit: *see* <https://uokik.gov.pl/news.php?news_id=12256>.

85 The maximum interest on delay is two times the sum of the NBP reference rate for interests on delay plus 5.5 percentage points; a different calculation exists for commercial transactions: *see* Kuchta, 'Changes'.

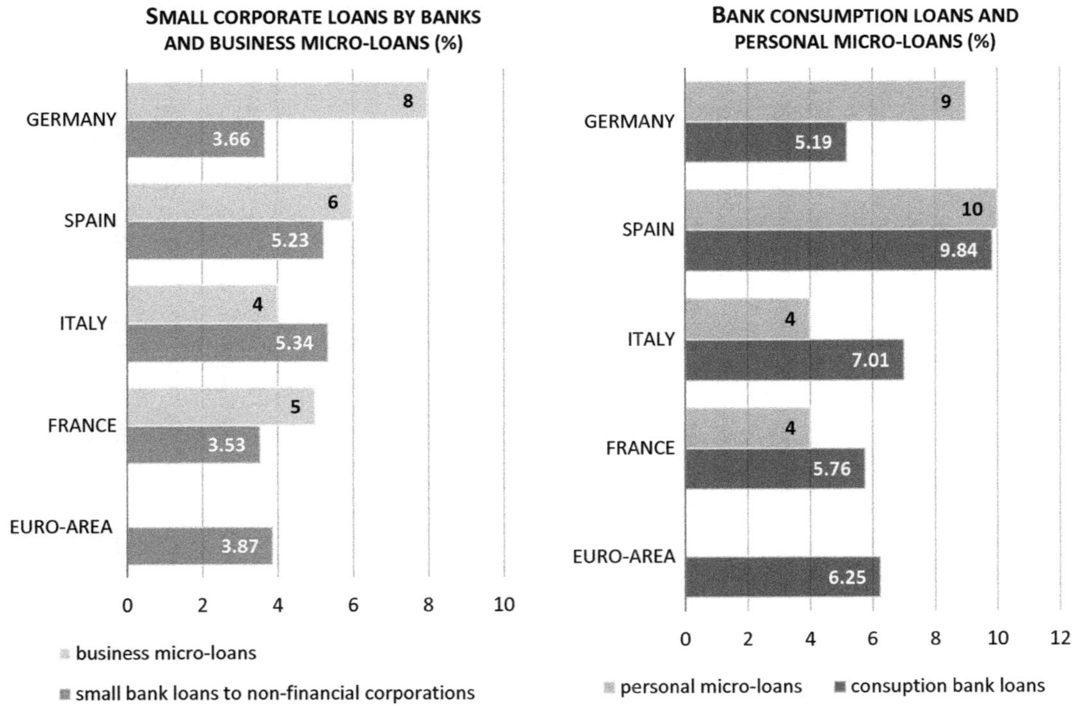

Figure 8.1 Average interest rate for bank loans and micro-loans in selected countries – 2013 (rough comparison)
(Author's elaboration using data from Bendig, 'Overview 2012/2013' and ECB statistics about December 2013 bank interest rates using as reference, for bank business loans, new loans up to €1 million and IRF 1–5 years to non-financial corporations and, for consumption loans, loans to households for consumption with IRF 1–5 years; interest rates do not include other charges; warning: this is just for a quick and approximate comparison but the two sets of data seem to present different calculation methods and the MFIs data are less precise and specific and rely on small samples for many countries)

charged in selected Euro-countries by MFIs and banks).[86] Sometimes, interest rate level depends also on the type of providers: in Germany, business loans provided by MFIs in partnership with banks generally carry an 8.9% interest rate, while promotional banks disburse loans with interest rates ranging between 3% and 7%.[87] Similarly, in Italy, some projects receiving subsidies apply no or very favourable interest rates while others use market-based interest rates (the average interest rate in 2012 was 3% but see below on the 2010 reform).[88]

In Western Europe, MFIs have to deal with the prevailing idea that microcredit should not be remunerative or not even sustainable (*see* Chapter 5, §1.b). For instance, in Italy, social microcredit cannot have an APR above the observed average APR for similar operations multiplied for a coefficient of 0.8 (Art. 5(6) decree 176/2014), therefore not only well below the usury level (corresponding to the observed average APR plus ¼ and 4 percentage points) but also to market prices. Italian not-for-profit MFIs are subject to even stricter rules: they have to apply a 'non-remunerative' APR, anyway below the observed average APR for similar operations multiplied for a 0.4 coefficient (Art. 11(5) decree 176/2014) (without considering the uncertain identification of 'comparable operations' since mainstream operators serve distinct clients with distinct products).[89]

The 'European MFIs Code' requires MFIs to disclose to their clients the APR prior to the conclusion of a contract (Clause 1.2) but not to publicly report such indicator and without an official APR calculation method for business loans, undermining again transparency, comparability and effectiveness.

5 Principles and guidelines for regulators

The EU financial sector has showed a renewed interest in client protection after the financial crisis, also in a stability perspective, this entailing also the adoption of intrusive and rather paternalistic measures, including instruments against over-indebtedness and responsible pricing.

86 For ECB data about 2013 bank interest rates visit <www.ecb.europa.eu/stats/money/interest/interest/html/interest_rates_2013-12.en.html> and <www.euro-area-statistics.org/bank-interest-rates-loans?cr=eur&lg=en&page=0&visited=1>.

87 Bendig, 'Overview', 65.

88 ENM, 'Le multiformi', 61–62 (82% of surveyed projects apply below-market interest rates).

89 Bank of Italy tends to assimilate social microcredit to 'personal loans' and commercial microcredit to 'other financing' but has recently exempted social microcredit from quarterly collection of APR data (to avoid distortive effects on APR calculation from including mandatory excessively low interest rates and reduce collection costs): *see* Banca d'Italia, 'Documento per la consultazione – Istruzioni per la rilevazione dei tassi effettivi globali medi ai sensi della legge sull'usura', (2015), 4–5, <www.bancaditalia.it/compiti/vigilanza/normativa/consultazioni/2015/istr-rilevazioni-tegm/istruz-rilevaz-tegm-documento-consultazione.pdf>. As of 30 September 2016, with a 'personal loans' average APR at 10.59% and a 17.23% anti-usury ceiling (<www.bancaditalia.it/media/comunicati/documenti/2016-01/CS-rilevazione-antiusura-lug-set-2016.pdf>), Italian for-profit MFIs' are subject to a 8.47% interest rate limit for social micro-loans while not-for-profit MFIs to a 4.24% one.

Client protection is even more important for microfinance in a funding and stability perspective since social responsibility contributes to justify MFIs' existence. Nonetheless, client protection regulation also entails relevant costs and might hinder microfinance activity and therefore financial inclusion. Consequently, we need to strike a balance between two equally fundamental microfinance goals, client protection and financial inclusion.

In particular, while microfinance clients receiving consumption/personal loans are protected by many EU consumer protection instruments, micro-entrepreneurs cannot be considered consumers. However, national laws are free to extend some or all of such measures to micro-entrepreneurs. Considering the common rationale for consumer protection, micro-entrepreneurs too would deserve protection but the above mentioned trade-off might justify a less protective regime in consideration also of the current sector's best practices and features in Europe (e.g. simple terms, financial education services, relationship-based lending).

Therefore, we might be willing to design a tailored regime to better balance conflicting goals. Such a regime might even be implemented through private regulation but only when the conditions for effectiveness exist (*see* Chapter 3).

As regards more specifically such a regime, we might want to impose pervasive pre-contractual disclosure and explanation duties (with a standardized summary sheet designed taking into account microfinance clients' characteristics), obligation to perform a repayment ability assessment (already in MFIs business model), client feed-back and redress mechanisms as well as adequate remuneration practices and pre-payment right but avoid imposing a withdrawal right (too burdensome considering the long and expensive evaluation process). Some requirements, even with reference to consumer microfinance clients, might need adjustments: for instance, a total annual or monthly cost expressed in euros instead of percentage has often proved more effective in a low-income context, therefore suggesting the use of both indicators for microfinance clients. Similarly, short and tailored forms about contractual terms and consequences from a breach might better respond to cognitive limits.

At the same time, we will need to reinforce other aspects that can indirectly protect microfinance clients. First, both social and financial indicators reporting needs to be potentiated and receive an improved enforcement framework (also thanks to the Commission and other institutions' role in financing and support programmes).

Second, credit bureaux relevance for the sector should be improved through a wider access to such databases by credit providers and the inclusion of data able to supplement the scarcity of low-income client traditional credit information (e.g. with utilities data). When this is not feasible considering the costs involved and the resistance related to different traditions and models among Member States, solutions entailing a broader sharing of data and even the use of big data should be envisaged, trying to overcome the obstacles recently created by the new Data Protection Regulation.

Such solutions should also eliminate the need for low or microfinance-specific interest rate ceilings (and their negative effects). In particular, we should, again, improve the disclosure regime, extending the same to pricing indicators but harmonizing APR calculation and in a way to reflect different costs of capital and credit markets among countries, as well as interest rate yield, in order to win MFIs' resistance and objections.

Such a regime should apply also to microfinance products offered by banks, when the conditions for the definition of microcredit stand (e.g. borrower's income, loan size, accompanying services, specific underwriting process) and therefore justify it.

9 Final conclusions

The present book has analysed microfinance (Chapter 2) and its different angles from a regulatory point of view, addressing many relevant legal issues and providing proposals for improving microfinance regulation at both national and EU level (Chapters 3–8). Although often referring to solutions adopted in developing countries, the book in fact focuses on Europe and its legal framework. In this geographic area, we have recently witnessed an increase in the demand for financial services for low-income and SMEs, also because of the post-crisis contraction in bank lending. Financial exclusion in Europe, although lower than in developing countries and partially explained by self-exclusion, is still significant, especially in some countries (e. g. in Eastern Europe), and requires better tailoring of products (Chapters 1 and 4).

Europe represents an interesting subject of study in this area for various reasons. First, European countries not only present very different microfinance models but also financial sectors, all nonetheless with pre-existing experiences of public policies and financial operators targeting low-income clients, this raising questions about the interaction of the same with microfinance, including with reference to competition and applicable law issues. Second, these differences in development, legal traditions and microfinance models have to deal with the current trend towards increasing harmonization and centralization in European financial regulation. Such a level of harmonization, together with other arguments, lays the ground for an European regulatory response under the Internal market strategy (as for basic payment accounts), to overcome the current legal fragmentation of national regimes and risk of violating EU laws in the financial regulation and state aid fields (Chapter 3, §4).

Looking at current trends in regulating microfinance and non-bank providers as well as in the application of other relevant laws affecting the sector, the EU Member States examined throughout the book show different patterns (*see* Table 9.1; Chapters 3–8). Except for the UK (traditionally characterized by an extensively liberalized regime and recently become, after Brexit, a non-EU country), Western Members tend to present also in the lending sector bank monopolies or public entities-led approach (Spain, Germany) or, as a post-crisis reaction, bank-like prudential regulation of NBFIs (Italy). Instead, Eastern and Central members (with the exception of Croatia and Hungary), likely more pressured by financial inclusion and development issues, generally exhibit more open regimes, with a general NBFI category subject to less strict and more flexible regulation, mostly non-prudential (Romania, Bulgaria, Poland) or liberalized sectors with even almost unregulated not-for-profit organizations allowed to provide loans (Poland, Bulgaria; but in part also the Western UK). In such countries, consequently, the need to create special windows for microfinance is less intense. Instead, some countries from the former group (France, Italy), together with one country from the Eastern and Central group with restrictive regulation (Hungary), have introduced special provisions to spur microfinance, exempting certain specialized entities, even not-for-profit (France, Italy, Hungary), and/or introducing special favourable regimes for the same (but in Italy the regime seems to end up reducing microcredit to a charitable dimension). The remaining countries (Germany, Spain and Croatia) appear rather closed towards non-bank providers traditionally (Germany, Spain) or in reaction to recent abuses (Croatia) (Chapters 4 and 6). MFIs might also find obstacles to their activity in a limited access to official credit information systems or in the limited range of data collected but some private databases are able to fill the void. However, Data Protection Regulation might limit data sharing and doubts are still casted on the possible recourse to big data in credit decisions (Chapters 6, §2.b; 8, §§1.b and 5). Even the application of certain consumer protection laws, protecting clients but raising costs without a tailored approach, can affect the sector. In almost all countries, the European consumer credit provisions only apply to personal loans (but in Italy micro-loans with below-market prices or more favourable conditions are exempted), not to business loans. Nonetheless, some countries have extended certain consumer rights provisions to micro-enterprises (e.g. sanctions against certain abusive clauses in Germany and misleading practices provisions in France) or the entire consumer credit regime to small loans disbursed to sole traders or unincorporated enterprises (UK). Interest rates ceilings, when existing (e.g. not in Romania and the UK) and set by the law (contrary to Hungary and Spain where the validity of interest rate clauses depend on a case-by-case Court assessment about their disproportionate or unfair nature) or *de facto* (by German Courts in a general way), tend to be limited to consumer loans (France, Bulgaria, Croatia). Especially in Eastern/Central Europe, they have been recently introduced to react to abuses (Poland, Croatia, Bulgaria). However, Italy not only applies anti-usury interest rate caps to all loans but also sets stricter maximum interest rates for social microcredit, especially when provided by not-for-profit entities (Chapter 8, §4).

Anyway, balancing stability, financial inclusion, competition and customer protection is not an easy task. Microfinance has received special attention in the aftermath of the financial crisis because of its perceived ability to improve financial access through business models, also in consideration of the expansion of financial regulators' purview to financial inclusion matters (Chapter 1). Nonetheless, it also raises regulatory concerns in the context of the larger debate about shadow banking and financial innovation regulation. In most mature markets, in fact, microfinance has showed features of complexity, client abuses and use of other financial innovations, also raising awareness on the potential risks coming from such a sector (Chapters 3–8).

In order to deal with microfinance's multiform nature (e.g. in terms of missions, business models, authorities and regulations involved: Introduction, Chapters 1–3) and tackle all relevant regulatory issues, I have examined it from different perspectives ('dimensions'; *see* Introduction). From such an analysis we can derive the following principles, here organized in a different order compared to the discussion of the single issues in the book to provide a clearer picture.

Microfinance can be regulated alone or as a part of a larger scheme targeting socially responsible financial services. In any case, to establish sound regulatory competition, regulators need to define microfinance and delimit the scope of its favourable regime focusing on social mission and social performance, targeted clients, supporting services, alternative risk-mitigation instruments, although allowing a certain level of flexibility (Chapter 3).

Regulation can be expensive, both for regulators and for operators, especially in a sector disregarded by mainstream operators because of its high operative costs. This can justify forms of private regulation, especially in the consumer protection and transparency fields, where transnational private regimes can effectively address certain issues under determined conditions (Chapters 3–5 and 8).

Favourable regimes for microfinance should be grounded on its social mission (e. g. serving financially excluded) and therefore subject to social performance transparency and monitoring, despite its difficult measurement (Chapters 4–6). Also private and hybrid measures can contribute spreading a social performance culture through enforceable clauses in articles of incorporation and investment contracts (Chapters 3–5). Such dedication and specialization also justify a partially different treatment from mainstream operators engaging in microfinance, also in the light of state aid law (as SGEI with a reasonable different treatment of operators: Chapters 3 and 6). Inputs for a flexible and favourable regime in case of social impact, based on *ex-post* (in case of risks for the system and consumers) controls and requirements escalating in strictness with complexity (tiered regime), derive also from analysing microfinance under the light of financial innovation regulation (Chapters 6 and 7).

An adequate regulation of microfinance should also take into account the type of activities conducted by MFIs, specific microfinance risks (e.g. high credit risk but use of unconventional instruments to manage it; fast decapitalization; higher reputational risk but also incentives; limited systemic risk and leverage, no typical shadow banking economic functions) and funding sources (Chapters 5 and 6). In particular, from the analysis of all such factors, current prudential bank-like regulation often conceived for large international banks and deposit-taking institutions appear inadequate, especially for non-deposit taking MFIs.

Nonetheless, in the absence of a harmonized framework for lending activities in EU, in some countries, as anticipated, non-deposit taking MFIs are subject to bank-like requirements because of a traditional banking monopoly on financial activities or of a post-crisis shadow banking fear, with consequently very different regimes among EU countries (Chapters 3, 4 and 6). However, most European non-deposit taking MFIs do not pose systemic risk nor conduct typical shadow banking economic functions and are typically funded long-term by sophisticated entities with reputational capital (Chapter 6). This, together with the social objective, justifies a regime focused on transparency and business conduct, in addition to, at least, registration requirements (conditional to the evidence of, for instance, adequate resources, fit and proper managers and owners, feasible business plan, low minimum capital or professional insurance, continuity plan), with financial authority's intervention when needed, proportional and flexible risk-management and governance requirements (*see* below and Chapter 6). Also to fulfil MFIs' social mission and response to their target clients' needs, such a regime should allow a varied range of permissible activities although characterized by basic features and simplicity, with escalating requirements for more varied and more complex services. Among permissible activities, we should also include non-financial supporting services, which however MFIs might decide to outsource (Chapter 4).

Instead, MFIs accepting deposits should be subject to prudential regulation (at present, highly harmonized at EU level) but with adaptations in consideration of the specific risks, business models and social goals (Chapter 6). Such adaptations can in fact be grouped into two categories: the first one gathers needed specifications to existing prudential requirements because of specific MFIs risks or features (such as shorter periods for loan-loss reporting and provisioning, definition of NPLs and resolution and recovery plans). The second group reunites instead facilitations justified by the limited size and systemic risk entailed as well as social goals, such as lower minimum capital, more flexible and proportional executives suitability, governance and risk-management requirements, more flexible CET1 rules, different evaluation of geographic, product and social concentration, liquidity and leverage requirements. In fact, many post-crisis reforms have been designed with large and complex banks in mind, currently raising concerns about the impact on small institutions. The proportionality principle, requiring adaptations of rules and requirements based on the size, complexity, systemically relevance of institutions, is internationally recognized (*see* Basel Core principles) and find some applications also in the CRD IV/CRR package. Nonetheless, these latter texts allow simplifications by competent authorities (Member States or ECB/Commission through EBA guidelines/RTS) but only to a limited extent, on a case by case basis and with reference only to specific aspects. A level 1 reform would instead be required for additional relevant aspects (e.g. SREP reporting, governance).

MFIs, especially when deposit-taking, present many features in common with small banks (such as SMEs and low-income specialization, geographic concentration, screening based on soft-information and business plan/personality of clients, relationship-lending, decentralized credit decisions) and consequently raise similar legal issues (Chapter 6). For instance, they are both penalized under the Basel capital adequacy framework (especially under the SA approach) because of their typical specialization on SME lending and SMEs unavailability of rating or collateral. Similar problems exist for lending to MFIs. Existing financial authorities trends (admitting a 75% SME consumer class risk-weight) and public and private microfinance guarantees partially solve the problem, while current proposals to ease up risk-weights for SME corporate class (85% instead of 100%) might be able to further respond to evidenced issues.

However, some large and mature MFIs also share with large banks some features and risks (e.g. over-indebtedness, standardization, excessive growth, lax underwriting standards), raising the question whether we should cap MFI size for stability reasons and to avoid mission drift. Nonetheless, setting an optimal size is even more difficult for MFIs than for mainstream banks, for which, despite current structural reforms, size caps are considered not optimal. Consequently, other measures, already or shortly to be discussed, should address such issues, such as through transparency about social and financial performance, governance and tiered regime based on the complexity of activities and structures.

Other requirements can be associated with non-prudential aspects of regulation (although now central in banking regulation and with prudential implications), such as corporate governance, transparency and consumer protection. Corporate governance is fundamental in managing the dual objective, balancing financial and social objectives, as evidenced even in the mainstream sector for composing shareholders' interest with stakeholders' ones, including stability (Chapter 5). In microfinance, relevant stakeholders are not only MFIs' clients and employees but also different types of funders (e.g. public entities, commercial banks and private investors, socially responsible investors) and relative objectives (as evidenced looking at hybrid legal forms). Consequently, MFIs need two different sets of rules in this field. A first set of rules, on the one hand, should incorporate social mission into internal organization and governance, through, for instance, specific bodies or board members responsible for social performance as well as financial and social performance reporting obligations also embedded in financing contracts. The legal form appears irrelevant in this regard, therefore regulators should not prescribe specific ones, nor impose on not-for-profit particular limits (e.g. on interest rates or profit-production since other rules can address such issues in a more efficient way). On the other hand, MFIs need rules spurring efficiency in their internal organization but adapted to their specificities. Therefore, a second set of rules should entail the proportionate application of current banking corporate governance rules and guidelines, conceived for large and complex banks, to MFIs, tailoring them to MFIs' specific features and missions (e.g. board composition and size rules: Chapter 5).

In fact, another fundamental aspect for microfinance is economic efficiency. This does not mean that MFIs always need to be profitable (which might or might not partially enter into conflict with its social mission) but that they should concretely aim at covering their costs and reach their mission in the most effective way possible. Financial self-sustainability has always represented an issue in microfinance, especially in Europe where several obstacles (e.g. mentality, complex regulation, social security policies, lower demand and scale) seem to impede such a target (Chapters 2 and 4). Therefore, to satisfy both social mission and the business model, while allowing subsidies (especially for non-financial services and serving the poorest as well as developing infrastructures), regulators need to implement measures and incentives towards efficiency. For instance, we need to spur transparency of financial (and social) performance, especially as regards expenses and yields. Second, regulators should allow a diverse range of financing options since access to funding has always represented an issue for MFIs because of typical obstacles (e.g. asymmetric information and adverse selection) but also regulatory restrictions for stability, investor protection and other objectives (Chapters 5 and 7). While available sources of funding also depend on the stage of development and other factors

(Eastern European MFIs relying more on deposits, investments and commercial loans while Western European one on grants and concessional loans), access to grants and EU funds should not be foreclosed because of the need to develop institutional capacity, non-financial services and social performance measurement. Instead, more complex operations such as IPOs and securitizations should be limited to the most mature and regulated MFIs, with measures to protect investors and subject to infrastructure improvements (e.g. liquidity facilities and back-up/continuity plans), although recognizing facilitations in case of simple activities and social objective. MIVs represent a fundamental source for large and established MFIs but the sector needs clarifications and simplifications of applicable regulation to spur investments also in smaller MFIs, without endangering investor and client protection (Chapter 5). Similarly, modifications of existing EU laws might be required to facilitate crowdfunding for MFIs while protecting clients and investors (Chapter 7). The recourse to new technologies for lowering costs (e.g. m-banking, big data in screening and other FinTech activities), in fact, adds complexity to the microfinance regulation enigma, which need to be addressed separately (Chapter 7).

Finally, microfinance clients deserve protection also because of their particularly vulnerable and unsophisticated nature (Chapter 8). Consumer protection in microfinance is also important for stability and funding reasons since social performance influences socially responsible and public investments, on which microfinance significantly relies, as well as regulatory reactions. Consumer protection measures entail relevant costs, especially in Europe where MFIs already strive for self-sustainability and many consumer protection laws apply, although not necessarily for micro-entrepreneurs since it depends on national choices (*see* above). Therefore we need to find a correct balance between consumer protection and financial inclusion, underlining that a tailored approach should be preferred to a mere extension of existing laws to microfinance, in order to protect MFIs' clients while granting financial access, also partially recurring to private regulation (Chapters 3 and 8).

As anticipated above, a special regime for MFIs can be justified but differentiations with mainstream providers of financial services should be based on reasonable grounds. Consequently, regulators should introduce facilitations (e.g. in terms of capital adequacy evaluation, supervisory review, transparency) also for banks and other mainstream providers in order to encourage cooperation, avoid competitive distortions and a complete separation of microfinance from traditional finance, as well as for not creating excuses for the latter not to serve certain parts of the population. Different degrees of facilitations should be entailed, based on the type and intensity of bank involvement (e.g. tax, Basel, SREP and reporting when MFI-partner: Chapter 6).

In conclusion, microfinance can represent an effective instrument of financial and social inclusion and should be encouraged but also needs an adequate regulatory regime to address the number of complex legal issues raised. EU institutions should make a step forward in their involvement in the sector, complementing their technical and financial support with the design of a tailored legal framework because of several obstacles in EU legal texts and the advantages in advancing harmonization also in this sub-sector of the financial field.

Table 9.1 Regulation applicable to microcredit in selected Member States

	France	*Germany*	*Italy*	*Spain*	*UK*	*Bulgaria*	*Croatia*	*Hungary*	*Poland*	*Romania*
a) Special regime for micro-credit/ micro-finance?	Yes, in part: special **exemption** from bank monopoly for not-for-profit entities providing micro-loans	No	Yes, **special regime** since 2010 (implemented in 2014 and effective 2016/ 2017)	No	No	No	No	Yes, in part: **special exemption** from bank monopoly for LEAs/ foundations participating to MC programs	No	No (yes between 2005-2009 for MC companies, but then revoked)
b) Entities authorized to provide (micro) loans	**(closed regime but MC exemption) Banks** and, only for loans and under certain conditions, **association and foundations**	**(very closed regime) only banks and development banks** (often partnerships among development banks, banks, business support centres and MFIs with public guarantee/ funds)	**(partially open plus quite-restrictive MC exemption) Banks, NBFIs, credit cooperatives, recently also authorized MC providers** (for-profit and not-for-profit). In the past frequent	**(very closed regime) only banks and savings banks**	(**very open** regime) **Liberalized** sector. MC typically provided by **CFDIs** (now Responsible Finance providers), under various legal forms	**(quite open regime) Banks, credit cooperatives and NBFIs. Not-for-profit entities** can offer loans if not principal activity, no deposit and no profits distribution	**(quite closed regime) Only banks, savings banks and credit unions**	**(quite closed regime) only banks, financial enterprises (also in the form of foundations) and credit cooperatives all subject to similar prudential regime** (interpretation of act No. CXII of 1996 on	(very open regime) **Liberalized** sector: **banks, credit unions, cooperative banks, companies, associations and foundations**	**(quite open regime) Banks, credit unions and NBFIS**

	France	*Germany*	*Italy*	*Spain*	*UK*	*Bulgaria*	*Croatia*	*Hungary*	*Poland*	*Romania*
			partnerships among banks, MFIs, public authorities.					Credit Institutions and Financial Enterprises with consequent involvement of banks in MC) but since 1998/2003 also **LEAs/ foundations** operating under MC program		
c) Prevailing regime applicable to MFIs	Since 2001 MC **associations and foundations** can be authorized to provide microloans of certain amount and to certain categories of people from own resources,	Banking law for **banks** and not-for-profit law for **MC organizations**	**NBFIs** (106 TUB) since 2010 subject to simplified but bank-like prudential requirements. **Specialized MC providers** (since 2010 but effective 2016; 111 TUB):	MC traditionally offered by **savings banks** (banking law) but after crisis public authorities and NGOs have stepped in	**CDFIs** tend to be unregulated since generally use: **not-for-profit form** (regulated only under consumer credit act which however covers also unincorporated entrepreneurs);	**NBFIs** need to **register** (when financial activities represent at least 30% of total activities) and conditional to joint stock company, limited liability company	**credit unions**: at least €70,000 funding capital from at least 30 members from same county, deposits unprotected, geographic restrictions, no external funding	**LEAs/** foundations subject to same regime as financial enterprises/ banks	Different regimes depending on the legal form (eg banks and credit unions regulated by 1997 Banking Act and subject to the	**NBFCs** have to register in the NBR **general registry** after verification of joint stock company form, €200,000 minimum capital, plan of activities, executives and

	France	*Germany*	*Italy*	*Spain*	*UK*	*Bulgaria*	*Croatia*	*Hungary*	*Poland*	*Romania*
	then also from bank loans (2003), private people loans (2008), and interest-free crowdfunding (2010) (Art. 511-6 (1) *CMF*) when evidence of competence and experience, guarantee fund, adequate internal controls (risk-management, management and control separation) **Regime**: certification of financial statements, annual report about their lending		**for-profit providers** authorized when limited liability company/ cooperative form, €250,000 minimum capital, executives and main shareholders requirements, business programme. No debt > 16 times net-worth. **Not-for-profit providers** authorized when associations, foundations, cooperatives, public agencies form,	MC traditionally offered by **savings banks** (banking law) but after crisis public authorities and NGOs have stepped in	**credit unions** (regulated by FCA); **company limited by guarantee** or Industrial and Provident societies (**IPSs**)	and association limited by shares form, BGN1 M/ €511,00 minimum capital, managers' and owners' requirements. But exemption from registration if EU programme (Art. 3.a l. on credit institutions; ordinance 26/2009) **NBFIs Regime**: simple own funds, organizational (internal structure and control) and reporting (financial statement)			Financial Supervision Authority-KNF-; limited liability companies subject to commercial code)	owners' requirements, audit committees (Art. 20 law 93/ 2009); **NBFIs Regime**: NBFIs subject to reporting (also about portfolio structure and other statistics, financial statements), accounting and auditing requirements (Artt. 14ff L. 93/ 2009) and NBR monitoring and inspection powers. But large

	France	*Germany*	*Italy*	*Spain*	*UK*	*Bulgaria*	*Croatia*	*Hungary*	*Poland*	*Romania*
	activities, management of non-performing assets, including own resources above 12% of loans not covered by guarantees or loan provisioning; favourable tax regime (Artt. R518-57ff *CMF*)		plan of activities, executives and owners' requirements. IR only to cover costs and anyway < TEGM for similar activities *0.4.**Credit cooperatives (MAG)**: simplified regime, IR only to cover expenses and cost of capital. **Regime for all**: disclosure and client information duties,			requirements as well as NBB monitoring. **Not-for-profit entities:** very favourable regime.				**NBFIs in special registry** (equity at least 50 M lei/€11 M, and outstanding portfolio of at least 25M lei/ €5M) need to have financial statements audited by NBR accredited auditors) and subject to bank-like requirements (capital requirements, large exposures, related party lending, organization, risk-management,

	France	*Germany*	*Italy*	*Spain*	*UK*	*Bulgaria*	*Croatia*	*Hungary*	*Poland*	*Romania*
			guarantee funds not covering >80%, Bank of Italy monitoring until creation of private body							internal control) and prudential surveillance by NBR (Artt. 29 ff L. 93/2009 and 58ff ordinance 20/2009). **Credit unions** do not have minimum capital requirement but report financial statements to Ministry of Public Finance and statistical indicators (on assets and debt) to NBR; no funding through external sources

	France	*Germany*	*Italy*	*Spain*	*UK*	*Bulgaria*	*Croatia*	*Hungary*	*Poland*	*Romania*
										(**not even borrowing; no use of deposits for lending**) (laws 122/ 1996 and 122/ 2004)
d) Permitted activities/ Products allowed	**Associations and foundations** can offer **business micro-credit** (to enterprises < 5-years old, no > 3 employees, loan amount < €12,000), **social micro-credit**	**Banks**: all bank services. **Non-bank MC organizations**: only partnerships with banks and development banks	**NBFIs** (106 TUB): all lending and (if authorized) payment services. **MC providers** (111 TUB): only MC and supporting services but **for-profit MFIs** can offer business MC	**Savings banks**: all bank services	Loans (consumer credit and mortgages subject to FCA regulation) but credit unions can also accept deposits	**NBFIs**: micro-credit, consumer lending, leasing, factoring, holding, guarantee. **Credit cooperatives**: also deposits for members.	**Credit unions** can offer deposits (but unprotected and seizable), **loans,** payments, exchange operations, collateral	**LEAs/ foundations** only MC (mainly business MC) ie loans < 7M forints (€24,000) to companies with < 10 employees and <200M forints (€690,000) revenue, < 8 years	**Banks and credit unions**: all services **Associations,** foundations, regional development agencies: business loans and BDS	**NBFIs**: micro-loans, larger loans, mortgages, consumer credit, leasing, factoring, guarantees and credit cards; manage public funds granted as micro-credit funds by governmental agencies and pledge

	France	*Germany*	*Italy*	*Spain*	*UK*	*Bulgaria*	*Croatia*	*Hungary*	*Poland*	*Romania*
	(to people with financing difficulties but repayment capacity and '*accompagnement social*' for re-employment or social inclusion, loan amount < €5,000), always charging IR, '*prêts d'honneur*'. Other providers also guarantees and micro-insurance		(to certain enterprises, for business purposes or self-employment, < €25,000, < 7 years, no real security, accompanying services) and social MC (to certain socially-excluded individuals, for primary needs, <10,000, no real security, supporting services, < 5 years, more favourable condition than market's and IR < TEGM* 0.4; credit cooperatives (MAG): can offer both business							own shares for their debts and grant loans secured by pledges over their shares **Credit unions**: also deposits (covered under national insurance protection scheme)

	France	*Germany*	*Italy*	*Spain*	*UK*	*Bulgaria*	*Croatia*	*Hungary*	*Poland*	*Romania*
			(and up to 75,000 and <10 years to members) and social MC							
e) Coaching services	By **MFIs** or **chambers** of commerce	[According to consumer protection laws, **MFIs** and business centres participating to loan provision **cannot provide advisory/ non-financial services (bundling prohibition)**]. Fees for services are financed, depending on the prior or post-start-up phase, by the Länder or the European Social Fund with KfW	Mix: traditionally by **public institutions** in combination with private actors such as **chambers of commerce** and business associations; now also directly by **MFIs** or through outsourcing	By **public** programmes and **MC** associations	by enterprise **agencies, CDFIs** and NGOs	by **agency** for SMEs promotion with the Minister of the Economy but also some **NGOs** and industry **associations** assist micro-entrepreneurs	no	Offered by **public authorities** (financial institutions can only offer financial and auxiliary services listed in banking law)	By national and regional **development agencies, EU contact points** and network of non-commercial **organizations**	**NBFIs cannot provide non-financial services** and so partnerships with **NGOs** (sometimes shareholder of MFIs): otherwise offered by **public** entities

	France	*Germany*	*Italy*	*Spain*	*UK*	*Bulgaria*	*Croatia*	*Hungary*	*Poland*	*Romania*
f) Credit bureaus	Since 2001 also **MFIs** have **duty to report and right to access the FCC** (*fichier central des chèques impayés*) and the **FICP** (*fichier des incidents des crédits aux particuliers*)	Bundesbank bureau is required by law to collect information only for loans above €1M. Private databases accessible by non-bank **MFIs when participating entities and borrower's counterparty or through a partner bank.**	**Only banks and NBFIs** (106 TUB) have to report to the Credit risk information system (Bank of Italy) and have access to database. Others can access **private credit information databases**.	Accessible **only by banks**. Non-bank MFIs have no obligations to provide data	Wide database of **private credit reference agencies** (also from telecommunication companies, government, Courts) accessible by lender submitting data and often part of a closed-user group (reciprocity) or on their behalf. But starting 2016, certain **banks have the duty to share data with designated CRAs and online platforms** (and their users)	**NBFIs and credit cooperatives' mandatory participation** (ordinance 22/2009 as amended in 2012)	Only one private credit bureau, **accessible only by banks**	**CCIS accessible only by banks** and **financial enterprises**	Main ones limited to banks, financial institutions and credit unions but other entities can access **many private databases,** with also data on utilities and telecommunication payments or from government departments, Courts or tax authorities	**Accessible only to banks and large NBFIs in special registry** (duty to report and right to access)

	France	*Germany*	*Italy*	*Spain*	*UK*	*Bulgaria*	*Croatia*	*Hungary*	*Poland*	*Romania*
g) Client protection	Consumer credit law; misleading practices provisions of unfair commercial practices law applies also to micro-enterprises	Consumer credit law (extended also to natural persons founders of start-up when loans > €75,000); "black list" of unfair commercial practices applies also to micro-enterprises; code of conduct;	**Consumer credit law but exemption for micro-loans** with IR below market prices or market prices but more favourable conditions; Unfair commercial practices also in B2B relations	Consumer credit law	**consumer credit protections mostly extended to micro-businesses (exempted only corporate bodies or loans for business purposes above £25,000)**	Consumer credit act (applicable also to loans below €200 except for the withdrawal right)	Consumer credit Act; unfair commercial practices and contractual terms	Consumer credit Act; code of conduct of financial institutions (banks, mortgage credit institutions, building societies, credit unions, financial enterprises)	Accurate disclosure and fair commercial practice and competition for all contracts; Personal Data Protection; consumer credit act	**NBFIs subject to consumer protection law** (truth-in-lending, anti-abusive collection) and **privacy/confidentiality** law

	France	*Germany*	*Italy*	*Spain*	*UK*	*Bulgaria*	*Croatia*	*Hungary*	*Poland*	*Romania*
h) Anti-usury law/ Interest rate ceilings	**Not IR ceilings for business loans** (IR cap only for personal loans at 1/3 of the average market rate: as of October 2016, 20.01% for loans up to €3,000 and 12.99% for loans up to €6,000)	**IR cap set only by case law** at the double or 12% market rate (based on section 138 of civil code) but currently debated	**IR ceilings for all loans (1/4 of the average market rate – TEGM – plus 4 percentage points) but more restrictive ceilings for social MC** (TEGM* 0.8 when by for profit and TEGM* 0.4 when by not-for-profit)	**No IR ceilings but disproportionate IR void** subject to Courts' interpretation	**No IR ceiling** except for credit unions (3% per months; 42.6% APR) and, since 2015, for short-term (<30-days) loans (initial cost cap at 0.8% per day and total cost cap at 100%) and, since 2015, for short term (<30-days) loans (initial cost capped at 0.8% per day and total cost capped at 100%)	**IR ceiling only on consumer loans** (annual IR, fees included, no > the legal rate set by the Cabinet for overdue payments, multiplied by 5 – now about 50.5%)	Since 2012 **effective IR cap on consumer loans** (up to 1% below statutory IR: currently **11%**)	**No IR ceilings** but civil code voids disproportionate/ unfair clauses and contracts	Since 2006 **IR regulatory cap on all loans** (2* the sum of the NBP reference rate plus 3.5 pp); since 2016 also caps on the non-interest cost of credit for consumer loans and on interest on delay (different calculation for commercial transactions)	**No IR ceilings** (except for government supported loans and credit unions': 15% all included) but **duty to disclose/ report IR.**

Bibliography

(All internet sources were last accessed August 2016.)

ACCIS, 'Proposal for Amendments to the Proposed Review of the EU's Data Protection Legal Framework', (2012), <www.accis.eu/fileadmin/filestore/position_ papers/ACCIS_Position_Paper_on_Proposed_Data_Protection_Regulation_May_2012.pdf>

ACCIS, 'ACCIS 2012 Survey of Members – An Analysis of Credit Bureaus in Europe', (2013), <www.accis.eu/fileadmin/filestore/newsflash/50923786_2_UKMATTERS_accis_2012_survey_of_members_.pdf>

Acharya, V., I. Hasan and A. Saunders, 'Should Banks Be Diversified? Evidence from Individual Bank Loan Portfolios', (2006) 79(3) *J Bus* 1355

Adams, R. and H. Mehran, 'Is Bank Holding Company Governance Different?', (2003) 9 *FRBNY Economic Policy Review* 123

ADIE, '20 Years of Microcredit in France the Knowledge Gained through Adie's Experience', (2008), <www.microfinancegateway.org/sites/default/files/mfg-en- paper-20-years-of-microcredit-in-france-the-knowledge-gained-through-adies-experience-oct-2008.pdf>

ADIE, 'Rapport Annuel 2011', <www.adie.org/sites/default/files/links/Adie_Rapport_Annuel_2011_0.pdf>

Aghion, P. and P. Bolton, 'A Theory of Trickle-Down Growth and Development', (1997) 64 *Rev Econ Stud* 151

Ahlin, C. and N. Jiang, 'Can Micro-credit Bring Development?', (2008) 86 *J Dev Econ* 1

Akerlof, G., 'The Market for "Lemons": Quality Uncertainty and the Market Mechanism', (1970) 84(3) *Q J Econ* 488

Akhigbe, A. and J. McNulty 'The Profit Efficiency of Small US Commercial Banks', (2003) 27*J Bank Finance* 307

Alarcón, D., 'Securitization in Microfinance. Creating Saving and Investments for the Poor', (2008), IDLO Microfinance Research Paper, www.idlo.int/microfinance/Documents/Publications/19E.pdf>

Albertazzi, U. and D. Marchetti, 'Credit Supply, Flight to Quality and Evergreening: An Analysis of Bank–Firm Relationships after Lehman', (2010), Banca d'Italia Working Paper 756, <www.bancaditalia.it/pubblicazioni/temi-discussione/2010/2010- 0756/en_tema_756.pdf?language_id=1>

Albertazzi, U. et al., *Securitisation Is Not That Evil After All*, (BIS 2011)

Allen, F., A. Demirgüç-Kunt, L. Klapper and M. Martinez-Peria, 'The Foundations of Financial Inclusion: Understanding Ownership and Use of Formal Accounts', (2012),

World Bank Policy Research Working Paper 6290, http://documents.worldbank.org/curated/en/348241468329061640/pdf/wps6290.pdf>

Allen, F. and R. Herring, 'Banking Regulation versus Securities Market Regulation', (2001), Wharton Financial Institutions Center Working Paper 29, 3, http://finance.wharton.upenn.edu/~allenf/download/Vita/0129.pdf>

Altunbas, Y., L. Evans and P. Molyneux, 'Bank Ownership and Efficiency', (2001) 33(4) *J Money Credit Bank* 926

AMF-ACP, 'Crowdfunding: A Guide for Funding Platforms and Project Owners', (2013), <http://acpr.banque-france.fr/fileadmin/user_upload/acp/Communication/Communiques%20de%20presse/20130514-guide-professionnel-crowdfunding.pdf>

Andenas, M. and I. Chiu, *The Foundations and Future of Financial Regulation*, (Routledge 2013)

Anderloni, L., M. Braga and E. Carluccio (eds), *New Frontiers in Banking Services Emerging Needs and Tailored Products for Untapped Markets*, (Springer 2007)

Andersen, J., 'Commercialization of Microfinance. Portfolio Aspects of Turning Banker to the Poor', (2009), Aarhus School of Business Thesis, http://theses.asb.dk/projekter/fbspretrieve/8073/THESIS_FINAL_CONTENTS.pdf>

Andreoni, A., M. Sassatelli and G. Vichi, *Nuovi bisogni finanziari. La risposta del micro-credito*, (Mulino 2013)

Arena, T., 'Social Corporate Governance and the Problem of Mission Drift in Socially-Oriented Microfinance Institutions', (2008) 41(3) *Columbia J Law Soc P* 269

Armendáriz, B. and A. Szafarz, 'On Mission Drift in Microfinance Institutions', (2011), MPRA Paper 31041, <https://mpra.ub.uni-muenchen.de/31041/1/MPRA_paper_31041.pdf>

Armendáriz, B. and J. Morduch, *The Economics of Microfinance*, (2nd , MIT Press 2010)

Armour, J. et al., *Principles of Financial Regulation*, (OUP 2016)

Arner, D., J. Barberis and R. Buckley, 'The Evolution of Fintech: A New Post-Crisis Paradigm?', (2015), University of Hong Kong Faculty of Law Research Paper 2015/047, <http://ssrn.com/abstract=2676553>

Ashta, A. 'Another "French Paradox": Explaining Why Interest Rates to Microenterprises did not Increase with the Change in French Usury Legislation', (2015) 40 *Eur J Law Econ* 479

Aspan, M., 'Lending Club Courts Small Banks as Personal-Loan Partners', *American Banker* (New York, 11 December 2013)

Aspinwall, R., 'On the "Specialness" of Banking', (1983) 7 *Issues in Bank Reg* 16

Athwal, N., 'The Disappearence of Peer-To-Peer Lending', *Forbes* (Jersey City, 14 October 2014), <www.forbes.com/sites/groupthink/2014/10/14/the-disappearance- of-peer-to-peer-lending/>

Attuèl-Mendes, L. and A. Ashta, 'French Legislation and the Development of Credit Availability for Microenterprise', (2008) 2(2) *GJBR* 123

Augsburg, B. and C. Fouillet, 'Profit Empowerment: The Microfinance Institution's Mission Drift', (2010) 9(3/4) *PGDT* 327

Avgouelas, E., 'Access to Finance, Microfinance, and International Capital Adequacy Standards for Banks: A New Approach to Development', (2007) 4 *Manchester J Int'l Econ L* 7

Avgouleas, E., 'The Global Financial Crisis and the Disclosure Paradigm in European Financial Regulation: The Case for Reform', (2009) 6(4) *ECFLR* 440

Awrey, D., 'The Dynamics of OTC Derivatives Regulation: Bridging The Public–Private Divide', (2010) 11 *EBOR* 155

Ayadi, R. et al., *Investigating Diversity in the Banking Sector in Europe – The Performance and Role of Savings Banks*, (CEPS 2009)

Ayadi, R. et al., *Banking Business Models Monitor 2015 Europe*, (IRCCF HEC Montréal 2016)

Bacon, K., *European Community Law of State Aid*, (OUP 2009)

Balkenhol, B. and C. Guézennec, 'Le microcrédit professionnel et l'accompagnement à la création d'entreprise en France: quel devenir des créateurs sur le marché du travail trois ans après?', (2014), France Stratégie note d'analyse 13, www.strategie.gouv.fr/sites/strategie.gouv.fr/files/atoms/files/na-fs-microcredit-juin201411.pdf>

Banca d'Italia, 'Documento per la consultazione – Istruzioni per la rilevazione dei tassi effettivi globali medi ai sensi della legge sull'usura', (2015), www.bancaditalia.it/compiti/vigilanza/normativa/consultazioni/2015/istr-rilevazioni-tegm/istruz-rilevaz- tegm -documento-consultazione.pdf

Banco de la Repùblica, 'Situación actual del microcrédito en Colombia: caracterìsticas y experiencias', (2010), <www.banrep.gov.co/docum/Lectura_finanzas/pdf/Tema1_sept.pdf>

Banerjee, A., D. Karlan and J. Zinman, 'Six Randomized Evaluations of Microcredit: Introduction and Further Steps', (2015) 7(1) *Am Econ J Appl Econ* 1

Bar-Gill, O., 'Bundling and Consumer Misperception', (2006) 73 *U Chicago Law Rev* 33

Bar-Gill, O., 'The Law, Economics and Psychology of Subprime Mortgage Contracts' (2009) 94 *Cornell L Rev* 1073

Barr, M., 'Banking the Poor', (2004) 21*Yale J on Reg* 121

Barr, M., 'Microfinance and Financial Development', (2004) 26*Mich J Int'l L* 271

Barr, M., 'Credit Where It Counts', (2005) 80*NYU L Rev* 101

Barr, M., J. Dokko and B. Keys, 'And Banking for All?', Federal Reserve Board Finance and Economics Discussion Series, (2009), <www.federalreserve.gov/pubs/feds/2009/200934/200934pap.pdf>

Barth, J. and A. Prabha, 'Breaking (Banks) Up is Hard to Do: New Perspective on Too Big To Fail', (2012), Wharton Financial Institutions Center Working Paper 12–16, <http://fic.wharton.upenn.edu/fic/papers/12/12-16.pdf>

Barth, J., C. Lin and C. Wihlborg (eds), *Research Handbook on International Banking and Governance*, (Edward Elgar 2012)

Barth, J., G. Caprio and R. Levine, *Rethinking Banking Regulation. Till Angels Govern*, (CUP 2006)

Barth, J., G. Caprio and R. Levine, 'Bank Regulation and Supervision in 180 Countries from 1999 to 2011', (2013), NBER Working Paper 18733, <www.nber.org/papers/w18733>

Barton, S. et al., 'Client-focused MFI Technologies Case Study', (2007), USAID Micro-Report 77, http://pdf.usaid.gov/pdf_docs/Pnadn418.pdf>

Basel Committee on Payments and Market Infrastructures (BCPMI)-WB, *Payment Aspects of Financial Inclusion*, (BIS/WB 2016)

Basu, S., 'Securitization and the Challenges Faced in Micro Finance', (2005), <http://ifmr.ac.in/cmf/publications/wp/2005/5_basu-Securitisation.pdf>

Bate, P., 'In Case of Emergency: Break Glass: ELF, an Innovative Fund that Helps MFIs Respond to all Kind of Disasters', (2007), www.iadb.org/micamericas/section/detail.cfm?id=4241&sectionID=SPCAL

Bateman, M. (ed.), *Confronting Microfinance: Undermining Sustainable Development*, (Kumarian Press 2011)

BCBS, 'Outsourcing in Financial Services', (2005), <www.bis.org/publ/joint12.pdf>

BCBS, *Basel Committee's Response to the Financial Crisis: Report to the G20*, (BIS 2010)

BCBS, *Basel II Document. Revisions to the Basel Securitisation Framework*, (BIS 2014, revised 2016)

BCBS, *Basel II: International Convergence of Capital Measurement and Capital Standards: A Revised Framework*, (BIS 2004)

BCBS, *Basel III Leverage Ratio Framework and Disclosure Requirements*, (BIS 2014)

BCBS, *Basel III: A Global Regulatory Framework for More Resilient Banks and Banking Systems*, (BIS 2011, revised December 2011)

BCBS, *Basel III: The Liquidity Coverage Ratio and Liquidity Risk Monitoring Tool*, (BIS 2013)

BCBS, *Basel III: The Net Stable Funding Ratio*, (BIS 2014)

BCBS, *Capital Treatment for 'Simple, Transparent and Comparable' Securitisation – Consultative Document*, (BIS 2015)

BCBS, *Core Principles for Effective Banking Supervision*, (BIS 2012)

BCBS, *Criteria for Identifying Simple, Transparent and Comparable Securitisations*, (BIS 2015)

BCBS, 'Enhancements to the Basel II framework', (2009), http://www.bis.org/publ/bcbs157.pdf

BCBS. 'Fundamental Review of the Trading Book – Outstanding Issues', (2014), www.bis.org/bcbs/publ/d305.htm

BCBS, *Guidance on the Application of the Core Principles for Effective Banking Supervision to the Regulation and Supervision of Institutions Relevant to Financial Inclusion – Consultative Document*, (BIS 2015)

BCBS, *Guidelines. Corporate Governance Principles for Banks*, (BIS 2015)

BCBS, *Microfinance Activities and the Core Principles for Effective Banking Supervision*, (BIS 2010)

BCBS, *Range of Practice in the Regulation and Supervision of Institutions Relevant to Financial Inclusion*, (BIS 2015)

BCBS, *Revisions to the Standardised Approach for Credit Risk – Standards. Second Consultative Document*, (BIS 2015)

BCBS, *Standards Supervisory Framework for Measuring and Controlling Large Exposures*, (BIS 2014)

BCBS–The Joint Forum, *Report on Asset Securitisation Incentives*, (BIS 2011)

Beck, T., A. Demirgüç-Kunt and M. S. Martinez Peria, 'Banking Services for Everyone? Barriers to Bank Access and Use around the World', (2008) 22(3) *World Bank Economic Review* 397 <http://siteresources.worldbank.org/DEC/Resources/WBER_Banking_services_for_everyone.pdf>

Beck, T., A. Demirgüç-Kunt and R. Levine, 'Finance, Inequality and the Poor' (2007) 12 *J Econ Growth* 27

Beck, T., A. Demirgüç-Kunt and V. Maksimovic, 'Financial and Legal Constraints to Firm Growth: Does Size Matter?', (2005) 60 *J Finance* 137

Bedson, J. and A. Renzaho, 'Good Practices in Microfinance and World Vision-funded Programs: The Challenges of a Poverty Focus in an Evolving Industry', (2006), <https://www.academia.edu/20614872/Good_Practice_In_Microfinance_and_World_Vision-funded_Programs_The_challenges_of_a_poverty_focus_in_an_evolving_industry>

Beisland, A., R. Mersland and T. Randøy, 'The Association between Microfinance Rating Scores and Corporate Governance: A Global Survey', (2014) *35 Int Rev Fin An* 268

Beltratti, A. and R. Stulz, 'Why Did Some Banks Perform Better during the Credit Crisis? A Cross-Country Study of the Impact of Governance and Regulation', (2009) Fisher

College of Business Working Paper 2009-03-012, <http://ssrn.com/abstract=1433502>

Bénard, M., 'European Microfinance and Social Performance: Where Do We Stand?', (Oct. 2014), <www.european-microfinance.org/docs/emn_publications/other_emn_publications/IL%20SPM%20-%20EU%20MF%20and%20SPM%20where%20do%20we%20stand%20-%2020141112.pdf>

Bendig, M., M. Unterberg and B. Sarpong, 'Overview of the Microcredit Sector in the European Union – 2012/2013', (2014), <www.european-microfinance.org/docs/emn_publications/emn_overview/Overview2012-2013_Nov2014.pdf>

Bendig, M., M. Unterberg and B. Sarpong, 'Overview of the Microfinance Sector in Europe 2010/2011', (2012), <www.european-microfinance.org/docs/emn_publications/emn_overview/1.overview2010-2011-final.pdf>

Benjamin, J., P. Bowden and D. Rouch, 'Law and Regulation for Global Financial Markets: Markets as Rule-Makers-Enforcement, Dispute Resolution and Risk', (2008) 2 *LFMR* 321

Ben-Shahar, O. and C. Schneider, 'The Failure of Mandated Disclosure', (2011) 159 *U Penn L Rev* 647

Berger, A. and G. Udell, 'Small Business Credit Availability and Relationship Lending: The Importance of Bank Organisational Structure', (2002) 112(477) *Econ J* F32

Berger, A. and R. DeYoung, 'The Effects of Geographic Expansion on Bank Efficiency', (2001) 19 *J Financ Serv Res* 163

Berger, A. et al., 'Does Function Follow Organizational Form? Evidence from the Lending Practices of Large and Small Banks', (2005) 76 *J Financ Econ* 237

Berger, A., A. Cowan and W. Frame, 'The Surprising Use of Credit Scoring in Small Business Lending by Community Banks and the Attendant Effects on Credit Availability and Risk', (2011) *39 J Financ Serv Res* 1

Berger, A., P. Molyneux and J. Wilson (eds), *The Oxford Handbook of Banking*, (1st edn., OUP 2012)

Berger, A., R. Rosen and G. Udell, 'Does Market Size Structure Affect Competition? The Case of Small Business Lending', (2007) 31(1) *J Bank Financ* 11

Berger, A., W. Frame and N. Miller, 'Credit Scoring and the Availability, Price, and Risk of Small Business Credit', (2005) 37(2) *J Money Credit Bank* 19

Berndt, A., and A. Gupta, 'Moral Hazard and Adverse Selection in the Originate to Distribute Model of Bank Credit', (2009) 56 *J Monetary Econ* 725

Bessis, J., *Risk Management in Banking*, (Wiley 2011)

Bhatt, N. and S. Tang, 'Making Microcredit Work in the United States: Social, Financial, and Administrative Dimensions', (2001) 15(3) *Econ Dev Q* 229

Binder, J., 'To Ring-Fence or Not, and How? Strategic Questions for Post-Crisis Banking Reform in Europe', (2014), <http://ssrn.com/abstract=2543860>

Biondi, A., P. Eeckhout and J. Flynn, *The Law of State Aid in the European Union*, (OUP 2004)

BIS, 'Recent Innovations in International Banking', (1986), <www.bis.org/publ/ecsc01a.pdf>

BIS, Proceedings from conference 'Financial Sector Regulation for Growth, Equity and Stability' (Mumbai, 15–16 Nov. 2011), <www.bis.org/publ/bppdf/bispap62j.pdf>

Black, J. and D. Rouch, 'The Development of the Global Markets as Rule-makers: Engagement and Legitimacy', (2008) 2 *Law and Fin Markets Rev* 218

Black, J., 'Constructing and Contesting Legitimacy and Accountability in Polycentric Regulatory Regimes', (2008) 2 *Regulation & Governance* 137

Black, T. and A. Martinez, 'Compartamos Draws Gartmore as UBS Projects 20% Rally', *Bloomberg* (20 April 2010), <www.bloomberg.com/news/2010-04-20/compartamos-draws-gartmore-on-mexico-s-rebound-as-ubs-projects-22-rally.html>

Blakenhol, B., 'Evaluating the Impact of European Microfinance – Business Models of Microfinance Institutions in Europe', (2015) Centre for Microfinance and Financial Inclusion, <http://microfinance.ucd.ie/images/Reports/BusinessModel.pdf>

Blitz, C. and M. Long, 'The Economics of Usury Regulation', (1965) 73(6) *J Polit Econ* 608

BNP, 'BNP Committee to Microfinance', (2016), http://rse2016.bnpparibas.com/microfinance-csr-booklet/#/pageNumber=1

Bogan, V., 'Microfinance Institutions: Does Capital Structure Matter?', (2008), http://ssrn.com/abstract=1144762

Bøhren, Ø. and M. Josefsen, 'Stakeholder Rights and Economic Performance: The Profitability of Nonprofits', (2013) 37 *J Bank Financ* 4073

Bolton, P., X. Freixas and J. Shapiro, 'The Credit Ratings Game', (2012) 67(1) *J Financ* 85

Bond, P. and A. Rai, 'Borrower Runs', (2009) *88 J Dev Econ* 185

Boot, A. and A. Thakor, 'Can Relationship Banking Survive Competition?', (2000) 55(2) *J Financ* 679

Borgomeo, C. et al., 'IX Rapporto sul microcredito in Italia – 2013', (2014), <http://www.fondazionedallefabbriche.coop/wp-content/uploads/2015/05/9%5E-Rapporto-sul-microcredito-in-Italia.pdf>

Borzic, J., 'Croatia', (2013) EMN Legislative Mapping Report12/2013, <www.european-microfinance.org/docs/emn_publications/other_emn_publications/mapping_croatia_2013.pdf>

Botti, F. and M. Corsi, 'Measuring the Social Performance of Microfinance in Europe', (2011), CEB Working Paper11/037, <https://yoursri.com/users/59e6c00a724f29e873a6985cafb31f04/eb7a64112144493e6a8304f4ec293afb/@@download/fs/wp11037%5B1%5D.pdf>

Brabant, M. et al., 'Rapport – Le Microcrédit', (2009) Inspection Générale des Finances 2009-M-085–003

Bradford, C., 'Crowdfunding and the Federal Securities Laws', (2012) *Col Bus L Rev* 1

Bradley, C., 'Private International Law-Making for the Financial Markets', (2005) *29 Fordham Int'l L J* 127

Bradley, D., 'Demutualization of Financial Exchanges: Business as Usual', (2001) 21 *Nw. J. Int'l L. & Bus.* 657

Brescia, R., 'The Community Reinvestment Act: Guilty, but Not as Charged', (2014) 88(1) *St. John's Law Review* 1

Brown, P., S. Arora and D. Turing, 'Microfinance Sector Transformation – Making Sense of the Basel II Capital Accord', (2008), <www.citifoundation.com/citi/microfinance/data/news080602a.pdf>

Bruhn-Leon, B., P. Eriksson and H. Kraemer-Eis, 'Progress in Microfinance in Europe', (2012), EIF Working Paper 13, <www.eif.org/news_centre/publications/eif_wp_2012_13_microfinance.pdf>

Brummer, C. and D. Gorfine, 'FinTech: Building a 21st Century Regulatory Toolkit', (2014) Milken Institute Report, <www.milkeninstitute.org/publications/view/665>

Brummer, C., 'Disruptive Technology and Securities Regulation', (2015) 84(3) *Fordham Law Rev* 977

Brusini, C., 'Microcredito. "La nuova legge costringe gli operatori a lavorare in perdita". Così l'albo degli intermediari resta vuoto', *Fatto Quotidiano* (6 March 2016), <www.ilfattoquotidiano.it/2016/03/06/microcredito-la-nuova-legge-costringe-gli-operatori-a-lavorare-in-perdita-cosi-lalbo-degli-intermediari-resta-vuoto/2496136/>.

Bülbül, D. et al., 'Savings Banks and Cooperative Banks in Europe', (2013) SAFE White Paper 5, http://safe-frankfurt.de/uploads/media/Schmidt_Buelbuel_Schuewer_Savings_ Banks_and_Cooperative_Banks_in_Europe.pdf>

Bumacov, V., A. Ashta and P. Singh, 'The Use of Credit Scoring in Microfinance Institutions', (2014) *23 Strat Change* 401

Burand, D., 'Microfinance Managers Consider Online Funding: Is It Finance, Marketing, or Something Else Entirely?', (2009) CGAP Focus Note 54, <www.cgap.org/sites/default/files/CGAP-Focus-Note-Microfinance-Managers-Consider-Online-Funding-Is-It-Finance-Marketing-or-Something-Else-Entirely-Apr-2009.pdf>

Busch, D. and G. Ferrarini (eds), *European Banking Union*, (OUP 2015)

Busch, D. and G. Ferrarini (eds), *Regulation of EU Financial Markets: MiFID II and MiFIR*, (OUP 2017)

Buyske, G., 'Microfinance Ratings Market Assessment', (2014), <www19.iadb.org/intal/intalcdi/PE/2014/14412.pdf>

Byström, H., 'The Microfinance Collateralized Debt Obligation: A Modern Robin Hood?', (2008) 36(11) *World Dev* 2109

Cafaggi, F., 'Gouvernance et responsabilité des régulateurs privés', (2005) EUI Working Paper Law 2005/6, <http://cadmus.eui.eu/bitstream/handle/1814/3326/law05-06.pdf?sequence=1>

Cafaggi, F., 'New Foundations of Transnational Private Regulation', (2011) 38(1) *J Law Soc* 20

Cafaggi, F., 'Private Regulation in European Private Law', in A. Hartkamp et al. (eds), *Towards a European Civil Code* (4th edn., Wolters Kluwer 2010)

Cafaggi, F., 'Rethinking Private Regulation in the European Regulatory Space', EUI Law Working Paper 2006/13, <http://ssrn.com/abstract=910870>

Camdessus, M., 'Rapport annuel 2012 de l'Observatoire de la microfinance', <www.banque-france.fr/fileadmin/user_upload/banque_de_france/publications/Rapport-annuel_2012_Observatoire-microfinance.pdf>

Camdessus, M., 'Rapport Annuel de l'Observatoire de la Microfinance 2009', (2010), <www.banque-france.fr/fileadmin/user_upload/banque_de_france/publications/ microfinance-2009.pdf>

Camdessus, M., 'Rapport Annuel de l'Observatoire de la Microfinance 2012', (2013), <www.banque-france.fr/fileadmin/user_upload/banque_de_france/publications/ Rapport-annuel-2012-Observatoire-microfinance.pdf>

Camerer, C. et al., 'Regulation for Conservatives: Behavioral Economics and the Case for "Asymmetric Paternalism"', (2003) 151 *U Penn Law Rev* 1211

Campbell, J. et al., 'Consumer Financial Protection', (2011) 25(1) *J Econ Perspect* 91

Campion, A. et al., 'Interest Rates and Implications for Microfinance in Latin America and the Caribbean', (2010) IDB Working Paper 177, http://idbdocs.iadb.org/wsdocs/getdocument.aspx?docnum=35121757>

Carbó, S., E. Gardener and P. Molyneux, *Financial Exclusion* (Palgrave Macmillan, 2005)

Carnell, R., J. Macey and G. Miller, *The Law of Banking and Financial Institutions*, (4th edn, Aspen Publisher 2009)

Carr, J. and Z. Yi Tong (eds), *Replicating Microfinance in the United States* (Woodrow Wilson Center Press 2002)

Carson, J., 'Self-Regulation in Securities Markets', (2011) World Bank Policy Research Working Paper 5542, <http://siteresources.worldbank.org/FINANCIALSECTOR/Resources/WPS5542_Self_Regulation_in_Securities_Markets.pdf>

Cassar, A., L. Crowley and B. Wydick, 'The Effect of Social Capital on Group Loan Repayment: Evidence from Field Experiments', (2007) 117*Econ J* 85

Catá Backer, L., 'Economic Globalization and the Rise of Efficient Systems of Global Private Law Making: Wal-Mart as Global Legislator', (2007) 39 *Conn L Rev* 1739

Caudill, S., D. Gropper and V. Hartarska, 'Which Microfinance Institutions are Becoming More Cost Effective With Time? Evidence From a Mixture Model', (2009) 41*J Money Credit Bank* 651

Cavalier, G., 'Is the Economic Crisis Driving Western Laws Closer to Islamic Laws on Interest Rate Prohibition?', (2013) 7(2) *IJEP* 47

Cavanna, H. (ed.), *Financial Innovation* (Routledge 1992)

CDFA, 'Inside Community Finance 2012', (2013), <http://responsiblefinance.org.uk/policy-research/publications/>

CEBS, 'Call for Technical Advice on the Effectiveness of a Minimum Retention Requirement for Securitisations', (2009), <www.eba.europa.eu/documents/Publications/Advice/2009/article-122a/Advice.aspx>

CEBS, 'Guidelines on Outsourcing', (2006), <www.eba.europa.eu/documents/10180/104404/GL02OutsourcingGuidelines.pdf.pdf>

CEBS, 'Guidelines on the Management of Concentration Risk under the Supervisory Review Process (GL31)', (2010), <www.eba.europa.eu/documents/10180/16094/Concentration.pdf/75fb2eca-955d-4c8e-a730-b491eef93188>

CFSI, *Microfinance Banana Skins 2009 – Confronting Crisis and Change*, (CFSI 2009)

CFSI, *Microfinance Banana Skins 2014 – Facing Reality*, (CFSI 2014)

CGAP, 'Annual Report 2002', 27, www.cgap.org/gm/document-1.9.41930/CGAP_Annual_Report_2002NoSig.pdf

CGAP, 'Access to Financial Services 2009. Measuring Access to Financial Services Around the World', (2009), <http://www.cgap.org/sites/default/files/CGAP-Financial-Access-2009.pdf>

CGAP, 'Financial Access 2009 – Measuring Access to Financial Services around the World', (2009), 8–9, <www.cgap.org/sites/default/files/CGAP-Financial-Access-2009.pdf>

CGAP, 'Financial Access 2010. The State of Financial Inclusion through the Crisis', (2010), <www.cgap.org/gm/document-1.9.47743/FA_2010_Financial_Access_2010_Rev.pdf>

CGAP, 'Securitization. A Technical Guide', (2010), <www.cgap.org/sites/default/files/CGAP-Technical-Guide-Securitization-Oct-2010.pdf>

CGAP and G20, 'Global Standard-Setting Bodies and Financial Inclusion for the Poor. Toward Proportionate Standards and Guidance', (2012), <www.gpfi.org/sites/default/files/documents/CGAP.pdf>

CGAP and IFC, 'Financial Access 2011. An Overview of the Supply-Side Data Landscape', 1, <www.cgap.org/sites/default/files/CGAP-Forum-Financial-Access-2011-An-Overview-of-the-Supply-Side-Data-Landscape-Jun-2012.pdf>

Chaia, A., A. Dala, T. Goland, M. Gonzalez, J. Morduch and R. Schiff, 'Half the World is Unbanked', (2009) Financial Access Initiative Framing Note, <www.mckinseyonsociety.com/downloads/reports/Economic-Development/Half_the_world_is_unbanked.pdf>

Chavez, R. and C. Gonzalez-Vega, 'Principles of Regulation and Prudential Supervision: Should They be Different for Microenterprise Finance Organizations?', (1992), <http:// pdf.usaid.gov/pdf_docs/PNABM578.pdf>

Chen, G. and X. Faz, 'The Potential of Digital Data: How Far Can It Advance Financial Inclusion?', (2015) CGAP Focus Note 100, <www.cgap.org/sites/default/files/Focus-Note-The-Potential-of-Digital-Data-Jan-2015.pdf>

Chen, G., S. Rasmussen and X. Reille, 'Growth and Vulnerabilities in Microfinance', (2010) CGAP Focus Note 61, <www.cgap.org/sites/default/files/CGAP- Focus-Note-Growth-and-Vulnerabilities-in-Microfinance-Feb-2010.pdf>

Chen, Z., 'Securitization Microcredit: The Implications of Securitisation for Microcredit Institutions' Human Rights Missions', (2008) 39 *Colum Hum Rts L Rev* 757

Cheng, S., 'Board Size and the Variability of Corporate Performance', (2008) 87(1) *J Financ Econ* 157

Chien, J., 'Designing Disclosure Regimes for Responsible Financial Inclusion', (2012) CGAP Focus Note 78, <www.cgap.org/sites/default/files/Focus-Note-Designing-Disclosure-Regimes-for-Responsible-Financial-Inclusion-Mar-2012.pdf>

Chiumya, C., 'The Regulation of Microcredit in Zambia', (International Conference 'Microfinance Regulations: Who Benefits?', 15–17 March 2010, Dhaka-Bangladesh), <www.microfinancegateway.org/sites/default/files/mfg-en-paper-the-regulation-of-microfinance-in-zambia-jan-2010.pdf>

Chow, J. and J. Surti, 'Making Banks Safer: Can Volcker and Vickers Do It?', (2011) IMF Working Paper 11/236, <www.imf.org/external/pubs/ft/wp/2011/wp11236.pdf>

Christen, R. and R. Rosenberg, 'The Rush to Regulate: Legal Frameworks for Microfinance', (2000) CGAP Occasional Paper 4, <www.cgap.org/sites/default/files/CGAP-Occasional-Paper-The-Rush-to-Regulate-Legal-Frameworks-for-Microfinance- Apr-2000.pdf>

Christen, R., T. Lyman and R. Rosenberg, 'Microfinance Consensus Guidelines – A Guide to Regulation and Supervision of Microfinance', (2012), <www.cgap.org/sites/default/files/Consensus-Guideline-A-Guide-to-Regulation-and-Supervision-of-Microfinance-Oct-2012_0.pdf>

Clark, H. and F. Sinha, 'Social Rating Guide', (2013) Rating Initiative, <http://sptf.info/images/social%20rating%20guide_english_nov%202014.pdf>

Clarke, G., 'More Evidence on Income Distribution and Growth', (1995) *47 J Dev Econ* 403

Coffee Jr., J., 'Market Failures and the Case for a Mandatory Disclosure System', (1984) 70 *Va Law Rev* 717

Cole, R., L. Goldberg and L. White, 'Cookie-Cutter versus Character: The Micro Structure of Small Business Lending by Large and Small Banks', (2004), 39(2) *J Financ Quant Anal* 227

Collins, D., J. Morduch, S. Rutherford and O. Ruthven, *Portfolios of the Poor. How the World's Poor Live on $2 a Day* (PUP 2010)

Commission and GBRW, 'Study on Asset-backed Securities: Impact and Use of ABS on SME Finance – Final Report', (2004), <http://ec.europa.eu/DocsRoom/documents/3342/attachments/1/translations/en/renditions/pdf>

Commission, 'Recommendation 2003/361/EC of 6 May 2003 Concerning the Definition of Micro, Small and Medium-sized Enterprises', [2003] OJL124/36

Commission, 'Recommendation 2011/442/EU of 18 July 2011 on Access to a Basic Payment Account', [2011] OJL190/87

Commission, '2013 SMEs' Action to Finance Survey. Analytical Report', (2013)', <http://ec.europa.eu/enterprise/policies/finance/files/2013-safe-analytical-report_en.pdf>

Commission, 'A European Agenda for the Collaborative Economy', (Communication) COM(2016) 356 final

Commission, 'A European Initiative for the Development of Micro-credit in Support of Growth and Employment', (Communication) COM(2007)708 final

Commission, 'A Quality Framework for Services of General Interest in Europe', (Communication) COM(2011)900 final

Commission, 'Action Plan on Building a Capital Markets Union', COM(2015)468 final

Commission, 'An Action Plan to Improve Access to Finance for SMEs' (Communication) COM(2011)870

Commission, 'Report on the application of Directive 2006/48/EC to Microcredit', (Report) COM(2012)769 final

Commission, 'Accompanying Document to the Decision of the European Parliament and of the Council Establishing a European Microfinance Facility for Employment and Social Inclusion (Progress Microfinance Facility)' SEC(2009)907

Commission, 'Capital Requirements – CRD IV/CRR – FAQs', MEMO/13/690

Commission, 'Commission Staff Working Document' SEC(2009)907

Commission, 'Common Principles for an Economic Assessment of the Compatibility of State Aid Under Article 87.3', (2009), <http://ec.europa.eu/competition/state_aid/reform/economic_assessment_en.pdf>

Commission, 'Crowdfunding in the EU Capital Markets Union', SWD(2016)154 final

Commission, 'Driving European Recovery, Volume 1', (Communication) COM(2009)114 final

Commission, 'European Financial Stability and Integration Report 2012', SWD(2013)156 final

Commission, 'European Union Framework for State aid in the Form of Public Service Compensation', (Communication) [2011] OJ C8/15

Commission, 'Evaluation of the JASMINE Technical Assistance Pilot Phase – Final Report', (2013), <http://ec.europa.eu/regional_policy/sources/thefunds/doc/instruments/ jasmine/jasmine_evaluation_final_report.pdf>

Commission, 'Financial Inclusion: Ensuring Access to a Basic Bank Account – Consultation Document', (2009), <http://ec.europa.eu/internal_market/consultations/docs/2009/fin_inclusion/consultation_en.pdf>

Commission, 'Financial Services Provision and Prevention of Financial Exclusion', (2008), <ec.europa.eu/social/BlobServlet?docId=760&langId=en>

Commission, 'Green Paper on Retail Financial Services. Better Products, More Choice, and Greater Opportunities for Consumers and Businesses', COM(2015)630 final

Commission, 'Green Paper on Services of General Interest', COM(2003)270 final

Commission, 'Green Paper on the Review of the Consumer Acquis', COM(2006)744 final

Commission, 'Green Paper. Building a Capital Markets Union', (Communication) COM (2015)63 final

Commission, 'Green Paper – Shadow Banking', (Communication) COM(2012)102 final

Commission, 'Guide to the Application of the European Union Rules on State Aid, Public Procurement and the Internal Market to Services of General Economic Interest, and in Particular to Social Services of General Interest', SWD(2013)53 final/2

Commission, 'Impact Assessment Accompanying the Document "Commission Recommendation of 18 July 2011 on Access to a Basic payment Account"', Staff Working Paper SEC(2011)906

Commission, 'Impact Assessment Accompanying the Proposal for a Directive on the Comparability of Fees Related to Payment Accounts, Payment Account Switching and Access to Payment Accounts with Basic Features', SWD(2013)164 final/53

Commission, 'Implementing the Community Lisbon Programme: Financing SME Growth – Adding European Value', (Communication) COM(2006)349 final

Commission, 'Legislative Package for Banking Supervision in the Eurozone' – 'FAQs', MEMO/13/780

Commission, 'Minimizing Regulatory Burden for SMEs. Adapting EU Regulation to the Needs of Micro-enterprises', (Report) (2011), <http://ec.europa.eu/governance/better_regulation/documents/minimizing_burden_sme_EN.pdf>

Commission, 'National Measures and Practices as Regards Access to Basic Payment Accounts – Follow-up to the Recommendation of 18 July 2011 on Access to a Basic Payment Account', SWD(2012)249 final

Commission, 'Notice on the Application of the State Aid Rules to Measures Relating to Direct Business Taxation', (1998) C384/3

Commission, 'Notice on the Notion of State Aid as Referred to in Article 107(1) of the Treaty on the Functioning of the European Union', (2016/C 262/01)

Commission, 'Proposal for a Regulation amending Regulation (EU) No 575/2013 on Prudential Requirements for Credit Institutions and Investment Firms', COM/2015/0473 final

Commission, 'Proposal for a Regulation of the European Parliament and of the Council amending Regulation (EU) 806/2014 in Order to Establish a European Deposit Insurance Scheme', COM(2015)586 final

Commission, 'Proposal for a Regulation of the European Parliament and of the Council on Structural Measures Improving the Resilience of EU Credit Institutions', COM/2014/043 final

Commission, 'Public Consultation on Responsible Lending and Borrowing in the EU', (2009), <http://ec.europa.eu/internal_market/consultations/docs/2009/responsible_lending/consultation_en.pdf>

Commission, 'Report of the Expert Group on Credit Histories', (2009), <http://ec.europa.eu/internal_market/consultations/docs/2009/credit_histories/egch_report_en.pdf>

Commission, 'Retail Financial Services Report', (2012) Special Eurobarometer 373http://ec.europa.eu/internal_market/finservices-retail/docs/policy/eb_special_373-report_en.pdf>

Commission, 'Services of General Economic Interest in the Banking Sector', Report (1998), http://ec.europa.eu/competition/state_aid/studies_reports/archive/report_bank_en.html

Commission, 'Services of General Interest in Europe of 2000', (Communication) [2001] OJ C 17/4

Commission, 'Services of General Interest, Including Social Services of General Interest: A New European Commitment', (Communication) COM(2007)725 final

Commission, 'Shadow Banking – Addressing New Sources of Risk in the Financial Sector', (Communication) COM/2013/0614 final

Commission, 'Social Business Initiative – Creating a Favourable Climate for Social Enterprises, Key Stakeholders in the Social Economy and Innovation', (Communication) COM(2011)682 final

Commission, 'State Aid Rules to Support Measures in Favour of Banks in the Context of the Financial Crisis', (Communication) [2013] OJ C 216/1

Commission, 'Study on the Costs and Benefits of Policy Actions in the Field of ensuring access to a Basic Bank Account – Final Report', (2010), <http://ec.europa.eu/internal_market/finservices-retail/docs/inclusion/abba_cses_en.pdf>

Commission, 'Summary of Contributions to the "Call for Evidence EU Regulatory Framework for Financial Services"', (2016), <http://ec.europa.eu/finance/consultations/2015/financial-regulatory-framework-review/docs/summary-of-responses_en.pdf>

Commission, 'Summary of the Responses to the Public Consultation on the Potential Impact of CRR and CRD IV on the Financing of the Economy', (2015), <http://ec.europa.eu/finance/consultations/2015/long-term-finance/docs/summary-of-responses_en.pdf>

Commission, 'Summary – Responses to the Public Consultation on Crowdfunding in the EU', (2014), <http://ec.europa.eu/internal_market/consultations/2013/crowdfunding/docs/summary-of-responses_en.pdf>

Commission, 'The Application of EU State Aid rules on Services of General Economic Interest since 2005 and the Outcome of the Public Consultation', Staff Working Paper SEC(2011)397

Commission, 'The Application of the European Union State Aid Rules to Compensation Granted for the Provision of Services of General Economic Interest', (Communication) [2012] OJ C8, 4

Commission, 'The Application of State Aid Rules to Measures Taken in Relation to Financial Institutions in the Context of the Current Global Financial Crisis', (Communication) [2008] OJ C-270/8

Commission, 'The Regulation of Microcredit in Europe', (Expert Group report) (2007), <http://ec.europa.eu/DocsRoom/documents/3669/attachments/1/translations/en/renditions/pdf>

Commission, 'Towards the Completion of the Banking Union', (Communication) COM (2015)587 final

Commission, 'Unleashing the Potential of Crowdfunding in the European Union', (Communication) COM(2014)172 final

Commission, 'Vademecum. Community Law on State Aid', (2008), <http://ec.europa.eu/competition/state_aid/studies_reports/vademecum_on_rules_09_2008_en.pdf>

Commission, *Annual Report on European SMEs 2014/2015. SMEs Start Hiring Again*, (EU 2015)

Commission, *Cyber Security. Special Eurobarometer 423*, (EU 2015)

Commission, *Methodology to Monitor the Implementation of the 'European Code of Good Conduct for Microcredit Provision' by Microcredit Providers. Microcredit Provider Guidelines*, (EU 2013)

Cooter, R. and H. Schaefer, *Solomon's Knot: How Law Can End the Poverty of Nations*, (2011), chapter 8 (manuscript), <http://works.bepress.com/cgi/viewcontent.cgi?article=1163&context=robert_cooter>;

Copisarow, R., 'An Example of Micro-finance in the North: Fundusz Mikro (Poland)', in C. Guene and E. Mayo (eds), *Banking and Social Cohesion. Alternative Responses to a Global Market*, (Carpenter 2001)

Council of Equity of Microfinance Equity Funds (CEMF), 'The Practice of Corporate Governance in Microfinance Institutions', (2012), <www.centerforfinancialinclusion.org/publications-a-resources/browse-publications/384-corporate-governance-in-microfinance-institutions-cmef>

Cozarenco, A., 'Microfinance Institutions and Banks in Europe: The Story to Date', (2015), <www.european-microfinance.org/docs/emn_publications/emn_research_papers/research_3.pdf>

Cozarenco, A. and A. Szafarz, 'Microcredit in Developed Countries: Unexpected Consequences of Loan Ceilings', (2013), http://ssrn.com/abstract=2269022

Cozarenco, A. and A. Szafarz, 'Microcredit in Developed Countries: Unexpected Consequences of Loan Ceilings', (2014), CEB Working Paper 14/015, www.iap- socent.be/sites/default/files/SOCENT%20Pub%202014-05%20(wp14015).pdf

Cranston, R., *Principles of Banking Law*, (2nd edn, OUP 2002)

Crespi, R. et al., 'Governance Mechanisms in Spanish Banks. Does Ownership Matter?', (2004) 28*J Bank Financ* 2311

CRISIL, 'Performance of ABS & MBS Pools', (May 2011), <www.crisil.com/Ratings/Commentary/CommentaryDocs/CRISIL-ratings_perf-of-ABS-MBS-pools_may11.pdf>

Croatian National Bank, 'Interest Rates', (2015), www.hnb.hr/en/-/kamate

CSFI, *Microfinance Banana Skins 2014. Facing Reality*, (CSFI 2014)

Cull, R. et al., 'Microfinance Tradeoffs. Regulation, Competition, and Financing', (2009) WB Policy Research Working Paper 5086, https://openknowledge.worldbank.org/bitstream/handle/10986/4278/WPS5086.pdf?sequence=1&isAllowed=y>

Cull, R., A. Demirgüç-Kunt and J. Morduch, 'Does Regulatory Supervision Curtail Microfinance Profitability and Outreach?', (2011) 39(6) *World Dev* 949

Cull, R., A. Demirgüç-Kunt and J. Morduch, 'Financial Performance and Outreach: A Global Analysis of Leading Microbanks', (2007) *117 Econ J* 107

Cull, R., A. Demirgüç-Kunt and J. Morduch, 'Microfinance Meets the Market', (2009) 23(1) *J Econ Perspect* 167

Daly, M., 'EU Social Policy after Lisbon', (2006) 44(3) *JCMS* 461

Das, P., 'Avoiding a Subprime-like Crises in Microfinance: Lessons from the Mexican and Bolivian Experience', (2009) 15*Law & Bus Rev Am* 819

Davis, J. and A. Gelpern, 'Peer-to-Peer Lending for Development: Regulating the Intermediaries', (2010) 42*NYU J Int'l L & Pol* 1209

Davis, K. and M. Trebilcock, 'The Relationship between Law and Development: Optimists versus Sceptics', (2009) 57(1) *Am J Comp Law* 895

Dayson, K. and P. Vik, 'Can MFIs in Western Europe be Sustainable?', (2009) 5*EMN-Microfinance Europe* 10

Dayson, K. and P. Vik, 'Toward an Architecture of Microcredit Regulation: The Case of the European Code of Good Conduct', (2014) 28(2) *Cost Management* 18

de Andrés, P. and E. Vallelado, 'Corporate Governance in Banking: The Role of the Board of Directors', (2008) 32(12) *J Bank Financ* 2570

de la Torre, A., J. Gozzi and S. Schmukler, 'Innovative Experiences in Access to Finance: Market Friendly Roles for the Visible Hand?', (2007) The World Bank Policy Research Working Paper 4326, http://documents.banquemondiale.org/curated/fr/861901468269684103/pdf/wps4326.pdf>

De Sousa-Shields, M. and B. King, 'MFI Financing Strategies and the Transition to Private Capital', (2005) microREPORT 32, <www.microlinks.org/sites/microlinks/files/resource/files/ML1776_mr8_financing_microfinance_institutions_1_.pdf>

De Sousa-Shields, M. and C. Frankiewicz, 'Financing Microfinance Institutions. The Context for Transitions to Private Capital', (2004) USAID microreport 8, http://pdf.usaid.gov/pdf_docs/Pnadc887.pdf>

De Vries Robbé, J., *Securitization Law and Practice in the Face of Credit Crunch* (Kluwer Law International 2008)

Degryse, H. and S. Ongena, 'The Impact of Competition on Bank Orientation', (2007) 16(3) *J Financ Intermed* 399

Dehejia, R. et al., 'Do Interest Rates Matter? Credit Demand in the Dhaka Slums', (2012) 97(2) *J Dev Econ* 437

Demirguc-Kunt, A. and L. Klapper, 'Measuring Financial Inclusion: The Global Findex Database', (2012), World Bank Policy Research Working paper 6025, www-wds.worldbank.org/servlet/WDSContentServer/WDSP/IB/2012/04/19/000158349_20120419083611/Rendered/PDF/WPS6025.pdf>

Demirgüç-Kunt, A. and R. Levine, 'Finance, Financial Sector Policies, and Long-Run Growth', (2008) World Bank Policy Research Working Paper 4469, http://ssrn.com/abstract=1081783>

Demirgüç-Kunt, A., T. Beck and P. Honohan, *Finance for all? Policies and Pitfalls in Expanding Access*, (WB 2008), <http://siteresources.worldbank.org/INTFINFORALL/Resources/4099583-1194373512632/FFA_book.pdf>

Department of the Treasury, 'Financial Regulatory Reform. A New Foundation: Rebuilding Financial Supervision and Regulation', (2009), <www.treasury.gov/initiatives/Documents/FinalReport_web.pdf>

Dermine, J. and D. Schoenmaker, 'In Banking: Is Small Beautiful?', (2009), DSF Policy Paper 2, <http://ssrn.com/abstract=1476764>

Devlin, J., 'A Detailed Study of Financial Exclusion in the UK', (2005), 28 *J Consum Policy* 75

DeYoung, R. and C. Roland, 'Product Mix and Earnings Volatility at Commercial Banks: Evidence from a Degree of Total Leverage Model', (2001) 10(1) *J Financ Intermed* 54

DeYoung, R., W. Hunter and G. Udell, 'The Past, Present and Probable Future for Community Banks', (2004) 25(2) *J Financ Serv Res*85

DG-FISMA, 'Consultation Paper on the Possible Impact of the CRR and CRD IV on Bank Financing of the Economy', (2015), <http://ec.europa.eu/finance/consultations/2015/long-term-finance/docs/consultation-document_en.pdf>

Di Bella, G., 'The Impact of the Global Financial Crisis on Microfinance and Policy Implications', (2011) IMF Working Paper 175, www19.iadb.org/intal/intalcdi/PE/2011/08802.pdf>

Di Benedetta, P., I. Lieberman and L. Ard, 'Corporate Governance in Microfinance Institutions', (2015), <https://openknowledge.worldbank.org/handle/10986/22059>

Dieckmann, R., 'Microfinance: An Emerging Investment Opportunity', (2007), <https://www.dbresearch.com/PROD/DBR_INTERNET_DE-PROD/PROD0000000000219174/Microfinance%3A+An+emerging+investment+opportunity.pdf>

Doiciu, M., 'Best practice in Microfinance in Romania', in A. Szabó, 'Microfinance for SMEs in the BSEC Region', (conference proceedings, 12–15 November 2014, Bucharest)

Doiciu, M., 'The Importance of the Regulatory Framework for Development of the Microfinance Sector: The Romanian Experience', (2007) MFC Microfinance Policy Monitor 11, <www.mfc.org.pl/sites/mfc.org.pl/files/PolMon11_2007_Eng.pdf>

Dominicé, R., *Microfinance Investments*, (Symbiotics 2012)

Donaldson, T. and L. Preston, 'The Stakeholder Theory of the Corporation: Concepts, Evidence, Implications', (1995) 20*Acad Manage Rev* 65

Dowla, A. and D. Barua, *The Poor Always Pay Back – The Grameen II Story* (Kumarian Press 2006)

Dragomir, L., 'Private Parties' Involvement in Prudential Banking Regulation – Some Thoughts on the Underlying Accountability Mechanisms', (2007), <www.iilj.org/GAL/documents/DragomirPrivateBankReg.pdf>

Dragomir, L., *European Prudential Banking Regulation and Supervision. The Legal Dimension*, (Routledge 2010)

Druschel, K., 'The Ultimate Balancing Act: Investor Confidence and Regulatory Considerations for Microfinance', (2005), USAID microNote 10, http://pdf.usaid.gov/pdf_docs/Pnadf314.pdf>

Duarte, J. et al., 'Do Individual Investors Form Rational Expectations? Evidence from Peer-to-Peer Lending', (2014), <http://ssrn.com/abstract=2473240>

Dupas, P. and J. Robinson, 'Savings Constraints and Microenterprise Development: Evidence from a Field Experiment in Kenya', (2013) 5(1) *Am Econ J Appl Econ* 163

Duwatripont, M. and J. Tirole, *The Prudential Regulation of Banks*, (MIT Press 1993)

Dyal-Chand, R., 'Reflection in a Distant Mirror: Why the West has Misperceived the Grameen Bank's Vision of Microcredit', (2005) 41*Stan J Int'l* 217

Easley, D. and M. O'Hara, 'The Economic Role of the Nonprofit Firm', (1983) 14(2) *Bell J Econ* 531

EBA, 'Assessment of SME Proposals for CRD IV/CRR', (2012), <www.eba.europa.eu/documents/10180/16148/EBA-SME-Report.pdf>

EBA, 'Consumer Trends Report 2016', (2016), <www.eba.europa.eu/documents/10180/1360107/Consumer+Trends+Report+2016.pdf>

EBA, 'Discussion Paper on innovative Uses of Consumer Data by Financial Institutions' (2016), EBA/DP/2016/01

EBA, 'Draft Guidelines on Remuneration Policies and Practices Related to the Sale and Provision of Retail Banking Products and Services', EBA/CP/2015/29

EBA, 'Final Draft regulatory technical standards on criteria for determining the minimum requirement for own funds and eligible liabilities under Directive 2014/59/EU', EBA/RTS/2015/05

EBA, 'Final Report – Guidelines on product oversight and governance arrangements for retail banking products', EBA/GL/2015/18

EBA, 'Guidelines on arrears and foreclosure', (2015) EBA/GL/2015/11

EBA, 'Guidelines on Common Procedures and Methodologies for the Supervisory Review and Evaluation Process (SREP)', EBA/GL/2014/13

EBA, 'Guidelines on Internal Governance', EBA/GL/44

EBA, 'Guidelines on Significant Credit Risk Transfer relating to Articles 243 and Article 244 of Regulation 575/2013', (2014)

EBA, 'Guidelines on the Application of Simplified Obligations under Article 4(5) of Directive 2014/59/EU', EBA/GL/2015/16

EBA, 'Guidelines on the Assessment of the Suitability of Members of the Management Body and Key Function Holders', EBA/GL/2012/06

EBA, 'Guidelines. Limits on Exposures to Shadow Banking Entities Which Carry Out Banking Activities Outside a Regulated Framework under Article 395(2) of Regulation (EU) No. 575/2013', EBA/GL/2015/20

EBA, 'Opinion on Lending-based Crowdfunding', EBA/Op/2015/03

EBA, 'Opinion on the application of the Principle of Proportionality to the Remuneration Provisions in Directive 2013/36/EU', EBA/Op/2015/25

EBA, 'Review of the Application of the Principle of Proportionality to the Remuneration Provisions in Directive 2013/36/EU', EBA/Op/2016/20

EBA, 'Report on Net Stable Funding Requirements under Article 510 of the CRR', <www.eba.europa.eu/documents/10180/983359/EBA-Op-2015-22+NSFR+Report.pdf>

EBA, 'Report on Qualifying Securitisation', (2014), <www.eba.europa.eu/documents/10180/950548/EBA+report+on+qualifying+securitisation.pdf>

EBA, 'Report on SMEs and SMEs Supporting Factor', (2016), <www.eba.europa.eu/documents/10180/1359456/EBA-Op-2016-04++Report+on+SMEs+and+SME+ supporting+factor.pdf>

EBA, 'Report to the European Commission on Matters Relating to the Perimeter of Credit Institutions', (2014), <www.eba.europa.eu/documents/10180/534414/2014+11+27+-+EBA+Report+-+Credit+institutions.pdf>

EBA, 'Report to the European Commission on Matters Relating to the Perimeter of Credit Institutions', (2014), <www.eba.europa.eu/documents/10180/534414/2014+11+27+-+EBA+Report+-+Credit+institutions.pdf>

EBA, 'Report – 2015 EU-wide Transparency Exercise', (2015), <www.eba.europa.eu/documents/10180/1280458/2015+EU-wide+Transparency+Exercise+Report+FINAL.pdf>

EBA, 'Report – Proposal for a Regulation of the European Parliament and of the Council Laying Down Common Rules on Securitisation and Creating a European Framework for Simple, Transparent and Standardised Securitisation', COM/2015/0472 final

EBA – Banking Stakeholders Group, 'Proportionality in Bank Regulation', (2015), <https://www.eba.europa.eu/documents/10180/807776/European+Banking+Authority+Banking+Stakeholder+Group-+Position+paper+on+proportionality.pdf>

Ebrahim, A., J. Battilana and J. Mair, 'The Governance of Social Enterprises: Mission Drift and Accountability Challenges in Hybrid Organizations', (2014) 34*Res Organ Behav* 81

ECA, *Is EU Financial Support Adequately Addressing the Needs of Micro-entrepreneurs?*, (EU 2015)

ECB, 'Financial Stability Review', (2013)

ECB, 'Financial Stability Review', (2014)

ECB, 'Financial Stability Review', (2015)

ECB, 'The Impact of the CRR and CRD IV on Bank Financing. Eurosystem Response to the DG FISMA Consultation Paper', (2015), <www.ecb.europa.eu/pub/pdf/other/impact_of_the_crr_and_crd_iv_on_bank_financing.en.pdf?88c21ee4d8283b0cbd 89a25700b32cda>

Egli, D., 'Progressive Lending as an Enforcement Mechanism in Microfinance Programs', (2004) 8*Rev Dev Econ* 505

EIF, 'Microfinance in Europe. A Market Overview', (2009), <www.eif.org/news_centre/publications/EIF_WP_2009_001_Microfinance.pdf>

EIM Business & Policy Research, 'Do SMEs Create More and Better Jobs?', (2011), <http://ec.europa.eu/enterprise/policies/sme/facts-figures-analysis/performance-review/files/supporting-documents/2012/do-smes-create-more-and-better-jobs_en.pdf>

Eisemberg, T. et al., 'Large Board Size and Decreasing Firm Value in Small Firms', (1998) 48*J Financ Econ* 35

Elliehausen, G. and R. Kurtz, 'Scale Economies in Compliance Costs for Federal Consumer Credit Regulations', (1988) 1(2) *J Financ Serv Res* 147

Elyasiani, E. and L. Goldberg, 'Relationship Lending: A Survey of the Literature', (2004) 56(4) *J Econ Bus* 315

El-Zoghbi, M., B. Gahwiler and K. Lauer, 'Cross-border Funding of Microfinance', (2011) CGAP Focus Note 70, <www.cgap.org/sites/default/files/CGAP-Focus-Note-Cross-border-Funding-of-Microfinance-Apr-2011.pdf>

Emmons, W., R. Gilbert, T. Yeager, 'Reducing the Risk at Small Community Banks: Is it Size or Geographic Diversification that Matters?', (2004) 25(2/3) *J Financ Serv Res* 259

EMN-EIF, 'Microfinance Market Studies in the framework of JEREMIE – Cross-Country Study on Western Europe. United Kingdom, Spain, Germany, Italy', (2009), <http://

www.emnconference.org/archives/data/file/EIF%20Study%20Microlending_Western%20Europe_March%202009.zip>

EMN Idea-Lab, 'Credit Scoring in the European (Micro)finance Sector', (2015), <http://www.european-microfinance.org/docs/activities/think_tanks_idea_labs/SCORING_EMN2015_LINKS_2.pdf>

EMN, 'A Collection of Case Studies on the Legal and Regulatory Framework for Microfinance Provision', (2012) 12(1) electronic Bulletin 16, <www.microfinancegateway.org/sites/default/files/mfg-en-case-study-a-collection-of-case-studies-on-the-legal-and-regulatory-framework-for-microfinance-provision-dec-2012.pdf>

EMN, 'Legislative Mapping Report – Spain', (2015), <www.european-microfinance.org/docs/emn_publications/other_emn_publications/Legislative%20Mapping%20Report%20Spain.pdf>

EMN, 'Policy Note on Sector Proposals to Increase the Impact of Microfinance in the EU', (2015), <www.european-microfinance.org/docs/emn_publications/policy_notes/Policy2015_EMN_oct.pdf>

EMN-EIF, 'EIF Market Studies on Micro Lending in the European Union – Cross-Country Study on Central and Eastern Europe: Bulgaria, Czech Republic, Romania, Slovakia', (2009), <www.emnconference.org/archives/data/file/EIF%20Study%20Microlending_Eastern%20Central%20Europe_March%2009.zip>

EMN-MFC, 'Policy Note on Sector Proposals to Increase the Impact of Microfinance in the EU', (2015), <www.european- microfinance.org/docs/emn_publications/policy_-notes/Policy2015_EMN_oct.pdf>

Enria, A. 'Opening Remarks by the Chairperson of the EBA', (EBA proportionality workshop, London, 3 July 2015), www.eba.europa.eu/documents/10180/1044289/Opening+remarks,%20Andrea+Enria,%20EBA+proportionality+workshop+-3+July+2015.pdf

Ente Nazionale per il Microcredito, 'Le multiformi caratteristiche del Microcredito. Rapporto finale di monitoraggio', (2013), <www.fgda.org/dati/ContentManager/files/Documenti_microfinanza/Le-multiformi-caratteristiche-del-microcredito—Rapporto-finale.pdf>

Estapé-Dubreuil, G. and C. Torreguitart-Mirada, 'Governance Mechanisms, Social Performance Disclosure and Performance in Microfinance: Does Legal Status Matter?', (2015) 86*Annals of Public and Cooperative Economics* 137

Etzensperger, R., 'Microfinance Market Outlook 2015. Growth Driven by Vast Market Potential', (2014), <www.responsability.com/funding/data/docs/es/10427/Microfinance-Market-Outlook-2015-DE.pdf>

Eurobarometer Report 2007, <www.bristol.ac.uk/media-library/sites/geography/migrated/documents/pfrc0808.pdf>

European Banking Federation, 'Microfinance within the EU Banking Industry: Policy and Practice', (2010), <www.ebf-fbe.eu/uploads/D1093k%20Microfinance%20EU%20banking%20industry.pdf>

European Parliament, 'Resolution of 24 March 2009 with Recommendations to the Commission on a European Initiative for the Development of Micro-credits in Support of Growth and Employment', [2010] OJC117E/85

European Parliament, 'Resolution of 20 November 2012 on Shadow Banking', (2012/2115(INI))

Evers, J., S. Lahn and M. Jung, 'Status of Microfinance in Western Europe – An Academic Review', (2007) EMN, www.microfinancegateway.org/sites/default/files/mfg-en-paper-status-of-microfinance-in-western-europe-an-academic-review-2007.pdf>

FATF, 'FATF Guidance. Anti-Money Laundering and Terrorist Financing Measures and Financial Inclusion', (2013), <www.fatf-gafi.org/media/fatf/documents/reports/AML_CFT_Measures_and_Financial_Inclusion_2013.pdf>

FCA, 'Detailed Rules for the FCA Regime for Consumer Credit', (2014) PS14/3

FDIC, '2013 FDIC National Survey of Unbanked and Underbanked Households', (2014), <www.fdic.gov/householdsurvey/2013report.pdf>

Federal Reserve Bank, 'Staff Analysis of the Relationship between the CRA and the Subprime Crisis', (2008) <www.federalreserve.gov/newsevents/speech/20081203_ ana lysis.pdf>

Fellowes, M. and M. Mabanta, 'Banking on Wealth: America's New Retail Banking Infrastructure and Its Wealth-Building Potential', (2008), <www.brookings.edu/~/media/resea rch/files/reports/2008/1/banking%20fellowes/01_banking_fellowes.pdf>

Fernandes, K., 'A Structured Finance Approach to Microfinance', in *Securitization and Structured Finance Handbook 2011/12* (Euromoney Yearbooks 2011), <www.ifmr.co.in/blog/wp-content/uploads/2011/08/Structured-finance-approach-to-Microfinance.pdf>

Fernando, N., 'Managing Microfinance Risks: Some Observations and Suggestions', (2008), <www.microfinancegateway.org/sites/default/files/mfg-en-paper-managing-m icrofinance-risks-some-observations-and-suggestions-jul-2008.pdf>

Fernando, N., 'Understanding and Dealing with High Interest Rates on Microcredit', (2006), <www.microfinancegateway.org/sites/default/files/mfg-en-paper-understanding-a nd-dealing-with-high-interest-rates-on-microcredit-a-note-to-policy-makers-in-the-asia -and-pacific-region-2006_0.pdf>

Fernando, N., *Micro Success Story? Transformation of Nongovernment Organizations into Regulated Financial Institutions*, (ADB 2004)

Ferrán, E. and V. Babis, *The European Single Supervisory Mechanism* (2013), University of Cambridge Faculty of Law Research Paper10/2013, <http://ssrn.com/abstract=2224538>

Ferran, E., 'Institutional Design. The Choices for National Systems', in Moloney et al. (eds), *The Oxford Handbook of Financial Regulation*, (OUP 2015)

Ferrarini, G. (ed.), *Prudential Regulation of Banks and Securities Firms*, (Springer 1995)

Ferrarini, G. and M. Ungureanu, 'Economics, Politics, and the International Principles for Sound Compensation Practices: An Analysis of Executive Pay at European Banks', (2011) 62(2) *Vanderbilt L Rev* 431

Ferreira, F. and J. Gyourko, 'A New Look at the U.S. Foreclosure Crisis: Panel Data Evidence of Prime and Subprime Borrowers from 1997 to 2012', (2015), NBER Working Paper 21261, <www.nber.org/papers/w21261>

Ferri, G. and G. Pesce, 'Regulation and the Viability of Cooperative Banks', (2011ICA Global Research Conference, Mikkeli–Finland), www.sommetinter.coop/sites/default/files/article-scientifique/files/22-ferri.pdf>

Fiebig, M., 'Prudential Regulation and Supervision for Agricultural Finance', (2001), <www.redcamif.org/uploads/tx_rtgfiles/afr5_e.pdf>

FinAlternatives, 'After Breakout Year, Peer-To-Peer Lending Still Evolving', (23 January 2014), <www.finalternatives.com/node/25928>

Financial Crisis Inquiry Commission, 'The Financial Crisis Inquiry Report', (2011), <www.gpo.gov/fdsys/pkg/GPO-FCIC/pdf/GPO-FCIC.pdf>

Financial Services User Group's (FSUG), '2012 FSUG Priorities Report – Ensuring Fair, Affordable and Safe Financial Products for Vulnerable Users', (2012), <http://ec.europa.eu/finance/finservices-retail/docs/fsug/papers/2012-priorities-report_en.pdf>

Fischer-Lescano, A., C. Joerges and A. Wonka (eds.), *The German Constitutional Court's Lisbon Ruling: Legal and Political Science Perspectives*, ZERP-Diskussionspapier 1/2010

FitchRatings, 'Indian Microfinance Securitizations Ratings Constrained by Unmitigated Risks', (2010), <https://asianbondsonline.adb.org/publications/external/2010/Indian_Microfinance_Securitisations_FR_16_Nov2010.pdf>

FitchRatings, 'Microfinance – Testing its Resilience to the Global Financial Crisis', (2009), <www.fitchratings.com>

FitchRatings, 'The Microfinance Sector: its Success Could be its Biggest Risk', (2008), <www.microfinancegateway.org/sites/default/files/mfg-en-paper-the-microfinance-sector-its-success-could-be-its-biggest-risk-jun-2008.pdf>

Flannery, M. 'Kiva at Four', *Innovations* (special edition for Skoll World Forum 2009), http://media.kiva.org/INNOV-SKOLL-2009_flannery.pdf

Fletcher, A., 'Small Businesses As Consumers: Are They Sufficiently Well Protected?', (2014), <http://competitionpolicy.ac.uk/documents/8158338/8264594/fsb+project_small_businesses_as-consumers.pdf/f1ed4da5-14cf-4b80-a1d8-ff76a0781def>

Fökehrer, C., 'Gaining Scale in Microcredit. Can Banks Make it Happen?', (2007) 2*EMN Bi-annual Magazine*

Fond de Cohesion Sociale, 'Rapport d'activité 2014', <www.france-microcredit.org/sites/www.france-microcredit.org/IMG/pdf/ra_2014_-_fcs.pdf>.

Fonteyne, W. 'Cooperative Banks in Europe – Policy Issues', (2007) IMF Working Paper 159, <www.imf.org/external/pubs/ft/wp/2007/wp07159.pdf>

Forcella, D., 'European Microfinance Credit Risk Management and Credit Scoring. State of Art and Perspective', (2015), <www.european-microfinance.org/docs/emn_ publications/other_emn_publications/EMN_RiskCredit%20v3C.pdf>

Ford, G., 'Microcredits in Europe', (*Finance Watch*, 30 October 2015), www.finance- watch.org/hot-topics/blog/1172-microcredits-in-the-eu

Forster, S. et al., 'Implementing the Client Protection Principles. A Technical Guide for Investors', (2011), <www.cgap.org/sites/default/files/CGAP-Technical- Guide-Implementing-the-Client-Protection-Principles-A-Technical-Guide-for-Investors- Jan-2011.pdf>

Fraisse, H., M. Lé and D. Thesmar, 'The Real Effect of Bank Capital Requirements', (2015) ACPR-Banque de France Débats économiques et financiers n. 8, <http://acpr.banque-france.fr/fileadmin/user_upload/acp/publications/Debats_economiques_et_financiers/20130802-The-Real-Effects-of-Bank-Capital-Requirements.pdf>

Frame, W., M. Padhi and L. Woosley, 'Credit Scoring and the Availability of Small Business Credit in Low- and Moderate-Income Areas', (2004) 39(1) *Financ Rev* 35

Frank, C., 'Stemming the Tide of Mission Drift: Microfinance Transformations and the Double Bottom Line', (2008) WWB Focus Note, <www.womensworldbanking.org/wp-content/uploads/imported/pdf/english/stemming_the_tide_of_mission_drift_ microfinance_transformations_and_the_double_bottom_line.pdf>

Freeman, R. and S. Velamuri, 'A New Approach to CSR: Company Stakeholder Responsibility', in A. Akabades and M. Morsing (eds), *Corporate Social Responsibility. Reconciling Aspiration with Application*, (Hampshire 2006)

Frisancho-Robles, V., 'Signaling Creditworthiness in Peruvian Microfinance Markets: The Role of Information Sharing', (2012) IDB Working Paper 347, <https://publications.iadb.org/bitstream/handle/11319/4084/Signaling%20Creditworthiness%20in%20Peruvian%20Microfinance%20Markets%3a%20The%20Role%20of%20Information%20Sharing.pdf;jsessionid=9FB826708E615054BB33CBA7BFBFDEA3?sequence=1>

FSB, 'Consumer Finance Protection with Particular Focus on Credit', (2011), <www.financialstabilityboard.org/wp-content/uploads/r_111026a.pdf>

FSB, 'Global Shadow Banking Monitoring Report 2015', (2015), <www.fsb.org/wp-content/uploads/global-shadow-banking-monitoring-report-2015.pdf>

FSB, 'FSB Principles for Sound Compensation Practices: Implementing Standards', (2009), <www.fsb.org/wp-content/uploads/r_090925c.pdf

FSB, 'Improving Financial Regulation. Report of the Financial Stability Board to G20 Leaders', (2009), <www.fsb.org/wp-content/uploads/r_090925b.pdf?page_moved=1>

FSB, 'Shadow Banking: Strengthening Oversight and Regulation – Recommendations of the Financial Stability Board', (2011), <www.financialstabilityboard.org>

FSF, 'FSF Principles for Sound Compensation Practices', (2009), <www.fsb.org/wp-content/uploads/r_0904b.pdf>

G.A.O., 'Person-to-Person Lending. New Regulatory Challenges Could Emerge as the Industry Grows', (2011), <www.gao.gov/new.items/d11613.pdf>

G-20, 'High-level Principles on Financial Consumer Protection', (2011), <www.oecd.org/g20/topics/financial-sector-reform/48892010.pdf>

G20, 'Leaders' Statement. The Pittsburgh Summit', (24–25 September 2009), <www.g20.org/Documents/pittsburgh_summit_leaders_statement_250909.pdf>

G20, 'Seoul Summit Document', (11–12 November 2010), <www.g20.utoronto.ca/2010/g20seoul-doc.pdf>

G-30, 'Banking Conduct and Culture. A Call for Sustained and Comprehensive Reform', (2015), <http://group30.org/images/PDF/BankingConductandCulture.pdf>

G-30, *Toward Effective Governance of Financial Institutions*, (G-30 2012)

Gabrielli, D. 'Les incidences de la réforme de l'usure sur les modalités de financement des PME', (2007) *Bulletin de la Banque de France* 157

Galema, R., R. Lensink and R. Mersland, 'Do Powerful CEOs Determine Microfinance Performance?', (2012) 49(4) *J Manage Stud* 718

Gambacorta, L. and A. van Rixtel, 'Structural Bank Regulation Initiatives: approaches and Implications', (2013) BIS Working Papers 412, <www.bis.org/publ/work412.pdf>

Gandhi, M., 'Enhancing Effectiveness of Directed Priority Sector Lending for Inclusive Growth Agenda for India', (2014) 3(4) *IJTGBP* 1298

Ganev, K., et al., 'Microcrediting of SMEs in Bulgaria', in A. Szabó (ed.), 'Microfinance for SMEs in the BSEC Region', (conference, 12–15 November 2014, Bucharest), <www.kas.de/wf/doc/kas_41327-1522-2-30.pdf?150513160755>

Gapper, J., 'The Lenders of the Revolution Look Familiar', *Financial Times* (London, 18 June 2015)

Garikipati, S., 'Microcredit and Women's Empowerment: Through the Lens of Time-Use Data from Rural India', (2012) *43 Dev Change* 719

Gehrig, T., 'Changing Business Models in Banking and Systemic Risk', in H. Albach et al. (eds.), *Management of Permanent Change*, (Springer 2015)

Gelpern, A., 'Wal-Mart Bank in Mexico: Money to the Masses and the Home-Host Hole', (2007) 39*Conn L Rev* 1513

Genet, M., 'Microfinance in Western Europe and Sustainability: Dream or Lack of Ambition?', (2009) 5*EMN-Microfinance Europe* 16

Gibbons, D. and J. Meehan, 'The Microcredit Summit's Challenge: Working Towards Institutional Financial Self-Sufficiency while Maintaining a Commitment to Serving the Poorest Families', (1999) 1(1) *J Microfinance* 131

Gietzen, T., 'The Exposure of Microfinance Institutions to Financial Risk', (2015) University of St. Gallen School of Finance Research Paper 2015/06, <http://ssrn.com/abstract=2590058>

Gilson, R. and R. Kraakman, 'The Mechanisms of Market Efficiency', (1984) 70 *Va Law Rev* 549

Giné, X. and R. Townsend, 'Evaluation of Financial Liberalization: A General Equilibrium Model with Constrained Occupation Choice' (2004) 74 *J Dev Econ* 269

Giné, X., P. Jakiela, D. Karlan, and J. Morduch, 'Microfinance Games', (2006), Yale University Economic Growth Center Discussion Paper 936, <http://ssrn.com/abstract=912301>

Glaeser, E. and A. Shleifer, 'Not-for-profit Entrepreneurs', (2001) 81 *J Public Econ* 99

Glaeser, E., 'The Governance of Not-for-Profit Firms', (2002) HIER Discussion Paper 1954, <http://scholar.harvard.edu/files/glaeser/files/the_governance_of_not-for-profit_firms.pdf?m=1360041717>

Gleeson, S., *International Regulation of Banking-Capital and Risk Requirements*, (OUP 2012)

Gloukoviezoff, G. and N. Rebière, 'Etude d'impacts des microcrédits personnels garanti – Livret 6 L'impact global sur les emprunteurs', (2013), <http://comptrasec.u-bordeaux.fr/sites/default/files/pdf_book/livret-6-impact-global.pdf>

Gloukoviezoff, G., 'Evaluating the Impact of European Microfinance. The Foundations', (2016) EIF Working Paper 2016/033, <http://comptrasec.u-bordeaux.fr/sites/default/files/pdf_book/livret-6-impact-global.pdf>

Gokhale, K., 'A Global Surge in Tiny Loans Spurs Credit Bubble in a Slum', *Wall St. J.* , (New York, 13 August 2009) A1

Goldberg, M. and E. Palladini, *Managing Risk and Creating Value with Microfinance*, (WB 2010)

Goldstein, M. and N. Véron, 'Too Big to Fail: the Transatlantic Debate', (2011) Bruegel Working Paper 2011/3, <http://bruegel.org/wp-content/uploads/imported/publications/Nicolas_Veron_WP_Too_big_to_fail_2011_03.pdf>

Gonzalez, A., 'Resilience of Microfinance Institutions to National Macroeconomic Events: An Econometric Analysis of MFI Asset Quality', (2010) MIX Exchange Research 1, <http://ssrn.com/abstract=1004568>

Gonzalez, A., 'Sources of Revenue and Assets Allocation at MFIs', (2008) 17 *MicroBanking Bulletin*

Gonzalez, A. and R. Rosenberg, 'The State of Microfinance – Outreach, Profitability, and Poverty: Findings from a Database of 2300 Microfinance Institution', (2006), <http://ssrn.com/abstract=1400253>

González-Hernández, E., 'Microcréditos y nuevas formas de financiación en España', (2015), <https://repositorio.comillas.edu/xmlui/bitstream/handle/11531/6393/TFM000193.pdf?sequence=1&isAllowed=y>

Goodhart, C. et al., *Financial Regulation. Why, How and Where Now?*, (Routledge 1998)

Goodhart, C., 'The Vickers Report: An Assessment', (2012) 6 *Law and Fin Markets L Rev* 32

Greenwood, J. and B. Jovanovic, 'Financial Development, Growth, and the Distribution of Income', (1990) 98 *J Pol Econ* 1076

Gretch, E. and G. Kochubka, 'Methodology and Assumptions: Standard & Poor's Approach to Rating Microfinance Securitizations', (2008), <www.researchandmarkets.com/reports/3168154/archive-criteria-structured-finance-abs>

Groeneveld, H., 'Governance of European Cooperative Banks: Overview, Issues and Recommendations', (2015) TIAS School for Business and Society Working paper,

<www.globalcube.net/clients/eacb/content/medias/publications/annual_reports/20160411_HG_EACB_FINAL_Snapshot.pdf>

Groeneveld, H., 'The Value of European Cooperative Banks for the Future Financial System', (2011), <http://www.helsinki.fi/ruralia/materiaalit/ICA2011/Groeneveld.pdf >

Group of Thirty, 'The Structure of Financial Supervision: Approaches and Challenges in a Global Marketplace', (2008), <www.group30.org/images/PDF/The%20Structure%20of%20Financial%20Supervision.pdf>

Guene, C., 'Microcredit Networks and Existing National Legislations with a View to the Implementation of the Microfinance Instrument', (2010) European Parliament Report IP/A/EMPL/NT/2009–2008, <www.europarl.europa.eu/RegData/etudes/note/join/2010/451479/IPOL-EMPL_NT(2010)451479_EN.pdf>

Guichandut, P., 'Europe Occidentale et reste du monde: parle-t-on des mêmes pratiques?', (2006) 25 *Finance & the Common Good/Bien Commun* 54

Haber, S. (ed.), *How Latin America Fell Behind?* (SUP 2005)

Hakenes, H., I. Hasan, P. Molyneux and R. Xie, 'Small Banks and Local Economic Development', (2009), <http://ssrn.com/abstract=1343048>

Haliassos, M. (ed.), *Financial Innovation: Too Much or Too Little?*, (MIT Press 2013)

Han, R. and M. Melecky, 'Financial Inclusion for Financial Stability: Access to Bank Deposits and the Growth of Deposits in the Global Financial Crisis', (2013) World Bank Policy Research Working Paper 6577, <https://openknowledge.worldbank.org/handle/10986/16010>

Handy, F., 'Reputation as Collateral: An Economic Analysis of the Role of Trustees of Nonprofits', (1995) 24 *Nonprof Volunt Sec Q* 293

Hannig, A. and S. Jansen, 'Financial Inclusion and Financial Stability: Current Policy Issues', (2010) ADB Institute Working Paper 259 <www.adbi.org/files/2010.12.21.wp259.financial.inclusion.stability.policy.issues.pdf>

Hanouch, M. and S. Rotman, 'Microfinance and Mobile Banking. Blurring the Lines', (2013) CGAP Focus Note 88, <www.cgap.org/sites/default/files/Focus-Note-Microfinance-and-Mobile-Banking-August-2013.pdf>

Hansmann, H., 'Ownership and Organizational Form', in R. Gibbons and J. Roberts (eds.), *The Handbook of Organizational Economics*, (PUP 2012)

Hansmann, H., 'The Role of Non Profit Enterprise', (1980) 89 *Yale L.J.* 835

Hartarska, V. and D. Nadolnyak, 'Do Regulated Microfinance Institutions Achieve Better Sustainability and Outreach? Cross-Country Evidence', (2007) 9 *Appl Econ* 1207

Hartarska, V., 'Governance and Performance of Microfinance Institutions in Central and Eastern Europe and the Newly Independent States', (2005) 33(10) *World Devel* 1627

Helms, B. and X. Reille, 'Interest Rate Ceilings and Microfinance: The Story So Far', (2004) CGAP Occasional Paper 9, <www.cgap.org/sites/default/files/CGAP- Occasional-Paper-Interest-Rate-Ceilings-and-Microfinance-The-Story-So-Far-Sep-2004.pdf>

Hermes, N., R. Lensink and A. Meesters, 'Outreach and Efficiency of Microfinance Institutions', (2008), <http://som.eldoc.ub.rug.nl/FILES/reports/2008/08002/08002.pdf>

Hishigsuren, G., 'Transformation of Micro-finance Operations from NGO to Regulated MFI', (2006), <www.microfinancegateway.org/sites/default/files/mfg-en-paper-transformation-of-micro-finance-operations-from-ngo-to-regulated-mfi-2006_0.pdf>

HM Treasury, 'A New Approach to Financial Regulation: Summary of Consultation Responses', (2010), <www.gov.uk/government/uploads/system/uploads/attachment_data/file/190261/summaryofcondocresponses241110.pdf>

Hollis, A. and A. Sweetman, 'Microcredit: What Can we Learn from the Past?', (1998) 26(10) *World Dev* 1875

Hopt, K., 'Better Governance of Financial Institutions', (2013) ECGI Law Working Paper 207, <http://ssrn.com/abstract=2212198>

Hopt, K., 'Comparative Corporate Governance: The State of the Art and International Regulation', (2011) 59(1) *Am J Comp L* 1

Horwitz, J. and R. Culley, 'Profits v. Purpose: Hybrid Companies and the Charitable Dollar', (2014) Law & Economics Working Paper 48, <http://repository.law.umich.edu/law_econ_current/art48>

Hoskins, S. and M. Labonte, 'An Analysis of the Regulatory Burden on Small Banks', (2015) Congressional Research Service Report, <www.fas.org/sgp/crs/misc/R43999.pdf>

Hu, H., 'Disclosure Universes and Modes of Information: Banks, Innovation, and Divergent Regulatory Quests', (2014) 31(3) *Yale J on Reg* 565

Hudon, M., 'Management of Microfinance Institutions: Do Subsidies Matter?', (2010) 22(7) *J Int Dev* 890

Hudon, M. and D. Traca, 'On the Efficiency Effects of Subsidies in Microfinance: An Empirical Inquiry', (2011) 39(6) *World Dev* 966

Hughes, J., L. Mester and C. Moon, 'Are Scale Economies in Banking Elusive or Illusive? Evidence Obtained by Incorporating Capital Structure and Risk-Taking into Models of Bank Production', (2001) 25*J Bank Financ* 2169

Hui-Huang, R. and D. Schoenmaker (eds), *Institutional Structure of Financial Regulation*, (Routledge 2015)

Iacobucci, E. and R. Winter, 'Asset Securitization and Asymmetric Information', (2005) 34*J Legal Stud* 161

Iannotta, G., G. Nocera and A. Sironi, 'Ownership Structure, Risk and Performance in the European Banking Industry' (2007), <http://ssrn.com/abstract=1020306>

IFMR Capital, 'IFMR Capital Structures the First Multi Originator Securitisation in Microfinance', (18 January 2010), <www.ifmr.co.in/blog/wp-content/uploads/2010/01/Mosec_press_release.pdf>

IFMR, 'IFMR Capital's Response to Fitch Ratings Report on Indian Microfinance Securitisations', (IFMR, 29 November 2010), <www.ifmr.co.in/blog/2010/11/>

Imai, K. et al., 'Micro-finance and Poverty: A Macro Perspective', (2012) 40(8) *World Dev* 1675

Imboden, K., 'Basel II and Microfinance: Exercising National Prerogatives', (2005), <www.microfinancegateway.org/sites/default/files/mfg-en-paper-basel-ii-and-microfinance-exercising-national-prerogatives-2005.pdf>

IMF, BIS and FSB, 'Guidance to Assess the Systemic Importance of Financial Institutions, Markets and Instruments: Initial Considerations', (2009), <www.bis.org/publ/othp07.pdf>

IMF, *Global Financial Stability Report. Navigating the Financial Challenges Ahead*, (IMF 2009), Ch. 2, <www.imf.org/external/pubs/ft/gfsr/2009/02/pdf/text.pdf>

Imp-Act and MFC, 'Social Performance Management in Microfinance. Guidelines', (2005), <www.microfinancegateway.org/sites/default/files/mfg-en-paper-social-performance-management-in-microfinance-guidelines-2005.pdf

Independent Evaluation Group, 'The World Bank's Country Policy and Institutional Assessment', (2009), <http://siteresources.worldbank.org/EXTCPIA/Resources/cpia_full.pdf>

IOSCO, 'Objectives and Principles of Securities Regulation', (2003), <www.iosco.org/library/pubdocs/pdf/IOSCOPD154.pdf

IOSCO Technical Committee, 'Unregulated Financial Markets and Products', (2009), <www.fsa.go.jp/inter/ios/20090911/02.pdf>

Isern, J. and T. Cook, 'What is a Network? The Diversity of Networks in Microfinance Today', (2004), CGAP Focus Note 26, <www.cgap.org/sites/default/files/CGAP-Focus-Note-What-Is-a-Network-The-Diversity-of-Networks-in-Microfinance-Today-Jul-2004.pdf>

Jackson, H., 'Centralization, Competition, and Privatization in Financial Regulation', (2001) 2*Theoretical Inq L* 649

Jain, A. and C. Norton, 'Microfinance: Where Do We Stand Today?', (2009) 18*Micro-Banking Bulletin* 9, <www.themix.org/sites/default/files/MBB%2018%20Spring%202009.pdf>

Jansson, T., 'Microfinance Regulation Sweeping Latin America', (2002) 5*Microenterprise Development Review* 1

Jansson, T., R. Rosales and G. Westley, 'Principles and Practices for Regulating and Supervising Microfinance', (2004), <https://publications.iadb.org/handle/11319/5582?locale-attribute=en>

Jayo Carboni, B. et al. (eds), *Handbook of Microcredit in Europe. Social Inclusion through Microenterprise Development*, (Edward Elgar 2010)

Jobst, A., 'Mobilising Structured Finance for New Fields – Ready for New Applications?', (2007) KfW Financial Sector Development Symposium, available through researchgate.net

John, K., T. John and A. Saunders, 'Universal Banking and Firm Risk Taking', (1994) 18*J Bank Financ* 307

Joint Forum, 'Review of the Differentiated Nature and Scope of Financial Regulation Key Issues and Recommendations', (2010), <www.bis.org/publ/joint24.pdf>

Jones-Harvard, C., 'To Lend or not to Lend: What the CRA Ought to Say about Sub-prime and Predatory Lending', (2005) *7 Fla Coastal L Rev* 1

Judge, K., 'Fragmentation Nodes: A Study in Financial Innovation, Complexity, and Systemic Risk', (2012) 64*Stan L Rev* 657

Judge, K., 'The Future of Direct Finance: The Diverging Paths of Peer-to-Peer Lending and Kickstarter', (2015), Columbia Law and Economics Working Paper 520, <http://ssrn.com/abstract=2662697>

Jung, M., S. Lahn and M. Unterberg, 'EIF Market Studies on Micro Lending in the European Union: Capacity Building and Policy Recommendations', (2009), <www.emnconference.org/archives/data/file/EIF%20MF%Studies%20-%20Capacity%20Building%20final.pdf>

Kane, E., 'Financial Regulation and Market Forces', (1991) 127*Swiss J Econ & Stat* 325

Kane, E., 'Impact of Regulation on Economic Behavior. Accelerating Inflation, Technological Innovation, and the Decreasing Effectiveness of Banking Regulation', (1981) 36(2) *J Financ* 355

Karlan, D. and J. Zinman, 'Credit Elasticities in Less-Developed Economies: Implications for Microfinance', (2008) 98*Am Econ Rev* 1040

Karlan, D. and J. Zinman, 'Expanding Credit Access: Using Randomized Supply Decisions to Estimate the Impacts', (2010) 23(1) *Rev Financ Stud* 433

Karlan, D. and M. Valdivia, 'Teaching Entrepreneurship: Impact of Business Training on Microfinance Clients and Institutions', (2006) Yale University Economic Growth Center Discussion Paper 941, <www.econ.yale.edu/growth_pdf/cdp941.pdf>

Karlan, D., 'Social Connections and Group Banking', (2007) 117*Econ J* F52

Kasala, M., 'Labeling Microfinance as Socially Responsible Investing: What's the Risk?', ('The United Nations Principles for Responsible Investing conference', Copenhagen, 2010)

Kendall, J., N. Mylenko and A. Ponce, 'Measuring Financial Access around the World', World Bank Policy Research Working Paper 5537, <www.cgap.org/gm/document-1.9.43130/Measuring_Financial_Access_Around_World.pdf>

Kettel, B., *Introduction to Islamic Banking and Finance*, (Wiley 2011)

Kettering, K., 'Securitization and its Discontents: the Dynamics of Financial Product Development', (2008) 29 *Cardozo L Rev* 1553

Khan, M. and M. Porzio (eds.), *Islamic Banking and Finance in the European Union. A Challenge*, (Edward Elgar 2010)

Khan, S. and A. Ashta, 'Managing Multi-Faceted Risks in Microfinance Operations', (2013) 22*Strat Change* 1

King, M., Speech, (Lord Mayor's Banquet for Bankers and Merchants of the City of London, 17 June 2009), <www.bankofengland.co.uk/archive/Documents/historicpubs/speeches/2009/speech394.pdf>

Kirby, E. and S. Worner, 'Crowdfunding: An Infant Industry Growing Fast', OICV-IOSCO Staff Working Paper 3/2014, <www.iosco.org/research/pdf/swp/Crowd-funding-An-Infant-Industry-Growing-Fast.pdf>

Klausner, M., 'Market Failure and Community Investment: A Market-Oriented Alternative to the Community Reinvestment Act', (1995) 143*U Pa L Rev* 1561

Kleinberger, D., 'A Myth Deconstructed: The Emperor's New Clothes on the Low-Profit Limited Liability Company', (2010) 35*Del J Corp L* 879

Komarova Loureiro, Y. and L. Gonzalez, 'Competition against Common Sense: Insights on Peer-to-Peer Lending as a Tool to Allay Financial Exclusion', (2015) forthcoming IJBM (special issue on financial exclusion), <http://ssrn.com/abstract=2533520>

Kono, H. and K. Takahashi, 'Microfinance Revolution: Its Effects, Innovations, and Challenges', (2010) 48(1) *Dev Econ* 15

KPMG, 'Mobile banking 2015', <https://assets.kpmg.com/content/dam/kpmg/pdf/2015/08/mobile-banking-report-2015.pdf>

Krauss, N. and I. Walter, 'Can Microfinance Reduce Portfolio Volatility?', (2009) 58(1) *Econ Dev Cult Change* 85

Kroszner, R., 'The Community Reinvestment Act and the Recent Mortgage Crisis', (2008), <www.frbsf.org/publications/community/cra/cra_recent_mortgage_crisis.pdf>

Kruijff, D. and S. Hartenstein, 'Microfinance and the Global Financial Crisis – A Call for Basel', (2013), <www.ifc.org/wps/wcm/connect/afc335804294f279bf01bf0dc33b630b/Microfinance+and+Global+Financial+Crisis+BASEL+Report-Final.pdf?MOD=AJPERES>

Kuchta, R. 'Changes in Maximum and Statutory Interest Rates', (2016), <www.codozasady.pl/en/changes-in-maximum-and-statutory-interest-rates/>

Kumar, K. et al., 'Microfinance and Mobile Banking: The Story So Far', (2010) CGAP Focus Note 62, <www.cgap.org/sites/default/files/CGAP-Focus-Note-Microfinance-and-Mobile-Banking-The-Story-So-Far-Jul-2010.pdf>

Kustin, B., 'Islamic (Micro)Finance: Culture, Context, Promise, Challenges', (2015), <https://docs.gatesfoundation.org/Documents/Islamic%20(Micro)%20Finance%20Culture,%20Context,%20Promise,%20Challenges.pdf>

Labie, M. and B. Armendáriz (eds), *The Handbook of Microfinance* (World Scientific Publishing 2011)

Labie, M., 'Corporate Governance in the Non-profit Sector: A Framework for Microfinance Organization', (2001) 39 *Manage Decis* 296

Lacalle-Calderón, M. and S.Rico, *Microfinanzas en España: impacto y recomendaciones a futuro* (Cromoimagen 2012)

Laeven, L. and R. Levine, 'Bank Governance, Regulation and Risk Taking', (2009) 93(2) *J Financ Econ* 259

Laeven, L., L. Ratnovski and H. Tong, 'Bank Size and Systemic Risk', (2014) IMF Staff Discussion Note 14/04, <www.imf.org/external/pubs/ft/sdn/2014/sdn1404.pdf>

Lagoa, S. and A. Suleman, 'Types of Financial Institution and Their Supply of Financial Services: The Case of Microfinance in Europe', (2013) FESSUD Working paper 72, <http://www.fessud.eu/wp-content/uploads/2013/04/Types-of-financial-institution-and-their-supply-of-financial-services-the-case-of-microfinance-in-Europe_WP-72.pdf>

Lagoa, S., 'Financial institutions and Supply of Financial Services in the European Microcredit Market: A Survey of Selected Countries' Experiences', (2014) FESSUD Working Paper 73 <www.fessud.eu/wp-content/uploads/2013/04/Financial-institutions-supply-of-financial-services_European-microcredit-market_WP-73.pdf>

Lahaye, E. and E. Dashi, 'Spotlight on International Funders' Commitments to Financial Inclusion', (2015), <www.cgap.org/sites/default/files/Brief-Spotlight-on- International-Funders%27-Commitments-to-Financial-Inclusion-Mar-2015%20.pdf>

Lahaye, E. and K. McKee, 'Investors Implementing the Client Protection Principles in Microfinance', (2010) <https://openknowledge.worldbank.org/bitstream/handle/10986/9465/567260BRI0CGAP1rotection1Principles.pdf?sequence=1&isAllowed=y>

Lämmermann, S., 'Microfinance in Europe and its Outreach to Target Groups', (2011) EMN Working Paper, <www.european-microfinance.org/data/file/Librairy/emn- target-overview-study.pdf

Lämmermann, S. and G. Ribbink, 'Microfinance and Business Development Services in Europe. What Can We Learn from the South?', (2011), <www.european-microfinance.org/docs/emn_publications/emn_research_papers/4.af-bds-handbook-lowres2.pdf>

Lamoreaux, N., *Insider Lending: Banks, Personal Connections, and Economic Development in Industrial New England* (CUP 1994)

Lang, F., 'The Role of Cooperative Banks and Smaller Institutions for the Financing of SMEs and Small Midcaps in Europe', (2016) EIF Working Paper 36, <www.eif.org/news_centre/publications/eif_wp_36.pdf>

Langevoort, D., 'Global Securities Regulation after the Financial Crisis', (2010) 13(3) *J Int Econ Law* 799

Lapenu, C. and D. Pierret, 'Handbook for the Analysis of the Governance of Microfinance Institutions', (2006), <www.ifad.org/ruralfinance/pub/handbook.pdf>

Larosière Group, 'The High Level Group on Financial Supervision in the EU – Report 6', (2009), <http://ec.europa.eu/internal_market/finances/docs/de_larosiere_report_en.pdf>

Lauer, K., 'Transforming NGO MFIs: Critical Ownership Issues to Consider', (2008) CGAP Occasional Paper 13, <www.cgap.org/sites/default/files/CGAP-Occasional-Paper-Transforming-NGO-MFIs-%20Critical-Ownership-Issues-to-Consider-Jun-2008.pdf>

Ledgerwood, J. (ed.), *Microfinance Handbook: An Institutional and Financial Perspective*, (1st edn, WB 1998)

Ledgerwood, J. (ed.), *The New Microfinance Handbook*, (WB 2013)

Ledgerwood, J. and V. White, *Transforming Microfinance Institutions. Providing Full Financial Services to the Poor*, (WB 2006)

Lehmann, M., 'Volcker Rule, Ring-Fencing or Separation of Bank Activities: Comparison of Structural Reform Acts around the World', (2014) LSE Working Paper 25, <https://www.lse.ac.uk/collections/law/wps/WPS2014-25_Lehmann.pdf>

Lentz, C., 'Trends in the Microfinance Sector in Europe', in Microfinance Barometer 2014, 11, <www.citi.com/citi/microfinance/data/lebarometre.pdf>

Lerario, D., 'The Basel Committee and the International Organization of Securities Commissions' "Criteria for Identifying Simple, Transparent and Comparable Securitisations": Not So Simple', (2016), <http://ssrn.com/abstract=2727772>

Levine, R., 'Finance and Growth: Theory and Evidence', (2004) NBER Working Paper 10766, <www.nber.org/papers/w10766>

Levine, R. 'Function, Not Form', (*Economist*, 11 July 2009) Lin roundtable, <www.economist.com/blogs/freeexchange/2009/07/ross_levine_is_james_and>

Levy, R. and A. Schütte, '2011 Underbanked Seizing Market Study', (2011) CFSI, <www.cfsinnovation.com/Document-Library/2011-Underbanked-Market-Sizing-Study.aspx>

Levy, R. and J. Sledge, 'A Complex Portrait: An Examination of Small-Dollar Credit Consumers', (2012), <www.cfsinnovation.com/Document-Library/A-Complex-Portrait-An-Examination-of-Small-Dollar>

Liikanen, E. et al., 'High-level Expert Group on Reforming the Structure of the EU Banking Sector', (2012)

Limone, A. and P. Vitali, *Banche e microfinanza. Esperienze e strumenti innovativi*, (Bancaria 2006)

Llewellyn, D., 'Fifty Years in the Evolution of Bank Business Models', in M. Balling and E. Gnan, *50 Years of Money and Finance: Lessons and Challenges*, (Larcier 2013), chapter 9

Llewellyn, D., 'The Economic Rationale for Financial Regulation', (1999) FSA Occasional Paper 1, <www.fep.up.pt/disciplinas/pgaf924/PGAF/Texto_2_David_Llewellyn.pdf>

Llewellyn, D., 'Financial Innovation and a New Economics of Banking: Lessons from the Financial Crisis', (2010), <http://frank-oertel-math.de/Financial_crisis_and_new_economics_of_banking_Aug_2009.pdf>

Lobbezoo, M., 'Lessons Learnt from the EMN Workshop: What Do We Really Know about BDS in Relation to Microfinance?', (2012) (February) EMN eRB2

Lobbezoo, M., 'Volunteer versus Paid Coaches within Microfinance Initiatives: What Do We Actually Know about Effectiveness?', (2012) (February) EMN eRB8

Lohr, S., 'Creditworthy? Let's Consider Capitalization', *The New York Times* (New York, 19 January 2015) A1

Lubambu, K., *The Impacts of Remittances on Developing Countries*, (EU 2014)

Lützenkirchen, C. and C. Weistroffer, 'Microfinance in Evolution. An Industry between Crisis and Advancement', (2012), <www.dbresearch.com/PROD/DBR_INTERNET_EN-PROD/PROD0000000000294314/Microfinance+in+evolution%3A+An+industry+between+crisis+and+advancement.pdf>

Lyman, T. et al., 'Regulating Transformational Branchless Banking: Mobile Phones and Other Technology to Increase Access to Finance', (2008), <www.cgap.org/sites/default/files/CGAP-Focus-Note-Regulating-Transformational-Branchless-Banking-Mobile-Phones-and-Other-Technology-to-Increase-Access-to-Finance-Jan-2008.pdf>

Maas, B. and S. Lämmermann, 'Designing Microfinance Operations in the EU', (2013), <www.microfinancegateway.org/sites/default/files/mfg-en-toolkit-designing- microfina

nce-operations-in-the-eu-a-manual-on-how-to-build-and-implement-microfinance-support-programmes-using-the-esf-2013.pdf>

Macchiavello, E., 'Microfinance Regulation and Supervision: A Multi-faced Prism of Structures, Levels and Issues', (2012) 9(1) *NYU J L & Bus* 125

Macchiavello, E., 'Peer-to-peer Lending and the "Democratization" of Credit Markets: Another Financial Innovation Puzzling Regulators', (2015) 21(3) *Colum J Eur L* 521

Macchiavello, E., 'Private Regulation and Enforcement in Microfinance: a Multi-Layered and Polycentric Puzzle', in F. Cafaggi and G. Miller (with T. Andreotti, M. Borowicz, A. Janczuk, E. Macchiavello and P. Saguato), *The Governance and Regulation of International Finance*, (Edward Elgar Publishing 2013)

Macchiavello, E., 'Securitisation in Microfinance and Global Financial Crisis: Innovation or Trojan Horse?', (2013) 28(3) *JIBLR* 109

Macey, J. and M. O'Hara, 'The Corporate Governance of Banks', (2003) 9(1) *FRBNY Economic Policy Review* 91

Macey, J., 'Public and Private Ordering and the Production of Legitimate and Illegitimate Legal Rules', (1997) Faculty Scholarship Paper 144, <http://digitalcommons.law.yale.edu/fss_papers/1449>

Majone, G., 'The European Community between Social Policy and Social Regulation', (1993) 31(9) *JCMS* 153

Mak, V. and J. Braspenning, '*Errare humanum est*: Financial Literacy in European Consumer Credit Law', (2012) 35*J Consum Policy* 307

Malani, A. and E. Posner, 'The Case For For-Profit Charities', (2007) 93*Va L Rev* 2017

Marti, A., 'Rating Guide', (2012) Rating Initiative, <http://sptf.info/images/Rating%20Guide_English_20150825.pdf>

Marulanda, B. et al., 'Failures in Microfinance: lessons learned', (2010), <www. calmeadow.com/pdf/failures.pdf>

Mason, J., 'Regulating for Financial System Development, Financial Institutions Stability, and Financial Innovation', (2009), <http://ssrn.com/abstract=2101731>

MasSolution, '2015CF: 2015 Crowdfunding Industry Report', (2014)

Matthäus-Maier, I. and J. D. von Pischke (eds.), *Microfinance Investment Funds: Leveraging Private Capital for Economic Growth and Poverty Reduction*, (Springer 2005)

Matthäus-Maier, I. and J. D. von Pischke (eds.), *New Partnerships for Innovation in Microfinance*, (Springer 2009)

Mazer, R., 'Applying Behavioral Insights in Consumer Protection Policy' (2014) CGAP Focus Note 95, <www.cgap.org/sites/default/files/Focus-Note-Applying-Behavioral-Insights-in-Consumer-Protection-Policy-Jun-2014.pdf>

McAllister, P. and D. Dezso, 'Building Vibrant and Inclusive Financial Sectors: Success Indicators for Microfinance Associations', (2010), <www.seepnetwork.org/filebin/SuccessIndicatorsforMFAs_web_en.pdf>

McAllister, P. and D. McManus, 'Resolving the Scale Efficiency Puzzle in Banking', (1993) 17(2/3) *J Bank Financ* 389

McIntosh, C. and B. Wydick, 'Competition and Microfinance', (2005) 78(2) *J Dev Econ* 271

McKay, C., and M. Pickens, 'Branchless Banking 2010: Who's Served? At What Price? What's Next?', (2010) CGAP Focus Note 66, <www.cgap.org/sites/default/files/CGAP-Focus-Note-Branchless-Banking-2010-Who-Is-Served-At-What-Price-What-Is-Next-Sep-2010.pdf>

McKernan, S., 'The Impact of Micro-Credit Programs on Self-Employment Profits: Do Non-Credit Program Aspects Matter?', (2002) 84(1) *Rev Econ Stat* 93

Meagher, P., 'Microfinance Regulation in Developing Countries: A Comparative Review of Current Practice', (2002), <www.arabic.microfinancegateway.org/sites/default/files/mfg-en-paper-microfinance-regulation-in-developing-countries-a-comparative-review- of-current-practice-2002.pdf>

Mehrotra, A. and J. Yetman, 'Financial Inclusion – Issues for Central Banks', 2015 (March) *BIS Quarterly Review*

Meidinger, E., 'Competitive Supragovernmental Regulation: How Could It Be Democratic?', (2008) *8 Chi J of Int'l L* 513

Mercieca, S., K. Schaeck and S. Wolfe, 'Small European Banks: Benefits from Diversification?', (2007) 31(7) *J Bank Financ* 1975

Mersland, R. and R. Strøm, 'Performance and Trade-offs in Microfinance Organizations – Does Ownership Matter?', (2008) *20 J Int Dev* 598

Mersland, R. and R. Strøm, 'Performance and Corporate Governance in Microfinance Institutions', (2009) 33(4) *J Bank Finan* 662

Mersland, R., 'The Cost of Ownership in Microfinance Organizations', (2009) 37 *World Devel* 469

Mersland, R., 'The Governance of Not-For-Profit Institutions: Lessons From History', (2008), <http://ssrn.com/abstract=1298613>

Meslier-Crouzille, C., D. Morgan, K. Samolyk, A. Tarazi, 'The Benefits of Geographic Diversification in Banking', (2015), <https://hal-unilim.archives-ouvertes.fr/hal-01155170>

Mester, L., L. Nakamura and M. Renault, 'Checking Accounts and Bank Monitoring', (2002), Wharton Financial Institutions Center Working Paper 99–02C, <http://fic.wharton.upenn.edu/fic/papers/99/9902.pdf>

MFC, EMN and CDFA, 'From Exclusion to Inclusion through Micro Finance', (2007), Report 3, <www.emnconference.org/archives/data/file/programmes/from-exclusion-to-inclusion-through-microfinance-benchmarks-and-performance-measurement.pdf>

MicroBank, 'Report on the Impact of Microcredits. Institute for Social Innovation', (2013), <http://itemsweb.esade.es/wi/research/iis/publicacions/Microbank_Informe_impacto_ microcreditos_2013_en.PDF>

Microfinance Focus, '6 Microfinance Crises that the Sector Does not Want to Remember', (22 April 2010), <www.microfinancefocus.com/6-microfinance-crises-sector- does-not-want-remember>

MicroRate, 'State of Microfinance Investment – 2010 MicroRate MIV Survey', (2010), <www.microrate.com/media/docs/archived/The-MicroRate-2010-MIV-Survey-Report.pdf>

MicroRate, 'The State of Microfinance Investment 2013 – Survey and Analysis of MIVs', <www.microrate.com/media/downloads/2013/11/MicroRate-The-State-of-Microfinance-Investment-2013.pdf>

Miled, K. and J. Rejeba, 'Microfinance and Poverty Reduction: A Review and Synthesis of Empirical Evidence', (2015) 195 *Procedia – Social and Behavioral Sciences* 705

Miller, G. and G. Rosenfeld, 'Intellectual Hazard: How Conceptual Biases in Complex Organizations Contributed to the Crisis of 2008', (2010) 33 *Harvard J Law and Publ P* 807

Milne, A. and P. Parboteeah, 'The Business Models and Economics of Peer-to-Peer Lending', (2016) ECRI Research Report 17, <www.ceps.eu/system/files/ECRI%20RR17%20P2P%20Lending.pdf>

Mirchandani, B. and H. Finkelstein, 'Microfinance Investment Vehicles: Best Practices and Lessons Learned', (2009) 13 *Microfinance Insights* 35

Molenaar, K., 'Microfinance, its Concepts and Development, Lessons to Draw from Europe', (2009), <http://www.microfinancegateway.org/sites/default/files/mfg-en-paper-micro finance-its-concepts-and-development-lessons-to-draw-for-europe-jan-2009_0.pdf>

Moloney, N., EU *Securities and Financial Markets Regulation* (3rd edn, OUP 2014)

Moloney, N., 'European Banking Union: Assessing its Risks and Resilience', (2014) 51(6) *CML Rev* 1609

Moloney, N., 'The Legacy Effects of the Financial Crisis on Regulatory Design in the EU', in E. Ferran et al. (eds), *The Regulatory Aftermath of the Global Financial Crisis*, (CUP 2012)

Moloney, N., 'New Frontiers in EC Capital Markets Law: From Market Construction to Market Regulation', (2003) 40(4) *CML Rev* 809

Molyneux, P. and N. Shamroukh, *Financial Innovation*, (Wiley 1999)

Monti, M., 'A New Strategy for the single market at the service of Europe's economy and society', (2010), <http://ec.europa.eu/bepa/pdf/monti_report_final_10_05_2010_en.pdf>

Morduch, J., T. Ogden and R. Schneider, 'An Invisible Finance Sector: How Households Use Financial Tools of Their Own Making', (2014), <http://www.usfinancialdiaries.org/issue3-informal/>

Morduch, J., 'The Microfinance Schism', (2000) 28(4) *World Dev* 617

Morduch, J., 'The Promise of Microfinance', (1999) 37 *J Econ Lit* 1569

Morduch, J., 'The Role of Subsidies in Microfinance: Evidence from the Grameen Bank', (1999) 60(1) *J Dev Econ* 229

Morgan, P., 'Legal Form, Performance and Risk in the Microfinance Industry', (Master Thesis, Utrecht University, 2015), <http://dspace.library.uu.nl/bitstream/handle/1874/317523/MorganMasters2015.pdf?sequence=1>

Moro Visconti, R. 'Global Recession and Microfinance in Developing Countries: Threats And Opportunities', (2012), <http://ssrn.com/abstract=1318581>

Morse, A., 'Peer-to-Peer Crowdfunding: Information and the Potential for Disruption in Consumer Lending', (2015), <http://ssrn.com/abstract=2551272>

Mosley, P. and D. Hulme, 'Micro Enterprise Finance: Is There a Conflict between Growth and Poverty Alleviation?', (1998) 26(5) *World Dev* 783

Moss, T. 'The Value of Stock Markets', (2009) Lin roundtable (*Economist*, 11 July 2009), <www.economist.com/blogs/freeexchange/2009/07/todd_moss_is_senior_fellow>

Mostowfi, M., 'Mobilising Structured Finance for Development – Added Value or Just More of the Same?', (2007), <www.kfw-entwicklungsbank.de/EN_Home/Sectors/Financial_system_development/Events/Pdf_documents_Symposium_2007/Session_4_Expert_Paper_-_Mehdi_Mostowfi.pdf>

Mülbert, P., 'Corporate Governance of Banks after the Financial Crisis – Theory, Evidence, Reforms', (2010) ECGI Law Working Paper 130/2009, <http://ssrn.com/abstract=1448118>

Mullainathan, S. and S. Krishnan, 'Psychology and Economics: What it Means for Microfinance', (2008), <www.microfinancegateway.org/sites/default/files/mfg-en-paper-psychology-and-economics-what-it-means-for-microfinance-apr-2008.pdf>

Muller, P. et al., 'Consumer Protection Aspects of Financial Services – Study', (2014), <www.europarl.europa.eu/RegData/etudes/etudes/join/2014/507463/IPOL-IMCO_ET(2014)507463_EN.pdf>

Muller, P. et al., *Non-bank Financial Institutions: Assessment of their Impact on the Stability of the Financial System*, (EC 2012)

Mullineux, A., 'Financial Innovation and Social Welfare', (2010) 18 *Jfr & C* 243

Mullineux, A., 'The Corporate Governance of Banks', (2006) 14*Jfr & C* 375

Munzele Maimbo, S. and C. Henriquez Gallegos, 'Interest Rate Caps around the World. Still Popular, but a Blunt Instrument', (2014) WB Policy Research Working Paper 7070, <www-wds.worldbank.org/external/default/WDSContentServer/WDSP/IB/2014/10/17/000158349_20141017143420/Rendered/PDF/WPS7070.pdf>

Muthiora, B., 'Enabling Mobile Money Policies in Kenya Fostering a Digital Financial Revolution', (2015) Bill & Melinda Gates Foundation – GSMA, <www.itu.int/en/ITU-T/focusgroups/dfs/Documents/2015_MMU_Enabling-Mobile-Money-Policies- in-Kenya.pdf>

Nagaraju, J., 'MFI Agents Forcing Debtors to Commit Suicide: Study', *Times of India*, (Delhi, 20 October 2010), <http://articles.timesofindia.indiatimes.com/2010-10-20/india/28247030_1_mfi-agents-loan-amount-elimination-of-rural-poverty>

Nakamura, L., 'Small Borrowers and the Survival of the Small Bank: Is Mouse Bank Mighty or Mickey?', (1994) *FRBP Economic Review Recent* 3

Narayan, D., L. Pritchett and S. Kapoor, *Moving Out of Poverty – Volume 2. Success from the Bottom Up*, (Palgrave-WB 2009)

Nassr, I. and G. Wehinger, 'Unlocking SME Finance through Market-based Debt: Securitisation, Private Placements and Bonds', (2014) 2*OECD Journal: Financial Market Trends* 89

Nawaz, A., 'Issues in Subsidies and Sustainability of Microfinance: An Empirical Investigation', (2010) CEB Working Paper 10/2010, <https://dipot.ulb.ac.be/dspace/bitstream/2013/54393/1/RePEc_sol_wpaper_10-010.pdf>

Newman, A. and D. Bach, 'Self-Regulatory Trajectories in the Shadow of Public Power: Resolving Digital Dilemmas in Europe and the U.S.', (2004) 17(3) *Governance* 387

Nitsche, R. and P. Heidhues, *Study on Methods to Analyse the Impact of State Aid on Competition*, (Commission 2006)

Nowak, M. and P. Valentin, 'Helenos – Supporting, Financing and Strengthening Equity of Small and Start-up Microfinance Institutions. A Project for Europe and Neighbouring Countries', ('Workshop on Regulations and laws for microfinance in the EU', Bruxelles, 20 October 2015), <www.european-microfinance.org/docs/events/15-10-20_Helenos%20Presentation_1st%20EMD.pdf>

Obstfeld, M. and A. Taylor, 'The Great Depression as a Watershed: International Capital Mobility over the Long Run', (1997) NBER Working Paper 5960, <www.nber.org/papers/w5960>

Odell, K., 'Measuring the Impact of Microfinance. Taking Another Look', (2010), <www.grameenfoundation.org/resource/measuring-impact-microfinance>

OECD, 'Financing SMEs and Entrepreneurs 2013: An OECD Scoreboard – Final Report' (2013), <www.oecd.org/officialdocuments/publicdisplaydocumentpdf/?cote=CFE/SME(2012)12/FINAL&docLanguage=En>

Omarova, S., 'License To Deal: Mandatory Approval of New Complex Financial Products', (2012) 90*Wash U L Rev* 63

Ostrom, E., *Governing the Commons: The Evolution of Institutions for Collective Action*, (CUP 1990)

Packin, N. and Y. Lev Aretz, 'Big Data and Social Netbanks: Are You Ready to Replace Your Bank?', (2015) Columbia Public Law Research Paper 14–460, <http://ssrn.com/abstract=2567135>

Périlleux, E., E. Bloy and M. Hudon, 'Productivity Surplus Distribution in Microfinance: Does Ownership Matter?', (2010) CEB Working Paper 10/036, <https://dipot.ulb.ac.be/dspace/bitstream/2013/60442/1/wp10036.pdf>

Perron, J., 'Dans le cadre de la Social Business Initiative de la Commission Européenne: Lever les freins au développement du Peer to Peer de microcrédit solidaire en Europe', (2012), <http://ec.europa.eu/internal_market/social_business/docs/expert-group/geces/perron_fr.pdf>

Person, T. and G. Tabellini, 'Is Inequality Harmful for Growth?', (1994) 84*Am Econ Rev* 600

Petersen, M. and R. Rajan, 'The Benefits of Lending Relationships: Evidence from Small Business Data', (1994) 49(1) *J Financ* 3

Pickens, M. et al., 'Scenarios for Branchless Banking in 2020', (2009) CGAP Focus Note 57, <www.cgap.org/sites/default/files/CGAP-Focus-Note-Scenarios-for-Branch less-Banking-in-2020-Oct-2009.pdf>

Pinar Ardic, O., M. Heimann and N. Mylenko, 'Access to Financial Services and the Financial Inclusion Agenda around the World. A Cross-Country Analysis with a New Data Set', (2011), World Bank Policy Research Working Paper 5537, <http://ssrn.com/abstract=1747440>

Pistelli, M., A. Pierantozzi and M. Hamadi, 'Beyond Good Intentions: Measuring Impact Investment and Social Performance in Microfinance', (2014), <www.themix.org/sites/default/files/Beyond%20Good%20Intentions%20Publication.pdf>

Pistelli, M., S. Geake and A. Gonzalez, 'Measuring Governance in Microfinance: Initial Findings from a Pilot Project', (2012) 4*MicroBanking Bulletin*, <www.themix.org/publications/microbanking-bulletin/2012/04/measuring-governance-microfinance>

Pistor, K., 'Into the Void: Governing Finance in Central & Eastern Europe', Columbia Law and Economics Working Paper 356, <http://ssrn.com/abstract=1476889>

Pistor, K., 'Law in Finance', (2013) 41(2) *J Comp Econ* 311

Pistor, K., M. Raiser and S. Gelfer, 'Law and Finance in Transition Economies', (2000) 8*Econ Transit* 325

Pop, C. and P. Buys, 'Microfinance in Romania', (2015) *5 Contemporary Legal & Economic Issues* 307

Pope, D. and J. Sydnor, 'What's in the Picture? Evidence of Discrimination from Prosper.com', (2011) 46(1) *J Hum Resour* 53

Porteous, D. et al., 'Interest Rate Policy', (2010) FAI Policy Framing Note 4, <www.microfinancegateway.org/sites/default/files/mfg-en-paper-interest-rate-policy-jan- 2010.pdf>

Porteous, D., 'Competition and Microcredit Interest Rates', (2006) CGAP Focus Note 33, <https://www.cgap.org/sites/default/files/CGAP-Focus-Note-Competition-and-Microcredit-Interest-Rates-Feb-2006.pdf>

Porteous, D., 'Consumer Protection in Credit Markets', (2009) FAI Policy Focus Note 2, <www.microfinancegateway.org/sites/default/files/mfg-en-paper-consumer-protection-in-credit-markets-jul-2009.pdf>

Porteous, D., D. Collins and J. Abrams, 'Prudential Regulation in Microfinance', (2010) FAI Policy Framing Note 3, <www.microfinancegateway.org/sites/default/files/mfg-en-paper-prudential-regulation-in-microfinance-jan-2010.pdf>

Posner, E. and E. Wey, 'An FDA for Financial Innovation: Applying the Insurable Interest Doctrine to 21st-Century Financial Markets', (2012), <http://ssrn.com/abstract=2010606>

Pouncy, C., 'Contemporary Financial Innovation: Orthodoxy and Alternatives', (1998) 51*SMUL Rev* 505

PwC, 'The Sustainability of Community Development Finance Institutions', (2015), <www.pwc.co.uk/assets/pdf/the-sustainability-of-community-development.pdf>

Rahman, R. and S. Mohammed, 'BRAC Micro Credit Securitization Series I: Lessons from the World's First Micro-Credit Backed Security (MCBS)', (2007) MF Analytics , <www8.gsb.columbia.edu/sites/socialenterprise/files/BRAC_Micro_Credit_Securitization_MFA.pdf>

Rajan, R. and L. Zingales, 'Financial Development and Growth', (1998) 88*Am Econ Rev* 559

Rajan, R., 'Separate and Unequal', (2006) 43(1) *Finan Dev* 58

Ramsay, G., 'Regulation of Consumer Credit', in G. Howells et al., *Handbook of Research on International Consumer Law*, (Edward Elgar 2010)

Ramsay, I., *Consumer Law and Policy: Text and Materials on Regulating Consumer Markets*, (3rd edn, Hart 2012)

Rasmusen, E., 'Stock Banks and Mutual Banks', (1988) 31*J Law Econ* 395

Ravaillon, M., 'Pro-Poor Growth: A Primer', (2004) World Bank Policy Research Working Paper 3242, <www-wds.worldbank.org/servlet/WDSContentServer/WDSP/IB/2004/06/09/000009486_20040609104122/Rendered/PDF/wps3242growth.pdf>

RBI, 'FAQs on Non-Banking-Financial-Company-Micro-Finance-Institutions (NBFC-MFIs)', <www.rbi.org.in/scripts/FAQView.aspx?Id=102>

Reifner, U. et al, 'Study on Interest Rate Restrictions in the EU – Final Report for the EU Commission DG Internal Market and Services', (2010), <http://ec.europa.eu/internal_market/finservices-retail/docs/credit/irr_report_en.pdf>

Reifner, U., 'Micro-Lending – A Case for Regulation', (2002), <www.emnconference.org/archives/data/file/Micro-lending_-_A_case_for_Regulation.pdf>

Reille, X., C. Kneiding, and M. Martinez, 'The Impact of the Financial Crisis on Microfinance and Their Clients. Results from CGAP's 2009 Opinion Survey', (2009), <www.cgap.org/sites/default/files/CGAP-Brief-The-Impact-of-the-Financial-Crisis-on- Microfinance-Institutions-and-Their-Clients-May-2009.pdf>

Reinke, J. and K. Druschel, 'Finance for the Poor: Regulatory Challenges to Private Sector Investment', (2005) 7*MFC Policy Monitor* 11

Rhyne, E., 'Toward a Distributed Global Banking Grid', *The New York Times* (New York, 27 January 2009)

Richardson, M., 'Increasing Microlending Potential In the United States through A Strategic Approach to Regulatory Reform', (2009) 34*J Corp L*923

Rock, R., M. Otero and S. Saltzman, 'Principles and Practices of Microfinance Governance', (1998), <www.jointokyo.org/mfdl/readings/MFGovernance.pdf>

Rodrik, D., A. Subramanian and F. Trebbi, 'Institutions Rule. The Primacy of Institutions Over Geography and Integration in Economic Development', (2004) 9 *J Econ Growth* 131

Rogers, H., *The Global Financial Crisis and Development Thinking*, (2010), World Bank Policy Research Working Paper 5353, <http://elibrary.worldbank.org/content/workingpaper/10.1596/1813-9450-5353>

Roodman, D. and J. Morduch, 'The Impact of Microcredit on the Poor in Bangladesh: Revisiting the Evidence', (2009) Center for Global Development Working Paper 174, <www.cgdev.org/files/1422302_file_Roodman_Morduch_Bangladesh.pdf>

Roodman, D., 'Kiva Is Not Quite What It Seems', (Center for Global Development, 2 October 2009), <www.cgdev.org/blog/kiva-not-quite-what-it-seems>

Rosenberg, R. et al., 'Microcredit Interest Rates and Their Determinants – 2004–2011', (2013), <www.cgap.org/sites/default/files/Forum-Microcredit%20Interest%20Rates%20and%20Their%20Determinants-June-2013.pdf>

Rosenberg, R., 'CGAP Reflections on the Compartamos Initial Public Offering: A Case Study on Microfinance Interest Rates and Profits', (2007), CGAP Focus Note 42, <www.cgap.org/sites/default/files/CGAP-Focus-Note-CGAP-Reflections-on-the-Compartamos-Initial-Public-Offering-A-Case-Study-on-Microfinance-Interest-Rates-and-Profits-Jun-2007.pdf>

Rosenberg, R., 'Measuring Microcredit Delinquency: Ratios Can Be Harmful to Your Health', (1999) CGAP Occasional Paper 3, <www.cgap.org/sites/default/files/CGA P-Occasional-Paper-Measuring-Microcredit-Delinquency-Ratios-Can-Be-Harmful-to-Your-Health-Jun-1999.pdf>

Rosenberg, R., 'Measuring Results of Microfinance Institutions. Minimum Indicators That Donors and Investors Should Track – A Technical Guide', (2009), <www.cgap.org/sites/default/files/CGAP-Technical-Guide-Measuring-Results-of-Microfinance-In stitutions-Minimum-Indicators-That-Donors-and-Investors-Should-Track-Jul-2009.pdf>

Rosenberg, R., 'Mohammed Yunus and Michael Chu debate commercialization', (*World Bank*, 14 October 2008), http://blogs.worldbank.org/psd/mohammed-yunus-and-michael-chu-debate-commercialization

Rosenberg, R., A. Gonzalez and S. Narain, 'The New Moneylenders: Are the Poor Being Exploited by High Microcredit Interest Rates?', (2009), CGAP Occasional Paper 15, <www.cgap.org/sites/default/files/CGAP-Occasional-Paper-The-New-Money lenders-Are-the-Poor-Being-Exploited-by-High-Microcredit-Interest-Rates-Feb-2009. pdf>

Rossi-Maccanico, P. and V. Sansonetti, 'Survey of State Aid in the Lending Sector: A Comprehensive Review of Main State Aid Cases', (2007) 18(6) *EBL Rev* 1353

Rott, P., 'Consumer Credit', in H.-W. Micklitz et al. (eds), *Understanding EU Consumer Law*, (Hart 2009)

Rozas, D., 'Throwing in the Towel: Lessons from MFI Liquidations', (2009), <www. microfinancegateway.org/sites/default/files/mfg-en-case-study-throwing-in-the-towel-lessons-from-mfi-liquidations-sep-2009_0.pdf>

Rozas, D. and V. Kothari, 'Preparing for Failure: Strategies for Challenging Times in Microfinance', (7 November 2010), <www.danielrozas.com/2010/11/08/preparing-for-failure-strategies-for-challenging-times/>

Rozas, D. and S. Sinha, 'Avoiding a Microfinance Bubble in India: Is Self-Regulation the Answer?', *Microfinance Focus* (10 January 2010), <www.microfinancefocus.com/news/2010/01/10/a voiding-a-microfinance-bubble-in-india-is-self-regulation-the-answer/>

Rutledge, S. (ed.), *Croatia – Diagnostic Review of Consumer Protection and Financial Literacy. Volume – Key Findings and Recommendations*, (WB 2010)

Sahasranaman, A., 'Securitization in Microfinance', (25 May 2012), <www.vinodkothari. com/Session%204_Securitisation%20in%20Micro%20Finance%20sector_Mr.%20Anand% 20Sahasranaman_IFMR.pdf>

Saltuk, Y. et al., 'Spotlight on the Market: The Impact Investor Survey', J.P. Morgan–GIIN (2014), <www.jpmorganchase.com/corporate/socialfinance/document/140502- Sp otlight_on_the_market-FINAL.pdf>

Sapundzhieva, R., '*Funding Microfinance. A Focus on Debt Financing*', (2011), <www. themix.org/publications/microbanking-bulletin/2011/11/microfinance-funding-micro finance-debt-financing#ixzz3zKlnsaH9>

Sauter, W., 'Services of General Economic Interest and Universal Service in EU Law', TILEC Discussion Paper 2008–017, <http://ssrn.com/abstract=1136105>

Scharpf, F., 'The European Social Model: Coping with the Challenges of Diversity', (2002) 40(4) *JCMS* 645

Schoar, A. 'Scale Matters', (*Economist*, 11 July 2009) Lin roundtable, <www.economist.com/blogs/freeexchange/2009/07/antoinette_schoar_is_michael_k>

Schoenmaker, D., 'Financial Trilemma', (2011) 111(1) *Economics Letters* 57

Schooner, H. and M. Taylor, *Global Bank Regulation. Principles and Policies*, (Academic Press/Elsevier 2010)

Schwarcz, S., 'Systemic Risk', (2008) 97*Geo L J* 193

Schwarcz, S., 'Disintermediating Avarice: A Legal Framework for Commercially Sustainable Microfinance', (2011) 4*U Illinois L Rev* 1165

Schwarcz, S., 'Helping Microfinance Become Commercially Sustainable', (2010) 46(2) *Gonz L Rev* 495

Schwarcz, S., 'Regulating Complexity in Financial Markets', (2009) 87(2) *Wash U L Rev* 211

Schwarcz, S., 'Regulating Financial Change: A Functional Approach', (2015) Duke Law School Public Law & Legal Theory Series Paper, <http://ssrn.com/abstract=2469467>

Schwarcz, S., 'Regulating Financial Change: A Functional Approach', (2016) 100*Minnesota Law Review* 1441

Schwarcz, S., 'Securitisation and Post-Crisis Financial Regulation', (2016) Duke Law School Public Law & Legal Theory Paper 2016–2017, <http://ssrn.com/abstract=2701556>

Schwarcz, S., 'The Future of Securitization', (2009) 41*Conn L Rev* 1313

Schwarcz, S., *Structured Finance* (3rd edn, Practicing Law Institute 2002)

Scully, M., 'Banks Heat Up Bidding for Peer-to-Peer Loans', *American Banker* (New York, 10 October 2014)

SEEP, 'Financial Reporting Standards Initiative. Survey Results Brief', (2008), <www.seepnetwork.org/filebin/pdf/resources/MFRS_Survey_Brief_English.pdf>

Segoviano, M. et al., 'Securitization: The Road Ahead', (2015) IMF Staff Discussion Note 15/01, <www.imf.org/external/pubs/ft/sdn/2015/sdn1501.pdf>

Sen, A., *Development as Freedom*, (1st edn, OUP 1999)

Servin, R., 'Ownership and Technical Efficiency of Microfinance Institutions: Empirical Evidence from Latin America', (2012) 36*J Bank Financ* 2136

Servon, L., 'Microenterprise Programs in U.S. Inner Cities: Economic Development or Social Welfare?', (1997) 11(2) *Econ Dev Q* 166

Shankar, S. and M. Asher, 'Regulating Microfinance: A Suggested Framework', (2010) 45*Economic & Political Weekly* 15 <http://ssrn.com/abstract=1607704>

Sheikh, S. et al., 'Support Services for Micro, Small and Sole Proprietor's Businesses of the EC – Final Report', (2002), www.microfinancegateway.org/sites/default/files/mfg-en-paper-support-services-for-micro-small-and-sole-proprietors-businesses-2002_0.pdf

Sievers, M. and P. Vandenberg, 'Synergies through Linkages: Who Benefits from Linking Micro-finance and Business Development Services?', (2007), <www.ilo.org/wcmsp5/groups/public/@ed_emp/@emp_ent/@ifp_seed/documents/publication/wcms_143167.pdf>

Singh, D., *Banking Regulation of UK and US Financial Markets*, (2nd edn, Routledge 2012)

Smaga, P., 'The Concept of Systemic Risk', (2014) SRC Special Paper 5, <http://eprints.lse.ac.uk/61214/1/sp-5.pdf>

SmartCampaign, 'Putting the Principles to Work: Detailed Guidance on the Client Protection Principles – Version 2.0', (2011), <www.smartcampaign.org/storage/documents/20110916_SC_Principles_Guidance_Draft_Final.pdf>

Snyder, D., 'Private Lawmaking', (2003) 64*Ohio St LJ* 371

Solaiman, S., 'Revisiting Securities Regulation in the Aftermath of the Global Financial Crisis: Disclosure – Panacea or Pandora's Box?', (2013) 14(4) *JWIT* 646

Soursourian, M. and E. Dashi, 'Current Trends in International Funding for Financial Inclusion', (2015), <www.cgap.org/sites/default/files/Brief-Current-Trends-in- International-Funding-Dec-2015.pdf>

Srinivasan, N., 'Microfinance India. State of the Sector Report 2008', (2009), <http://indiamicrofinance.com/wp-content/uploads/2009/08/state_of_the_sector_report_2008.pdf>

Sriram, M., V. Chaturvedi and A. Neti, 'Too Big to Fail versus Too Small to be Counted', (2012) BIS Paper 62, <http://ssrn.com/abstract=2028905>

Staschen, S., 'Regulatory Requirements for Microfinance: A Comparison of Legal Frameworks in 11 Countries Worldwide' (2003), <www.izdihar-iraq.com/resources/mfsummit/ref_RegulatoryRequirementsInMicrofinance_GTZ.pdf>

Stein, C., 'Information Production and Capital Allocation: Decentralized versus Hierarchical Firms', (2002) 57(5) *J Financ* 1891

Stieber, S., 'Is Securitisation Right for Microfinance?', (2007) 2 *Innovations* 202

Stiglitz, J. and A. Weiss, 'Credit Rationing in Markets with Imperfect Information', (1981) 71(3) *The Am Econ Rev*, 393

Strom, S., 'Confusion On Where Money Lent via Kiva Goes', *The New York Times* (New York, 9 November 2009)

Symbiotics, '2015 Microfinance Investment Vehicles Survey', (2015), <www.symbioticsgroup.com/media/79151/2015_09_symbiotics-2015-miv-survey.pdf>

Symbiotics, 'Swiss Microfinance Investments. From Early Growth Stage to Maturity: History, Current Developments and New Challenges', (2011), <www.eda.admin.ch/content/dam/deza/en/documents/themen/privatsektorentwicklung/212462-swiss- microfinance-investments_EN.pdf>

Szabó, A. (ed.), 'Microfinance for SMEs in the BSEC Region', (conference, 12–15 November 2014, Bucharest), <www.kas.de/wf/doc/kas_41327-1522-2-30.pdf?150513160755>

Szekfu, T., 'Hungary', (2013) EMN Legislative Mapping Report 12/2013, <www.european-microfinance.org/docs/emn_publications/e_bulletins/Microfinance_MappingHungary.pdf>

Szekfu, T., 'The Hungarian Microfinance Legislation', in J. Durán Navarro et al., *The Importance of a Microfinance Legislation for the Development of the Sector in Spain*, (Cromoimagen 2013)

Tarazi, A., L. Lepetit, E. Nys and P. Rous, 'Bank Income Structure and Risk: An Empirical Analysis of European Banks', (2008) 32(8) *J Bank Financ* 1452

Tarullo, D., 'Rethinking the Aims of Prudential Regulation', (Federal Reserve Bank of Chicago 'Bank Structure' Conference, Chicago, 8 May 2014), <https://www.federalreserve.gov/newsevents/speech/tarullo20140508a.pdf>

Tarullo, D., 'Tailoring Community Bank Regulation and Supervision', (Independent Community Bankers of America Policy Summit, Washington, 30 April 2015), <www.federalreserve.gov/newsevents/speech/tarullo20150430a.pdf>

Tarullo, D., *Banking on Basel: The Future of International Financial Regulation*, (Institute for International Economics 2008)

Tchakoute-Tchuigoua, H., 'Determinants of the Governance Quality of Microfinance Institutions', (2015) 58*Q Rev Econ Financ* 32

Tchakoute-Tchuigoua, H., 'Is There a Difference in Performance by the Legal Status of Microfinance Institutions?', (2010) 50*Q Rev Econ Financ* 436

Thoma, M. 'Small Banks Need Help', (*Economist*, 11 July 2009) Lin roundtable, <www.economist.com/blogs/freeexchange/2009/07/lin_roundtable_small_banks_nee>

Thorat, U., 'Financial Regulation and Financial Inclusion – Working Together or at Cross-purposes', (10th annual international seminar on Policy challenges for the financial sector, 4 June 2010), <http://rbidocs.rbi.org.in/rdocs/Speeches/PDFs/GDUTWE070610.pdf>

Trant, J., 'Microfinance: Investing with an Impact. International Investment and Securities Review', (2009), <www.microfinancegateway.org/sites/default/files/mfg-en-paper-microfinance-investing-with-an-impact-2009_0.pdf>

Trigo-Loubière, J., P. Lee Devaney and E. Rhyne, 'Supervising & Regulating Microfinance in the Context of Financial Liberalization. Lessons from Bolivia, Colombia and Mexico', (2004), <www.microfinancegateway.org/sites/default/files/mfg-en-paper- supervising-and-regulating-microfinance-in-the-context-of-financial-sector-liberalization-lessons-from-bolivia-colombia-and-mexico-aug-2004.pdf>

Trubeck, D. and M. Galanter, 'Scholars in Self-Estrangement: Some Reflections on the Crisis in Law and Development Studies in the United States', (1974) 4 *Wisc Law Rev* 1062

TrustLaw, 'Creating Jobs in Europe Legal and Regulatory Frameworks of Microenterprises and Microcredit in Europe', (2011), <www.trust.org/contentAsset/raw-data/ ac56cbae-2724-4226-bbfe-1903c01bb68b/file>

Tucker, M., 'Financial Performance of Selected Microfinance Institutions: Benchmarking Progress to Sustainability', (2001) 3 *J Microfinance* 107

UN DESA-UNCDF, *Building Inclusive Financial Sectors for Development*, (UN 2006), <www.uncdf.org/sites/default/files/Documents/bluebook_1.pdf>

United Nations, 'Microfinance and Millennium Development Goals', (2005), <www.yearofmicrocredit.org/docs/MF_MDGs.pdf>;

United Nations, 'The Monterrey Consensus', (2003), <www.un.org/esa/ffd/monterrey/MonterreyConsensus.pdf>

Unnikrishnan, D., 'MFIs See Sharp Rise in Securitization Deals', *LiveMint* (Mumbai, 1 April 2012), <www.livemint.com/Politics/DAC3gIVnMJOUFi5KrE7prK/MFIs-see-sharp-rise-in-securitization-deals.html>

Unterberg, M., 'Microfinance as a European Policy Issue – Policy Images and Venues', (2008) EMN Annual Conference, <http://tk.eversjung.de/www/downloads/Microfinance_as_a_European_policy_issue.pdf>

Unterberg, M., M. Bendig and B. Sarpong, *Study on the Imperfections in the Area of Microfinance and Options How to Address Them through an EU Financial Instrument – Final Progress Report*, (EU 2014)

Valentin, P. et al., 'Le microcrédit', (2011) Rapport d'un groupe de travail du CNIS 125, <www.unaf.fr/IMG/pdf/RAP_2011_125_microcredit.pdf>

Van Greuning, H. and S. Brajovic Bratanovic, *Analyzing and Managing Banking Risk: A Framework for Assessing and Corporate Governance and Financial Risk*, (3rd ., WB 2009)

Vanroose, A. and B. D'Espallier, 'Do Microfinance Institutions Accomplish their Mission? Evidence from the Relationship between Traditional Financial Sector Development and Microfinance Institutions' Outreach and Performance', (2013) 45(15) *Appl Econ* 1965

Vernstein, A., 'The Misregulation of Person-to-Person Lending', (2011) 45(2) *UC Davis L Rev* 445

Véron, N., 'Defining Europe's Capital Markets Union', (2014) Bruegel Policy Contribution 2014/12, <http://bruegel.org/wp-content/uploads/imported/publications/pc_2014_12_cmu.pdf>.

Vidan, H. 'Amendments to the Consumer Loans Act', (*Lexology*, 23 August 2013), <www.lexology.com/library/detail.aspx?g=54381349-08f8-40c0-b3d3-804f2d85b740

Viganò, L., L. Bonomo and P. Vitali, 'Microfinance in Europe', (2004) Working Paper, <www.microfinancegateway.org/sites/default/files/mfg-en-paper-microfinance-in-europe-2004.pdf>

Wagner, C. and A. Winkler, 'The Vulnerability of Microfinance to Financial Turmoil. Evidence from the Global Financial Crisis', (2013) 51 *World Dev* 71

Walker, O., 'The Future of Microlending in the United States: a Shift from Charity to Profits?', (2011) 6*Ohio St Entrepen Bus LJ* 383

Warwick Commission, 'The Warwick Commission on International Financial Reform: In Praise of Un-level Playing Fields', (2009), <www2.warwick.ac.uk/research/warwick commission/financialreform/report/uw_warcomm_intfinreform_09.pdf>

Waterfield, C., 'Responsible Pricing – Where There is no Will, There is no Way', (2015), <www.mftransparency.org/responsible-pricing-where-there-is-no-will-there-is-no-way/>

Westaway, K. and D. Sampselle, 'The Benefit Corportation: An Economic Analysis with Recommendations to Courts, Boards, and Legislatures', (2013) 62*Emory L J* 1002

Wheelock, D. and P. Wilson, 'Do Large Banks have Lower Costs? New Estimates of Returns to Scale for US Banks', (2012) 44(1) *J Money Credit Bank* 171

Wheelock, D. and P. Wilson, 'New Evidence on Returns to Scale and Product Mix among U.S. Commercial Banks', (2001) 47*J Monetary Econ* 653

White, V. and A. Campion, 'Transformation – Journey from NGO to Regulated MFI', in D. Drake and E. Rhyne (eds), *The Commercialization of Microfinance* (Kumarian Press 2002)

White, W., 'The Prudential Regulation of Financial Institutions: Why Regulatory Responses to the Crisis Might Not Prove Sufficient', (2013), <www.policyschool.ucalgary.ca/sites/default/files/research/prudential-regulation-white.pdf>

Whiteman, L., 'Small Banks Say One-on-One Beats Credit Scoring Models', (1998) 163 (193) *American Banker* 13

Wisniewski, J., 'Important Changes in the Regulatory Landscape of the Consumer (Personal) Loans Market in Poland', (2016), <www.squirepattonboggs.com/~/media/files/insights/publications/2016/03/important-changes-in-the-regulatory- landscape-of-the-consumer-loans-market-in-poland/poland-loans-marketthought-leadership-(2).pdf>

Wolkowitz, E., '2013 Underserved Market Size', (2014) CFSI, <www.cfsinnovation.com/Document-Library/2013-Financially-Underserved-Market-Size>

Worton, S., S. Grew and C. Jessett, 'Consumer Credit Research: Low Income Consumers', (2014), <www.fca.org.uk/your-fca/documents/research/consumer-credit-research-low-income>

Wymeersch, E., 'The Structure of Financial Supervision in Europe: About Single Financial Supervisors, Twin Peaks and Multiple Financial Supervisors', (2007) 8(2) *EBOR* 237

Wymeersh, E. 'How Far Should Financial Regulation Go? Shadow Banking and Related Phenomena', (International Working Group on MIFID II conference, Amsterdam, 28–29 January 2016)

Wymeersch, E., K. Hopt, and G. Ferrarini, *Financial Regulation and Supervision*, (OUP 2012)

Yeager, T., 'The Demise of Community Banks? Local Economic Shocks are Not to Blame', (2004) 28*J Bank Financ* 2135

Yee, A., 'Buzz Around India's Maturing Microfinance Sector Quietens', *Financial Times* (London, 23 March 2009) 8

Yermack, D., 'Higher Valuation of Companies with Small Board of Directors', (1996) 40*J Financ Econ* 185

Yunus, M., *Banker to the Poor: Microlending and the Battle against World Poverty* (Public Affairs 1998)

Zaman, S. and S. Kairy, 'Building Domestic Capital Markets: BRAC's AAA Securitization', (2007) 14 *Micro-Banking Bulletin* 13

Zhang, B. et al., 'Moving Mainstream-The European Alternative Finance Benchmarking Report 2015', (2015), <http://www.jbs.cam.ac.uk/fileadmin/user_upload/research/centres/alternative-finance/downloads/2015-uk-alternative-finance-benchmarking-report.pdf>

Zhang, B. et al., 'Pushing Boundaries. The 2015 UK Alternative Finance Industry Report', (2016), <http://www.nesta.org.uk/sites/default/files/pushing_boundaries_0.pdf>

Zhuang, J. et al., 'Financial Sector Development, Economic Growth, and Poverty Reduction: A Literature Review', (2009) ADB Economics Working Paper 173, <http://www.adb.org/publications/financial-sector-development-economic-growth-and-poverty-reduction-literature-review>

Zimmerman, E., et al. 'Responsible Bundling of Microfinance Services. A Mixed Method Evaluation of the Impact of Timing, Pressure, and Information' (2015), http://www.cgap.org/sites/default/files/Working-Paper-Responsible-Bundling-of-Microfinance-Services-Mar-2016.pdf

Zingales, L. 'Leave Room for Growth', (*Economist*, 11 July 2009) Lin roundtable <http://www.economist.com/blogs/freeexchange/2009/07/the_devastation_produced_by_th>

Index

For Product Safety Concerns and Information please contact our EU
representative GPSR@taylorandfrancis.com
Taylor & Francis Verlag GmbH, Kaufingerstraße 24, 80331 München, Germany

www.ingramcontent.com/pod-product-compliance
Ingram Content Group UK Ltd.
Pitfield, Milton Keynes, MK11 3LW, UK
UKHW022011180926
475701UK00003B/308

* 9 7 8 0 3 6 7 5 9 4 8 6 2 *